# HTML in Plain English

## SECOND EDITION

**SANDRA E. EDDY**

MIS:
PRESS

**Henry Holt & Co., Inc. • New York, NY**

**MIS:Press**
A Division of Henry Holt and Company, Inc.
115 West 18th Street
New York, New York 10011
http://www.mispress.com

First Edition—1998

ISBN 1-55828-587-3

MIS:Press and M&T Books are available at special discounts for bulk purchases for sales promotions, premiums, and fundraising.

For details contact:          Special Sales Director
                              MIS:Press and M&T Books
                              Divisions of Henry Holt and Company, Inc.
                              115 West 18th Street
                              New York, New York 10011

10 9 8 7 6 5 4 3 2 1

**Associate Publisher:** *Paul Farrell*

**Managing Editor:** *Shari Chappell*          **Production Editor:** *Anthony Washington*
**Editor:** *Debra Williams Cauley*            **Technical Editor:** *Simon St. Laurent*
**Copy Edit Manager:** *Karen Tongish*         **Copy Editor:** *Winifred Davis*

## DEDICATION

For E. A. S.

> He that has patience may compass any-
> thing.
> —*Rabelais*

## ACKNOWLEDGMENTS

In almost every acknowledgments section of any computer book, you can read a reference to a support team of editors, experts, family, and friends. However, there's no getting around it: producing the best possible book is a team effort. When you're "deadlined out" and trying to make sense of what's displayed on your computer screen in the middle of an all-nighter or you're attempting to understand and then explain a technical concept that is way over your head, it's great to know that you have a group of people urging you on and helping you in many ways. In this section, I'd like to thank all those whose support has been so important.

Special thanks go to editor Debra Williams Cauley, who has been a joy to work with in our three projects.

Thanks to the other people at MIS:Press for making this a rewarding experience. Thanks to the copyediting team of Karen Tongish, Matthew Casper, and Winifred Davis. And thanks very much to the production editor, Anthony Washington.

For his expertise and attention to detail, an enthusiastic thank you to the technical editor, Simon St. Laurent, who is the author of *Dynamic HTML: A Primer*, also published by MIS:Press.

A special thank you for the patience and persistence of my agent, Matt Wagner of Waterside Productions.

For their continued encouragement, thanks to my family and friends—especially the ever-growing group of Perseids people, who continue to make three days in August so much fun.

*A friend may well be reckoned the master-*

*piece of Nature.*

*—Ralph Waldo Emerson*

For their special and continuing contributions—Toni, Bart, and Eli. Always in loving memory of Indy.

*Recollect that the Almighty, who gave the*
*dog to be companion of our pleasures and*
*our toils, hath invested him with a nature*
*noble and incapable of deceit.*
    —*Sir Walter Scott*

Finally, thanks to the readers of *HTML in Plain English.* I hope that you'll let me know what you think of the book and how I can make the next edition even better.

Sandra E. Eddy

eddygrp@sover.net

# Contents

# INTRODUCTION

Welcome to the second edition of *HTML in Plain English*. I hope that you enjoy using this book as much as I have enjoyed researching and writing it. This reference handbook has been crafted to provide you with quick yet comprehensive information about all HTML 4.0 elements (commonly known as *tags*), the elements of its predecessors, HTML 3.2 and HTML 2.0, Netscape and Microsoft extensions, and the Universal Character Set (UCS), or Unicode 2.0, the supported character set. Also included are all associated attributes and many examples, which you can use as templates for coding World Wide Web pages.

Although you can find comprehensive HTML references on the Web and in many other HTML books, this handbook cuts to the heart of HTML. When you want to write an HTML document, you don't need to learn about the background; all you need is the element name and purpose, its syntax, attributes, and practical examples. Are you writing a page specifically for Netscape Navigator or the Microsoft Internet Explorer browser? Or are you creating a document that you want the whole online world to be able to view? *HTML in Plain English* identifies elements and attributes that are tailored for particular browsers or ones that you can safely use for a much wider audience.

Although *HTML in Plain English* does not cover CGI scripting and Java programming, it leads you right up to those levels and then points you to online CGI and Java resources and other HTML information. So, this book is for all levels of HTML page creators, from first-time users to the most advanced.

*HTML in Plain English* is the essential HTML reference that should have a special place next to your personal computer.

# How This Book Is Organized

Finding HTML information online or in a book can be daunting. *HTML in Plain English* is designed to be easy to use, regardless of your level of experience.

*HTML in Plain English* is organized as follows:

- *Part 1: Overview.* If you want to learn more about the origins of HTML and find out how to create, post, and test HTML documents, read through this part of the book.

- *Part 2: HTML in Plain English.* If you know what you want to do but can't remember the element name, view this thumbnail list of plain-English tasks and related elements.

- *Part 3: HTML Elements A to Z.* If you know the name of the element you want to use, scan this alphabetically arranged list with brief descriptions.

- *Part 4: HTML Elements and Codes, Organized by Group.* If you know the element name but want to learn more about it or how to use one of its attributes, browse through these pages of elements grouped by type. In this part, you'll find each element along with its purpose, its complete syntax and attributes, the element set or extension set that supports it, usage notes, related elements, and plenty of examples and illustrations of the results.

- *Part 5: Cascading Style Sheets.* Throughout most of personal computing history, individuals creating word processor documents have set standard paragraph formats using style sheets. Then, they have applied individual properties, or styles, from the style sheets to paragraphs in both new and old documents. Now, you are witnessing the beginning of the style sheet era for HTML document formats. This part provides an introduction and overview of cascading style sheets. In this part, you'll find each property along with its purpose, its complete syntax, usage notes, related styles, and examples.

- *Part 6: Glossary.* HTML and the Internet have their own unique vocabularies. If you have never seen a particular term or you want a clarification, browse through this glossary of HTML and Internet terms.
- *Part 7: Webliography.* If you want to learn more about any of the information covered or mentioned in this book, look in the extensive "Webliography," a Web bibliography of HTML and HTML-related resources. The headings in the Webliography follow those in the rest of the book. The entry for each resource includes an address and brief description.
- *Appendix A: Elements by Version and Activity.* This appendix provides lists of elements organized under HTML versions or extensions. Also included are lists of the elements that are deprecated and obsolete in HTML 4.0.
- *Appendix B: Attributes in Depth.* HTML 4.0 now includes more attributes than ever—on the most simple to most complex element. This appendix lists HTML 4.0 attributes alphabetically. Each entry describes the attribute, tells how it works, and names valid and default values.
- *Appendix C: HTML Editors and Utilities.* You can use a wide variety of HTML editors and utilities to create and edit HTML documents easily and efficiently on many computer platforms. This appendix lists many editors and utilities along with the names of the developers and the URLs at which you can learn more about the programs.

## CONVENTIONS USED IN THIS BOOK

The conventions used in *HTML in Plain English* are as follows:

- Throughout the book, element names are in UPPER-CASE or **boldface UPPERCASE**. However, HTML is not case sensitive; any combination of uppercase and lowercase characters is acceptable when you create an HTML document.

- Elements and attributes that are to be typed into an HTML document are displayed in a `monospaced` typeface.

- *Italics* are used to identify both new terms and variables (such as file names, paths, colors, numbers, or URLs) that you name and enter. For example, in the following syntax `BGCOLOR="#`*rrggbb*`"|"`*color*`"]`, *rrggbb* and *color* represent a hexadecimal code and color name, respectively, that you give for an HTML document page background color. Substitute a code (such as "`#FFFFFF`") or color ("`white`") for the italicized text.

- Default values, which are automatically supplied when you do not use a particular attribute, are <u>underlined</u>.

**NOTE** At the beginning of Part 4, "HTML Elements and Codes, Organized by Group," you will find a complete explanation of the syntax conventions for the elements documented in that part. At the beginning of Part 5, "Cascading Style Sheets," you will find a similar explanation of style sheet syntax.

## HOW TO REACH THE AUTHOR

I would like to hear from you—especially if you can furnish tips, shortcuts, and tricks that you have used to create imaginative and innovative Web pages. If I have missed an attribute or an important example for a particular element, be sure to let me know. My e-mail address is eddygrp@sover.net, or you can send a note in care of MIS:Press at http://www.mispress.com.

# PART 1

## Overview

# Overview

*HTML in Plain English,* Second Edition explains HTML at the most basic level. It is tailor-made for those who "code" documents using word processors and text editors. However, those who create documents using HTML editors, such as Microsoft FrontPage, Adobe PageMill, Sausage Software's HotDog Professional, and SoftQuad's HoTMetaL PRO, should know that underneath the polished documents shown on their desktops are the same HTML statements and attributes that the "coders" see.

For a variety of reasons, many HTML documents must be edited at the HTML level—regardless of the way in which they were originally created. For example, to tailor a page for a particular browser, a page writer could add nonstandard HTML statements not currently supported by the HTML editor with which he or she is working. Or, a writer who wanted to search for and replace all second-level headings in a document with third-level headings could use a full-featured word processor to perform a one-step search-and-replace-all operation rather than using an HTML editor, which might allow only a search-and-replace for text shown on-screen.

This part of *HTML in Plain English* not only covers the basics of HTML and document creation, but also provides the background and history of HTML, information about page validation, the steps used to register a domain name, and the process of uploading a page to a server. The sections in this part are:

- "The History of Hypertext, the World Wide Web, and HTML," which briefly describes each HTML version, past and present.
- "Creating an HTML Document," which describes the tools used to create and edit a document, HTML elements syntax, and the contents of an HTML document. Four HTML editors, Microsoft FrontPage, SoftQuad's HoTMetaL PRO, Sausage Software's HotDog Professional, and Adobe PageMill, are featured.
- "Using Graphics and Multimedia," which includes supported multimedia formats.
- "Testing a Page," which summarizes how to validate an HTML document.
- "Registering a Domain Name," which provides the step-by-step process of choosing and registering a name.
- "Posting a Page," which lists the typical steps for uploading a page to a server.

## THE HISTORY OF HYPERTEXT, THE WORLD WIDE WEB, AND HTML

The interest in hypertext is a relatively recent development, due to the introduction and rapidly increasing popularity of the World Wide Web and its language, HTML.

### Hypertext

*Hypertext* allows a user to connect disconnected chunks of text and multimedia—graphics, animation, audio, and video—into an informal network of information. In essence, the user builds a temporary document tailored to his or her own needs.

The concept of hypertext is more than 50 years old. In July 1945, Vannevar Bush wrote an article for *Atlantic Monthly*. In "As We May Think," he described a machine for "browsing and making notes in an extensive online text and graphics system."

Theodor Holm Nelson coined the terms *hypertext* and *hypermedia* (which encompasses both text and multimedia) in 1960. He wrote the book *Computer Lib/Dream Machines* (originally published by Mindful Press in 1974 and reprinted in 1987 by

Microsoft Press), which influenced the introduction of the World Wide Web. In the late 1970s, Nelson introduced Project Xanadu, which produced digital library and hypertext publishing systems—another pioneering effort, but unfortunately one that did not reach fruition.

Although universities and other institutions experimented with hypertext during the 60s and 70s, it generally faded into the background until Apple introduced Hypercard in 1987 and Apple and Microsoft developed their Mac and Windows help systems, with which users can click on hypertext terms to jump from one topic to another or open a description box.

## The World Wide Web

The World Wide Web demonstrates the true and best nature of hypertext. You can link to most pages on the Web by clicking on hyperlinks on Web pages or by typing in their URLs, or addresses, regardless of the server on which they reside—anywhere in the world. For example, you can start a session on the Web by viewing a document in California, clicking on a link to jump to one in Australia or Japan, going to the next in France or Sweden, and so on, until you weave your way around the world several times in just a few minutes. Hypertext, the feature that differentiates the Web from all other Internet resources, allows you to leave the traditional way of reading a series of printed or online pages sequentially, line by line, from top to bottom, and page by page until you reach the end of the document or the end of your attention span, whichever happens first.

The Web is a relatively new part of the Internet. In the late 1980s, researchers at the European Laboratory for Particle Physics (CERN) in Switzerland developed the Web to make their jobs easier; they wanted easy access to research documents networked at their laboratory. By 1990, they introduced a text-only browser and developed HTML, and in 1991, they implemented the Web at CERN. They introduced the Web to the Internet community in 1992. Thus started the revolution.

## HTML

*HTML*, HyperText Markup Language, has been designed to handle the World Wide Web's hypermedia functionality. Within a simple text document, an HTML writer inserts an *element*, or command, that links one site on the Internet to another; describes the document to browsers, search indexes, computers, networks, and people; and defines the look of the document. HTML provides elements with which you can define, format, or enhance pages for the Web:

- You can select text and change its typeface or font size, or enhance it with boldface, italics, underlines, or strikethroughs.

- You can insert links to other sections of the current document, documents at other sites, audio files, and video files.

- You can decorate a document with graphics of all shapes and sizes, or use them as image maps a user can click on to link to other pages. You can also embed *GIF animations*, which are series of several graphic files incorporated into a single file.

- You can construct fill-out forms, which allow the user to send you mail, answer questionnaires, and even order from your online catalog.

- You can create tables, which allow you to have more control over a document's formats and arrange data in easy-to-understand columns.

- You can specify background colors for an HTML document, entire table, table row, or even a particular table cell.

- Instead of single pages onscreen, you can use *frames*, which are multiple panes, each of which can display its own HTML document. For example, you can display two small static frames with a site title and table of contents linking to individual pages displayed one at a time in a larger third frame.

HTML has gone through several iterations during its brief lifetime. The following sections provide a short history, starting with SGML (the parent of HTML), and including Netscape and Microsoft extensions.

## SGML

*Standard Generalized Markup Language* (SGML) was made an ISO (International Organization for Standardization) standard in 1986. Because it is a standard, commercial organizations worldwide use SGML for document publishing and distribution. SGML documents can contain text and multimedia elements and can also include headings of all levels, paragraphs, and a few formatted elements. Unlike HTML documents, those written in SGML do not contain formats or enhancements, such as boldface, center alignment, and so on. Each SGML document has an associated *document type definition* (DTD), which defines rules for document contents. DTDs can stand by themselves; for example, each version of HTML has been defined in a DTD.

Part 7, "Webliography" includes a section titled "SGML," which lists online resources.

## HTML 1.0 and HTML+

The first version of HTML, 1.0, appeared in 1990, and an unofficial version, HTML+, was introduced in late 1993. HTML+ features included fill-out forms, tables, and captioned figures, but did not include paragraph formatting or text enhancements. HTML+ contained 78 elements, many of which no longer remain in HTML. Many of the obsolete elements defined document components such as abstracts, notes, and bylines.

## HTML 2.0

HTML 2.0, released in 1994, was the first version to have a formal specification and be an official standard (see RFC 1866). This version contained 49 elements.

Part 7, "Webliography" includes a section titled "HTML 2.0," which lists online resources. Most HTML 2.0 elements are included in HTML 4.0.

## HTML 3.0

In March 1995, HTML 3.0 appeared. New features included tables, the capability to have text flow around images, the FIG element for inline figures, and mathematical elements. Also included were formatting features, such as horizontal tabs, and banners, which remained in place as a user scrolled down or up a page. The NOTE element, which was a feature of HTML+ but had disappeared from HTML 2.0, reappeared. Attributes for the FORM element appeared in this version. HTML 3.0 (and a number of its elements) has expired and is no longer supported.

## HTML 3.2

Introduced in May 1996, HTML 3.2 was regarded as the true successor to HTML 2.0 (in other words, bypassing HTML 3.0). According to a quotation from a May 8, 1996, *Inter@ctive Week* article by Joe McGarvey, Dan Connolly, the editor of the HTML 2.0 specification at the World Wide Web Consortium, said, "The main purpose of the specification is to get everyone on the same page of the map." HTML 3.2, which added 19 new elements, kept the tables and text flow attributes from HTML 3.0, and incorporated many Netscape extensions.

## HTML 4.0

The new version of HTML, which was code-named Cougar during its development, has added support for the OBJECT element, a powerful image and multimedia embedding element. In addition, HTML 4.0 supports cascading style sheets (see Part 5), enhancements to fill-out forms and tables, client-side scripting, *internationalization* (that is, recognition of languages made up of special-characters alphabets that may be readable in the right-to-left direction), and additional special characters for mathematics and advanced publishing.

Part 7, "Webliography" includes a section titled "HTML 4.0," which lists online resources.

## Netscape Extensions

For both HTML 2.0 and HTML 3.0, the Netscape Communications Corporation developed proprietary elements that were supported by some, but not all, browsers. HTML 2.0 extensions included five new elements, including FONT and CENTER, and several new attributes for existing elements. For HTML 3.0, Netscape added the BIG, SMALL, SUB, and SUP elements and client-side image maps, all of which moved to HTML 3.2. Other Netscape extensions, such as frames, have been added to HTML 4.0.

Part 7, "Webliography" includes a section titled "Netscape Extensions,"which lists online resources. For a complete list of Netscape extensions, see *Appendix A.*

## Microsoft Extensions

At the same time Netscape was developing its extensions, the Microsoft Corporation created and supported its own extensions for its browser, Microsoft Internet Explorer Versions 2.0 and 3.0. Some Microsoft extensions, such as the OBJECT multimedia element, frames, and some table elements, have been added to HTML 4.0.

Part 7, "Webliography" includes a section titled "Microsoft Extensions," which lists online resources. For a complete list of Microsoft extensions, see Appendix A.

## CREATING AN HTML DOCUMENT

An HTML document combines text and optional graphics with HTML elements.

You can construct an HTML document any way you wish. Some people write the document first, editing and polishing it as they would any word processing document. Then, they insert the elements and attributes to prepare the document for publishing on the Web. Others insert elements and attributes as they write the document.

### Word Processors and Text Processors vs. HTML Editors

You can create a World Wide Web page using a word processor or text editor or by using an HTML editor. Both have advantages and disadvantages.

- If you use a word processor or text editor, you have to remember to include some of the boilerplate statements that HTML editors automatically include in the HEAD section at the top of an HTML document.

- An HTML editor automatically inserts an **HTM** or **HTML** extension when you save an HTML document; a word processor may add a **DOC** extension and a text editor may add a **TXT** extension. Then you will have to rename the document as an **HTM** or **HTML** document before uploading it to a server.

**NOTE** A word processor adds formats as you work on a document. When you save a document as a word processing file, the formats remain. Browsers viewing this file may display some of the formatting codes—an undesirable result.

- If you use an HTML editor, you can't always easily view the elements and attributes in the underlying HTML code, especially in the HEAD section at the top of the document. So, if you need to edit your document, you might have to make a greater effort to select attributes (such as filling in one or two dialog boxes) rather than overtyping a number or a color name or code in the document itself.
- An HTML editor will construct an HTML statement using the appropriate syntax and the attributes that you have selected. If you use a word processor or text editor, you have to understand how to use the syntax.
- Many HTML editors can automatically validate your syntax as you enter it.
- The software publishers that develop HTML editors want you to upgrade whenever they release a new version. So, they add many functions that make document creation easier. They often provide templates and graphics, spell checkers, thesauruses, and dictionaries.

## Creating HTML Documents with an HTML Editor

This section provides overviews of using four popular HTML editors—Microsoft FrontPage, Adobe PageMill, HotDog Professional, and HoTMetaL PRO—to create HTML documents.

## Using Microsoft FrontPage

If you want to keep track of a *web*, a set of pages, the FrontPage applications are excellent choices. Using FrontPage Explorer, FrontPage Editor, and the To Do List, you can create webs and WYSIWYG (in the "what you see is what you get" format that visitors to the page will see) HTML documents, view the relationship of each page to the others in the web, and keep a to-do list of future page creation and maintenance. Note that FrontPage also includes the Microsoft Personal Web Server, so that you can run your own "microserver" on your PC.

To create a web, start the FrontPage Explorer. If this is your first web, select options from the New FrontPage Web dialog box. Choose the type of web, its title, and click on the Change button to specify the web's location. Then, click on OK to create the new web.

 **You must have a server on the current computer to create a web.**

NOTE

To create an individual page, whether or not you have created a web, start the FrontPage Editor by choosing **Show FrontPage Editor** from the Tools menu. Add elements to the page using the commands on the Insert, Format, Table, and Frame menus and style and format the elements using the Edit and Format menus. You can add or remove applicable toolbars from the FrontPage Editor window by selecting from the View menu. When you have completed the page (see Figure 1.1), save it, and return to FrontPage Explorer.

**Figure 1.1** *The FrontPage Editor displaying part of a page as it is being created and all the toolbars on view.*

To edit a document, you can open the FrontPage Editor and edit the page in the same way that you created it. To edit HTML statements in a document, click on the HTML tab at the bottom of the window, and to preview the document as it will look to visitors, click on the Preview tab.

## Using HoTMetaL PRO

HoTMetaL PRO, a suite of programs and utilities (including a cascading style sheet editor), focuses on creating World Wide Web pages and web sites, using both HTML 4.0 elements and Netscape and Microsoft extensions, and with the support of a robust help system. Almost every element has its own toolbar button or item on a drop-down list. HoTMetaL PRO validates your statements as you add them to a document and allows you to view your document using up to four browsers, started with the click of a toolbar button.

To create a page, start HoTMetaL PRO Editor. Then, choose the **New** command from the File menu or press **Ctrl+N** to open the New dialog box, from which you can select one of many templates. Select a template and click on **OK**.

**NOTE** If you want to open a blank page and bypass the New dialog box, click on the New toolbar button.

You can add elements and attributes to the page in three ways:

- Click on a toolbar button. When HoTMetaL PRO inserts icons representing *start tags* and *end tags* which represent the beginning and ending of an element statement, type text within the tags.
- Choose the **Element** command from the Insert menu or press **Ctrl+Shift+I**. From the Insert Element dialog box, either double-click on an element or choose the element and click on **OK**.
- Choose a command from the Insert, Format, Tools, Table, Forms, or Edit menu.

You can apply formatting using the commands on the Format menu and select attributes for a selected element by pressing **F6** or choosing the **Attribute Inspector** command from the View menu. When you have completed the page (see Figure 1.2), save it, and then preview it by either selecting **Preview in Browser** from the File menu or clicking on a button representing one of the browsers installed on your computer.

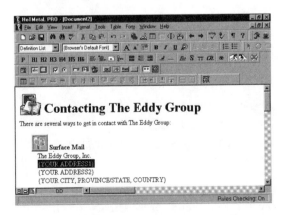

**Figure 1.2** *HoTMetaL PRO showing part of a page.*

You can view and edit a document in three viewing modes, with commands on the View menu: choose **HTML Source** or press **Alt+Ctrl+H** to view the HTML source code, choose **Tags On** or press **Alt+Ctrl+T** to add the elements to the document, or choose **WYSIWYG** or press **Alt+Ctrl+W** to view the document as it will look to visitors to your site. You can edit a document in any of the three modes.

## Using HotDog Professional

HotDog Professional has been a popular choice with Web page developers for a long time. Using HotDog, you can create World Wide Web pages using HTML 4.0 elements. You can customize the HotDog window using commands on the View menu. For example, you can display up to four toolbars and add Resource Manager windows. As you add more windows and toolbars to the application window, you will have more tools at your disposal yet less space in which to work (Figure 1.3). HotDog validates your statements as you add them to a document; if you enter an invalid element (for example, misspell it), HotDog highlights the problem in bright red.

**Figure 1.3** *HotDog Professional showing four toolbars and two windows, one displaying a new document.*

To create a page, start HotDog. Then, choose the **New** command from the File menu, press **Ctrl-N**, or click on the New toolbar button. You can add elements and attributes to a document in the following ways:

- Click on a toolbar button. When HotDog Professional inserts start tags and end tags which represent the beginning and end of element statements, type text within the tags. You may be able to insert particular attributes (such as document colors) using a toolbar button.
- Choose commands from the Insert menu.
- Drag elements and attributes from the HTML Tags window into the document. After you add attributes, you will probably have to edit them.
- Type elements and attributes in the document window.

You can format the document by using the commands on the Format menu and clicking on buttons from one of the four toolbars. When you have completed the page, save it, and then view it by clicking on the External Preview toolbar button or selecting **Preview Document** from the File menu. HotDog previews a document using a browser installed on your computer.

## Using Adobe PageMill

PageMill applies Adobe's document management techniques to the Web, giving you full access to HTML elements while making it easy to create complex documents including frames, tables, plug-ins, and more. You can switch quickly between an edit and a preview mode to see what a document should look like, or open a document in another browser for a more thorough examination.

In many ways, PageMill looks more like a word processor than an HTML editor; its menus and toolbars reflect this (see Figure 1.4). It's easy to format text with the top toolbar and some buttons on the bottom toolbar, while the bottom toolbar also provides tools for form and table creation. The program includes an Inspector window, which lets you manipulate the details of your HTML code without having to make changes directly to the code, and has a complete set of color pickers to simplify choosing colors.

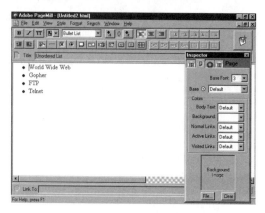

**Figure 1.4** *An HTML document in the PageMill window and the Inspector window with default color values.*

To create a page, choose **New Page** from the File menu. A new untitled document appears; you can type or copy anything you like into it.

Adding elements is simple. To format text, just select it and choose formatting from either the toolbars or the Style or Format menu. You can insert other objects—plug-ins, graphics, Java applets, sounds, or Adobe's own Acrobat files—with the **Place** command on the File menu. The **Insert Invisibles** command on the Edit menu lets you insert line breaks, anchors, comments, and hidden fields. The Inspector allows you to fine-tune your colors, sizes, backgrounds, and object properties. If you want to edit your HTML codes directly, though, there's always the **HTML Source** command on the Edit menu.

PageMill is great for modifying pages, but isn't as useful for managing entire webs, verifying links, or automating sites. Users who want those features with the convenience of Adobe's easy editing will have to get SiteMill, an enhanced version with many more management features.

## Creating Pages with a Word Processor or Text Editor

Constructing a page using a word processor or text editor is as simple as creating any other document. Launch the program and start typing elements, attributes, and text. Don't worry about spaces or margins; browsers do not interpret carriage returns or anything but HTML margin settings. When you save the HTML document, name it, give it a file type of text or ASCII, and make sure that it has an **HTM** or **HTML** extension.

A word processor adds formats as you work on a document. When you save a document as a word processing file, the formats remain. Browsers viewing this file may display some of the formatting codes—an undesirable result.

## Creating Pages with an HTML Editor

To create an HTML document using an HTML editor, launch the editor, and use a combination of toolbar buttons, menu commands, and shortcut keys to insert elements on-screen (see Figure 1.5).

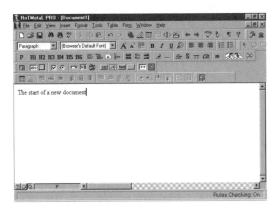

**Figure 1.5** *The initial HTML document and four toolbars in HoTMetaL PRO.*

Either type text within the start tags, which indicate the beginning of an element statement, and end tags, which indicate the end of an element statement, or select attributes from dialog boxes. When you have finished, save the HTML document as you would any other file.

Part 7, "Webliography" includes a section titled "HTML Editors," which lists online resources.

## HTML Elements

Regardless of how you create an HTML document, knowing the syntax of an element statement is important. The most elementary element uses the following syntax:

`<element>`

Two examples are `<P>`, which causes a paragraph break, and `<BR>`, which starts a new line. Both of these examples are *start tags*, the beginning of an HTML element. Although `<P>` has an *end tag* (the end of an HTML element), `</P>`, it is optional; you are not required to use it. `<BR>` does not have an end tag.

**XML, a Web page language and a "child" of SGML, just like HTML, requires end tags. So, whenever an end tag is optional, it's a good idea to add it—for future compatibility with XML.**

NOTE

Browsers and HTML editors are programmed to know that the less than (<) symbol marks the beginning of a start or end tag and the greater than (>) symbol marks the end. The text within the two symbols is the actual element and attributes on which the browser acts.

**`<BR>` indicates the end of one line and the beginning of the next. If you think about it, there is no reason for an end tag in this situation. Where would you put it? Common sense can get you a long way in HTML.**

NOTE

Sometimes, an element has both a start tag and an end tag:

`<start-element>element-contents</end-element>`

In the example:

`<TITLE>Chocolate Chip Cookies</TITLE>`

- `<` marks the beginning of the start tag.
- `TITLE` is the element enclosed within the start tag, the command that the browser will interpret.
- `>` marks the completion of the start tag.

- `Chocolate Chip Cookies` is the text that will appear in the browser title bar when the page is loaded.
- `<` marks the beginning of the end tag.
- `/TITLE` marks the end of the element, the required end of a `TITLE` element. The slash (`/`) symbol is included in all end tags.
- `>` marks the completion of the end tag.

**Some HTML references and tutorials refer to elements with required start tags and end tags as containers. In the prior example, the end tag states very clearly that the title text is complete; it is contained within the start tag and end tag. Without the `</TITLE>`, a browser would treat all following text as part of the title, until it encountered any start tag.**

More complex elements may add attributes, usually using the following syntax:

```
<start-element option1="value1" option2="value2"></end-element>
```

Notice that the start tag, within the less than and greater than symbols, includes all the attributes. For example:

```
<TABLE BORDER WIDTH="120" HEIGHT="80">
```

where:

- `<` marks the beginning of the start tag.
- `TABLE` is the element name.
- `BORDER` is an attribute that turns on a table border.
- `WIDTH="120"` is an attribute that sets the table width to 120 pixels.
- `HEIGHT="80"` is an attribute that sets the table height to 80 pixels.
- `>` marks the completion of the start tag.

**The required end tag, which completes the definition of the table, is several table rows below the start tag and does not appear in this example.**

You can embed many HTML elements within other elements. For example:

```
<FONT COLOR="red" SIZE="5"><B><I>Watch this
space!</I></B></FONT>
```

These FONT element attributes change text color to red and increase the size of the text from the default size of 3. The start and end B (boldface) elements are nested within the FONT elements, and the I (italics) elements are embedded within the B elements. Notice that the nesting is completely symmetrical and does not overlap:

```
<FONT>              </FONT>
   <B>          </B>
      <I>   <I>
```

When creating an HTML document, one of the few rules that you can violate is to overlap nested elements. Using the previous example, if you change the elements layout to this:

```
<FONT COLOR="red" SIZE="5"><B><I>Watch this
space!</FONT></B></I>
```

and overlap nested elements:

```
<FONT>              ˋ</I>
   <B>          </B>
      <I>   </FONT>
```

your document might look strange, and the HTML police might take you away.

**NOTE** Most browsers ignore elements and attributes that they don't recognize. For example, when you use Netscape extensions and Microsoft extensions that are not included in the HTML 4.0 element set, Netscape Navigator or Microsoft Internet Explorer can interpret the elements and their attributes, but many other browsers won't. You'll find several examples of this in Part 4, Chapter 7, "Netscape and Microsoft Extensions."

## The Contents of an HTML Document

An HTML document contains two parts: the HEAD section and the BODY section.

### The HEAD Section

The HEAD section of an HTML document, started and ended with the optional HEAD element, describes the document to programs, such as browsers, search indexes, and HTML validators; to other HTML documents; and to people. HEAD section elements are TITLE, ISINDEX, BASE, STYLE, SCRIPT, META, and LINK.

Use the META element to provide the name of the author, the date on which the document was created, and the last date it was edited. It is important to mention that the META element can also include a list of keywords that search indexes will use to match keywords that people have entered and to rank your document with other documents on a list. Search indexes also use the TITLE element as a document identifier. Some browsers use styles within the STYLE elements to specify document formats. (See Part 5, "Cascading Style Sheets," for more information.)

Except for the title, the contents of the HEAD section do not appear on the Web page when it's loaded. Some detail-oriented people (a much friendlier term than quibbler or hairsplitter) might argue that the title is not actually on the page; it's above the page in the title bar. Whatever.

Except for the title (depending on your opinion of its location on-screen), about the only way to see the contents of the HEAD section is to view the document in an HTML editor, word processor, or text editor. In a typical browser, viewing the source code only shows you the BODY section of the document—not the HEAD section.

### The BODY Section

The BODY section of an HTML document, started and ended with the optional BODY element, contains all the parts of the document that visitors can see, including text, links, and multimedia. It's easy to identify BODY section elements: simply subtract the HEAD elements (TITLE, ISINDEX, BASE, STYLE, SCRIPT, META, and LINK) from the rest of the HTML 4.0 element set, and there you have it.

Part 7, "Webliography" includes a section titled "Creating an HTML Document," which lists online resources.

## A Sample HTML Document

This section contains a short HTML document (see Figure 1.6), which demonstrates links, lists, and a graphic.

```
<!DOCTYPE HTML PUBLIC "-//W3C//DTD HTML 4.0//EN">

<HTML>

<HEAD>

<TITLE>A Sample HTML Document</TITLE>

</HEAD>

<BODY BGCOLOR="white">

<H1>Lists</H1>

Thanks for visiting. On this page, you'll see an

<A HREF="http://www.eddygrp.com/OL">ordered list</A> and
an

<A HREF="http://www.eddygrp.com/UL">unordered list.</A>

<H3>An Ordered List</H3>

<OL>

<LI>Do this step.

<LI>Then do this step.

<LI>Do it all over again starting at the top.

</OL>

<H3>An Unordered List</H3>

<UL>

<LI>Planes

<LI>Trains

<LI>Automobiles

</UL>

<CENTER><IMG SRC="scene.gif"></CENTER>

</BODY>

</HTML>
```

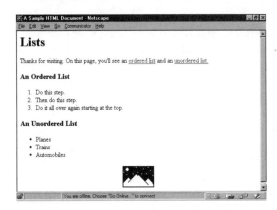

**Figure 1.6** *The sample HTML document as viewed in a browser program.*

 **NOTE** As you probably have noticed, some Web sites allow users to download files to their computers. The protocol used for file downloads is FTP (file transfer protocol), and the programs that you use to add FTP to your site are FTP clients. To learn more about FTP, visit the following sites: FTP Tools: Stock Up Today, To Be Ready for Tomorrow (http://www.hotfiles.com/toolkits/ftp/tlk0797.html), A Crash Course in FTP Clients (http://www.hotfiles.com/toolkits/ftp/side797.html), and Anonymous FTP FAQ (http://www.iss.net/vd/anonftp.html).

## Using Graphics and Multimedia

Use the A, IMG, or OBJECT element to insert graphics or multimedia files in an HTML document. Note the following:

- Always remember that many users access the Web with a 14.4 modem. Loading speed is critically important; most users are not willing to wait more than a minute or two.
- To accelerate graphic loading, use the IMG tag's HEIGHT and WIDTH attributes to specify height and width, respectively. Then, the browser knows how much space to reserve for the graphic, and can go ahead and

load other parts of the page on-screen. You can also use HEIGHT and WIDTH to scale a graphic as it loads.

- For Netscape Navigator users only, you can load a low resolution and high resolution version of a JPEG graphic file using the IMG element and the LOWSRC and SRC attributes. To load a low resolution, faster-loading version of a graphic file, use the LOWSRC attribute, unique to Netscape. Then load the higher resolution version using the SRC attribute. The low-resolution version gives the user a chance to get a first look before deciding to stay at your page.

- JPEG files are usually smaller than GIF files, which makes them faster to load.

- One way of getting around having a large graphic in a document is to use a thumbnail version instead. Then, the user can either see the large graphic by clicking on a link, or ignore the graphic altogether.

- You can reduce loading time for a graphic file by reducing its number of colors.

- You can reduce loading time for audio and video files by setting a lower sampling frequency.

- The newest browsers have built-in audio and video players. However, users with older browsers must download special sound video players or video players, install them, and perhaps configure them before they will operate.

- Downloading or accessing a large multimedia file should be the user's choice. So, either insert a text or graphic link.

- It's a good idea to show the size of a large file before a user commits to loading it or downloading it.

- If you are writing an HTML document for Microsoft Internet Explorer users, you can use the BGSOUND element to play an audio file when a user first visits your site. Choose the sound file carefully; some users will be annoyed by certain tunes, and others will not be willing to wait extra time for the sound file to load.

Part 4, Chapter 1, "General-Purpose Elements" includes an entry for the A element. Part 4, Chapter 6, "Multimedia and

Special Effects Elements" includes entries for the IMG and OBJECT elements.

## Supported Multimedia Formats

This section lists supported formats for graphics, audio, and video files.

### Graphics Formats

The most used graphics formats are GIF and JPEG. In addition you can use PNG (Portable Network Graphics), XBM bitmaps (a UNIX graphics standard), and Adobe's Portable Document Format (PDF), which requires the Adobe Acrobat reader.

NOTE    For more information about the PNG file format which is growing in popularity, refer to "PNG (Portable Network Graphics)," a W3C document, at http://www.w3.org/pub/WWW/Graphics/PNG/Overview.htmland the "PNG Specification", at http://www.w3.org/pub/WWW/TR/REC-png-multi.html.

### Audio Formats

AU is the most commonly used audio format because it has both Windows and Macintosh support. Macintosh supports the AIFF format, and Windows supports both MID (MIDI) and WAV (waveform) files. MPEG (Motion Pictures Expert Group) audio is another valid format.

### Video Formats

Popular video formats include MPEG (Motion Pictures Expert Group), QuickTime, and AVI, which is a Windows-only format.
    Part 7, "Webliography" includes a section titled "Using Graphics and Multimedia," which lists online resources.

## TESTING A PAGE

Before posting a page, it is imperative to test it to make sure that you have used appropriate syntax, chosen supported HTML elements and attributes, and properly named the URLs for links and graphics. You also want to see how your page looks under various browsers.

HTML validators, available as online services or as programs installed on your computer, check syntax, elements, and URLs, using built-in or user-specified criteria. To use a validator, simply fill in a form, click a button, and receive the results. Then, correct your HTML document and run the validator again until the document is error-free.

 **When creating HTML documents, it's a good idea to stick by the latest HTML standard rather than using extensions, which are not supported by most browsers. In most cases, a browser will ignore syntax that it can't interpret. Sometimes, a browser will misinterpret HTML statements with unpredictable results.**

N O T E

After validation is clean, look at your document using as many browsers as possible. Also, make sure that your graphics load in a reasonable time.

*Part 7, Webliography* includes the section "Testing a Page," a list of online resources.

## REGISTERING A DOMAIN NAME

Many businesses and individuals want to use their own domain name rather than their Internet provider's name. Would you rather have this address:

```
http://www.provider.net/~example/
```

or this?

```
http://www.example.com/
```

You or your provider can register a domain name by following these steps:

1. Choose one or two acceptable names.
2. At the InterNIC (at http://rs.internic.net/rs-internic.html), check to see if one of the chosen names is available.
3. If the domain name is already in use, repeat steps 1 and 2 until you identify a unique name.

4. Complete a registration template and select a payment type. You can even use a credit card.
5. Wait up to three weeks for the InterNIC to process your application.

**Many Internet service providers (ISPs) offer to register your domain name at no cost or for a nominal charge.**

N O T E

Part 7, "Webliography" includes a section titled "Registering a Domain Name," which lists online resources.

## Posting a Page

Internet providers have different procedures for uploading an HTML document and associated files to a server. You may need to establish a telnet connection, enter UNIX commands, use an FTP utility, a terminal emulator, or a combination of two or three of these. However, all uploads follow these steps:

1. From the Web or via e-mail or fax, obtain and read your provider's instructions for uploading. (This may also include directions for specifying *permissions*, whether you will allow others to read or even edit your HTML files.)
2. Place the HTML document and all files associated with it—graphics, audio, and video—in a single directory or folder on your computer.
3. On your computer, open the HTML document and change directory, folder, filenames, and URLs to the names of the assigned folders or directories on your provider's server.
4. On your computer, save the edited HTML document. If you have created an HTML document, you may have to change the extension to HTM, depending on your provider's instructions.
5. If necessary, on your computer, install utilities that your provider requires to upload files.

6. Using your provider's instructions, log onto the assigned server and create one or more folders or directories.

7. Upload the HTML document and associated files into the newly created folders or directories. You may have to rename the HTML document and other files to conform with the provider's standards.

# PART 2

# HTML in Plain English

If a writer's worst nightmare is a blank sheet of paper, a Web page designer's bad dream is a blank computer screen. To compound the terror, HTML elements are not always easy to remember. For example, what do OL and UL do? Are DL, DT, DD, and DH related? What about TH and THEAD? What's the difference between CAPTION and LEGEND? You get the idea.

This part is for those of you who know what HTML can do but don't always remember the name of the element or extension. This part is composed of two columns: in the left column, you'll find tasks to be performed with italicized key words; the right column contains the element or extension with which you'll accomplish your goal.

**NOTE**

You will find all entities (that is, special characters) in Part 4, Chapter 2, "Special Characters."

| IF YOU WANT TO... | USE THIS ELEMENT |
| --- | --- |
| identify an *acronym* | ACRONYM |
| provide author *address* information | ADDRESS |
| *anchor* a hypertext link | A |
| embed a Java *applet* | APPLET |
| define an image map *area* | AREA |
| include a *background sound* | BGSOUND |
| define the *base* (default) *font* size | BASEFONT |
| define the base (absolute) URL | BASE |
| change to a *bigger* font | BIG |
| *blink* text on and off | BLINK |

**35**

| **IF YOU WANT TO...** | **USE THIS ELEMENT** |
| --- | --- |
| define the *body* of the document | BODY |
| specify *boldface* text | B |
| *break a line* of text | BR |
| *break a word* or line in a nonbreak line | WBR |
| insert a *button* in a form | BUTTON |
| place a table *caption* | CAPTION |
| place a form controls *caption* | LEGEND |
| *center* a line of text between the margins | CENTER |
| *cite* a book or other source | CITE |
| define a *column group* | COLGROUP |
| align a table *column* | COL |
| insert a non-displaying *comment* | ! |
| insert a *definition* | DFN |
| start a *definition* (glossary) *list* | DL |
| insert a *definition description* in a definition list | DD |
| insert a *definition term* in a definition list | DT |
| indicate *deleted* text | DEL |
| specify text *direction* | BDO |
| start a *directory* list | DIR |
| mark a *division* in a document | DIV |
| state the *document type* | !DOCTYPE |
| *embed* an object | EMBED |
| code *embed alternates* for nonembed browsers | NOEMBED |
| *emphasize* text | EM |
| mark a *field set* | FIELDSET |
| insert an inline *floating frame* | IFRAME |
| assign a *font* characteristic | FONT |
| insert a fill-out *form* | FORM |
| specify a *frame* | FRAME |
| code *frame alternates* for nonframe browsers | NOFRAMES |

| IF YOU WANT TO... | USE THIS ELEMENT |
| --- | --- |
| specify a *frames set* | FRAMESET |
| place a *horizontal rule* | HR |
| describe an *HTML* document | HEAD |
| start and end an *HTML* document | HTML |
| create a unique *identifier* | NEXTID |
| define an *inflow layer* | ILAYER |
| specify an *inline image* | IMG |
| specify an *input field* in a form | INPUT |
| indicate *inserted* text | INS |
| specify *italic* text | I |
| generate a public *key* | KEYGEN |
| indicate *keyboard input* | KBD |
| *label* an input control | LABEL |
| define a *layer* of HTML content | LAYER |
| code a *layer alternate* for nonlayer browsers | NOLAYER |
| make a *level 1* heading | H1 |
| make a *level 2* heading | H2 |
| make a *level 3* heading | H3 |
| make a *level 4* heading | H4 |
| make a *level 5* heading | H5 |
| make a *level 6* heading | H6 |
| *link* to another document | LINK |
| define a *list item* | LI |
| define an image *map* | MAP |
| add a scrolling *marquee* | MARQUEE |
| identify a *menu* list | MENU |
| provide *meta* information | META |
| format *multiple columns* | MULTICOL |
| specify an area with *no line breaks* | NOBR |

| IF YOU WANT TO... | USE THIS ELEMENT |
|---|---|
| embed a multimedia *object* | OBJECT |
| insert a list *option* in a form | OPTION |
| specify an *ordered* (numbered) *list* | OL |
| start a new *paragraph* | P |
| define *parameters* for a Java applet | PARAM |
| specify a *predefined* layout and font | PRE |
| identify a long *quotation* | BLOCKQUOTE |
| identify a short *quotation* | Q |
| display text as *sample* computer output | SAMP |
| define a client-side *script* | SCRIPT |
| include a LiveWire-compiled *script* | SERVER |
| code *script alternates* for nonscript browsers | NOSCRIPT |
| identify a simple *search index* | ISINDEX |
| start a *selection* list in a form | SELECT |
| change to a *smaller* font | SMALL |
| display as *source* program code | CODE |
| mark a *span* of text | SPAN |
| specify *strikethrough* text | S or STRIKE |
| *strongly* emphasize text | STRONG |
| define a *style* or style sheet | STYLE |
| specify *subscript* text | SUB |
| specify *superscript* text | SUP |
| identify a *table* | TABLE |
| define the *table body* | TBODY |
| indicate *table data* | TD |
| define a *table footer* | TFOOT |
| define a *table header* | THEAD |
| define a *table heading* | TH |
| define a *table row* | TR |
| specify *teletype* (monospaced) text | TT |

| IF YOU WANT TO... | USE THIS ELEMENT |
|---|---|
| define a multiline *text field* in a form | TEXTAREA |
| specify an HTML document *title* | TITLE |
| specify *underlined* text | U |
| specify an *unordered* (bulleted) *list* | UL |
| display text indicating a *variable* | VAR |
| insert a *white-space* area | SPACER |

# PART 3

# HTML Elements A to Z

This part is basically a table of the elements covered comprehensively in the chapters in Part 4. Here, you'll find an alphabetically arranged master list of HTML elements and the chapters in which they are located.

You will find all entities (that is, special characters) in Part 4, Chapter 2, "Special Characters."

NOTE

| ELEMENT | CHAPTER |
|---|---|
| ! | General-Purpose (Ch. 1) |
| !DOCTYPE | General-Purpose (Ch. 1) |
| A | General-Purpose (Ch. 1) |
| ACRONYM | General-Purpose (Ch. 1) |
| ADDRESS | General-Purpose (Ch. 1) |
| APPLET | Multimedia/Special Effects (Ch. 6) |
| AREA | Multimedia/Special Effects (Ch. 6) |
| B | General-Purpose (Ch. 1) |
| BASE | General-Purpose (Ch. 1) |
| BASEFONT | General-Purpose (Ch. 1) |
| BDO | General-Purpose (Ch. 1) |
| BGSOUND | Netscape/Microsoft (Ch. 7) |
| BIG | General-Purpose (Ch. 1) |
| BLINK | Netscape/Microsoft (Ch. 7) |
| BLOCKQUOTE | General-Purpose (Ch. 1) |
| BODY | General-Purpose (Ch. 1) |

| ELEMENT | CHAPTER |
|---------|---------|
| BR | General-Purpose (Ch. 1) |
| BUTTON | Forms (Ch. 4) |
| CAPTION | Tables (Ch. 3) |
| CENTER | General-Purpose (Ch. 1) |
| CITE | General-Purpose (Ch. 1) |
| CODE | General-Purpose (Ch. 1) |
| COL | Tables (Ch. 3) |
| COLGROUP | Tables (Ch. 3) |
| DD | General-Purpose (Ch. 1) |
| DEL | General-Purpose (Ch. 1) |
| DFN | General-Purpose (Ch. 1) |
| DIR | General-Purpose (Ch. 1) |
| DIV | General-Purpose (Ch. 1) |
| DL | General-Purpose (Ch. 1) |
| DT | General-Purpose (Ch. 1) |
| EM | General-Purpose (Ch. 1) |
| EMBED | Netscape/Microsoft (Ch. 7) |
| FIELDSET | Forms (Ch. 4) |
| FONT | General-Purpose (Ch. 1) |
| FORM | Forms (Ch. 4) |
| FRAME | Frames (Ch. 5) |
| FRAMESET | Frames (Ch. 5) |
| H1 | General-Purpose (Ch. 1) |
| H2 | General-Purpose (Ch. 1) |
| H3 | General-Purpose (Ch. 1) |
| H4 | General-Purpose (Ch. 1) |
| H5 | General-Purpose (Ch. 1) |
| H6 | General-Purpose (Ch. 1) |
| HEAD | General-Purpose (Ch. 1) |
| HR | General-Purpose (Ch. 1) |

| ELEMENT | CHAPTER |
|---|---|
| HTML | General-Purpose (Ch. 1) |
| I | General-Purpose (Ch. 1) |
| IFRAME | Frames (Ch. 5) |
| ILAYER | Netscape/Microsoft (Ch. 7) |
| IMG | Multimedia/Special Effects (Ch. 6) |
| INPUT | Forms (Ch. 4) |
| INS | General-Purpose (Ch. 1) |
| ISINDEX | Forms (Ch. 4) |
| KBD | General-Purpose (Ch. 1) |
| KEYGEN | Netscape/Microsoft (Ch. 7) |
| LABEL | Forms (Ch. 4) |
| LAYER | Netscape/Microsoft (Ch. 7) |
| LEGEND | Forms (Ch. 4) |
| LI | General-Purpose (Ch. 1) |
| LINK | General-Purpose (Ch. 1) |
| MAP | Multimedia/Special Effects (Ch. 6) |
| MARQUEE | Netscape/Microsoft (Ch. 7) |
| MENU | General-Purpose (Ch. 1) |
| META | General-Purpose (Ch. 1) |
| MULTICOL | Netscape/Microsoft (Ch. 7) |
| NEXTID | Netscape/Microsoft (Ch. 7) |
| NOBR | Netscape/Microsoft (Ch. 7) |
| NOEMBED | Netscape/Microsoft (Ch. 7) |
| NOFRAMES | Frames (Ch. 5) |
| NOLAYER | Netscape/Microsoft (Ch. 7) |
| NOSCRIPT | Multimedia/Special Effects (Ch. 6) |
| OBJECT | Multimedia/Special Effects (Ch. 6) |
| OL | General-Purpose (Ch. 1) |
| OPTION | Forms (Ch. 4) |
| P | General-Purpose (Ch. 1) |

| ELEMENT | CHAPTER |
| --- | --- |
| PARAM | Multimedia/Special Effects (Ch. 6) |
| PRE | General-Purpose (Ch. 1) |
| Q | General-Purpose (Ch. 1) |
| S/STRIKE | General-Purpose (Ch. 1) |
| SAMP | General-Purpose (Ch. 1) |
| SCRIPT | Multimedia/Special Effects (Ch. 6) |
| SELECT | Forms (Ch. 4) |
| SERVER | Netscape/Microsoft (Ch. 7) |
| SMALL | General-Purpose (Ch. 1) |
| SPACER | Netscape/Microsoft (Ch. 7) |
| SPAN | General-Purpose (Ch. 1) |
| STRONG | General-Purpose (Ch. 1) |
| STYLE | General-Purpose (Ch. 1) |
| SUB | General-Purpose (Ch. 1) |
| SUP | General-Purpose (Ch. 1) |
| TABLE | Tables (Ch. 3) |
| TBODY | Tables (Ch. 3) |
| TD | Tables (Ch. 3) |
| TEXTAREA | Forms (Ch. 4) |
| TFOOT | Tables (Ch. 3) |
| TH | Tables (Ch. 3) |
| THEAD | Tables (Ch. 3) |
| TITLE | General-Purpose (Ch. 1) |
| TR | Tables (Ch. 3) |
| TT | General-Purpose (Ch. 1) |
| U | General-Purpose (Ch. 1) |
| UL | General-Purpose (Ch. 1) |
| VAR | General-Purpose (Ch. 1) |
| WBR | Netscape/Microsoft (Ch. 7) |

# PART 4

# HTML Tags and Codes, Organized by Group

This part groups HTML elements and special characters by function. The groups are:

- General-purpose
- Special characters
- Tables
- Forms
- Frames
- Multimedia/Special effects
- Netscape and Microsoft extensions

This part is the cornerstone of *HTML in Plain English,* Second Edition. Here, you will find detailed information about each element and entity in the 4.0 set as well as Netscape and Microsoft extensions, many of which will be added to the next version of HTML.

Each element's description uses the same format. The heading includes the name of the element and a very brief description. Following that are the purpose, syntax and attributes, notes about using the element, one or more examples, and a list of related elements.

The syntax uses certain conventions:

Required attributes are listed before optional attributes. Each type of attributes is arranged in alphabetical order.

{}      You must choose one of the attributes, values, or punctuation within the braces.

[]      You can choose one or more of the attributes, values, or punctuation within the brackets.

|      A pipe symbol indicates an OR. Choose one attribute or value OR another. In other words, just choose one.

...     An ellipsis indicates a continuation of the preceding attribute and that the next attribute is the end of the series.

<u>default</u>   If an attribute or value is underlined, it is the default. In other words, if you do not use the attribute, your browser will automatically use the default attribute or value.

*Italics*   Italicized text represents a variable (such as a file name, path, color, number, URL, and so on) that you enter. Most times, enclose a variable within double quotes (" ") or single quotes (' '); do not mix double and single quotes.

Appendix B, "Attributes in Depth," describes all attributes in the HTML 4.0 standard and for Netscape and Microsoft extensions. With each entry, you'll find valid values and usage notes.

If an attribute is supported only by the Netscape Navigator or Microsoft Internet Explorer browser, its description will be preceded by an icon:

indicates that Netscape Navigator can read and use the attribute but most other browsers cannot. Use this attribute sparingly or not at all.

indicates that Microsoft Internet Explorer can read and use the attribute but most other browsers cannot. Use this attribute sparingly or not at all.

**1**

# General-Purpose Elements

These general-purpose elements are those that you will use to create typical HTML documents and will utilize most often.

| **!** | **Comment** |
| --- | --- |

## Purpose

Places a comment in the document.

## Syntax

```
<!- comment text->
```

## Where

- *comment text* is the text comprising the comment.

## Notes

This element is an SGML standard—not part of HTML 4.0.

Use a comment to document a line or part of an HTML document. For example, you can state the reason for using a particular element rather than another. Or, for someone who will maintain this document, you can describe how you created a complex table or form. Comments are very useful if one individual creates an HTML document and another maintains it.

You can see the comment in the source file but not in the published document.

You cannot nest a comment within another comment.

## Examples

Example 1

```
<!- watch the following alignment ->
```

Example 2

```
<!- This comment overflows to a second line, but that's OK
with me. ->
```

| !DOCTYPE | Document Declaration |
|---|---|

## Purpose

Identifies the type of document.

## Syntax

```
<!DOCTYPE HTML PUBLIC "-//W3C//DTD HTML 4.0[ spec]//lang">
```

## Where

- *spec* is the specification: Draft, Final, Strict. The default is Final.
- *lang* is the two-letter HTML DTD language. EN represents English.

## Notes

This element originated in HTML 2.0 but is actually an SGML standard, not part of HTML 4.0.

The `<!DOCTYPE` declaration, which leads a document and which is automatically placed at the top of a new HTML document created using an HTML editor, is not required. However, it is a good idea to include this line, so that individuals, browser software, validation software, and other programs can read that you are using HTML 4.0.

You can see this comment in the source file but not in the published document.

## Examples

Example 1

```
<!DOCTYPE HTML PUBLIC "-//W3C//DTD HTML 4.0//EN">
```

Example 2

```
<!DOCTYPE HTML PUBLIC "-//W3C//DTD HTML 4.0 Draft//EN">
```

## Example 3

```
<!DOCTYPE HTML PUBLIC "-//W3C//DTD HTML 4.0 Final//EN">
```

## Example 4

```
<!DOCTYPE HTML PUBLIC "-//W3C//DTD HTML 4.0 Strict//EN">
```

| A | Hypertext Link |
|---|---|

## Purpose

Specifies a link and/or *anchor* (location to which you can jump either within the current HTML document or to another HTML document).

## Syntax

```
<A[ ACCESSKEY="shortcut_key"][ CHARSET="ISO-8859-
1"]["char_set"][ CLASS="class_name"][ COORDS="coords_1,
coords_2, coords_3[..., coords_n]"][
DATAFLD="ds_col_name"][ DATASRC="ds_identifier"][
DIR="LTR"|"RTL"][ HREF="link_url"][ ID="id_name"][
LANG="lang_code"][
LANGUAGE="JAVASCRIPT"|"JSCRIPT"|"VBS[CRIPT]"][
METHODS="functions_perf"][ NAME="anchor_name"][
ONBLUR="bl_script_data"][ ONCLICK="cl_script_data"][ OND-
BLCLICK="dc_script_data"][ ONFOCUS="fc_script_data"][
ONHELP="hlp_script_data"][ ONKEYDOWN="kd_script_data"][
ONKEYPRESS="kp_script_data"][ ONKEYUP="ku_script_data"][
ONMOUSEDOWN="md_script_data"][
ONMOUSEMOVE="mm_script_data"][
ONMOUSEOUT="mo_script_data"][
ONMOUSEOVER="mov_script_data"][
ONMOUSEUP="mu_script_data"][
ONSELECTSTART="ss_script_data"][
REL="Contents"|"Index"|"Glossary"|"Copyright"|"Next"|"Prev
ious"|"Start"|"Help"|"Bookmark"|"Stylesheet"|"Alternate"|"
Same"|"Parent"|"link_type_1"[
"link_type_2"[..."link_type_n"]]][
REV="Contents"|"Index"|"Glossary"|"Copyright"|"Next"|"Prev
ious"|"Start"|"Help"|"Bookmark"|"Stylesheet"|"Alternate"|"
link_type_3"[ "link_type_4"[..."link_type_m"]]][
SHAPE="RECT[ANGLE]"|"CIRC[LE]"|"POLY[GON]"|"DEFAULT"][
STYLE="name_1: value_1"[; "name_2: value_2"][...; "name_n:
value_n"]][ TABINDEX="position_number"][ TARGET="win-
dow"|"_blank"|"_parent"|"_self"|"_top"][ TITLE="title"][
URN="urn"]>anchor</A>
```

## Where

- **ACCESSKEY** assigns a shortcut key to the link in order to focus on it.
- **CHARSET** specifies the character set for the hypertext link.
- **CLASS** specifies a class identification for the link.
- **COORDS** is a list containing the coordinates of a shape.
- **Microsoft** **DATAFLD** specifies the column name from the file that provides the data source object for the link.
- **Microsoft** **DATASRC** specifies the identifier of the data source object for the link.
- **DIR** specifies the direction in which the link text is displayed: left-to-right or right-to-left.
- **HREF** specifies a URL for the link.
- **ID** provides a unique identifier name for the link.
- **LANG** provides the code representing the language used for the link text.
- **Microsoft** **LANGUAGE** declares the scripting language of the current script.
- **Microsoft** **METHODS** indicates the functions to be performed on the data source object.
- **NAME** is the unique name of an anchor.
- **Microsoft** **ONBLUR** specifies that the referred-to script runs when the link loses focus (that is, it is no longer the active element).
- **ONCLICK** specifies that the referred-to script runs when a user moves the mouse pointer or other pointing device over the link and clicks the device button.
- **ONDBLCLICK** specifies that the referred-to script runs when a user moves the mouse pointer or other pointing device over the link and double-clicks the device button.

-  ONFOCUS specifies that the referred-to script runs when the current element receives focus (that is, is made active) by the mouse pointer or other pointing device.

-  ONHELP specifies that the referred-to script runs when a user presses the **F1** or **Help** key over the current element.

- ONKEYDOWN specifies that the referred-to script runs when a user presses and holds a key down over the link.

- ONKEYPRESS specifies that the referred-to script runs when a user presses and releases a key over the link.

- ONKEYUP specifies that the referred-to script runs when a user releases a key over the link.

- ONMOUSEDOWN specifies that the referred-to script runs when a user moves the mouse pointer or other pointing device over the link and presses and holds down the device button.

- ONMOUSEMOVE specifies that the referred-to script runs when a user moves the mouse pointer or other pointing device over the link.

- ONMOUSEOUT specifies that the referred-to script runs when a user moves the mouse pointer or other pointing device away from the link.

- ONMOUSEOVER specifies that the referred-to script runs the first time a user moves the mouse pointer or other pointing device over the link.

- ONMOUSEUP specifies that the referred-to script runs when a user moves the mouse pointer or other pointing device over the link and releases a pressed-down device button.

- ONSELECTSTART specifies that the referred-to script runs when a user starts selecting an object.

- REL specifies a forward link type; that is, the type of relationship of the current link forward to the anchor.

57

- REV specifies a backward link type; that is, the type of relationship of the anchor back to the current link.
- SHAPE is the shape of an area within a link.
- STYLE sets styles for the link.
- TABINDEX defines the position of the current element in all the elements that a user can navigate using a Tab or Shift+Tab key.
- TARGET loads a linked and named document in a particular window or frame. (For examples of the TARGET attribute, see Part V, Chapter 5, "Frames.")
- TITLE provides a title or title information about the link.
- **Microsoft** URN names a uniform resource name (URN) for the target document specified with the TARGET attribute.

- *anchor* is a named location within the document to which you can jump.

## Notes

This element originated in HTML 2.0.

Any text or element within the A element becomes a link. If you want to link to a document under the current document, there is no need to enter the complete URL. Simply enter the file name (for example, **child.html**).

You cannot nest links and anchors within the A element.

If the link is on the current page, don't use its complete address; doing so tells the browser to reload the page, which is costly in time and resources.

URLs to which you can link include files on your computer (file), on the World Wide Web (http), at a file transfer protocol (FTP) site (ftp), at a Gopher site (gopher), at a Usenet newsgroup (news), on a WAIS site (wais), or a Telnet connection (telnet).

When creating a text link, use meaningful words, such as the title of the page of the top-level heading. Do not use "Click here" or even "here." Make a text link part of the text on a page rather than breaking the flow for a reader. All but the newest users can identify a link without being prompted to click.

The HTML 4.0 DTD categorizes this as an inline element.

The TARGET attribute allows a user to visit a target window without leaving your site. For example, a user can click on an advertising icon at your site and return to your site without retyping your URL.

## Examples

Example 1 (Figure 4.1)

```
<P>Click on <A HREF="http://www.yahoo.com/">Yahoo</A> to
go to a master directory.
```

Click on Yahoo to go to a master directory

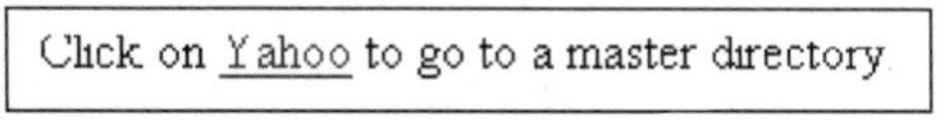

*Figure 4.1 A standard text link.*

Example 2 (Figure 4.2)

```
<P>Click on <A HREF="http://www.yahoo.com/">Yahoo <IMG
SRC="buttons.gif"></A> to go to a master directory.
```

Click on Yahoo 🔘 to go to a master directory.

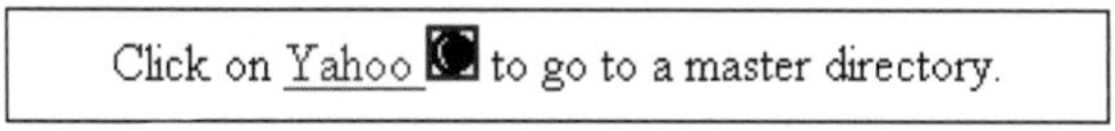

*Figure 4.2 A text link with a graphic link to its right.*

Example 3 (Figure 4.3)

```
<P>Click on <A HREF="http://www.yahoo.com/"><IMG SRC="but-
tons.gif">Yahoo </A> to go to a master directory.
```

Click on 🔘Yahoo to go to a master directory.

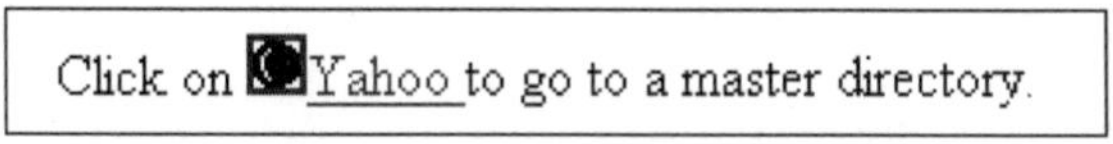

*Figure 4.3 A text link with a graphic link to its left.*

Example 4 (Figure 4.4)

```
<P><A HREF="http://www.yahoo.com/"><IMG
SRC="buttons.gif"></A> Click on <A
HREF="http://www.yahoo.com/"> Yahoo </A> to go to a master
directory.
```

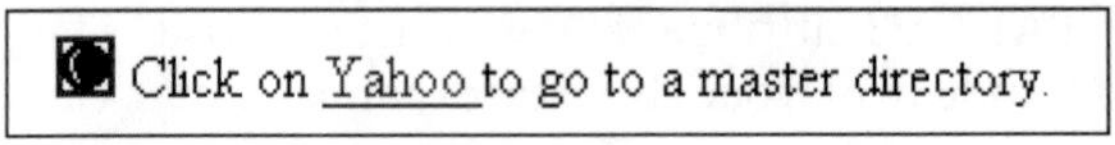

> ▓ Click on <u>Yahoo</u> to go to a master directory.

*Figure 4.4 A graphic link preceding a line that includes a text link.*

Example 5 (Figure 4.5)

```
<P>Send me a message at <A
HREF="mailto:eddygrp@sover.net">eddygrp@sover.net</A>.
```

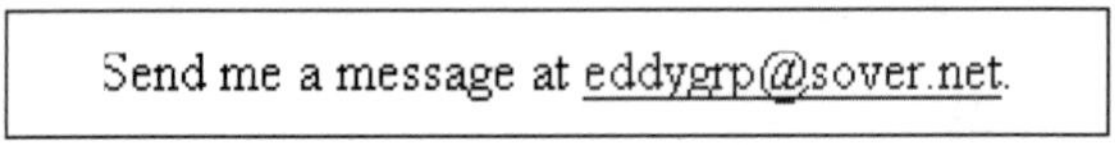

> Send me a message at <u>eddygrp@sover.net</u>.

*Figure 4.5 A link on which you click to send a message.*

Example 6 (Figure 4.6)

```
<P><A HREF="#a">A</A> <A HREF="#b">B</A> <A
HREF="#c">C</A>

<A NAME="a"><H2>A</H2></A>

<A NAME="b"><H2>B</H2></A>

<A NAME="c"><H2>C</H2></A>
```

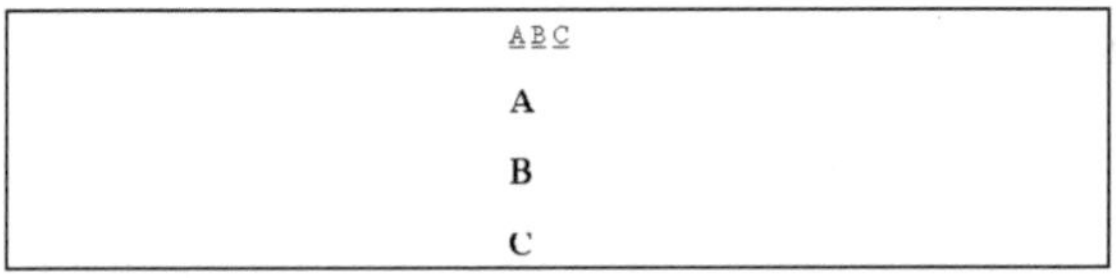

> <u>A B C</u>
>
> **A**
>
> **B**
>
> **C**

*Figure 4.6 Links used to jump to sections of a document.*

Example 7 (Figure 4.7)

```
<H2>Chapter 2</H2>

<A HREF="contents.htm">Top</A> 

<A HREF="ch01.htm" REV="previous">Previous</A> 

<A HREF="ch03.htm" REL="next">Next</A>
```

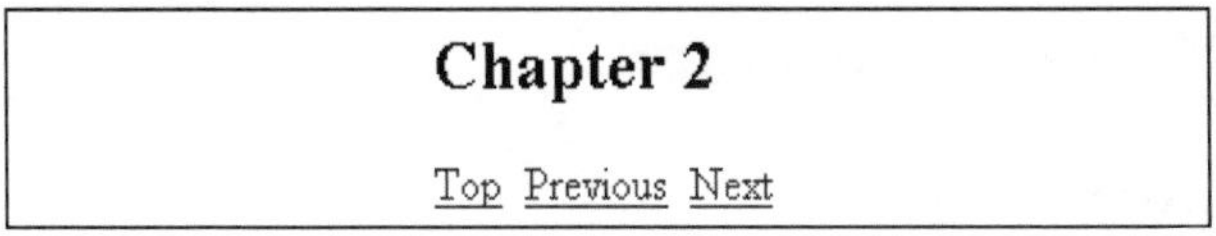

> # Chapter 2
>
> Top  Previous  Next

*Figure 4.7 A page with links to the previous, next, and top pages.*

## Related Element

LINK

| **ACRONYM** | **Acronym** |
| --- | --- |

## Purpose

Indicates an acronym, such as FBI, CIA, FTP, URL, WWW, and so on.

## Syntax

```
<ACRONYM[ CLASS="class_name"][ DIR="LTR"|"RTL"][
ID="id_name"][ LANG="lang_code"][
ONCLICK="cl_script_data"][ ONDBLCLICK="dc_script_data"][
ONKEYDOWN="kd_script_data"][ ONKEYPRESS="kp_script_data"][
ONKEYUP="ku_script_data"][ ONMOUSEDOWN="md_script_data"][
ONMOUSEMOVE="mm_script_data"][
ONMOUSEOUT="mo_script_data"][
ONMOUSEOVER="mov_script_data"][
ONMOUSEUP="mu_script_data"][ STYLE="name_1: value_1"[;
"name_2: value_2"][...; "name_n: value_n"]][
TITLE="title"]></ACRONYM>
```

## Where

- CLASS specifies a class identification for the acronym.
- DIR specifies the direction in which the acronym text is displayed: left-to-right or right-to-left.
- ID provides a unique identifier name for the acronym.
- LANG provides the code representing the language used for the acronym.
- ONCLICK specifies that the referred-to script runs when a user moves the mouse pointer or other pointing device over the acronym and clicks the device button.
- ONDBLCLICK specifies that the referred-to script runs when a user moves the mouse pointer or other pointing device over the acronym and double-clicks the device button.
- ONKEYDOWN specifies that the referred-to script runs when a user presses and holds a key down over the acronym.

- ONKEYPRESS specifies that the referred-to script runs when a user presses and releases a key over the acronym.
- ONKEYUP specifies that the referred-to script runs when a user releases a key over the acronym.
- ONMOUSEDOWN specifies that the referred-to script runs when a user moves the mouse pointer or other pointing device over the acronym and presses and holds down the device button.
- ONMOUSEMOVE specifies that the referred-to script runs when a user moves the mouse pointer or other pointing device over the acronym.
- ONMOUSEOUT specifies that the referred-to script runs when a user moves the mouse pointer or other pointing device away from the acronym.
- ONMOUSEOVER specifies that the referred-to script runs the first time a user moves the mouse pointer or other pointing device over the acronym.
- ONMOUSEUP specifies that the referred-to script runs when a user moves the mouse pointer or other pointing device over the acronym and releases a pressed-down device button.
- STYLE sets styles for the acronym.
- TITLE provides a title or title information about the acronym.

## Notes

This is an HTML 4.0 element. The HTML 4.0 DTD categorizes this as an inline element.

## Related Elements

CITE, CODE, DFN, EM, KBD, STRONG, VAR

63

| ADDRESS | Address |
|---------|---------|

## Purpose

Shows address information, particularly e-mail addresses.

## Syntax

```
<ADDRESS[ CLASS="class_name"][ DIR="LTR"|"RTL"][
ID="id_name"][ LANG="lang_code"][
LANGUAGE="JAVASCRIPT"|"JSCRIPT"|"VBS[CRIPT]"][
ONCLICK="cl_script_data"][ ONDBLCLICK="dc_script_data"][
ONHELP="hlp_script_data"][ ONKEYDOWN="kd_script_data"][
ONKEYPRESS="kp_script_data"][ ONKEYUP="ku_script_data"][
ONMOUSEDOWN="md_script_data"][
ONMOUSEMOVE="mm_script_data"][
ONMOUSEOUT="mo_script_data"][
ONMOUSEOVER="mov_script_data"][
ONMOUSEUP="mu_script_data"][
ONSELECTSTART="ss_script_data"][ STYLE="name_1: value_1"[;
"name_2: value_2"][...; "name_n: value_n"]][
TITLE="title"]>text</ADDRESS>
```

## Where

- CLASS specifies a class identification for the address.
- DIR specifies the direction in which the address text is displayed: left-to-right or right-to-left.
- ID provides a unique identifier name for the address.
- LANG provides the code representing the language used for the address.
- **Microsoft** LANGUAGE declares the scripting language of the current script.
- ONCLICK specifies that the referred-to script runs when a user moves the mouse pointer or other pointing device over the address and clicks the device button.
- ONDBLCLICK specifies that the referred-to script runs when a user moves the mouse pointer or other

pointing device over the address and double-clicks the device button.

-  ONHELP specifies that the referred-to script runs when a user presses the **F1** or **Help** key over the address.

- ONKEYDOWN specifies that the referred-to script runs when a user presses and holds a key down over the address.

- ONKEYPRESS specifies that the referred-to script runs when a user presses and releases a key over the address.

- ONKEYUP specifies that the referred-to script runs when a user releases a key over the address.

- ONMOUSEDOWN specifies that the referred-to script runs when a user moves the mouse pointer or other pointing device over the address and presses and holds down the device button.

- ONMOUSEMOVE specifies that the referred-to script runs when a user moves the mouse pointer or other pointing device over the address.

- ONMOUSEOUT specifies that the referred-to script runs when a user moves the mouse pointer or other pointing device away from the address.

- ONMOUSEOVER specifies that the referred-to script runs the first time a user moves the mouse pointer or other pointing device over the address.

- ONMOUSEUP specifies that the referred-to script runs when a user moves the mouse pointer or other pointing device over the address and releases a pressed-down device button.

-  ONSELECTSTART specifies that the referred-to script runs when a user starts selecting an object.

- STYLE sets styles for the address.

- TITLE provides a title or title information about the address.

- *text* represents one or more characters.

## Notes

This element originated in HTML 2.0.

The HTML 4.0 DTD categorizes this as an inline element. The cascading style sheet specification categorizes ADDRESS as a block-level element.

## Example

```
<ADDRESS>For more information, contact us at
eddygrp@sover.net.</ADDRESS>
```

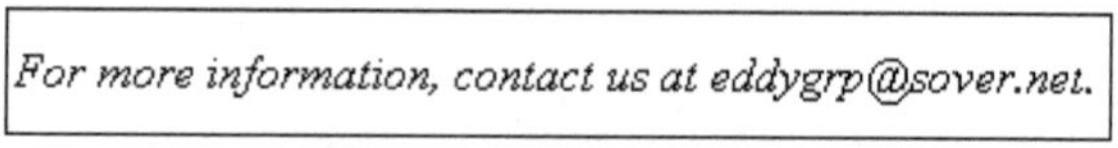

> *For more information, contact us at eddygrp@sover.net.*

*Figure 4.8 A sample ADDRESS line.*

## Related Elements

ACRONYM, B, EM, CITE, CODE, DFN, I, KBD, PRE, SAMP, STRONG, TT, VAR

| B | Bold |
|---|------|

## Purpose

Applies boldface to selected text.

## Syntax

```
<B[ CLASS="class_name"][ DIR="LTR"|"RTL"][ ID="id_name"][
LANG="lang_code"][
LANGUAGE="JAVASCRIPT"|"JSCRIPT"|"VBS[CRIPT]"][
ONCLICK="cl_script_data"][ ONDBLCLICK="dc_script_data"][
ONHELP="hlp_script_data"][ ONKEYDOWN="kd_script_data"][
ONKEYPRESS="kp_script_data"][ ONKEYUP="ku_script_data"][
ONMOUSEDOWN="md_script_data"][
ONMOUSEMOVE="mm_script_data"][
ONMOUSEOUT="mo_script_data"][
ONMOUSEOVER="mov_script_data"][
ONMOUSEUP="mu_script_data"][
ONSELECTSTART="ss_script_data"][ STYLE="name_1: value_1"[;
"name_2: value_2"][...; "name_n: value_n"]][
TITLE="title"]>text</B>
```

## Where

- CLASS specifies a class identification for the current text.
- DIR specifies the direction in which the current text is displayed: left-to-right or right-to-left.
- ID provides a unique identifier name for the current text.
- LANG provides the code representing the language used for the current text.
- **Microsoft** LANGUAGE declares the scripting language of the current script.
- ONCLICK specifies that the referred-to script runs when a user moves the mouse pointer or other pointing device over the boldface text and clicks the device button.

- ONDBLCLICK specifies that the referred-to script runs when a user moves the mouse pointer or other pointing device over the boldface text and double-clicks the device button.
- **Microsoft** ONHELP specifies that the referred-to script runs when a user presses the **F1** or **Help** key over the boldface text.
- ONKEYDOWN specifies that the referred-to script runs when a user presses and holds a key down over the boldface text.
- ONKEYPRESS specifies that the referred-to script runs when a user presses and releases a key over the boldface text.
- ONKEYUP specifies that the referred-to script runs when a user releases a key over the boldface text.
- ONMOUSEDOWN specifies that the referred-to script runs when a user moves the mouse pointer or other pointing device over the boldface text and presses and holds down the device button.
- ONMOUSEMOVE specifies that the referred-to script runs when a user moves the mouse pointer or other pointing device over the boldface text.
- ONMOUSEOUT specifies that the referred-to script runs when a user moves the mouse pointer or other pointing device away from the boldface text.
- ONMOUSEOVER specifies that the referred-to script runs the first time a user moves the mouse pointer or other pointing device over the boldface text.
- ONMOUSEUP specifies that the referred-to script runs when a user moves the mouse pointer or other pointing device over the boldface text and releases a pressed-down device button.
- **Microsoft** ONSELECTSTART specifies that the referred-to script runs when a user starts selecting an object.
- STYLE sets styles for the boldface text.
- TITLE provides a title or title information about the boldface text.
- *text* represents one or more characters.

## Notes

This element originated in HTML 2.0.

The EM and STRONG elements are logical styles, which allow a browser to emphasize selected text in the way in which it is programmed to do. This is in contrast with I and B, their counterpart physical styles, which command a browser to apply italics and boldface, respectively.

The HTML 4.0 DTD categorizes this as an inline element.

## Example

```
This is <B>bold</B> text.
```

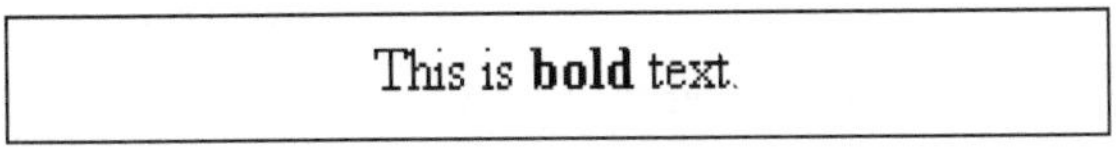

This is **bold** text.

*Figure 4.9 A sample of text emphasized with the B element.*

## Related Elements

STRONG, I, U, S, EM, SUB, SUP, BIG, SMALL, FONT

| BASE | Base URL |
|------|----------|

## Purpose

Specifies the URL of the home page of the current document.

## Syntax

```
<BASE HREF="base_URL"[ CLASS="class_name"][
ID="id_name"][ LANG="lang_code"][ TARGET="win-
dow"|"_blank"|"_parent"|"_self"|"_top"][
TITLE="title"]>
```

## Where

- HREF specifies an absolute URL for the current document.

- 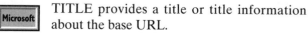 CLASS specifies a class identification for the base URL.

- ID provides a unique identifier name for the base URL.

- LANG provides the code representing the language used for the base URL.

- TARGET loads a linked and named document in a particular window or frame.

- TITLE provides a title or title information about the base URL.

## Notes

This element originated in HTML 2.0.

The BASE element is valid only at the top of the document within the opening and closing HEAD elements.

The TARGET attribute allows a user to visit a target window without actually leaving your site. For example, a user can click on an advertising icon at your site, automatically open a window, view its contents, close the window, and be able to return to your site without retyping your URL.

## Examples

Example 1

```
<BASE HREF="http://www.eddygrp.com/home.htm">
```

Example 2

```
<BASE HREF="http://www.eddygrp.com/home.htm" TARGET="abou-
tus.htm">
```

| **BASEFONT** | **Base Font** |

## Purpose

Defines the size of the font for the entire document from the BASEFONT element to the end of the current document.

## Syntax

```
<BASEFONT SIZE="[+|-]1|2|3|4|5|6|7"[ CLASS="class_name"][
COLOR="#rrggbb"|"color"][ FACE="typeface"][ ID="id_name"][
LANG="lang_code"][ TITLE="title"]>
```

## Where

- SIZE indicates that you will change the actual (1-7) size of the text.
- **Microsoft** CLASS specifies a class identification for the text.
- COLOR is the color of the text.
- FACE specifies the name of a typeface installed on your computer.
- **Microsoft** ID provides a unique identifier name for the text.
- **Microsoft** LANG provides the code representing the language used for the text.
- **Microsoft** TITLE provides a title or title information about the text.

## Notes

This HTML 4.0 element was a Netscape extension and a Microsoft extension.

The HTML 4.0 DTD categorizes this as an inline element.

Although BASEFONT is supported by HTML 4.0, it has been deprecated (that is, it will eventually be obsolete). Use style sheets to specify font attributes.

Many browsers do not support extensions.
Use the FONT element to change the typeface, size, and/or color of the base font.

## Example

```
<BASEFONT SIZE="1">This is size 1 text.<BR>

<BASEFONT SIZE="2">This is size 2 text.<BR>

<BASEFONT SIZE="3">A base font of 3 is the default.<BR>

<BASEFONT SIZE="4">This is size 4 text.<BR>

<BASEFONT SIZE="4"><B>This is size 4 bold text.</B><BR>

<BASEFONT SIZE="5">This is size 5 text.<BR>

<BASEFONT SIZE="6">This is size 6 text.<BR>

<BASEFONT SIZE="6"><B>This is size 6 bold text.</B><BR>

<BASEFONT SIZE="7">This is size 7 text.<BR>
```

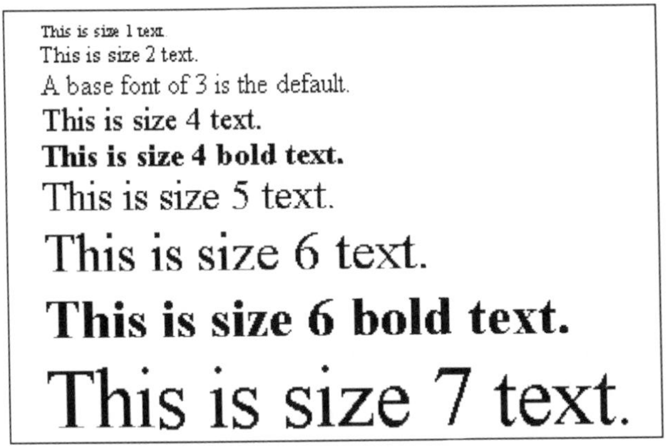

This is size 1 text.
This is size 2 text.
A base font of 3 is the default.
This is size 4 text.
**This is size 4 bold text.**
This is size 5 text.
This is size 6 text.
**This is size 6 bold text.**
This is size 7 text.

*Figure 4.10 BASEFONT text in various sizes and bold emphases.*

## Related Element

FONT

| **BDO** | **Bidirectional Text** |
|---------|------------------------|

## Purpose

Changes the direction of an area of text.

## Syntax

`<BDO DIR="LTR"|"RTL"[ LANG="lang_code"]>text</BDO>`

## Where

- DIR specifies the direction in which the current text is displayed: left-to-right or right-to-left. (For example, English is displayed from left to right, and Hebrew is displayed from right to left.)
- LANG provides the code representing the language used for the current text.

## Notes

This is an HTML 4.0 element.

Use BDO to manually set text direction. This element is part of the internationalization effort of the World Wide Web Consortium (W3C). Using BDO, you can use languages that flow from left to right as well as those that flow from right to left.

The HTML 4.0 DTD categorizes this as an inline element.

BDO is related to the DIR attribute.

You can change the direction of text by inserting the Unicode characters: LEFT-TO-RIGHT OVERRIDE (hexadecimal code 202D), RIGHT-TO-LEFT OVERRIDE (hexadecimal code 202E). You can end the effect of these codes by inserting the POP DIRECTIONAL FORMATTING character (hexadecimal 202C). However, if you use these characters while the DIR attribute is in effect, you may experience unusual results.

| BIG | Big Text |
|-----|----------|

## Purpose

Displays text in a larger font than the base font or than the currently set font.

## Syntax

```
<BIG[ CLASS="class_name"][ DIR="LTR"|"RTL"][
ID="id_name"][ LANG="lang_code"][
LANGUAGE="JAVASCRIPT"|"JSCRIPT"|"VBS[CRIPT]"][
ONCLICK="cl_script_data"][ ONDBLCLICK="dc_script_data"][
ONHELP="hlp_script_data"][ ONKEYDOWN="kd_script_data"][
ONKEYPRESS="kp_script_data"][ ONKEYUP="ku_script_data"][
ONMOUSEDOWN="md_script_data"][
ONMOUSEMOVE="mm_script_data"][
ONMOUSEOUT="mo_script_data"][
ONMOUSEOVER="mov_script_data"][
ONMOUSEUP="mu_script_data"][
ONSELECTSTART="ss_script_data"][ STYLE="name_1: value_1"[;
"name_2: value_2"][...; "name_n: value_n"]][
TITLE="title"]>text</BIG>
```

## Where

- CLASS specifies a class identification for the big text.
- DIR specifies the direction in which the big text is displayed: left-to-right or right-to-left.
- ID provides a unique identifier name for the big text.
- LANG provides the code representing the language used for the big text.
- **Microsoft** LANGUAGE declares the scripting language of the current script.
- ONCLICK specifies that the referred-to script runs when a user moves the mouse pointer or other pointing device over the big text and clicks the device button.
- ONDBLCLICK specifies that the referred-to script runs when a user moves the mouse pointer or other

75

pointing device over the big text and double-clicks the device button.

- **Microsoft** ONHELP specifies that the referred-to script runs when a user presses the **F1** or **Help** key over the current element.

- ONKEYDOWN specifies that the referred-to script runs when a user presses and holds a key down over the big text.

- ONKEYPRESS specifies that the referred-to script runs when a user presses and releases a key over the big text.

- ONKEYUP specifies that the referred-to script runs when a user releases a key over the big text.

- ONMOUSEDOWN specifies that the referred-to script runs when a user moves the mouse pointer or other pointing device over the big text and presses and holds down the device button.

- ONMOUSEMOVE specifies that the referred-to script runs when a user moves the mouse pointer or other pointing device over the big text.

- ONMOUSEOUT specifies that the referred-to script runs when a user moves the mouse pointer or other pointing device away from the big text.

- ONMOUSEOVER specifies that the referred-to script runs the first time a user moves the mouse pointer or other pointing device over the big text.

- ONMOUSEUP specifies that the referred-to script runs when a user moves the mouse pointer or other pointing device over the big text and releases a pressed-down device button.

- **Microsoft** ONSELECTSTART specifies that the referred-to script runs when a user starts selecting an object.

- STYLE sets styles for the big text.

- TITLE provides a title or title information about the big text.

- *text* represents one or more characters.

## Notes

This element originated in HTML 3.2.
The HTML 4.0 DTD categorizes this as an inline element.

## Example

```
This is <BIG>big</BIG> text.
```

This is **big** text.

*Figure 4.11 A sample of BIG text.*

## Related Elements

SMALL, FONT, STRONG, I, U, S, EM, SUB, SUP

| **BLOCKQUOTE** | **Long Quote** |

## Purpose

Formats a long quotation.

## Syntax

```
<BLOCKQUOTE[ CITE="cite_url"][ CLASS="class_name"][
DIR="LTR"|"RTL"][ ID="id_name"][ LANG="lang_code"][ LAN-
GUAGE="JAVASCRIPT"|"JSCRIPT"|"VBS[CRIPT]"][
ONCLICK="cl_script_data"][ ONDBLCLICK="dc_script_data"][
ONHELP="hlp_script_data"][ ONKEYDOWN="kd_script_data"][
ONKEYPRESS="kp_script_data"][ ONKEYUP="ku_script_data"][
ONMOUSEDOWN="md_script_data"][
ONMOUSEMOVE="mm_script_data"][
ONMOUSEOUT="mo_script_data"][
ONMOUSEOVER="mov_script_data"][
ONMOUSEUP="mu_script_data"][
ONSELECTSTART="ss_script_data"][ STYLE="name_1: value_1"[;
"name_2: value_2"][...; "name_n: value_n"]][
TITLE="title"]>text</BLOCKQUOTE>
```

## Where

- CITE provides a URL for a document or message that contains information about a BLOCKQUOTE.
- CLASS specifies a class identification for the current text.
- DIR specifies the direction in which the current text is displayed: left-to-right or right-to-left.
- ID provides a unique identifier name for the current text.
- LANG provides the code representing the language used for the current text.
- **Microsoft** LANGUAGE declares the scripting language of the current script.

- ONCLICK specifies that the referred-to script runs when a user moves the mouse pointer or other pointing device over the quote and clicks the device button.

- ONDBLCLICK specifies that the referred-to script runs when a user moves the mouse pointer or other pointing device over the quote and double-clicks the device button.

- **Microsoft** ONHELP specifies that the referred-to script runs when a user presses the **F1** or **Help** key over the current element.

- ONKEYDOWN specifies that the referred-to script runs when a user presses and holds a key down over the quote.

- ONKEYPRESS specifies that the referred-to script runs when a user presses and releases a key over the quote.

- ONKEYUP specifies that the referred-to script runs when a user releases a key over the quote.

- ONMOUSEDOWN specifies that the referred-to script runs when a user moves the mouse pointer or other pointing device over the quote and presses and holds down the device button.

- ONMOUSEMOVE specifies that the referred-to script runs when a user moves the mouse pointer or other pointing device over the quote.

- ONMOUSEOUT specifies that the referred-to script runs when a user moves the mouse pointer or other pointing device away from the quote.

- ONMOUSEOVER specifies that the referred-to script runs the first time a user moves the mouse pointer or other pointing device over the quote.

- ONMOUSEUP specifies that the referred-to script runs when a user moves the mouse pointer or other pointing device over the quote and releases a pressed-down device button.

- **Microsoft** ONSELECTSTART specifies that the referred-to script runs when a user starts selecting an object.

- STYLE sets styles for the quote.

- TITLE provides a title or title information about the quote.
- *text* represents one or more characters.

## Notes

This element originated in HTML 2.0.

Within the BLOCKQUOTE elements, text is indented from the left margin and is ragged on the right margin.

The HTML 4.0 DTD categorizes this as a block-level element.

The BLOCKQUOTE element causes a paragraph break.

## Example

```
<P>Mark Twain said:

<BLOCKQUOTE>The common eye sees only the outside of
things, and judges by that, but the seeing eye pierces
through and reads the heart and the soul, finding there
capacities which the outside didn't indicate or promise,
and which the other kind couldn't detect.</BLOCKQUOTE>
```

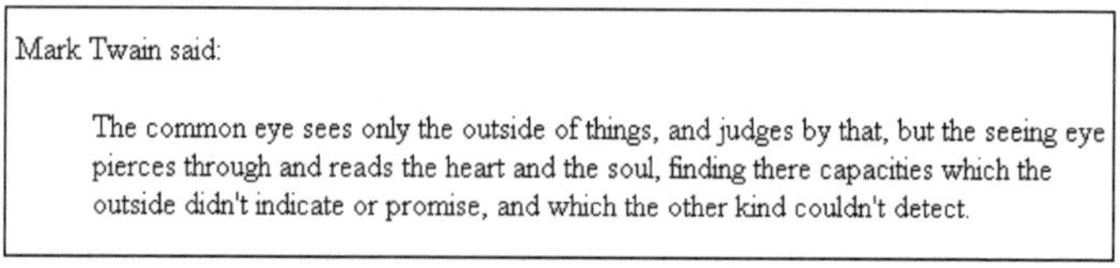

Mark Twain said:

> The common eye sees only the outside of things, and judges by that, but the seeing eye pierces through and reads the heart and the soul, finding there capacities which the outside didn't indicate or promise, and which the other kind couldn't detect.

*Figure 4.12 A quotation that demonstrates the BLOCKQUOTE element.*

## Related Elements

CODE, KBD, PRE, Q, SAMP, TT

| BODY | Document Body |
|------|---------------|

## Purpose

Indicates the start and end of the body, or the contents, of the document immediately after the head.

## Syntax

```
[<BODY[ ACCESSKEY="shortcut_key"][
ALINK="#rrggbb"|"color"][ BACKGROUND="picture_url"][
BGCOLOR="#rrggbb"|"color"][ BGPROPERTIES="FIXED"][ BOTTOM-
MARGIN="bot_mar_pix"][ CLASS="class_name"][
DIR="LTR"|"RTL"][ ID="id_name"][ LANG="lang_code"][ LAN-
GUAGE="JAVASCRIPT"|"JSCRIPT"|"VBS[CRIPT]"][
LEFTMARGIN="lmar-num"]  [ LINK="#rrggbb"|"color"][
ONAFTERUPDATE="au_script_data"][
ONBEFOREUPDATE="bu_script_data"][
ONBLUR="bl_script_data"][ ONCLICK="cl_script_data"][ OND-
BLCLICK="dc_script_data"][ ONDRAGSTART="ds_script_data"][
ONFOCUS="fc_script_data"][ ONHELP="hlp_script_data"][
ONKEYDOWN="kd_script_data"][ ONKEYPRESS="kp_script_data"][
ONKEYUP="ku_script_data"][ ONLOAD="ol_script_data"][
ONMOUSEDOWN="md_script_data"][
ONMOUSEMOVE="mm_script_data"][
ONMOUSEOUT="mo_script_data"][
ONMOUSEOVER="mov_script_data"][
ONMOUSEUP="mu_script_data"][ ONRESIZE="rsz_script_data"][
ONROWENTER="re_script_data"][
ONROWEXIT="rex_script_data"][ ONSCROLL="sc_script_data"][
ONSELECTSTART="ss_script_data"][
ONUNLOAD="un_script_data"][ RIGHTMARGIN="rmar-num"][
SCROLL="YES"|"NO"][ STYLE="name_1: value_1"[; "name_2:
value_2"][...; "name_n: value_n"]][
TEXT="#rrggbb"|"color"][ TITLE="title"][ TOPMARGIN="tmar-
num"][ VLINK="#rrggbb"|"color"]]>body-contents[</BODY>]
```

## Where

-  ACCESSKEY assigns a shortcut key to the element in order to focus on it.

- ALINK defines the color of the text and graphics borders of the link that has just been clicked.

- BACKGROUND specifies an image file that is displayed in the background of each page of the current document.

- BGCOLOR specifies the background color for the document body.

-  BGPROPERTIES specifies that the background picture does not move when you scroll the document.

-  BOTTOMMARGIN specifies the measurement, in pixels, of the bottom margin of the document.

- CLASS specifies a class identification for the document body.

- DIR specifies the direction in which the document body text is displayed: left-to-right or right-to-left.

- ID provides a unique identifier name for the document body.

- LANG provides the code representing the language used for the document body text.

- LANGUAGE declares the scripting language of the current script.

- LEFTMARGIN specifies the left margin, in pixels, of this document.

- LINK defines the color of the text and graphics borders of links that have not been visited or that have been visited but have been made inactive again from within your browser.

- ONAFTERUPDATE specifies that the referred-to script runs after data has been transferred from the element to the data repository.

ONBEFOREUPDATE specifies that the referred-to script runs before data is transferred from the element to the data repository.

 ONBLUR specifies that the referred-to script runs when the current element loses focus.

- ONCLICK specifies that the referred-to script runs when a user moves the mouse pointer or other pointing device over the document body and clicks the device button.

- ONDBLCLICK specifies that the referred-to script runs when a user moves the mouse pointer or other pointing device over the document body and double-clicks the device button.

-  ONDRAGSTART specifies that the referred-to script runs when the user starts dragging a selection or element.

-  ONFOCUS specifies that the referred-to script runs when the current element receives focus (that is, is made active) by the mouse pointer or other pointing device.

-  ONHELP specifies that the referred-to script runs when a user presses the **F1** or **Help** key over the current element.

- ONKEYDOWN specifies that the referred-to script runs when a user presses and holds a key down over the document body.

- ONKEYPRESS specifies that the referred-to script runs when a user presses and releases a key over the document body.

- ONKEYUP specifies that the referred-to script runs when a user releases a key over the document body.

- ONLOAD specifies that the referred-to script runs after the active browser has finished loading the window.

- ONMOUSEDOWN specifies that the referred-to script runs when a user moves the mouse pointer or other pointing device over the document body and presses and holds down the device button.

- ONMOUSEMOVE specifies that the referred-to script runs when a user moves the mouse pointer or other pointing device over the document body.
- ONMOUSEOUT specifies that the referred-to script runs when a user moves the mouse pointer or other pointing device away from the document body.
- ONMOUSEOVER specifies that the referred-to script runs the first time a user moves the mouse pointer or other pointing device over the document body.
- ONMOUSEUP specifies that the referred-to script runs when a user moves the mouse pointer or other pointing device over the document body and releases a pressed-down device button.
- Microsoft   ONRESIZE specifies that the referred-to script runs when the user resizes the selected object.
- Microsoft   ONROWENTER specifies that the referred-to script runs when the body has been modified.
- Microsoft   ONROWEXIT specifies that the referred-to script runs before the body is modified.
- Microsoft   ONSCROLL specifies that the referred-to script runs when a user moves the scroll box within the scroll bar.
- Microsoft   ONSELECTSTART specifies that the referred-to script runs when a user starts selecting an object.
- ONUNLOAD specifies that the referred-to script runs after the active browser has removed thea document from a window.
- Microsoft   SCROLL turns on or off document scroll-bars.
- STYLE sets styles for the entire document body.
- TEXT defines the color of all nonlink text in the current document.

- TITLE provides a title or title information about the document body.

- ▮Microsoft▮ TOPMARGIN specifies the top margin, in pixels, of this document.

- VLINK defines the color of the text and graphics borders of links that have been visited.

- *body-contents* is the contents of the BODY section of the document.

## Notes

This element originated in HTML 2.0.

The HTML 4.0 DTD categorizes this as an inline element.

If you use the BODY element, the starting element should be immediately after the HEAD end tag, and the BODY end tag should be immediately above the HTML end tag.

If you omit the quotation marks from the color values or the picture file URL, some HTML editors automatically insert them.

Background pictures can take time to load and can interfere with a user's ability to view text and links, so use them carefully.

If you do not accept the default colors for links, try to specify a bright color for links that have not been visited and a darker, duller color for visited links. Make sure that the text, links, and body colors are compatible.

Both Netscape and Microsoft provide many more color names. However, keep in mind that many other browsers do not support Netscape and Microsoft attributes.

JPG pictures tend to be much smaller than GIF pictures of the same size.

## Examples

The following example inserts a background file, sets teal as the color for links not visited, maroon for visited links, and yellow for a clicked-on link. (To learn how you can use styles to assign the same colors, see Part 5, "Cascading Style Sheets.")

```
<BODY BACKGROUND="70.GIF" TEXT="black" LINK="teal"
VLINK="maroon" ALINK="yellow">

<DL>
```

**85**

```
<DT>File</DT>
```

```
<DD>A set of organized and related information stored
with a unique filename.</DD>
```

```
<DT>Menu</DT>
```

```
<DD>A list of commands available from a horizontal bar
immediately below the title bar.</DD>
```

```
</DL>
```

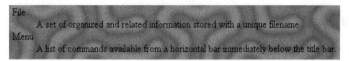

*Figure 4.13 Part of a glossary with a background GIF file.*

## Related Element

HEAD

*Table 4.1 Selected Colors and Their Hexadecimal Values*

| | |
|---|---|
| black | #000000 |
| bright cyan | #00FFFF |
| bright fuchsia | #FF00FF |
| bright medium yellow | #FFFF00 |
| dark blue | #0000AA |
| dark blue-green | #006666 |
| dark gray | #808080 |
| dark lime green | #00AA00 |
| dark purple | #880088 |
| dark red | #AA0000 |
| gray-white | #DDDDDD |
| light rose | #FFB6C1 |
| medium blue | #0000CC |
| medium cyan | #00CCCC |
| medium fuchsia | #CC00CC |

| | |
|---|---|
| medium gold | #FFFFAA |
| medium gold-green | #CCCC00 |
| medium gray | #999999 |
| medium dull green | #22AA22 |
| medium lime green | #00CC00 |
| medium peach | #FAAAAC |
| medium red | #CC0000 |
| medium rose | #FFADDA |
| navy blue | #0000FF |
| off white 1 | #F0F7F7 |
| off white 2 | #FFFFF2 |
| off white 3 | #F0F0F0 |
| orange-red | #FF6347 |
| pale blue | #AAADEA |
| pale cyan | #C0FFEE |
| pale gold | #FFFFCC |
| pale green | #ADEADA |
| pale green-gray | #AADEAD |
| pale purple | #ADAADA |
| pumpkin | #FF8127 |
| reddish brown | #550000 |
| strong blue | #0000FF |
| strong lime green | #00FF00 |
| strong red | #FF0000 |
| white | #FFFFFF |

| BR | Line Break |
|---|---|

## Purpose

Starts a new line of text.

## Syntax

```
text<BR[ CLASS="class_name"][
CLEAR="none"|"left"|"all"|"right"][ ID="id_name"][ LAN-
GUAGE="JAVASCRIPT"|"JSCRIPT"|"VBS[CRIPT]"][ STYLE="name_1:
value_1"[; "name_2: value_2"][...; "name_n: value_n"]][
TITLE="title"]>
```

## Where

- *text* represents one or more characters.
- CLASS specifies a class identification for the break.
- CLEAR clears previous alignment settings depending on the location of floating images (placed with the IMG element).
- ID provides a unique identifier name for the break.
- **Microsoft** LANGUAGE declares the scripting language of the current script.
- STYLE sets styles for the break.
- TITLE provides a title or title information about the break.

## Notes

This element originated in HTML 2.0.

The HTML 4.0 DTD categorizes this as an inline element.

The CLEAR attribute is an HTML 3.2 feature.

The P element is the equivalent of two BR elements.

## Examples

Example 1 (Figure 4.14)

```
<P>My crown is in my heart, not on my head;<BR>Not decked
```

```
with diamonds and Indian stones,<BR>Nor to be seen: my
crown is called content;<BR>A crown it is that seldom
kings enjoy.<P ALIGN="center">William Shakespeare
```

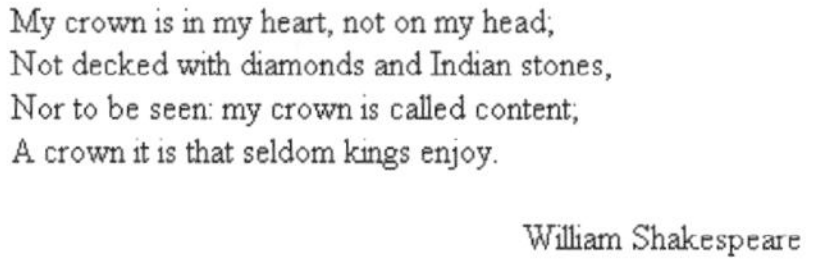

My crown is in my heart, not on my head;
Not decked with diamonds and Indian stones,
Nor to be seen: my crown is called content;
A crown it is that seldom kings enjoy.

William Shakespeare

*Figure 4.14 A quotation with line breaks inserted.*

## Example 2 (Figure 4.15)

```
<BLOCKQUOTE>My crown is in my heart, not on my
head;<BR>Not decked with diamonds and Indian
stones,<BR>Nor to be seen: my crown is called
content;<BR>A crown it is that seldom kings enjoy.</BLOCK-
QUOTE><CENTER>William Shakespeare</CENTER>
```

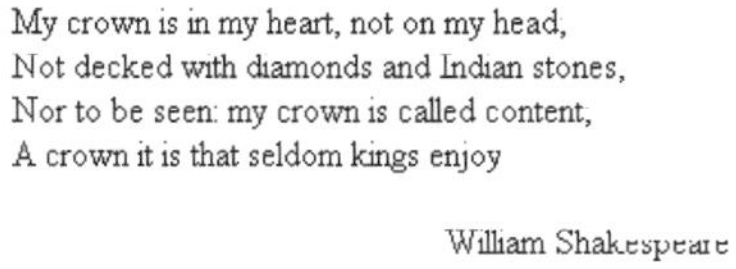

My crown is in my heart, not on my head,
Not decked with diamonds and Indian stones,
Nor to be seen: my crown is called content,
A crown it is that seldom kings enjoy

William Shakespeare

*Figure 4.15 A quotation with line breaks within BLOCKQUOTE elements.*

For examples showing the BR element (with the CLEAR attribute), see the IMG element.

## Related Element

P

| CENTER | Center Text |
| --- | --- |

## Purpose

Centers a line of text between the left margin and the right margin.

## Syntax

```
<CENTER[ CLASS="class_name"][ DIR="LTR"|"RTL"][
ID="id_name"][ LANG="lang_code"][
LANGUAGE="JAVASCRIPT"|"JSCRIPT"|"VBS[CRIPT]"][
ONCLICK="cl_script_data"][ ONDBLCLICK="dc_script_data"][
ONHELP="hlp_script_data"][ ONKEYDOWN="kd_script_data"][
ONKEYPRESS="kp_script_data"][ ONKEYUP="ku_script_data"][
ONMOUSEDOWN="md_script_data"][
ONMOUSEMOVE="mm_script_data"][
ONMOUSEOUT="mo_script_data"][
ONMOUSEOVER="mov_script_data"][
ONMOUSEUP="mu_script_data"][
ONSELECTSTART="ss_script_data"][ STYLE="name_1: value_1"[;
"name_2: value_2"][...; "name_n: value_n"]][
TITLE="title"]>text-line</CENTER>
```

## Where

- CLASS specifies a class identification for the current text.
- DIR specifies the direction in which the current text is displayed: left-to-right or right-to-left.
- ID provides a unique identifier name for the current text.
- LANG provides the code representing the language used for the current text.
- **Microsoft** LANGUAGE declares the scripting language of the current script.
- ONCLICK specifies that the referred-to script runs when a user moves the mouse pointer or other pointing

device over the centered text and clicks the device button.

- ONDBLCLICK specifies that the referred-to script
  runs when a user moves the mouse pointer or other
  pointing device over the centered text and double-clicks
  the device button.

- ONHELP specifies that the referred-to script
  runs when a user presses the **F1** or **Help** key
  over the current element.

- ONKEYDOWN specifies that the referred-to script
  runs when a user presses and holds a key down over the
  centered text.

- ONKEYPRESS specifies that the referred-to script
  runs when a user presses and releases a key over the
  centered text.

- ONKEYUP specifies that the referred-to script runs
  when a user releases a key over the centered text.

- ONMOUSEDOWN specifies that the referred-to script
  runs when a user moves the mouse pointer or other
  pointing device over the centered text and presses and
  holds down the device button.

- ONMOUSEMOVE specifies that the referred-to script
  runs when a user moves the mouse pointer or other
  pointing device over the centered text.

- ONMOUSEOUT specifies that the referred-to script
  runs when a user moves the mouse pointer or other
  pointing device away from the centered text.

- ONMOUSEOVER specifies that the referred-to script
  runs the first time a user moves the mouse pointer or
  other pointing device over the centered text.

- ONMOUSEUP specifies that the referred-to script runs
  when a user moves the mouse pointer or other pointing
  device over the centered text and releases a pressed-
  down device button.

- ONSELECTSTART specifies that the
  referred-to script runs when a user starts
  selecting an object.

- STYLE sets styles for the centered text.

- TITLE provides a title or title information about the centered text.
- *text-line* represents a line of text in the document.

## Notes

This element originated in HTML 3.2.

The HTML 4.0 DTD categorizes this as a block-level element.

Although CENTER is supported by HTML 4.0, it has been deprecated (that is, it will eventually be obsolete). Use style sheets to lay out documents.

Some browsers do not recognize the CENTER element; some HTML editors convert this element to <CENTER><P>text</P></CENTER>.

Using the CENTER element is analogous to entering <P ALIGN="center">.

## Example

See the prior element, BR.

## Related Attribute

ALIGN

| CITE | Citation |
| --- | --- |

## Purpose

Indicates a citation, such as a book, paper, or the name of an expert, by emphasizing it, usually with italics.

## Syntax

```
<CITE[ CLASS="class_name"][ DIR="LTR"|"RTL"][
ID="id_name"][ LANG="lang_code"][
LANGUAGE="JAVASCRIPT"|"JSCRIPT"|"VBS[CRIPT]"][
ONCLICK="cl_script_data"][ ONDBLCLICK="dc_script_data"][
ONHELP="hlp_script_data"][ ONKEYDOWN="kd_script_data"][
ONKEYPRESS="kp_script_data"][ ONKEYUP="ku_script_data"][
ONMOUSEDOWN="md_script_data"][
ONMOUSEMOVE="mm_script_data"][
ONMOUSEOUT="mo_script_data"][
ONMOUSEOVER="mov_script_data"][
ONMOUSEUP="mu_script_data"][
ONSELECTSTART="ss_script_data"][ STYLE="name_1: value_1"[;
"name_2: value_2"][...; "name_n: value_n"]][
TITLE="title"]>text</CITE>
```

## Where

- CLASS specifies a class identification for the current text.
- DIR specifies the direction in which the current text is displayed: left-to-right or right-to-left.
- ID provides a unique identifier name for the current text.
- LANG provides the code representing the language used for the current text.
- **Microsoft** LANGUAGE declares the scripting language of the current script.

93

- ONCLICK specifies that the referred-to script runs when a user moves the mouse pointer or other pointing device over the citation and clicks the device button.

- ONDBLCLICK specifies that the referred-to script runs when a user moves the mouse pointer or other pointing device over the citation and double-clicks the device button.

- | Microsoft | ONHELP specifies that the referred-to script runs when a user presses the **F1** or **Help** key over the current element.

- ONKEYDOWN specifies that the referred-to script runs when a user presses and holds a key down over the citation.

- ONKEYPRESS specifies that the referred-to script runs when a user presses and releases a key over the citation.

- ONKEYUP specifies that the referred-to script runs when a user releases a key over the citation.

- ONMOUSEDOWN specifies that the referred-to script runs when a user moves the mouse pointer or other pointing device over the citation and presses and holds down the device button.

- ONMOUSEMOVE specifies that the referred-to script runs when a user moves the mouse pointer or other pointing device over the citation.

- ONMOUSEOUT specifies that the referred-to script runs when a user moves the mouse pointer or other pointing device away from the citation.

- ONMOUSEOVER specifies that the referred-to script runs the first time a user moves the mouse pointer or other pointing device over the citation.

- ONMOUSEUP specifies that the referred-to script runs when a user moves the mouse pointer or other pointing device over the citation and releases a pressed-down device button.

- | Microsoft | ONSELECTSTART specifies that the referred-to script runs when a user starts selecting an object.

- STYLE sets styles for the citation.

- TITLE provides a title or title information about the citation.
- *text* represents one or more characters.

## Notes

This element originated in HTML 2.0.

CITE is a logical element, in which particular browsers are programmed to apply a certain style to the selected text. This is in contrast to a physical element in which you "code" the styles yourself.

Many browsers use the same enhancement for the I, CITE, EM, and VAR elements.

The HTML 4.0 DTD categorizes this as an inline element.

## Example

```
Many examples of animations are included in <CITE>The GIF
Animator's Guide</CITE>, published by MIS:Press.
```

Many examples of animations are included in *The GIF Animator's Guide*, published by MIS:Press.

*Figure 4.16 An example of a citation.*

## Related Elements

ACRONYM, B, CODE, DFN, EM, I, KBD, PRE, S, SAMP, STRIKE, STRONG, TT, U, VAR

**95**

| CODE | Source Code |
| --- | --- |

## Purpose

Applies a computer code (monospace) font to selected text.

## Syntax

```
<CODE[ CLASS="class_name"][ DIR="LTR"|"RTL"][
ID="id_name"][ LANG="lang_code"][
LANGUAGE="JAVASCRIPT"|"JSCRIPT"|"VBS[CRIPT]"][
ONCLICK="cl_script_data"][ ONDBLCLICK="dc_script_data"][
ONHELP="hlp_script_data"][ ONKEYDOWN="kd_script_data"][
ONKEYPRESS="kp_script_data"][ ONKEYUP="ku_script_data"][
ONMOUSEDOWN="md_script_data"][
ONMOUSEMOVE="mm_script_data"][
ONMOUSEOUT="mo_script_data"][
ONMOUSEOVER="mov_script_data"][
ONMOUSEUP="mu_script_data"][
ONSELECTSTART="ss_script_data"][ STYLE="name_1: value_1"[;
"name_2: value_2"][...; "name_n: value_n"]][
TITLE="title"]>text</CODE>
```

## Where

- CLASS specifies a class identification for the current text.
- DIR specifies the direction in which the current text is displayed: left-to-right or right-to-left.
- ID provides a unique identifier name for the current text.
- LANG provides the code representing the language used for the current text.
- **Microsoft** LANGUAGE declares the scripting language of the current script.
- ONCLICK specifies that the referred-to script runs when a user moves the mouse pointer or other pointing

device over the source code and clicks the device button.

- ONDBLCLICK specifies that the referred-to script runs when a user moves the mouse pointer or other pointing device over the source code and double-clicks the device button.

- **Microsoft** ONHELP specifies that the referred-to script runs when a user presses the **F1** or **Help** key over the current element.

- ONKEYDOWN specifies that the referred-to script runs when a user presses and holds a key down over the source code.

- ONKEYPRESS specifies that the referred-to script runs when a user presses and releases a key over the source code.

- ONKEYUP specifies that the referred-to script runs when a user releases a key over the source code.

- ONMOUSEDOWN specifies that the referred-to script runs when a user moves the mouse pointer or other pointing device over the source code and presses and holds down the device button.

- ONMOUSEMOVE specifies that the referred-to script runs when a user moves the mouse pointer or other pointing device over the source code.

- ONMOUSEOUT specifies that the referred-to script runs when a user moves the mouse pointer or other pointing device away from the source code.

- ONMOUSEOVER specifies that the referred-to script runs the first time a user moves the mouse pointer or other pointing device over the source code.

- ONMOUSEUP specifies that the referred-to script runs when a user moves the mouse pointer or other pointing device over the source code and releases a pressed-down device button.

- **Microsoft** ONSELECTSTART specifies that the referred-to script runs when a user starts selecting an object.

- STYLE sets styles for the source code.

- TITLE provides a title or title information about the source code.
- *text* represents one or more characters.

## Notes

This element originated in HTML 2.0.

CODE is a logical element, in which particular browsers are programmed to apply a certain style to the selected text. This is in contrast to a physical element in which you "code" the styles yourself.

The HTML 4.0 DTD categorizes this as an inline element.

Many browsers use the same font for the CODE, KBD, PRE, SAMP, and TT elements.

To display two or more lines of preformatted text, use the PRE element.

## Example

```
This is <CODE>computer code</CODE> text.
```

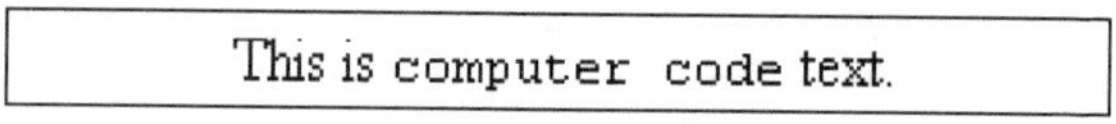

This is computer code text.

*Figure 4.17 A sample of text changed with the CODE element.*

## Related Elements

ACRONYM, B, CITE, DFN, EM, I, KBD, PRE, S, SAMP, STRIKE, STRONG, TT, U, VAR

| DD | Definition Description |
|----|------------------------|

## Purpose

States a description in a definition list.

## Syntax

```
<DD[ CLASS="class_name"][ DIR="LTR"|"RTL"][ ID="id_name"][
LANG="lang_code"][
LANGUAGE="JAVASCRIPT"|"JSCRIPT"|"VBS[CRIPT]"][
ONCLICK="cl_script_data"][ ONDBLCLICK="dc_script_data"][
ONHELP="hlp_script_data"][ ONKEYDOWN="kd_script_data"][
ONKEYPRESS="kp_script_data"][ ONKEYUP="ku_script_data"][
ONMOUSEDOWN="md_script_data"][
ONMOUSEMOVE="mm_script_data"][
ONMOUSEOUT="mo_script_data"][
ONMOUSEOVER="mov_script_data"][
ONMOUSEUP="mu_script_data"][
ONSELECTSTART="ss_script_data"][ STYLE="name_1: value_1"[;
"name_2: value_2"][...; "name_n: value_n"]][
TITLE="title"]definition[</DD>]
```

## Where

- CLASS specifies a class identification for the definition description.
- DIR specifies the direction in which the definition description is displayed: left-to-right or right-to-left.
- ID provides a unique identifier name for the definition description.
- LANG provides the code representing the language used for the definition description text.
- **Microsoft** LANGUAGE declares the scripting language of the current script.
- ONCLICK specifies that the referred-to script runs when a user moves the mouse pointer or other pointing

device over the definition description and clicks the device button.

- ONDBLCLICK specifies that the referred-to script runs when a user moves the mouse pointer or other pointing device over the definition description and double-clicks the device button.

- **Microsoft** ONHELP specifies that the referred-to script runs when a user presses the **F1** or **Help** key over the current element.

- ONKEYDOWN specifies that the referred-to script runs when a user presses and holds a key down over the definition description.

- ONKEYPRESS specifies that the referred-to script runs when a user presses and releases a key over the definition description.

- ONKEYUP specifies that the referred-to script runs when a user releases a key over the definition description.

- ONMOUSEDOWN specifies that the referred-to script runs when a user moves the mouse pointer or other pointing device over the definition description and presses and holds down the device button.

- ONMOUSEMOVE specifies that the referred-to script runs when a user moves the mouse pointer or other pointing device over the definition description.

- ONMOUSEOUT specifies that the referred-to script runs when a user moves the mouse pointer or other pointing device away from the definition description.

- ONMOUSEOVER specifies that the referred-to script runs the first time a user moves the mouse pointer or other pointing device over the definition description.

- ONMOUSEUP specifies that the referred-to script runs when a user moves the mouse pointer or other pointing device over the definition description and releases a pressed-down device button.

- **Microsoft** ONSELECTSTART specifies that the referred-to script runs when a user starts selecting an object.

- STYLE sets styles for the definition description.

- TITLE provides a title or title information about the definition description.
- *definition* represents a description paired with a term (DT).

## Notes

This element originated in HTML 2.0.

Each DD element in a definition list must be paired with a DT element.

Pairs of terms (DT) and descriptions (DD) are embedded within DL elements.

To present multiple terms in a definition description, insert line breaks using the BR element.

A paragraph break automatically occurs at the end of a DD element and its contents.

## Examples

See the DL element.

## Related Elements

DL, DT, UL, OL, LI, DIR, MENU

| **DEL** | **Mark Deletion** |

## Purpose

Marks document sections that have been deleted since the original document was created and posted.

## Syntax

```
<DEL[ CITE="url"][ CLASS="class_name"][ DATETIME="YYYY-MM-
DD[Thh:mm:ssTZD]"][ DIR="LTR"|"RTL"][ ID="id_name"][
LANG="lang_code"][ ONCLICK="cl_script_data"][
ONDBLCLICK="dc_script_data"][ ONKEYDOWN="kd_script_data"][
ONKEYPRESS="kp_script_data"][ ONKEYUP="ku_script_data"][
ONMOUSEDOWN="md_script_data"][
ONMOUSEMOVE="mm_script_data"][
ONMOUSEOUT="mo_script_data"][
ONMOUSEOVER="mov_script_data"][
ONMOUSEUP="mu_script_data"][ STYLE="name_1: value_1"[;
"name_2: value_2"][...; "name_n: value_n"]][
TITLE="title"]>deleted-section</DEL>
```

## Where

- CITE provides a URL for a document that contains the reason for a document change.
- CLASS specifies a class identification for the text marked as deleted.
- DATETIME names the date and time at which a change in the document was made.
- DIR specifies the direction in which the text marked as deleted is displayed: left-to-right or right-to-left.
- ID provides a unique identifier name for the text marked as deleted.
- LANG provides the code representing the language used for the text marked as deleted.
- ONCLICK specifies that the referred-to script runs when a user moves the mouse pointer or other pointing

device over the text marked as deleted and clicks the device button.

- ONDBLCLICK specifies that the referred-to script runs when a user moves the mouse pointer or other pointing device over the text marked as deleted and double-clicks the device button.
- ONKEYDOWN specifies that the referred-to script runs when a user presses and holds a key down over the text marked as deleted.
- ONKEYPRESS specifies that the referred-to script runs when a user presses and releases a key over the text marked as deleted.
- ONKEYUP specifies that the referred-to script runs when a user releases a key over the text marked as deleted.
- ONMOUSEDOWN specifies that the referred-to script runs when a user moves the mouse pointer or other pointing device over the text marked as deleted and presses and holds down the device button.
- ONMOUSEMOVE specifies that the referred-to script runs when a user moves the mouse pointer or other pointing device over the text marked as deleted.
- ONMOUSEOUT specifies that the referred-to script runs when a user moves the mouse pointer or other pointing device away from the text marked as deleted.
- ONMOUSEOVER specifies that the referred-to script runs the first time a user moves the mouse pointer or other pointing device over the text marked as deleted.
- ONMOUSEUP specifies that the referred-to script runs when a user moves the mouse pointer or other pointing device over the text marked as deleted and releases a pressed-down device button.
- STYLE sets styles for the text marked as deleted.
- TITLE provides a title or title information about the text marked as deleted.
- *deleted-section* is the text marked as deleted.

## Notes

This is an HTML 4.0 element.

Browsers may mark deleted text in various ways: by changing to a special font, by striking it through, and so on.

## Example

```
This is active text.<DEL DATETIME="1998-08-06"> This is
deleted text.</DEL> This is active text.
```

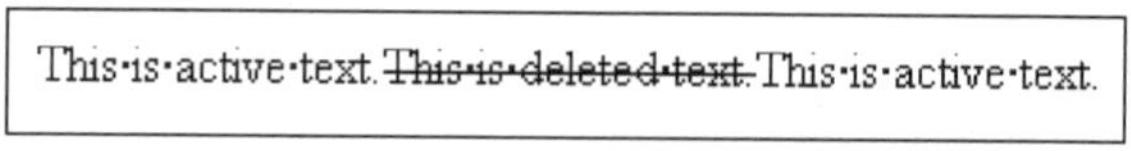

This·is·active·text. ~~This·is·deleted·text.~~ This·is·active·text.

*Figure 4.18 A section of timestamped text marked as deleted.*

## Related Element

INS

| DFN | Definition |
|-----|-----------|

## Purpose

Identifies a definition term using emphasized text.

## Syntax

```
<DFN[ CLASS="class_name"][ DIR="LTR"|"RTL"][
ID="id_name"][ LANG="lang_code"][
LANGUAGE="JAVASCRIPT"|"JSCRIPT"|"VBS[CRIPT]"][
ONCLICK="cl_script_data"][ ONDBLCLICK="dc_script_data"][
ONHELP="hlp_script_data"][ ONKEYDOWN="kd_script_data"][
ONKEYPRESS="kp_script_data"][ ONKEYUP="ku_script_data"][
ONMOUSEDOWN="md_script_data"][
ONMOUSEMOVE="mm_script_data"][
ONMOUSEOUT="mo_script_data"][
ONMOUSEOVER="mov_script_data"][
ONMOUSEUP="mu_script_data"][
ONSELECTSTART="ss_script_data"][ STYLE="name_1: value_1"[;
"name_2: value_2"][...; "name_n: value_n"]][
TITLE="title"]>text</DFN>
```

## Where

- CLASS specifies a class identification for the definition.
- DIR specifies the direction in which the definition text is displayed: left-to-right or right-to-left.
- ID provides a unique identifier name for the definition.
- LANG provides the code representing the language used for the definition text.
- **Microsoft** LANGUAGE declares the scripting language of the current script.
- ONCLICK specifies that the referred-to script runs when a user moves the mouse pointer or other pointing device over the definition and clicks the device button.
- ONDBLCLICK specifies that the referred-to script runs when a user moves the mouse pointer or other

pointing device over the definition and double-clicks the device button.

- **Microsoft** ONHELP specifies that the referred-to script runs when a user presses the **F1** or **Help** key over the current element.

- ONKEYDOWN specifies that the referred-to script runs when a user presses and holds a key down over the definition.

- ONKEYPRESS specifies that the referred-to script runs when a user presses and releases a key over the definition.

- ONKEYUP specifies that the referred-to script runs when a user releases a key over the definition.

- ONMOUSEDOWN specifies that the referred-to script runs when a user moves the mouse pointer or other pointing device over the definition and presses and holds down the device button.

- ONMOUSEMOVE specifies that the referred-to script runs when a user moves the mouse pointer or other pointing device over the definition.

- ONMOUSEOUT specifies that the referred-to script runs when a user moves the mouse pointer or other pointing device away from the definition.

- ONMOUSEOVER specifies that the referred-to script runs the first time a user moves the mouse pointer or other pointing device over the definition.

- ONMOUSEUP specifies that the referred-to script runs when a user moves the mouse pointer or other pointing device over the definition and releases a pressed-down device button.

- **Microsoft** ONSELECTSTART specifies that the referred-to script runs when a user starts selecting an object.

- STYLE sets styles for the definition.

- TITLE provides a title or title information about the definition.

- *text* represents one or more characters.

## Notes

This element originated in HTML 3.2.

DFN is a logical element, in which particular browsers are programmed to apply a certain style to the selected text. This is in contrast to a physical element in which you "code" the styles yourself.

The HTML 4.0 DTD categorizes this as an inline element.

## Example

```
The <DFN>DFN</DFN> element identifies a defined term.
```

The *DFN* element identifies a defined term.

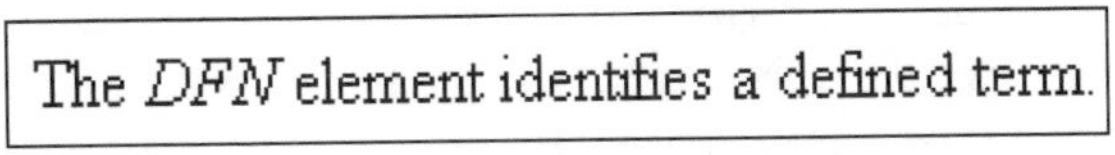

*Figure 4.19 A sample of the DFN element.*

## Related Elements

ACRONYM, B, CITE, CODE, EM, I, KBD, PRE, S, SAMP, STRIKE, STRONG, TT, U, VAR

| DIR | Directory List |
|-----|----------------|

## Purpose

Displays a word list.

## Syntax

```
<DIR[ CLASS="class_name"][ COMPACT][ DIR="LTR"|"RTL"][
ID="id_name"][ LANG="lang_code"][
LANGUAGE="JAVASCRIPT"|"JSCRIPT"|"VBS[CRIPT]"][
ONCLICK="cl_script_data"][ ONDBLCLICK="dc_script_data"][
ONHELP="hlp_script_data"][ ONKEYDOWN="kd_script_data"][
ONKEYPRESS="kp_script_data"][ ONKEYUP="ku_script_data"][
ONMOUSEDOWN="md_script_data"][
ONMOUSEMOVE="mm_script_data"][
ONMOUSEOUT="mo_script_data"][
ONMOUSEOVER="mov_script_data"][
ONMOUSEUP="mu_script_data"][
ONSELECTSTART="ss_script_data"][ STYLE="name_1: value_1"[;
"name_2: value_2"][...; "name_n: value_n"]][
TITLE="title"]>directory-list</DIR>
```

## Where

- CLASS specifies a class identification for the directory list.
- COMPACT indicates that a browser might decrease the size of the space between a number or bullet and the list item.
- DIR specifies the direction in which the directory list text is displayed: left-to-right or right-to-left.
- ID provides a unique identifier name for the directory list.
- LANG provides the code representing the language used for the directory list text.
- **Microsoft** LANGUAGE declares the scripting language of the current script.

- ONCLICK specifies that the referred-to script runs when a user moves the mouse pointer or other pointing device over the directory list and clicks the device button.

- ONDBLCLICK specifies that the referred-to script runs when a user moves the mouse pointer or other pointing device over the directory list and double-clicks the device button.

- **Microsoft** ONHELP specifies that the referred-to script runs when a user presses the **F1** or **Help** key over the current element.

- ONKEYDOWN specifies that the referred-to script runs when a user presses and holds a key down over the directory list.

- ONKEYPRESS specifies that the referred-to script runs when a user presses and releases a key over the directory list.

- ONKEYUP specifies that the referred-to script runs when a user releases a key over the directory list.

- ONMOUSEDOWN specifies that the referred-to script runs when a user moves the mouse pointer or other pointing device over the directory list and presses and holds down the device button.

- ONMOUSEMOVE specifies that the referred-to script runs when a user moves the mouse pointer or other pointing device over the directory list.

- ONMOUSEOUT specifies that the referred-to script runs when a user moves the mouse pointer or other pointing device away from the directory list.

- ONMOUSEOVER specifies that the referred-to script runs the first time a user moves the mouse pointer or other pointing device over the directory list.

- ONMOUSEUP specifies that the referred-to script runs when a user moves the mouse pointer or other pointing device over the directory list and releases a pressed-down device button.

- **Microsoft** ONSELECTSTART specifies that the referred-to script runs when a user starts selecting an object.

- STYLE sets styles for the directory list.
- TITLE provides a title or title information about the directory list.
- *directory-list* represents one or more LI (list item) elements containing one or more characters.

## Notes

This element originated in HTML 2.0.

The HTML 4.0 DTD categorizes this as a block-level element.

Although DIR is supported by HTML 4.0, it has been deprecated (that is, it will eventually be obsolete). Use other list elements (OL or UL) instead.

Some browsers arrange DIR lists in columns, which is the element's intended format.

Each of the words in the list should be 20 characters or less long.

Items on a directory list may or may not be preceded with bullets, depending on the browser.

## Example

```
<DIR>
<LI>Astronomy
<LI>Biology
<LI>Chemistry
<LI>Mathematics
<LI>Physics
</DIR>
```

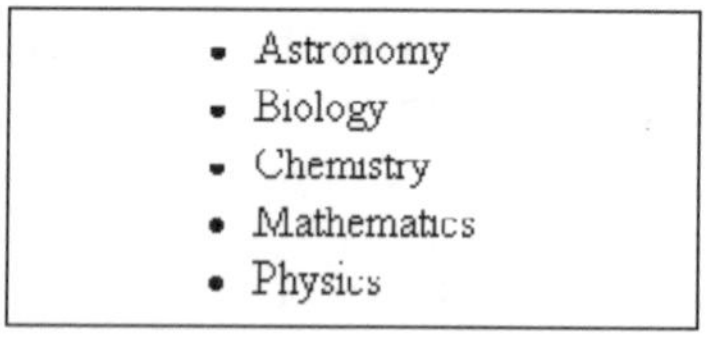

- Astronomy
- Biology
- Chemistry
- Mathematics
- Physics

*Figure 4.20 A short list within DIR elements.*

## Related Elements

UL, OL, MENU

| DIV | Division |
|-----|----------|

## Purpose

Marks the beginning of a new division in a document.

## Syntax

```
<DIV[ ALIGN="left"|"center"|"right"|"justify"][
CLASS="class_name"][ DATAFLD="ds_col_name"][ DATAFOR-
MATAS="HTML"|"TEXT"][ DATASRC="ds_identifier"][
DIR="LTR"|"RTL"][ ID="id_name"][ LANG="lang_code"][
NOWRAP][ ONAFTERUPDATE="au_script_data"][
ONBEFOREUPDATE="bu_script_data"][
ONBLUR="bl_script_data"][ ONCLICK="cl_script_data"][ OND-
BLCLICK="dc_script_data"][ ONDRAGSTART="ds_script_data"][
ONFOCUS="fc_script_data"][ ONHELP="hlp_script_data"][
ONKEYDOWN="kd_script_data"][ ONKEYPRESS="kp_script_data"][
ONKEYUP="ku_script_data"][ ONMOUSEDOWN="md_script_data"][
ONMOUSEMOVE="mm_script_data"][
ONMOUSEOUT="mo_script_data"][
ONMOUSEOVER="mov_script_data"][
ONMOUSEUP="mu_script_data"][ ONRESIZE="rsz_script_data"][
ONROWENTER="re_script_data"][
ONROWEXIT="rex_script_data"][ ONSCROLL="sc_script_data"][
ONSELECTSTART="ss_script_data"][ STYLE="name_1: value_1"[;
"name_2: value_2"][...; "name_n: value_n"]][
TITLE="title"]>text</DIV>
```

## Where

* **ALIGN** horizontally aligns the contents of the entire division.
* **CLASS** specifies a class identification for the division.
* **Microsoft** **DATAFLD** specifies the column name from the file that provides the data source object.

-  DATAFORMATAS indicates whether the data for this element is formatted as *plain text* (that is, unformatted ASCII) or HTML.

-  DATASRC specifies the identifier of the data source object.

- DIR specifies the direction in which the text in the division is displayed: left-to-right or right-to-left.

- ID provides a unique identifier name for the division.

- LANG provides the code representing the language used for the division text.

-  NOWRAP disables word wrap within the current document division.

-  ONAFTERUPDATE specifies that the referred-to script runs after data has been transferred from the element to the data repository.

-  ONBEFOREUPDATE specifies that the referred-to script runs before data is transferred from the element to the data repository.

-  ONBLUR specifies that the referred-to script runs when the link loses focus (that is, it is no longer the active element).

- ONCLICK specifies that the referred-to script runs when a user moves the mouse pointer or other pointing device over the division and clicks the device button.

- ONDBLCLICK specifies that the referred-to script runs when a user moves the mouse pointer or other pointing device over the division and double-clicks the device button.

- ONDRAGSTART specifies that the referred-to script runs when the user starts dragging a selection or element.

- ONFOCUS specifies that the referred-to script runs when the current element receives focus (that is, is made active) by the mouse pointer or other pointing device.

113

-  ONHELP specifies that the referred-to script runs when a user presses the **F1** or **Help** key over the current element.

- ONKEYDOWN specifies that the referred-to script runs when a user presses and holds a key down over the division.

- ONKEYPRESS specifies that the referred-to script runs when a user presses and releases a key over the division.

- ONKEYUP specifies that the referred-to script runs when a user releases a key over the division.

- ONMOUSEDOWN specifies that the referred-to script runs when a user moves the mouse pointer or other pointing device over the division and presses and holds down the device button.

- ONMOUSEMOVE specifies that the referred-to script runs when a user moves the mouse pointer or other pointing device over the division.

- ONMOUSEOUT specifies that the referred-to script runs when a user moves the mouse pointer or other pointing device away from the division.

- ONMOUSEOVER specifies that the referred-to script runs the first time a user moves the mouse pointer or other pointing device over the division.

- ONMOUSEUP specifies that the referred-to script runs when a user moves the mouse pointer or other pointing device over the division and releases a pressed-down device button.

-  ONRESIZE specifies that the referred-to script runs when the user resizes the selected object.

-  ONROWENTER specifies that the referred-to script runs when the current row has been modified.

-  ONROWEXIT specifies that the referred-to script runs before the current row is modified.

- **Microsoft** ONSCROLL specifies that the referred-to script runs when a user moves the scroll box within the scroll bar.
- **Microsoft** ONSELECTSTART specifies that the referred-to script runs when a user starts selecting an object.
- STYLE sets styles for the division.
- TITLE provides a title or title information about the division.
- *text* represents one or more characters.

## Notes

This element originated in HTML 3.2.

The DIV element simply marks the location of a new chapter or section within a document; it does not change or reset alignment, enhancements, or anything else in the document unless you specify the alignment using the ALIGN attribute.

The HTML 4.0 DTD categorizes this as a block-level element.

You can use the DIV element to apply styles to a particular section of a document.

The DIV element usually causes a line break.

You cannot use the DIV element within a paragraph set with the P element; it will terminate the paragraph.

## Example

```
<DIV ALIGN="center">
<H2>Starting a Centered Division</H2>
This is the start of a new centered section.
</DIV>
```

---

**Starting a Centered Division**

This is the start of a new centered section.

---

*Figure 4.21 A centered new division.*

# Related Element

BODY

| DL | Definition List |
|---|---|

## Purpose

Defines a glossary or definition list.

## Syntax

```
<DL[ CLASS="class_name"][ COMPACT][ DIR="LTR"|"RTL"][
ID="id_name"][ LANG="lang_code"][
LANGUAGE="JAVASCRIPT"|"JSCRIPT"|"VBS[CRIPT]"][
ONCLICK="cl_script_data"][ ONDBLCLICK="dc_script_data"][
ONHELP="hlp_script_data"][ ONKEYDOWN="kd_script_data"][
ONKEYPRESS="kp_script_data"][ ONKEYUP="ku_script_data"][
ONMOUSEDOWN="md_script_data"][
ONMOUSEMOVE="mm_script_data"][
ONMOUSEOUT="mo_script_data"][
ONMOUSEOVER="mov_script_data"][
ONMOUSEUP="mu_script_data"][
ONSELECTSTART="ss_script_data"][ STYLE="name_1: value_1"[;
"name_2: value_2"][...; "name_n: value_n"]][
TITLE="title"]>definition-list</DL>
```

## Where

- CLASS specifies a class identification for the definition list.
- COMPACT indicates that a browser might decrease the size of the space between the term and the definition description.
- DIR specifies the direction in which the text in the definition list is displayed: left-to-right or right-to-left.
- ID provides a unique identifier name for the definition list.
- LANG provides the code representing the language used for the definition list text.
- LANGUAGE declares the scripting language of the current script.

- ONCLICK specifies that the referred-to script runs when a user moves the mouse pointer or other pointing device over the definition list and clicks the device button.

- ONDBLCLICK specifies that the referred-to script runs when a user moves the mouse pointer or other pointing device over the definition list and double-clicks the device button.

- **Microsoft** ONHELP specifies that the referred-to script runs when a user presses the **F1** or **Help** key over the current element.

- ONKEYDOWN specifies that the referred-to script runs when a user presses and holds a key down over the definition list.

- ONKEYPRESS specifies that the referred-to script runs when a user presses and releases a key over the definition list.

- ONKEYUP specifies that the referred-to script runs when a user releases a key over the definition list.

- ONMOUSEDOWN specifies that the referred-to script runs when a user moves the mouse pointer or other pointing device over the definition list and presses and holds down the device button.

- ONMOUSEMOVE specifies that the referred-to script runs when a user moves the mouse pointer or other pointing device over the definition list.

- ONMOUSEOUT specifies that the referred-to script runs when a user moves the mouse pointer or other pointing device away from the definition list.

- ONMOUSEOVER specifies that the referred-to script runs the first time a user moves the mouse pointer or other pointing device over the definition list.

- ONMOUSEUP specifies that the referred-to script runs when a user moves the mouse pointer or other pointing device over the definition list and releases a pressed-down device button.

- **Microsoft** ONSELECTSTART specifies that the referred-to script runs when a user starts selecting an object.

- STYLE sets styles for the definition list.
- TITLE provides a title or title information about the definition list.
- *definition-list* represents one or more pairs of terms (DT) and definitions (DD).

## Notes

This element originated in HTML 2.0.

Each definition term (DT) in a definition list is paired with a definition description (DD).

The HTML 4.0 DTD categorizes this as a block-level element.

You can nest other lists within a definition list.

Not all browsers recognize the COMPACT attribute.

Embed the DD, DL, and DT elements within the DL element. However, some browsers do not support the nesting of elements. See also the DD and DT elements.

## Example

```
<DL>
<DT><B>File</B>
<DD>A set of organized and related information stored with
a unique file name.
<DT><B>Menu</B>
<DD>A list of commands available from a horizontal bar
immediately below the title bar.
</DL>
```

> **File**
> > A set of organized and related information stored with a unique file name.
>
> **Menu**
> > A list of commands available from a horizontal bar immediately below the title bar.

*Figure 4.22 A definition list with embedded B elements.*

## Related Elements

DD, DT

| DT | Definition Term |
|---|---|

## Purpose

Names a term in a definition list.

## Syntax

```
<DT[ CLASS="class_name"][ DIR="LTR"|"RTL"][ ID="id_name"][
LANG="lang_code"][
LANGUAGE="JAVASCRIPT"|"JSCRIPT"|"VBS[CRIPT]"][
ONCLICK="cl_script_data"][ ONDBLCLICK="dc_script_data"][
ONHELP="hlp_script_data"][ ONKEYDOWN="kd_script_data"][
ONKEYPRESS="kp_script_data"][ ONKEYUP="ku_script_data"][
ONMOUSEDOWN="md_script_data"][
ONMOUSEMOVE="mm_script_data"][
ONMOUSEOUT="mo_script_data"][
ONMOUSEOVER="mov_script_data"][
ONMOUSEUP="mu_script_data"][
ONSELECTSTART="ss_script_data"][ STYLE="name_1: value_1"[;
"name_2: value_2"][...; "name_n: value_n"]][
TITLE="title"]>definition-term[</DT>]
```

## Where

- CLASS specifies a class identification for the definition term.
- DIR specifies the direction in which the definition term text is displayed: left-to-right or right-to-left.
- ID provides a unique identifier name for the definition term.
- LANG provides the code representing the language used for the definition term text.
- **Microsoft** LANGUAGE declares the scripting language of the current script.
- ONCLICK specifies that the referred-to script runs when a user moves the mouse pointer or other pointing

device over the definition term and clicks the device button.

- ONDBLCLICK specifies that the referred-to script runs when a user moves the mouse pointer or other pointing device over the definition term and double-clicks the device button.

-  ONHELP specifies that the referred-to script runs when a user presses the **F1** or **Help** key over the current element.

- ONKEYDOWN specifies that the referred-to script runs when a user presses and holds a key down over the definition term.

- ONKEYPRESS specifies that the referred-to script runs when a user presses and releases a key over the definition term.

- ONKEYUP specifies that the referred-to script runs when a user releases a key over the definition term.

- ONMOUSEDOWN specifies that the referred-to script runs when a user moves the mouse pointer or other pointing device over the definition term and presses and holds down the device button.

- ONMOUSEMOVE specifies that the referred-to script runs when a user moves the mouse pointer or other pointing device over the definition term.

- ONMOUSEOUT specifies that the referred-to script runs when a user moves the mouse pointer or other pointing device away from the definition term.

- ONMOUSEOVER specifies that the referred-to script runs the first time a user moves the mouse pointer or other pointing device over the definition term.

- ONMOUSEUP specifies that the referred-to script runs when a user moves the mouse pointer or other pointing device over the definition term and releases a pressed-down device button.

-  ONSELECTSTART specifies that the referred-to script runs when a user starts selecting an object.

- STYLE sets styles for the definition term.

- TITLE provides a title or title information about the definition term.
- *definition-term* represents a name paired with a definition description.

## Notes

This element originated in HTML 2.0.

Each DD element in a definition list must be paired with a DT element.

Pairs of terms (DT) and descriptions (DD) are embedded within DL elements.

A paragraph break automatically occurs at the end of a DT element and its contents.

## Examples

See the DL element.

## Related Elements

DL, DD

| EM | Emphasis |
|---|---|

## Purpose

Emphasizes selected text, usually with italics.

## Syntax

```
<EM[ CLASS="class_name"][ DIR="LTR"|"RTL"][ ID="id_name"][
LANG="lang_code"][
LANGUAGE="JAVASCRIPT"|"JSCRIPT"|"VBS[CRIPT]"][
ONCLICK="cl_script_data"][ ONDBLCLICK="dc_script_data"][
ONHELP="hlp_script_data"][ ONKEYDOWN="kd_script_data"][
ONKEYPRESS="kp_script_data"][ ONKEYUP="ku_script_data"][
ONMOUSEDOWN="md_script_data"][
ONMOUSEMOVE="mm_script_data"][
ONMOUSEOUT="mo_script_data"][
ONMOUSEOVER="mov_script_data"][
ONMOUSEUP="mu_script_data"][
ONSELECTSTART="ss_script_data"][ STYLE="name_1: value_1"[;
"name_2: value_2"][...; "name_n: value_n"]][
TITLE="title"]>text</EM>
```

## Where

- CLASS specifies a class identification for the emphasized text.
- DIR specifies the direction in which the current text is displayed: left-to-right or right-to-left.
- ID provides a unique identifier name for the emphasized text.
- LANG provides the code representing the language used for the emphasized text.
- **Microsoft** LANGUAGE declares the scripting language of the current script.
- ONCLICK specifies that the referred-to script runs when a user moves the mouse pointer or other pointing

device over the emphasized text and clicks the device button.

- ONDBLCLICK specifies that the referred-to script runs when a user moves the mouse pointer or other pointing device over the emphasized text and double-clicks the device button.

- [Microsoft] ONHELP specifies that the referred-to script runs when a user presses the **F1** or **Help** key over the current element.

- ONKEYDOWN specifies that the referred-to script runs when a user presses and holds a key down over the emphasized text.

- ONKEYPRESS specifies that the referred-to script runs when a user presses and releases a key over the emphasized text.

- ONKEYUP specifies that the referred-to script runs when a user releases a key over the emphasized text.

- ONMOUSEDOWN specifies that the referred-to script runs when a user moves the mouse pointer or other pointing device over the emphasized text and presses and holds down the device button.

- ONMOUSEMOVE specifies that the referred-to script runs when a user moves the mouse pointer or other pointing device over the emphasized text.

- ONMOUSEOUT specifies that the referred-to script runs when a user moves the mouse pointer or other pointing device away from the emphasized text.

- ONMOUSEOVER specifies that the referred-to script runs the first time a user moves the mouse pointer or other pointing device over the emphasized text.

- ONMOUSEUP specifies that the referred-to script runs when a user moves the mouse pointer or other pointing device over the emphasized text and releases a pressed-down device button.

- [Microsoft] ONSELECTSTART specifies that the referred-to script runs when a user starts selecting an object.

- STYLE sets styles for the emphasized text.

- TITLE provides a title or title information about the emphasized text.
- *text* represents one or more characters.

## Notes

This element originated in HTML 2.0.

The EM and STRONG elements are logical styles, which allow a browser to emphasize selected text in the way in which it is programmed to do. This is in contrast with I and B, their counterpart physical styles, which command a browser to apply italics and boldface, respectively.

The HTML 4.0 DTD categorizes this as an inline element.

## Example

```
This is text with <EM>emphasis</EM>.
```

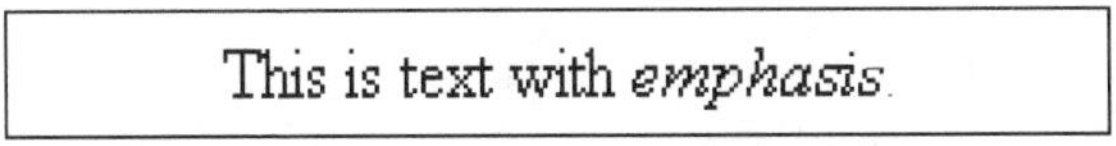

This is text with *emphasis*

*Figure 4.23 A sample of emphasized text.*

## Related Elements

ACRONYM, B, CITE, CODE, DFN, I, KBD, PRE, S, SAMP, STRIKE, STRONG, TT, U, VAR

| FONT | Font |
|------|------|

## Purpose

Changes the size, color, or typeface of selected text.

## Syntax

```
<FONT[ CLASS="class_name"][ COLOR="#rrggbb"|"color"][
FACE="typeface"][ ID="id_name"][ LANG="lang_code"][ LAN-
GUAGE="JAVASCRIPT"|"JSCRIPT"|"VBS[CRIPT]"][
ONCLICK="cl_script_data"][ ONDBLCLICK="dc_script_data"][
ONHELP="hlp_script_data"][ ONKEYDOWN="kd_script_data"][
ONKEYPRESS="kp_script_data"][
ONMOUSEMOVE="mm_script_data"][
ONMOUSEOUT="mo_script_data"][
ONMOUSEOVER="mov_script_data"][
ONMOUSEUP="mu_script_data"][
ONSELECTSTART="ss_script_data"][ SIZE="[+|-
]1|2|3|4|5|6|7"][ STYLE="name_1: value_1"[; "name_2:
value_2"][...; "name_n: value_n"]][
TITLE="title"]>text</FONT>
```

## Where

- **Microsoft** CLASS specifies a class identification for the element.
- COLOR is the color of the selected text.
- FACE specifies the name of a typeface installed on your computer
- **Microsoft** ID provides a unique identifier name for the element.
- **Microsoft** LANG provides the code representing the language used for the element.
- **Microsoft** LANGUAGE declares the scripting language of the current script.

-  ONCLICK specifies that the referred-to script runs when a user moves the mouse pointer or other pointing device over the selected text and clicks the device button.

-  ONDBLCLICK specifies that the referred-to script runs when a user moves the mouse pointer or other pointing device over the selected text and double-clicks the device button.

-  ONHELP specifies that the referred-to script runs when a user presses the **F1** or **Help** key over the current element.

-  ONKEYDOWN specifies that the referred-to script runs when a user presses and holds a key down over the selected text.

-  ONKEYPRESS specifies that the referred-to script runs when a user presses and releases a key over the selected text.

-  ONMOUSEDOWN specifies that the referred-to script runs when a user moves the mouse pointer or other pointing device over the selected text and presses and holds down the device button.

-  ONMOUSEMOVE specifies that the referred-to script runs when a user moves the mouse pointer or other pointing device over the selected text.

-  ONMOUSEOUT specifies that the referred-to script runs when a user moves the mouse pointer or other pointing device away from the selected text.

-  ONMOUSEOVER specifies that the referred-to script runs the first time a user moves the mouse pointer or other pointing device over the selected text.

- ■ Microsoft — ONMOUSEUP specifies that the referred-to script runs when a user moves the mouse pointer or other pointing device over the selected text and releases a pressed-down device button.

- ■ Microsoft — ONSELECTSTART specifies that the referred-to script runs when a user starts selecting an object.

- SIZE indicates that you will change the relative (+ or -) or actual (1-7) size of the selected text.

- ■ Microsoft — STYLE sets styles for the selected text.

- ■ Microsoft — TITLE provides a title or title information about the selected text.

## Notes

This element originated in HTML 3.2.

The HTML 4.0 DTD categorizes this as an inline element.

Although FONT is supported by HTML 4.0, it has been deprecated (that is, it will eventually be obsolete). Use style sheets to specify font attributes.

If you select a typeface not found on your computer system, the browser substitutes the default font, usually Times Roman.

If you omit the quotation marks from the color values or the typeface, some HTML editors automatically insert them.

## Examples

Example 1 (Figure 4.24)

```
<P>Small
<FONT SIZE="-1"> smaller</FONT>
<FONT SIZE="-2"> even smaller</FONT>
```

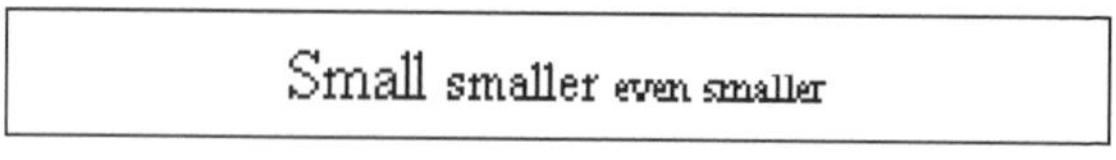

Small smaller even smaller

*Figure 4.24 Small, smaller, and smallest font sizes.*

Example 2 (Figure 4.25)

```
<P><FONT SIZE="1"> Smallest font size</FONT>
<BR><FONT SIZE="7">Largest font size</FONT>
```

smallest font size

# Largest font size

*Figure 4.25 The smallest and largest font sizes.*

Example 3 (Figure 4.26)

```
<BODY BGCOLOR="black">
<P><FONT COLOR="white">White text</FONT>
```

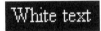

*Figure 4.26 White text on a black background.*

Example 4 (Figure 4.27)

```
<P>This is <FONT FACE="Courier"
SIZE="4"><B>Courier</B></FONT> text.
```

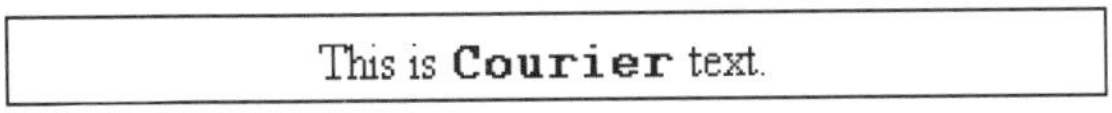

This is **Courier** text.

*Figure 4.27 A sample of larger, boldface, Courier text.*

## Related Elements

BASEFONT, BIG, SMALL

| H*n* | Heading |
|------|---------|

## Purpose

Applies one of six heading characteristics to selected text.

## Syntax

```
<Hn[ ALIGN="left"|"center"|"right"|"justify"][
CLASS="class_name"][ DIR="LTR"|"RTL"][ ID="id_name"][
LANG="lang_code"][
LANGUAGE="JAVASCRIPT"|"JSCRIPT"|"VBS[CRIPT]"][
ONCLICK="cl_script_data"][ ONDBLCLICK="dc_script_data"][
ONHELP="hlp_script_data"][ ONKEYDOWN="kd_script_data"][
ONKEYPRESS="kp_script_data"][ ONKEYUP="ku_script_data"][
ONMOUSEDOWN="md_script_data"][
ONMOUSEMOVE="mm_script_data"][
ONMOUSEOUT="mo_script_data"][
ONMOUSEOVER="mov_script_data"][
ONMOUSEUP="mu_script_data"][
ONSELECTSTART="ss_script_data"][ STYLE="name_1: value_1"[;
"name_2: value_2"][...; "name_n: value_n"]][
TITLE="title"]>heading-text</Hn>
```

## Where

- *n* represents a heading level from 1 to 6.
- ALIGN horizontally aligns the heading.
- CLASS specifies a class identification for the current heading.
- DIR specifies the direction in which the heading text is displayed: left-to-right or right-to-left.
- ID provides a unique identifier name for the heading.
- LANG provides the code representing the language used for the heading text.
- **Microsoft** LANGUAGE declares the scripting language of the current script.

- ONCLICK specifies that the referred-to script runs when a user moves the mouse pointer or other pointing device over the heading and clicks the device button.
- ONDBLCLICK specifies that the referred-to script runs when a user moves the mouse pointer or other pointing device over the heading and double-clicks the device button.
- **Microsoft** ONHELP specifies that the referred-to script runs when a user presses the **F1** or **Help** key over the current element.
- ONKEYDOWN specifies that the referred-to script runs when a user presses and holds a key down over the heading.
- ONKEYPRESS specifies that the referred-to script runs when a user presses and releases a key over the heading.
- ONKEYUP specifies that the referred-to script runs when a user releases a key over the heading.
- ONMOUSEDOWN specifies that the referred-to script runs when a user moves the mouse pointer or other pointing device over the heading and presses and holds down the device button.
- ONMOUSEMOVE specifies that the referred-to script runs when a user moves the mouse pointer or other pointing device over the heading.
- ONMOUSEOUT specifies that the referred-to script runs when a user moves the mouse pointer or other pointing device away from the heading.
- ONMOUSEOVER specifies that the referred-to script runs the first time a user moves the mouse pointer or other pointing device over the heading.
- ONMOUSEUP specifies that the referred-to script runs when a user moves the mouse pointer or other pointing device over the heading and releases a pressed-down device button.
- **Microsoft** ONSELECTSTART specifies that the referred-to script runs when a user starts selecting an object.
- STYLE sets styles for the heading.

- TITLE provides a title or title information about the heading.
- *head*ing-*text* represents a section or page heading.

## Notes

These elements originated in HTML 2.0.

The HTML 4.0 DTD categorizes these as block-level elements.

The number representing the heading level must match in the start tag and the end tag.

H1 elements are at the highest level and have the largest font size; H6 elements are at the lowest level and have the smallest font size.

By default, all Hn headings have line spaces above and below.

The Hn start and end elements both cause a line break.

When planning a document, be sure to select the proper heading elements. At the top of the document, place an H1 heading. As a rule, don't skip heading levels (for example, from H1 to H3). Think of how you would outline your document, and use the outline levels to plan your heading levels.

Some browsers can create tables of contents using the heading elements.

## Examples

```
<H1>Heading 1</H1>

<H2>Heading 2</H2>

<H3>Heading 3</H3>

<H4>Heading 4</H4>

<H5>Heading 5</H5>

<H6>Heading 6</H6>
```

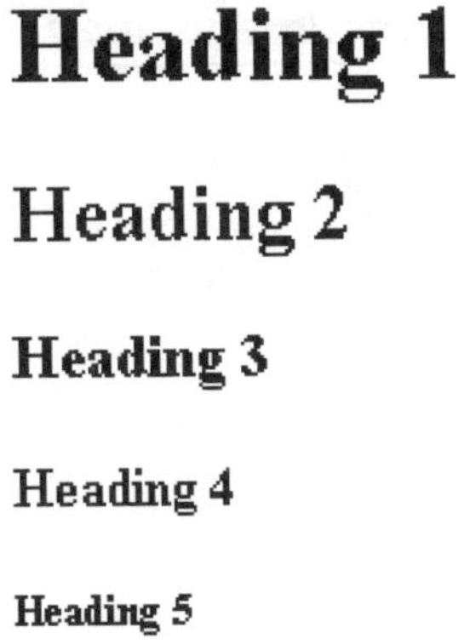

# Heading 1

## Heading 2

### Heading 3

#### Heading 4

##### Heading 5

*Figure 4.28 The five HTML headings in the Netscape Navigator window.*

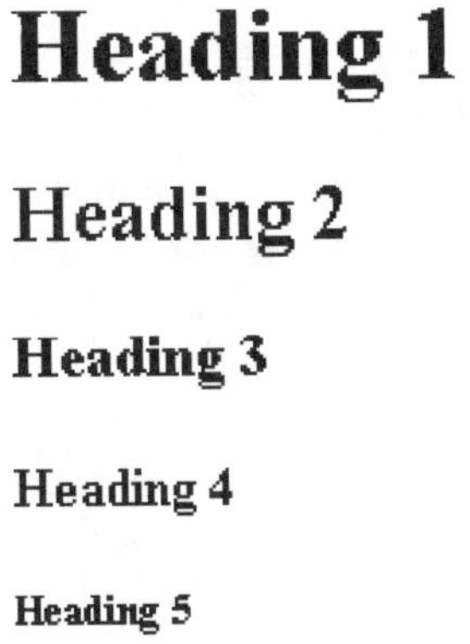

# Heading 1

## Heading 2

### Heading 3

#### Heading 4

##### Heading 5

*Figure 4.29 The five HTML headings in the Microsoft Internet Explorer window.*

| HEAD | Document Head |
|------|---------------|

## Purpose

Introduces and describes an HTML document, including its title.

## Syntax

```
[<HEAD[ CLASS="class_name"][ DIR="LTR"|"RTL"][
ID="id_name"][ LANG="lang_code"][ PROFILE="prof_url_1"[
"prof_url_2"[..."prof_url_n"]]][ TITLE="title"]>]head-sec-
tion[</HEAD>]
```

## Where

- **Microsoft** CLASS specifies a class identification for the element.

- DIR specifies the direction in which the text in the HEAD section is displayed: left-to-right or right-to-left.

- **Microsoft** ID provides a unique identifier name for the element.

- LANG provides the code representing the language used for the text in the HEAD section.

- PROFILE lists one or more URLs of files containing meta information, which describe the current document.

- *head-section* includes the title and other introductory lines of text.

## Notes

This element originated in HTML 2.0.

HTML documents are composed of two sections, headed by the HEAD and BODY elements. All other elements are included in one of these sections. Frames documents use the FRAMESET element and its contents rather than the BODY element and its contents.

The HEAD section of a document includes information that is not displayed when you open the document.

Many documents have only a TITLE element in the head section. However, you can also embed the following elements within the HEAD element: BASE, ISINDEX, LINK, META, SCRIPT, and STYLE.

The HEAD element is embedded within the HTML element.

## Example

```
<HEAD>
<TITLE>The Eddy Group Home Page</TITLE>
<!—Company="The Eddy Group, Inc."—>
<LINK HREF="mailto:eddygrp@sover.net">
<META name="Author" content="Sandra E. Eddy">
<META name="date" content="17 April 1998">
<META name="keywords" content="books, computer books,
business writing, articles, article writing, column writ-
ing, author, internet books, writing"
</HEAD>
```

## Related Elements

BODY, HTML

| HR | Horizontal Rule |
|---|---|

## Purpose

Inserts a horizontal rule line between sections of a document.

## Syntax

```
<HR[ ALIGN="center"|"left"|"right"][ CLASS="class_name"][
COLOR="#rrggbb"|"color"][ ID="id_name"][
LANG="lang_code"][
LANGUAGE="JAVASCRIPT"|"JSCRIPT"|"VBS[CRIPT]"][ NOSHADE][
ONBEFOREUPDATE="bu_script_data"][
ONBLUR="bl_script_data"][ ONCLICK="cl_script_data"][ OND-
BLCLICK="dc_script_data"][ ONDRAGSTART="ds_script_data"][
ONFOCUS="fc_script_data"][ ONHELP="hlp_script_data"][
ONKEYDOWN="kd_script_data"][ ONKEYPRESS="kp_script_data"][
ONKEYUP="ku_script_data"][ ONMOUSEDOWN="md_script_data"][
ONMOUSEMOVE="mm_script_data"][
ONMOUSEOUT="mo_script_data"][
ONMOUSEOVER="mov_script_data"][
ONMOUSEUP="mu_script_data"][ ONRESIZE="rsz_script_data"][
ONROWENTER="re_script_data"][
ONROWEXIT="rex_script_data"][
ONSELECTSTART="ss_script_data"][ SIZE="rule_height"][
STYLE="name_1: value_1"[; "name_2: value_2"][...; "name_n:
value_n"]][ TITLE="title"][ WIDTH="width_pix"|"width_%"]
```

## Where

- ALIGN horizontally aligns the horizontal rule.

- CLASS specifies a class identification for the horizontal rule.

- **Microsoft** COLOR defines the color of the horizontal rule.

- ID provides a unique identifier name for the horizontal rule.

-  LANG provides the code representing the language used for the element.

-  LANGUAGE declares the scripting language of the current script.

- NOSHADE removes the shading from the rule.

-  ONBEFOREUPDATE specifies that the referred-to script runs before data is transferred from the element to the data repository.

-  ONBLUR specifies that the referred-to script runs when the link loses focus (that is, it is no longer the active element).

- ONCLICK specifies that the referred-to script runs when a user moves the mouse pointer or other pointing device over the horizontal rule and clicks the device button.

- ONDBLCLICK specifies that the referred-to script runs when a user moves the mouse pointer or other pointing device over the horizontal rule and double-clicks the device button.

-  ONDRAGSTART specifies that the referred-to script runs when the user starts dragging a selection or element.

-  ONFOCUS specifies that the referred-to script runs when the current element receives focus (that is, is made active) by the mouse pointer or other pointing device.

-  ONHELP specifies that the referred-to script runs when a user presses the **F1** or **Help** key over the current element.

- ONKEYDOWN specifies that the referred-to script runs when a user presses and holds a key down over the horizontal rule.

- ONKEYPRESS specifies that the referred-to script runs when a user presses and releases a key over the horizontal rule.

137

- ONKEYUP specifies that the referred-to script runs when a user releases a key over the horizontal rule.
- ONMOUSEDOWN specifies that the referred-to script runs when a user moves the mouse pointer or other pointing device over the horizontal rule and presses and holds down the device button.
- ONMOUSEMOVE specifies that the referred-to script runs when a user moves the mouse pointer or other pointing device over the horizontal rule.
- ONMOUSEOUT specifies that the referred-to script runs when a user moves the mouse pointer or other pointing device away from the horizontal rule.
- ONMOUSEOVER specifies that the referred-to script runs the first time a user moves the mouse pointer or other pointing device over the horizontal rule.
- ONMOUSEUP specifies that the referred-to script runs when a user moves the mouse pointer or other pointing device over the horizontal rule and releases a pressed-down device button.
- **Microsoft** ONRESIZE specifies that the referred-to script runs when the user resizes the selected object.
- **Microsoft** ONROWENTER specifies that the referred-to script runs when the current row has been modified.
- **Microsoft** ONROWEXIT specifies that the referred-to script runs before the current row is modified.
- **Microsoft** ONSELECTSTART specifies that the referred-to script runs when a user starts selecting an object.
- SIZE is the height of the rule, in pixels.
- STYLE sets styles for the horizontal rule.
- TITLE provides a title or title information about the horizontal rule.
- WIDTH represents the width of the rule, in pixels or as a percentage of the width of the window.

## Notes

This element originated in HTML 2.0.

The HTML 4.0 DTD categorizes this as a block-level element.

The HR element causes a paragraph break.

The default horizontal rule is 600 pixels wide based on a 640x480 graphic resolution.

You cannot align a rule that is the full width of the computer screen.

## Examples

Example 1 (Figure 4.30)

```
<HR>
```

*Figure 4.30 The default HR rule shown in an Internet Explorer window.*

*Figure 4.31 The default HR rule shown in a Netscape Communicator window.*

Example 2 (Figure 4.32)

```
<HR WIDTH="400" ALIGN="left">
```

*Figure 4.32 A short left-aligned rule.*

Example 3 (Figure 4.33)

```
<HR SIZE="5">
```

*Figure 4.33 An example of a rule with a 5-pixel SIZE attribute.*

Example 4 (Figure 4.34)

`<HR NOSHADE>`

*Figure 4.34 A rule with no shading.*

## Related Element

IMG

| HTML | HTML Document |
|------|---------------|

## Purpose

Defines an HTML (HyperText Markup Language) document.

## Syntax

```
[<HTML[ DIR="LTR"|"RTL"][ LANG="lang_code"][
TITLE="title"][ VERSION="dtd_url"]>]HTML-document[</HTML>]
```

## Where

- DIR specifies the direction in which the HTML document text is displayed: left-to-right or right-to-left.
- LANG provides the code representing the language used for the text in the HTML document.
- [Microsoft] TITLE provides a title or title information about the element.
- VERSION specifies the URL for the Document Type Definition (DTD) of the HTML standard for the elements and attributes of the current document.
- *HTML-document* represents an entire document.

## Notes

This element originated in HTML 2.0.

The HTML 4.0 DTD categorizes this as an inline element.

The <HTML> start tag should be the first in a document, and the </HTML> end tag should be the last.

You can embed the HEAD and BODY elements within the HTML elements, but they are not required. However, if you are working on a frames document, the FRAMESET element is required.

## Example

The following is a skeleton HTML document:

```
<!DOCTYPE HTML PUBLIC "-//W3C//DTD HTML 4.0//EN">
```

141

```
<HTML>

<HEAD>

<TITLE>A Very Short and Simple Document</TITLE>

</HEAD>

<BODY>

<H2>A Heading

One paragraph

<P>Another paragraph

</BODY>

</HTML>
```

## Related Elements

BODY, FRAMESET, HEAD

| I | Italic Text |
|---|---|

## Purpose

Applies italics to selected text.

## Syntax

```
<I[ CLASS="class_name"][ DIR="LTR"|"RTL"][ ID="id_name"][
LANG="lang_code"][
LANGUAGE="JAVASCRIPT"|"JSCRIPT"|"VBS[CRIPT]"][
ONCLICK="cl_script_data"][ ONDBLCLICK="dc_script_data"][
ONHELP="hlp_script_data"][ ONKEYDOWN="kd_script_data"][
ONKEYPRESS="kp_script_data"][ ONKEYUP="ku_script_data"][
ONMOUSEDOWN="md_script_data"][
ONMOUSEMOVE="mm_script_data"][
ONMOUSEOUT="mo_script_data"][
ONMOUSEOVER="mov_script_data"][
ONMOUSEUP="mu_script_data"][
ONSELECTSTART="ss_script_data"][ STYLE="name_1: value_1"[;
"name_2: value_2"][...; "name_n: value_n"]][
TITLE="title"]>text</I>
```

## Where

- CLASS specifies a class identification for the italicized text.
- DIR specifies the direction in which the italicized text is displayed: left-to-right or right-to-left.
- ID provides a unique identifier name for the italicized text.
- LANG provides the code representing the language used for the italicized text.
- Microsoft LANGUAGE declares the scripting language of the current script.
- ONCLICK specifies that the referred-to script runs when a user moves the mouse pointer or other pointing

143

device over the italicized text and clicks the device button.

- ONDBLCLICK specifies that the referred-to script runs when a user moves the mouse pointer or other pointing device over the italicized text and double-clicks the device button.

- [Microsoft] ONHELP specifies that the referred-to script runs when a user presses the **F1** or **Help** key over the current element.

- ONKEYDOWN specifies that the referred-to script runs when a user presses and holds a key down over the italicized text.

- ONKEYPRESS specifies that the referred-to script runs when a user presses and releases a key over the italicized text.

- ONKEYUP specifies that the referred-to script runs when a user releases a key over the italicized text.

- ONMOUSEDOWN specifies that the referred-to script runs when a user moves the mouse pointer or other pointing device over the italicized text and presses and holds down the device button.

- ONMOUSEMOVE specifies that the referred-to script runs when a user moves the mouse pointer or other pointing device over the italicized text.

- ONMOUSEOUT specifies that the referred-to script runs when a user moves the mouse pointer or other pointing device away from the italicized text.

- ONMOUSEOVER specifies that the referred-to script runs the first time a user moves the mouse pointer or other pointing device over the italicized text.

- ONMOUSEUP specifies that the referred-to script runs when a user moves the mouse pointer or other pointing device over the italicized text and releases a pressed-down device button.

- [Microsoft] ONSELECTSTART specifies that the referred-to script runs when a user starts selecting an object.

- STYLE sets styles for the italicized text.

- TITLE provides a title or title information about the italicized text.
- *text* represents one or more characters.

## Notes

This element originated in HTML 2.0.

The HTML 4.0 DTD categorizes this as an inline element.

The EM and STRONG elements are logical styles, which allow a browser to emphasize selected text in the way in which it is programmed. This is in contrast with I and B, their counterpart physical styles, which command a browser to apply italics and boldface respectively.

## Example

```
This is <I>italicized</I> text.
```

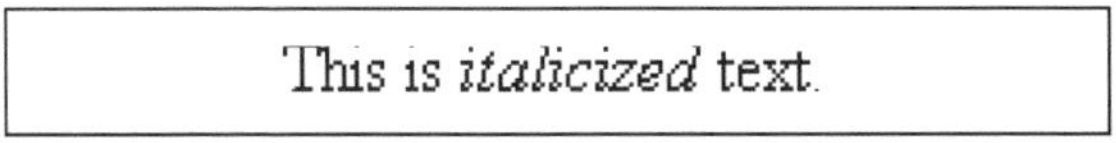

This is *italicized* text.

*Figure 4.35 An example of the I element.*

## Related Elements

EM, CITE, VAR, B, STRONG, U, S, SUB, SUP, BIG, SMALL, FONT

| INS | Mark Insertions |
|-----|-----------------|

## Purpose

Marks document sections that have been inserted since the original document was created and posted.

## Syntax

```
<INS[ CITE="url"][ CLASS="class_name"][
DATETIME="datetime"][ DIR="LTR"|"RTL"][ ID="id_name"][
LANG="lang_code"][ ONCLICK="cl_script_data"][
ONDBLCLICK="dc_script_data"][ ONKEYDOWN="kd_script_data"][
ONKEYPRESS="kp_script_data"][ ONKEYUP="ku_script_data"][
ONMOUSEDOWN="md_script_data"][
ONMOUSEMOVE="mm_script_data"][
ONMOUSEOUT="mo_script_data"][
ONMOUSEOVER="mov_script_data"][
ONMOUSEUP="mu_script_data"][ STYLE="name_1: value_1"[;
"name_2: value_2"][...; "name_n: value_n"]][
TITLE="title"]>inserted-section</INS>
```

## Where

- CITE provides a URL for a document that contains the reason for a document change.
- CLASS specifies a class identification for the text marked as inserted.
- DATETIME names the date and time at which a change in the document was made.
- DIR specifies the direction in which the text marked as inserted is displayed: left-to-right or right-to-left.
- ID provides a unique identifier name for the text marked as inserted.
- LANG provides the code representing the language used for the text marked as inserted.
- ONCLICK specifies that the referred-to script runs when a user moves the mouse pointer or other pointing

device over the text marked as inserted and clicks the device button.

- ONDBLCLICK specifies that the referred-to script runs when a user moves the mouse pointer or other pointing device over the text marked as inserted and double-clicks the device button.
- ONKEYDOWN specifies that the referred-to script runs when a user presses and holds a key down over the text marked as inserted.
- ONKEYPRESS specifies that the referred-to script runs when a user presses and releases a key over the text marked as inserted.
- ONKEYUP specifies that the referred-to script runs when a user releases a key over the text marked as inserted.
- ONMOUSEDOWN specifies that the referred-to script runs when a user moves the mouse pointer or other pointing device over the text marked as inserted and presses and holds down the device button.
- ONMOUSEMOVE specifies that the referred-to script runs when a user moves the mouse pointer or other pointing device over the text marked as inserted.
- ONMOUSEOUT specifies that the referred-to script runs when a user moves the mouse pointer or other pointing device away from the text marked as inserted.
- ONMOUSEOVER specifies that the referred-to script runs the first time a user moves the mouse pointer or other pointing device over the text marked as inserted.
- ONMOUSEUP specifies that the referred-to script runs when a user moves the mouse pointer or other pointing device over the text marked as inserted and releases a pressed-down device button.
- STYLE sets styles for the text marked as inserted.
- TITLE provides a title or title information about the text marked as inserted.
- *inserted-section* is the text marked as inserted.

## Notes

This is an HTML 4.0 element.

Browsers may mark inserted text in various ways: by changing to a special font, by inserting revision marks, and so on.

## Example

```
This text has been here for a while.<INS
CITE="docchg.htm"> This is newly inserted text.</INS> This
text has been here since creation.
```

This text has been here for a while. This is newly inserted text. This text has been here since creation.

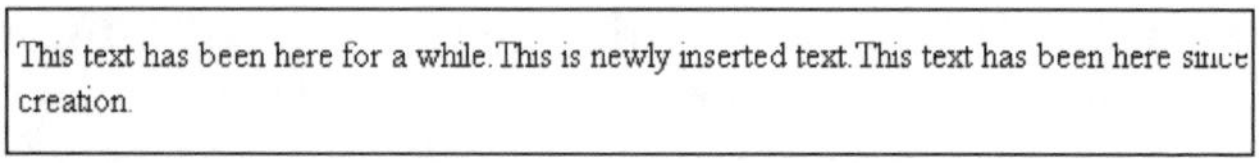

*Figure 4.36 In HotMetal Pro, inserted text is not marked.*

## Related Element

DEL

| KBD | Keyboard Input |
|-----|----------------|

## Purpose

Applies a keyboard input (monospace) font to selected text.

## Syntax

```
<KBD[ CLASS="class_name"][ DIR="LTR"|"RTL"][
ID="id_name"][ LANG="lang_code"][
LANGUAGE="JAVASCRIPT"|"JSCRIPT"|"VBS[CRIPT]"][
ONCLICK="cl_script_data"][ ONDBLCLICK="dc_script_data"][
ONHELP="hlp_script_data"][ ONKEYDOWN="kd_script_data"][
ONKEYPRESS="kp_script_data"][ ONKEYUP="ku_script_data"][
ONMOUSEDOWN="md_script_data"][
ONMOUSEMOVE="mm_script_data"][
ONMOUSEOUT="mo_script_data"][
ONMOUSEOVER="mov_script_data"][
ONMOUSEUP="mu_script_data"][
ONSELECTSTART="ss_script_data"][ STYLE="name_1: value_1"[;
"name_2: value_2"][...; "name_n: value_n"]][
TITLE="title"]>text</KBD>
```

## Where

- CLASS specifies a class identification for the keyboard input.
- DIR specifies the direction in which the keyboard input is displayed: left-to-right or right-to-left.
- ID provides a unique identifier name for the keyboard input.
- LANG provides the code representing the language used for the keyboard input.
- **Microsoft** LANGUAGE declares the scripting language of the current script.
- ONCLICK specifies that the referred-to script runs when a user moves the mouse pointer or other pointing

**149**

device over the keyboard input and clicks the device button.

- ONDBLCLICK specifies that the referred-to script runs when a user moves the mouse pointer or other pointing device over the keyboard input and double-clicks the device button.

- |Microsoft| ONHELP specifies that the referred-to script runs when a user presses the **F1** or **Help** key over the current element.

- ONKEYDOWN specifies that the referred-to script runs when a user presses and holds a key down over the keyboard input.

- ONKEYPRESS specifies that the referred-to script runs when a user presses and releases a key over the keyboard input.

- ONKEYUP specifies that the referred-to script runs when a user releases a key over the keyboard input.

- ONMOUSEDOWN specifies that the referred-to script runs when a user moves the mouse pointer or other pointing device over the keyboard input and presses and holds down the device button.

- ONMOUSEMOVE specifies that the referred-to script runs when a user moves the mouse pointer or other pointing device over the keyboard input.

- ONMOUSEOUT specifies that the referred-to script runs when a user moves the mouse pointer or other pointing device away from the keyboard input.

- ONMOUSEOVER specifies that the referred-to script runs the first time a user moves the mouse pointer or other pointing device over the keyboard input.

- ONMOUSEUP specifies that the referred-to script runs when a user moves the mouse pointer or other pointing device over the keyboard input and releases a pressed-down device button.

- |Microsoft| ONSELECTSTART specifies that the referred-to script runs when a user starts selecting an object.

- STYLE sets styles for the keyboard input.

- TITLE provides a title or title information about the keyboard input.
- *text* represents one or more characters.

## Notes

This element originated in HTML 2.0.

KBD is a logical element, in which particular browsers are programmed to apply a certain style to the selected text. This is in contrast to a physical element in which you "code" the styles yourself.

The HTML 4.0 DTD categorizes this as an inline element.

Many browsers use the same font for the CODE, KBD, PRE, SAMP, and TT elements.

To display two or more lines of preformatted text, use the PRE element.

## Example

```
This is <KBD>keyboard input</KBD> text.
```

```
This is keyboard input text
```

*Figure 4.37 A sample of keyboard input text using the KBD element.*

## Related Elements

ACRONYM, B, CITE, CODE, DFN, EM, I, PRE, S, SAMP, STRIKE, STRONG, TT, U, VAR

| LI | List Item |
|---|---|

## Purpose

Lists one item within an ordered (OL), unordered (UL), menu (MENU), or directory (DIR) list.

## Syntax

```
<LI[ CLASS="class_name"][ DIR="LTR"|"RTL"][ ID="id_name"][
LANG="lang_code"][
LANGUAGE="JAVASCRIPT"|"JSCRIPT"|"VBS[CRIPT]"][
ONCLICK="cl_script_data"][ ONDBLCLICK="dc_script_data"][
ONHELP="hlp_script_data"][ ONKEYDOWN="kd_script_data"][
ONKEYPRESS="kp_script_data"][ ONKEYUP="ku_script_data"][
ONMOUSEDOWN="md_script_data"][
ONMOUSEMOVE="mm_script_data"][
ONMOUSEOUT="mo_script_data"][
ONMOUSEOVER="mov_script_data"][
ONMOUSEUP="mu_script_data"][
ONSELECTSTART="ss_script_data"][ STYLE="name_1: value_1"[;
"name_2: value_2"][...; "name_n: value_n"]][
TITLE="title"][
TYPE="disk"|"square"|"circle"|"1"|"a"|"A"|"i"|"I"][
VALUE="cur_num"]>text[</LI>]
```

## Where

- CLASS specifies a class identification for the list item.
- DIR specifies the direction in which the list-item text is displayed: left-to-right or right-to-left.
- ID provides a unique identifier name for the list item.
- LANG provides the code representing the language used for the list item text.
- **Microsoft** LANGUAGE declares the scripting language of the current script.

- ONCLICK specifies that the referred-to script runs when a user moves the mouse pointer or other pointing device over the list item and clicks the device button.
- ONDBLCLICK specifies that the referred-to script runs when a user moves the mouse pointer or other pointing device over the list item and double-clicks the device button.
- [Microsoft] ONHELP specifies that the referred-to script runs when a user presses the **F1** or **Help** key over the current element.
- ONKEYDOWN specifies that the referred-to script runs when a user presses and holds a key down over the list item.
- ONKEYPRESS specifies that the referred-to script runs when a user presses and releases a key over the list item.
- ONKEYUP specifies that the referred-to script runs when a user releases a key over the list item.
- ONMOUSEDOWN specifies that the referred-to script runs when a user moves the mouse pointer or other pointing device over the list item and presses and holds down the device button.
- ONMOUSEMOVE specifies that the referred-to script runs when a user moves the mouse pointer or other pointing device over the list item.
- ONMOUSEOUT specifies that the referred-to script runs when a user moves the mouse pointer or other pointing device away from the list item.
- ONMOUSEOVER specifies that the referred-to script runs the first time a user moves the mouse pointer or other pointing device over the list item.
- ONMOUSEUP specifies that the referred-to script runs when a user moves the mouse pointer or other pointing device over the list item and releases a pressed-down device button.
- [Microsoft] ONSELECTSTART specifies that the referred-to script runs when a user starts selecting an object.
- STYLE sets styles for the list item.

- TITLE provides a title or title information about the list item.
- TYPE sets a number or a bullet format preceding a list item.
- VALUE sets the current number for a list item in an ordered list.
- *text* represents one or more words.

## Notes

This is an HTML 2.0 element, and the TYPE and VALUE attributes are HTML 3.2 features.

A paragraph break automatically occurs at the end of an LI element and its contents.

The Netscape Editor inserts the pound sign (#) and other placeholders in the place of numbers and bullets in ordered and unordered lists, respectively. To see the actual look of a list (that is, to view it as an actual document page), choose the **Open Page** command from the File menu.

Embed the LI element within the DIR, MENU, OL, and UL elements.

## Examples

Example 1 (Figure 4.38)

```
<OL>
<LI>Oranges
<LI>Apples
<LI>Pears
<LI VALUE="6">Peaches
<LI>Plums
<LI>Lemons
<LI TYPE="I">Limes
<LI>Kumquats
</OL>
```

1. Oranges
2. Apples
3. Pears
6. Peaches
7. Plums
8. Lemons
IX. Limes
X. Kumquats

*Figure 4.38 A demonstration of the VALUE and TYPE attributes.*

Example 2 (Figure 4.39)

```
<UL>

<LI>Plums

<LI TYPE="disk">Oranges

<LI TYPE="square">Apples

<LI TYPE="circle">Pears

</UL>
```

- Plums
- Oranges
- Apples
- Pears

*Figure 4.39 Three types of bullets preceding list items.*

See also examples under the entries for the OL and UL elements.

## Related Elements

DIR, MENU, OL, UL

**155**

| LINK | Link |
| --- | --- |

## Purpose

Shows a link from the current HTML document to another, primarily to provide internal documentation.

## Syntax

```
<LINK[ CLASS="class_name"][ DIR="LTR"|"RTL"][ DISABLED][
HREF="link_url"][ ID="id_name"][ LANG="lang_code"][
MEDIA=["screen"][,]["print"][,]["projection"][,]["braille"
][,]["speech"][,]["all"]][ ONCLICK="cl_script_data"][ OND-
BLCLICK="dc_script_data"][ ONKEYDOWN="kd_script_data"][
ONKEYPRESS="kp_script_data"][ ONKEYUP="ku_script_data"][
ONMOUSEDOWN="md_script_data"][
ONMOUSEMOVE="mm_script_data"][
ONMOUSEOUT="mo_script_data"][
ONMOUSEOVER="mov_script_data"][
ONMOUSEUP="mu_script_data"][
REL="Contents"|"Index"|"Glossary"|"Copyright"|"Next"|"Prev
ious"|"Start"|"Help"|"Bookmark"|"Stylesheet"|"Alternate"|"
link_type_1"[ "link_type_2"[..."link_type_n"]]][
REV="Contents"|"Index"|"Glossary"|"Copyright"|"Next"|"Prev
ious"|"Start"|"Help"|"Bookmark"|"Stylesheet"|"Alternate"|"
link_type_3"[ "link_type_4"[..."link_type_m"]]][
STYLE="name_1: value_1"[; "name_2: value_2"][...; "name_n:
value_n"]][
TARGET="window"|"_blank"|"_parent"|"_self"|"_top"][
TITLE="title"][ TYPE="content_type"]>
```

## Where

- CLASS specifies a class identification for the link.
- DIR specifies the direction in which the link text is displayed: left-to-right or right-to-left.
- **Microsoft** DISABLED prevents the link from receiving the focus.

- HREF specifies a URL for a link to another document.
- ID provides a unique identifier name for the link.
- LANG provides the code representing the language used for the link text.
- MEDIA indicates the type of destination.
- ONCLICK specifies that the referred-to script runs when a user moves the mouse pointer or other pointing device over the link and clicks the device button.
- ONDBLCLICK specifies that the referred-to script runs when a user moves the mouse pointer or other pointing device over the link and double-clicks the device button.
- ONKEYDOWN specifies that the referred-to script runs when a user presses and holds a key down over the link.
- ONKEYPRESS specifies that the referred-to script runs when a user presses and releases a key over the link.
- ONKEYUP specifies that the referred-to script runs when a user releases a key over the link.
- ONMOUSEDOWN specifies that the referred-to script runs when a user moves the mouse pointer or other pointing device over the link and presses and holds down the device button.
- ONMOUSEMOVE specifies that the referred-to script runs when a user moves the mouse pointer or other pointing device over the link.
- ONMOUSEOUT specifies that the referred-to script runs when a user moves the mouse pointer or other pointing device away from the link.
- ONMOUSEOVER specifies that the referred-to script runs the first time a user moves the mouse pointer or other pointing device over the link.
- ONMOUSEUP specifies that the referred-to script runs when a user moves the mouse pointer or other pointing device over the link and releases a pressed-down device button.
- REL specifies the link type; that is, the type of relationship of the current link forward to another document.

- REV specifies the link type; that is, the type of relationship of the anchor back to another document.
- STYLE sets styles for the link.
- TARGET loads a linked and named document in a particular window or frame.
- TITLE provides a title or title information about the link.
- TYPE specifies a type name of the link, for information within the current document.

## Notes

This element originated in HTML 2.0.

Use the LINK element within the HEAD of a document.

You can use multiple LINK statements in the HEAD section of an HTML document. For example, businesses can use the LINK element to identify the author, the author's e-mail address, and the documents and types of documents that are linked to the current document.

## Examples

Example 1

```
<LINK REV="main" TITLE="Sandra E. Eddy" HREF="mailto:eddy-grp@sover.net">
```

Example 2

```
<LINK REL="x_doc" TITLE="Companies Starting with X"
HREF="http://www.eddygrp.com/x_cos.htm">
```

| LISTING | Computer Listing |
|---------|------------------|

This element is obsolete; that is, it is no longer part of the HTML standard. Use the PRE element instead.

| MENU | Menu List |
|------|-----------|

## Purpose

Displays a menu list of items.

## Syntax

```
<MENU[ CLASS="class_name"][ COMPACT][ DIR="LTR"|"RTL"][
ID="id_name"][ LANG="lang_code"][
ONCLICK="cl_script_data"][ ONDBLCLICK="dc_script_data"][
ONHELP="hlp_script_data"][ ONKEYDOWN="kd_script_data"][
ONKEYPRESS="kp_script_data"][ ONKEYUP="ku_script_data"][
ONMOUSEDOWN="md_script_data"][
ONMOUSEMOVE="mm_script_data"][
ONMOUSEOUT="mo_script_data"][
ONMOUSEOVER="mov_script_data"][
ONMOUSEUP="mu_script_data"][
ONSELECTSTART="ss_script_data"][ STYLE="name_1: value_1"[;
"name_2: value_2"][...; "name_n: value_n"]][
TITLE="title"]>menu-list</MENU>
```

## Where

- CLASS specifies a class identification for the menu list.
- COMPACT indicates that a browser might decrease the size of the space between a number or bullet and the list item.
- DIR specifies the direction in which the menu list text is displayed: left-to-right or right-to-left.
- ID provides a unique identifier name for the menu list.
- LANG provides the code representing the language used for the menu list text.
- ONCLICK specifies that the referred-to script runs when a user moves the mouse pointer or other pointing device over the menu list and clicks the device button.
- ONDBLCLICK specifies that the referred-to script runs when a user moves the mouse pointer or other

pointing device over the menu list and double-clicks the device button.

-  ONHELP specifies that the referred-to script runs when a user presses the **F1** or **Help** key over the current element.

- ONKEYDOWN specifies that the referred-to script runs when a user presses and holds a key down over the menu list.

- ONKEYPRESS specifies that the referred-to script runs when a user presses and releases a key over the menu list.

- ONKEYUP specifies that the referred-to script runs when a user releases a key over the menu list.

- ONMOUSEDOWN specifies that the referred-to script runs when a user moves the mouse pointer or other pointing device over the menu list and presses and holds down the device button.

- ONMOUSEMOVE specifies that the referred-to script runs when a user moves the mouse pointer or other pointing device over the menu list.

- ONMOUSEOUT specifies that the referred-to script runs when a user moves the mouse pointer or other pointing device away from the menu list.

- ONMOUSEOVER specifies that the referred-to script runs the first time a user moves the mouse pointer or other pointing device over the menu list.

- ONMOUSEUP specifies that the referred-to script runs when a user moves the mouse pointer or other pointing device over the menu list and releases a pressed-down device button.

- ONSELECTSTART specifies that the referred-to script runs when a user starts selecting an object.

- STYLE sets styles for the menu list.

- TITLE provides a title or title information about the menu list.

- *text* represents one or more words following the LI (list item) element.

## Notes

This element originated in HTML 2.0.

The HTML 4.0 DTD categorizes this as a block-level element.

Although MENU is supported by HTML 4.0, it has been deprecated (that is, it will eventually be obsolete). Use other list elements (OL and UL) instead.

Items on a menu list may or may not be preceded with bullets, depending on the browser.

The MENU element is meant to list items in a single column.

## Example

```
<MENU>
<LI>Oranges
<LI>Apples
<LI>Pears
<LI>Peaches
</MENU>
```

- Oranges
- Apples
- Pears
- Peaches

*Figure 4.40 A MENU list, which looks like an unordered (UL) list.*

## Related Elements

```
DIR, OL, UL
```

| META | Meta |
|------|------|

## Purpose

Provides a description of the properties of the current document, including the author, an expiration date, and keywords, so that search engines can correctly identify it.

## Syntax

```
<META CONTENT="content-text"[ CHARSET=][ DIR="LTR"|"RTL"][
HTTP-EQUIV="HTTP-header-field-name"][ LANG="lang_code"][
NAME="name-text"][ SCHEME="format_id"]>
```

## Where

- CONTENT provides text or character information.
- DIR specifies the direction in which the meta text is displayed: left-to-right or right-to-left.
- HTTP-EQUIV indicates that the META information will be bound to an HTTP response header.
- LANG provides the code representing the language used for the meta text.
- NAME is the name, description, or identification of the contents of the current document.
- SCHEME identifies a particular format for the CONTENT attribute.
- *text* represents one or more words.

## Notes

This element originated in HTML 2.0.

The META element belongs in the HEAD section.

You can consider the data associated with a META element as an index to contents of the document. Search indexes use the META attributes and keywords, along with the document title (the TITLE element) and the first 250 or so words in the body of an HTML document to identify and rank documents that match search keywords.

The META element can also provide information about document creation and modification information. For example, you can include the following information within a document's META element: the author, the individual who maintains the document, the date the document was created, the last date the document was edited, and the document's expiration date.

You can use multiple META elements in an HTML document.

When using keywords within a META statement, check spelling to ensure that search engines will use all your keywords properly.

If you do not use the NAME attribute, a server uses the HTTP-EQUIV attributes as the name.

HTTP servers use the META information in various ways; there is no standard.

## Examples

Example 1

This example shows how you can use two META elements to describe a document and to define keywords.

```
<HEAD>

<TITLE>A Periodic Table of the Elements at Los Alamos
National Laboratory</TITLE>

<META name="description" content="The Chemical Science and
Technology division's Periodic Table describes the histo-
ry, properties, resources, uses, isotopes, forms, costs,
and other information for each element."

<META name="keywords" content="periodic table, elements,
chemistry, Los Alamos National Laboratory, Chemical
Science and Technology Division, chemicals, isotopes, ele-
ment history, CST, science, properties, forms, uses, mole-
cules, compounds, atoms, neutrons, electrons, protons,
discover, hydrogen, helium, carbon, organic, oxygen, sodi-
um, magnesium, aluminum, phosphorus, chlorine, potassium,
iron, nickel, copper, iodine, plutonium, uranium, hafnium,
silicon, argon, enamium, lithium, beryllium, boron, nitro-
gen, calcium, scandium, sulfur, krypton, gold, silver,
francium, californium, nuclear, H, HE, Li, Be, Mg, B, C,
N, O, noble gases, metalloids, metals, U, Ag, S, Cl, Ni,
```

```
K, Cf"
```

Example 2

This example uses the META element to display a new page after six seconds. This is an excellent way to automatically move from an introductory page to a site index or opening page of a document. Not all browsers support "refresh".

```
<META NAME="refresh"
content="6,http://www.eddygrp.com/intro.html">
```

| OL | Ordered List |
| --- | --- |

## Purpose

Starts an ordered (numbered) list.

## Syntax

```
<OL[ CLASS="class_name"][ COMPACT][ DIR="LTR"|"RTL"][
ID="id_name"][ LANG="lang_code"][
LANGUAGE="JAVASCRIPT"|"JSCRIPT"|"VBS[CRIPT]"][
ONCLICK="cl_script_data"][ ONDBLCLICK="dc_script_data"][
ONHELP="hlp_script_data"][ ONKEYDOWN="kd_script_data"][
ONKEYPRESS="kp_script_data"][ ONKEYUP="ku_script_data"][
ONMOUSEDOWN="md_script_data"][
ONMOUSEMOVE="mm_script_data"][
ONMOUSEOUT="mo_script_data"][
ONMOUSEOVER="mov_script_data"][
ONMOUSEUP="mu_script_data"][
ONSELECTSTART="ss_script_data"][ START="1"|"start_num"][
STYLE="name_1: value_1"[; "name_2: value_2"][...; "name_n:
value_n"]][ TITLE="title"][
TYPE="1"|"a"|"A"|"i"|"I"]>ordered-list-items</OL>
```

## Where

- CLASS specifies a class identification for the ordered list.
- COMPACT indicates that a browser might decrease the size of the space between the number and the list item.
- DIR specifies the direction in which the ordered list text is displayed: left-to-right or right-to-left.
- ID provides a unique identifier name for the ordered list.
- LANG provides the code representing the language used for the ordered list text.
- **Microsoft** LANGUAGE declares the scripting language of the current script.

- ONCLICK specifies that the referred-to script runs when a user moves the mouse pointer or other pointing device over the ordered list and clicks the device button.

- ONDBLCLICK specifies that the referred-to script runs when a user moves the mouse pointer or other pointing device over the ordered list and double-clicks the device button.

- **Microsoft** ONHELP specifies that the referred-to script runs when a user presses the **F1** or **Help** key over the current element.

- ONKEYDOWN specifies that the referred-to script runs when a user presses and holds a key down over the ordered list.

- ONKEYPRESS specifies that the referred-to script runs when a user presses and releases a key over the ordered list.

- ONKEYUP specifies that the referred-to script runs when a user releases a key over the ordered list.

- ONMOUSEDOWN specifies that the referred-to script runs when a user moves the mouse pointer or other pointing device over the ordered list and presses and holds down the device button.

- ONMOUSEMOVE specifies that the referred-to script runs when a user moves the mouse pointer or other pointing device over the ordered list.

- ONMOUSEOUT specifies that the referred-to script runs when a user moves the mouse pointer or other pointing device away from the ordered list.

- ONMOUSEOVER specifies that the referred-to script runs the first time a user moves the mouse pointer or other pointing device over the ordered list.

- ONMOUSEUP specifies that the referred-to script runs when a user moves the mouse pointer or other pointing device over the ordered list and releases a pressed-down device button.

- **Microsoft** ONSELECTSTART specifies that the referred-to script runs when a user starts selecting an object.

- START sets a numeric starting value for the current ordered list.
- STYLE sets styles for the ordered list.
- TITLE provides a title or title information about the ordered list.
- TYPE sets a number format for an ordered list.
- *ordered-list-items* represents one or more LI items.

## Notes

This element originated in HTML 2.0.

The HTML 4.0 DTD categorizes this as a block-level element.

Some browsers do not recognize the COMPACT attribute.

If you nest ordered lists, it's a good idea to indent each level of lists in the HTML document to make it easier for you to ensure that each of the start and end elements are on the same level. However, you are not required to indent elements for various list levels.

If you nest ordered lists, number types do not change automatically. To do so, use the TYPE attribute (see the third example).

To continue numbering from a previous list, set the VALUE attribute for the current list.

LI elements are embedded within OL elements.

## Examples

Example 1 (Figure 4.41)

```
<OL>
<LI>World Wide Web
<LI>Gopher
<LI>FTP
<LI>Telnet
</OL>
```

1. World Wide Web
2. Gopher
3. FTP
4. Telnet

*Figure 4.41 A default ordered list.*

## Example 2 (Figure 4.42)

```
<OL TYPE="A" START="3">
<LI>World Wide Web
<LI>Gopher
<LI>FTP
<LI>Telnet
</OL>
```

C. World Wide Web
D. Gopher
E. FTP
F. Telnet

*Figure 4.42 An ordered list with an A type and the starting number C.*

## Example 3 (Figure 4.43)

```
<OL TYPE="I">
    <LI>Computers
        <OL TYPE="A">
            <LI>Desktop
            <LI>Notebooks
        </OL>
    <LI>Printers
        <OL TYPE="A">
            <LI>Laser
                <OL TYPE="i">
                    <LI>Color
                    <LI>Black & White
```

```
        </OL>

    <LI>Inkjet

        <OL TYPE="i">

            <LI>Color

            <LI>Black & White

        </OL>

    </OL>

  <LI>Modems

</OL>
```

```
I. Computers
    A. Desktop
    B. Notebooks
II. Printers
    A. Laser
            i. Color
           ii. Black & White
    B. Inkjet
            i. Color
           ii. Black & White
III. Modems
```

*Figure 4.43 An example of a nested ordered list.*

## Related Elements

DIR, MENU, UL

| P | Paragraph |
|---|-----------|

## Purpose

Indicates the start of a new paragraph.

## Syntax

```
<P[ ALIGN="left"|"center"|"right"|"justify"][
CLASS="class_name"][ DIR="LTR"|"RTL"][ ID="id_name"][
LANG="lang_code"][
LANGUAGE="JAVASCRIPT"|"JSCRIPT"|"VBS[CRIPT]"][
ONCLICK="cl_script_data"][ ONDBLCLICK="dc_script_data"][
ONHELP="hlp_script_data"][ ONKEYDOWN="kd_script_data"][
ONKEYPRESS="kp_script_data"][ ONKEYUP="ku_script_data"][
ONMOUSEDOWN="md_script_data"][
ONMOUSEMOVE="mm_script_data"][
ONMOUSEOUT="mo_script_data"][
ONMOUSEOVER="mov_script_data"][
ONMOUSEUP="mu_script_data"][
ONSELECTSTART="ss_script_data"][ STYLE="name_1: value_1"[;
"name_2: value_2"][...; "name_n: value_n"]][
TITLE="title"]>text[</P>]
```

## Where

- ALIGN horizontally aligns the contents of a section of text.
- CLASS specifies a class identification for the paragraph break.
- DIR specifies the direction in which the paragraph text is displayed: left-to-right or right-to-left.
- ID provides a unique identifier name for the paragraph break.
- LANG provides the code representing the language used for the text in the paragraph after the break.
- Microsoft LANGUAGE declares the scripting language of the current script.

171

- ONCLICK specifies that the referred-to script runs when a user moves the mouse pointer or other pointing device over the paragraph break and clicks the device button.

- ONDBLCLICK specifies that the referred-to script runs when a user moves the mouse pointer or other pointing device over the paragraph break and double-clicks the device button.

- **Microsoft** ONHELP specifies that the referred-to script runs when a user presses the **F1** or **Help** key over the current element.

- ONKEYDOWN specifies that the referred-to script runs when a user presses and holds a key down over the paragraph break.

- ONKEYPRESS specifies that the referred-to script runs when a user presses and releases a key over the paragraph break.

- ONKEYUP specifies that the referred-to script runs when a user releases a key over the paragraph break.

- ONMOUSEDOWN specifies that the referred-to script runs when a user moves the mouse pointer or other pointing device over the paragraph break and presses and holds down the device button.

- ONMOUSEMOVE specifies that the referred-to script runs when a user moves the mouse pointer or other pointing device over the paragraph break.

- ONMOUSEOUT specifies that the referred-to script runs when a user moves the mouse pointer or other pointing device away from the paragraph break.

- ONMOUSEOVER specifies that the referred-to script runs the first time a user moves the mouse pointer or other pointing device over the paragraph break.

- ONMOUSEUP specifies that the referred-to script runs when a user moves the mouse pointer or other pointing device over the paragraph break and releases a pressed-down device button.

- **Microsoft** ONSELECTSTART specifies that the referred-to script runs when a user starts selecting an object.

- STYLE sets styles for the paragraph after the break.
- TITLE provides a title or title information about the paragraph break.
- *text* represents one or more characters, words, and/or sentences to be separated from the preceding paragraph.

## Notes

This is an HTML 2.0 element; the ALIGN attribute is an HTML 3.2 feature.

The P element is equivalent to two BR elements.

The HTML 4.0 DTD categorizes this as a block-level element.

The next block element that follows the paragraph acts as the P end tag if you have not inserted one.

If you have changed the alignment of the current paragraph, the end P element will turn off the alignment and return to an alignment of left (the default).

## Example

```
<P>The P element inserts<P>two line breaks.
```

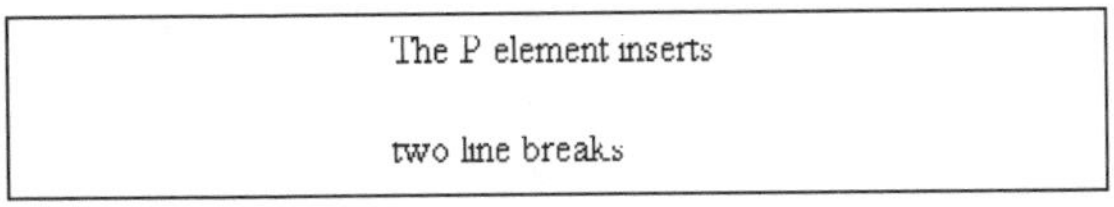

The P element inserts

two line breaks

*Figure 4.44 An example of two P elements.*

## Related Element

BR

## PLAINTEXT | Plain Text

This element is obsolete; that is, it is no longer part of the HTML standard. Use the PRE element instead.

| PRE | Preformatted Text |
|-----|-------------------|

## Purpose

Applies a monospace font to, and maintains the character-and-space formatting of, one or more lines of preformatted text.

## Syntax

```
<PRE[ CLASS="class_name"][ DIR="LTR"|"RTL"][
ID="id_name"][ LANG="lang_code"][
LANGUAGE="JAVASCRIPT"|"JSCRIPT"|"VBS[CRIPT]"][
ONCLICK="cl_script_data"][ ONDBLCLICK="dc_script_data"][
ONHELP="hlp_script_data"][ ONKEYDOWN="kd_script_data"][
ONKEYPRESS="kp_script_data"][ ONKEYUP="ku_script_data"][
ONMOUSEDOWN="md_script_data"][
ONMOUSEMOVE="mm_script_data"][
ONMOUSEOUT="mo_script_data"][
ONMOUSEOVER="mov_script_data"][
ONMOUSEUP="mu_script_data"][
ONSELECTSTART="ss_script_data"][ STYLE="name_1: value_1"[;
"name_2: value_2"][...; "name_n: value_n"]][
TITLE="title"][ WIDTH="text_block_width"]>text</PRE>
```

## Where

- CLASS specifies a class identification for the preformatted text.
- DIR specifies the direction in which the current text is displayed: left-to-right or right-to-left.
- ID provides a unique identifier name for the preformatted text.
- LANG provides the code representing the language used for the preformatted text.
- **Microsoft** LANGUAGE declares the scripting language of the current script.
- ONCLICK specifies that the referred-to script runs when a user moves the mouse pointer or other pointing

**175**

device over the preformatted text and clicks the device button.

- ONDBLCLICK specifies that the referred-to script runs when a user moves the mouse pointer or other pointing device over the preformatted text and double-clicks the device button.

- [Microsoft] ONHELP specifies that the referred-to script runs when a user presses the **F1** or **Help** key over the current element.

- ONKEYDOWN specifies that the referred-to script runs when a user presses and holds a key down over the preformatted text.

- ONKEYPRESS specifies that the referred-to script runs when a user presses and releases a key over the preformatted text.

- ONKEYUP specifies that the referred-to script runs when a user releases a key over the preformatted text.

- ONMOUSEDOWN specifies that the referred-to script runs when a user moves the mouse pointer or other pointing device over the preformatted text and presses and holds down the device button.

- ONMOUSEMOVE specifies that the referred-to script runs when a user moves the mouse pointer or other pointing device over the preformatted text.

- ONMOUSEOUT specifies that the referred-to script runs when a user moves the mouse pointer or other pointing device away from the preformatted text.

- ONMOUSEOVER specifies that the referred-to script runs the first time a user moves the mouse pointer or other pointing device over the preformatted text.

- ONMOUSEUP specifies that the referred-to script runs when a user moves the mouse pointer or other pointing device over the preformatted text and releases a pressed-down device button.

- [Microsoft] ONSELECTSTART specifies that the referred-to script runs when a user starts selecting an object.

- STYLE sets styles for the preformatted text.

- TITLE provides a title or title information about the preformatted text.
- WIDTH sets a maximum line width for the preformatted text.
- *text* represents one or more characters.

## Notes

This element originated in HTML 2.0.

The PRE element shows preformatted characters and spaces as typed.

The HTML 4.0 DTD categorizes this as a block-level element.

Each instance of <PRE> and </PRE> causes a new paragraph.

The WIDTH attribute is not accepted by all browsers.

The LISTING, PLAINTEXT, and XMP elements are all obsolete; use the PRE element instead.

PRE does not override text direction (the DIR attribute).

Do not use tabs within preformatted text—especially if you plan to use tabs in other parts of the document. The unwanted result may be clashing tab positions.

## Example

```
<PRE>
          W E L C O M E

          M E M B E R S

          W E L C O M E</PRE>
```

```
          W E L C O M E
          M E M B E R S
          W E L C O M E
```

*Figure 4.45 An example of preformatted text.*

## Related Elements

```
ACRONYM, B, CITE, CODE, DFN, EM, I, KBD, S, SAMP, STRIKE,
STRONG, TT, U, VAR
```

| Q | Short Quote |
|---|---|

## Purpose

Formats a short quotation.

## Syntax

```
<Q[ CITE="url"][ CLASS="class_name"][ DIR="LTR"|"RTL"][
ID="id_name"][ LANG="lang_code"][
ONCLICK="cl_script_data"][ ONDBLCLICK="dc_script_data"][
ONKEYDOWN="kd_script_data"][ ONKEYPRESS="kp_script_data"][
ONKEYUP="ku_script_data"][ ONMOUSEDOWN="md_script_data"][
ONMOUSEMOVE="mm_script_data"][
ONMOUSEOUT="mo_script_data"][
ONMOUSEOVER="mov_script_data"][
ONMOUSEUP="mu_script_data"][ STYLE="name_1: value_1"[;
"name_2: value_2"][...; "name_n: value_n"]][
TITLE="title"]>text</Q>
```

## Where

- CITE provides a URL for a document or message that contains information about a quote.
- CLASS specifies a class identification for the quote.
- DIR specifies the direction in which the quote is displayed: left-to-right or right-to-left.
- ID provides a unique identifier name for the quote.
- LANG provides the code representing the language used for the quote.
- ONCLICK specifies that the referred-to script runs when a user moves the mouse pointer or other pointing device over the quote and clicks the device button.
- ONDBLCLICK specifies that the referred-to script runs when a user moves the mouse pointer or other pointing device over the quote and double-clicks the device button.

- ONKEYDOWN specifies that the referred-to script runs when a user presses and holds a key down over the quote.
- ONKEYPRESS specifies that the referred-to script runs when a user presses and releases a key over the quote.
- ONKEYUP specifies that the referred-to script runs when a user releases a key over the quote.
- ONMOUSEDOWN specifies that the referred-to script runs when a user moves the mouse pointer or other pointing device over the quote and presses and holds down the device button.
- ONMOUSEMOVE specifies that the referred-to script runs when a user moves the mouse pointer or other pointing device over the quote.
- ONMOUSEOUT specifies that the referred-to script runs when a user moves the mouse pointer or other pointing device away from the quote.
- ONMOUSEOVER specifies that the referred-to script runs the first time a user moves the mouse pointer or other pointing device over the quote.
- ONMOUSEUP specifies that the referred-to script runs when a user moves the mouse pointer or other pointing device over the quote and releases a pressed-down device button.
- STYLE sets styles for the quote.
- TITLE provides a title or title information about the quote.
- *text* represents one or more characters.

## Notes

This is an HTML 4.0 element.

The HTML 4.0 DTD categorizes this as an inline element.

## Example

```
<Q>I love a dog. He does nothing for political
reasons.</Q>
```

> I love a dog. He does nothing for political reasons.

*Figure 4.46 A short quote from Will Rogers.*

## Related Elements

CODE, KBD, PRE, Q, SAMP, TT

| S|STRIKE | Strikethrough |
|---|---|

## Purpose

Strikes through selected text.

## Syntax

```
<S|STRIKE[ CLASS="class_name"][ DIR="LTR"|"RTL"][
ID="id_name"][ LANG="lang_code"][
LANGUAGE="JAVASCRIPT"|"JSCRIPT"|"VBS[CRIPT]"][
ONCLICK="cl_script_data"][ ONDBLCLICK="dc_script_data"][
ONHELP="hlp_script_data"][ ONKEYDOWN="kd_script_data"][
ONKEYPRESS="kp_script_data"][ ONKEYUP="ku_script_data"][
ONMOUSEDOWN="md_script_data"][
ONMOUSEMOVE="mm_script_data"][
ONMOUSEOUT="mo_script_data"][
ONMOUSEOVER="mov_script_data"][
ONMOUSEUP="mu_script_data"][
ONSELECTSTART="ss_script_data"][ STYLE="name_1: value_1"[;
"name_2: value_2"][...; "name_n: value_n"]][
TITLE="title"]>text</S|STRIKE>
```

## Where

- CLASS specifies a class identification for the strikethrough text.
- DIR specifies the direction in which the strikethrough text is displayed: left-to-right or right-to-left.
- ID provides a unique identifier name for the strikethrough text.
- LANG provides the code representing the language used for the strikethrough text.
- **Microsoft** LANGUAGE declares the scripting language of the current script.
- ONCLICK specifies that the referred-to script runs when a user moves the mouse pointer or other pointing

**181**

device over the strikethrough text and clicks the device button.

- ONDBLCLICK specifies that the referred-to script runs when a user moves the mouse pointer or other pointing device over the strikethrough text and double-clicks the device button.

-  ONHELP specifies that the referred-to script runs when a user presses the **F1** or **Help** key over the current element.

- ONKEYDOWN specifies that the referred-to script runs when a user presses and holds a key down over the strikethrough text.

- ONKEYPRESS specifies that the referred-to script runs when a user presses and releases a key over the strikethrough text.

- ONKEYUP specifies that the referred-to script runs when a user releases a key over the strikethrough text.

- ONMOUSEDOWN specifies that the referred-to script runs when a user moves the mouse pointer or other pointing device over the strikethrough text and presses and holds down the device button.

- ONMOUSEMOVE specifies that the referred-to script runs when a user moves the mouse pointer or other pointing device over the strikethrough text.

- ONMOUSEOUT specifies that the referred-to script runs when a user moves the mouse pointer or other pointing device away from the strikethrough text.

- ONMOUSEOVER specifies that the referred-to script runs the first time a user moves the mouse pointer or other pointing device over the strikethrough text.

- ONMOUSEUP specifies that the referred-to script runs when a user moves the mouse pointer or other pointing device over the strikethrough text and releases a pressed-down device button.

-  ONSELECTSTART specifies that the referred-to script runs when a user starts selecting an object.

- STYLE sets styles for the strikethrough text.

- TITLE provides a title or title information about the strikethrough text.
- *text* represents one or more characters.

## Notes

This element originated in HTML 2.0.

S and STRIKE are identical elements.

The HTML 4.0 DTD categorizes this as an inline element.

Although S and STRIKE are supported by HTML 4.0, they have been deprecated (that is, they will eventually be obsolete).

## Example

```
This is <STRIKE>strikeout</STRIKE> text.
```

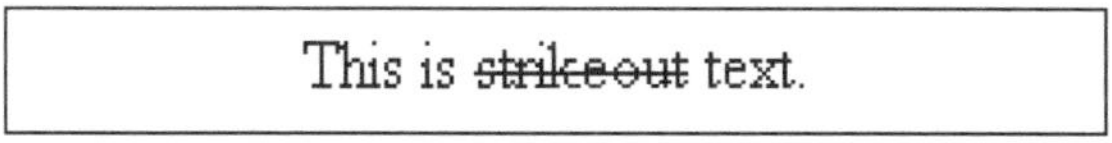

This is ~~strikeout~~ text.

*Figure 4.47 Text enhanced with a strikethrough.*

## Related Elements

B, BIG, EM, FONT, I, SMALL, STRONG, SUB, SUP, U

| SAMP | Sample Output |

## Purpose

Applies a sample program output (monospace) font to selected text.

## Syntax

```
<SAMP[ CLASS="class_name"][ DIR="LTR"|"RTL"][
ID="id_name"][ LANG="lang_code"][
LANGUAGE="JAVASCRIPT"|"JSCRIPT"|"VBS[CRIPT]"][
ONCLICK="cl_script_data"][ ONDBLCLICK="dc_script_data"][
ONHELP="hlp_script_data"][ ONKEYDOWN="kd_script_data"][
ONKEYPRESS="kp_script_data"][ ONKEYUP="ku_script_data"][
ONMOUSEDOWN="md_script_data"][
ONMOUSEMOVE="mm_script_data"][
ONMOUSEOUT="mo_script_data"][
ONMOUSEOVER="mov_script_data"][
ONMOUSEUP="mu_script_data"][
ONSELECTSTART="ss_script_data"][ STYLE="name_1: value_1"[;
"name_2: value_2"][...; "name_n: value_n"]][
TITLE="title"]>text</SAMP>
```

## Where

- CLASS specifies a class identification for the sample output.
- DIR specifies the direction in which the sample output text is displayed: left-to-right or right-to-left.
- ID provides a unique identifier name for the sample output.
- LANG provides the code representing the language used for the sample output text.
- **Microsoft** LANGUAGE declares the scripting language of the current script.
- ONCLICK specifies that the referred-to script runs when a user moves the mouse pointer or other pointing

device over the sample output and clicks the device button.

- ONDBLCLICK specifies that the referred-to script runs when a user moves the mouse pointer or other pointing device over the sample output and double-clicks the device button.

- Microsoft ONHELP specifies that the referred-to script runs when a user presses the **F1** or **Help** key over the current element.

- ONKEYDOWN specifies that the referred-to script runs when a user presses and holds a key down over the sample output.

- ONKEYPRESS specifies that the referred-to script runs when a user presses and releases a key over the sample output.

- ONKEYUP specifies that the referred-to script runs when a user releases a key over the sample output.

- ONMOUSEDOWN specifies that the referred-to script runs when a user moves the mouse pointer or other pointing device over the sample output and presses and holds down the device button.

- ONMOUSEMOVE specifies that the referred-to script runs when a user moves the mouse pointer or other pointing device over the sample output.

- ONMOUSEOUT specifies that the referred-to script runs when a user moves the mouse pointer or other pointing device away from the sample output.

- ONMOUSEOVER specifies that the referred-to script runs the first time a user moves the mouse pointer or other pointing device over the sample output.

- ONMOUSEUP specifies that the referred-to script runs when a user moves the mouse pointer or other pointing device over the sample output and releases a pressed-down device button.

- Microsoft ONSELECTSTART specifies that the referred-to script runs when a user starts selecting an object.

- STYLE sets styles for the sample output.

- TITLE provides a title or title information about the sample output.
- *text* represents one or more characters.

## Notes

This element originated in HTML 2.0.

SAMP is a logical element, in which particular browsers are programmed to apply a certain style to the selected text. This is in contrast to a physical element in which you "code" the styles yourself.

The HTML 4.0 DTD categorizes this as an inline element.

Many browsers use the same font for the CODE, KBD, PRE, SAMP, and TT elements.

To display two or more lines of preformatted text, use the PRE element.

## Example

```
This is <SAMP>sample output</SAMP> text.
```

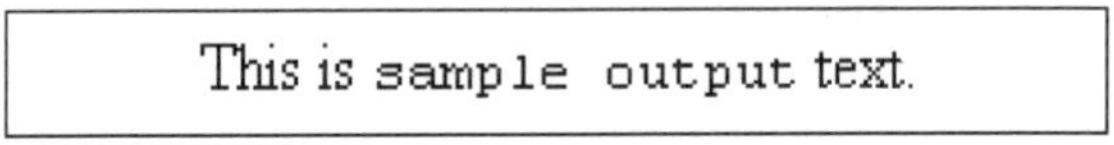

This is sample output text.

*Figure 4.48 The SAMP element in use.*

## Related Elements

ACRONYM, B, EM, CITE, CODE, DFN, I, KBD, PRE, STRONG, TT, VAR

| SMALL | Small Text |
|-------|-----------|

## Purpose

Displays text in a smaller font than the default starting font.

## Syntax

```
<SMALL[ CLASS="class_name"][ DIR="LTR"|"RTL"][
ID="id_name"][ LANG="lang_code"][
LANGUAGE="JAVASCRIPT"|"JSCRIPT"|"VBS[CRIPT]"][
ONCLICK="cl_script_data"][ ONDBLCLICK="dc_script_data"][
ONHELP="hlp_script_data"][ ONKEYDOWN="kd_script_data"][
ONKEYPRESS="kp_script_data"][ ONKEYUP="ku_script_data"][
ONMOUSEDOWN="md_script_data"][
ONMOUSEMOVE="mm_script_data"][
ONMOUSEOUT="mo_script_data"][
ONMOUSEOVER="mov_script_data"][
ONMOUSEUP="mu_script_data"][
ONSELECTSTART="ss_script_data"][ STYLE="name_1: value_1"[;
"name_2: value_2"][...; "name_n: value_n"]][
TITLE="title"]>text</SMALL>
```

## Where

- CLASS specifies a class identification for the small text.
- DIR specifies the direction in which the small text is displayed: left-to-right or right-to-left.
- ID provides a unique identifier name for the small text.
- LANG provides the code representing the language used for the small text.
- ![Microsoft] LANGUAGE declares the scripting language of the current script.
- ONCLICK specifies that the referred-to script runs when a user moves the mouse pointer or other pointing device over the small text and clicks the device button.
- ONDBLCLICK specifies that the referred-to script runs when a user moves the mouse pointer or other

pointing device over the small text and double-clicks the device button.

-  ONHELP specifies that the referred-to script runs when a user presses the **F1** or **Help** key over the current element.

- ONKEYDOWN specifies that the referred-to script runs when a user presses and holds a key down over the small text.

- ONKEYPRESS specifies that the referred-to script runs when a user presses and releases a key over the small text.

- ONKEYUP specifies that the referred-to script runs when a user releases a key over the small text.

- ONMOUSEDOWN specifies that the referred-to script runs when a user moves the mouse pointer or other pointing device over the small text and presses and holds down the device button.

- ONMOUSEMOVE specifies that the referred-to script runs when a user moves the mouse pointer or other pointing device over the small text.

- ONMOUSEOUT specifies that the referred-to script runs when a user moves the mouse pointer or other pointing device away from the small text.

- ONMOUSEOVER specifies that the referred-to script runs the first time a user moves the mouse pointer or other pointing device over the small text.

- ONMOUSEUP specifies that the referred-to script runs when a user moves the mouse pointer or other pointing device over the small text and releases a pressed-down device button.

-  ONSELECTSTART specifies that the referred-to script runs when a user starts selecting an object.

- STYLE sets styles for the small text.

- TITLE provides a title or title information about the small text.

- *text* represents one or more characters.

## Notes

This element originated in HTML 3.2.

The HTML 4.0 DTD categorizes this as an inline element.

Some HTML editors convert the SMALL element to <FONT SIZE=-1>text</FONT>, its equivalent.

## Example

```
This is <SMALL>small</SMALL> text.
```

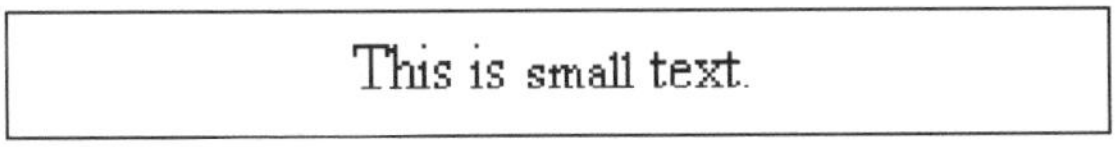

This is small text.

*Figure 4.49 An example of small text.*

## Related Elements

BIG, FONT

| SPAN | Spanned Section |
|------|-----------------|

## Purpose

Marks the beginning of a new section in a document.

## Syntax

```
<SPAN[ CLASS="class_name"][ DATAFLD="ds_col_name"][
DATAFORMATAS="HTML"|"TEXT"][ DATASRC="ds_identifier"][
DIR="LTR"|"RTL"][ ID="id_name"][ LANG="lang_code"][ LAN-
GUAGE="JAVASCRIPT"|"JSCRIPT"|"VBS[CRIPT]"][
ONCLICK="cl_script_data"][ ONDBLCLICK="dc_script_data"][
ONHELP="hlp_script_data"][ ONKEYDOWN="kd_script_data"][
ONKEYPRESS="kp_script_data"][ ONKEYUP="ku_script_data"][
ONMOUSEDOWN="md_script_data"][
ONMOUSEMOVE="mm_script_data"][
ONMOUSEOUT="mo_script_data"][
ONMOUSEOVER="mov_script_data"][
ONMOUSEUP="mu_script_data"][
ONSELECTSTART="ss_script_data"][ STYLE="name_1: value_1"[;
"name_2: value_2"][...; "name_n: value_n"]][
TITLE="title"]>span-text</SPAN>
```

## Where

- CLASS specifies a class identification for the span section of the document.
- **Microsoft** DATAFLD specifies the column name from the file that provides the data source object.
- **Microsoft** DATAFORMATAS indicates whether the data for this element is formatted as *plain text* (that is, unformatted ASCII) or HTML.
- **Microsoft** DATASRC specifies the identifier of the data source object.
- DIR specifies the direction in which the span section text is displayed: left-to-right or right-to-left.

- ID provides a unique identifier name for the span section.
- LANG provides the code representing the language used for the span text.
- [Microsoft] LANGUAGE declares the scripting language of the current script.
- ONCLICK specifies that the referred-to script runs when a user moves the mouse pointer or other pointing device over the span section and clicks the device button.
- ONDBLCLICK specifies that the referred-to script runs when a user moves the mouse pointer or other pointing device over the span section and double-clicks the device button.
- [Microsoft] ONHELP specifies that the referred-to script runs when a user presses the **F1** or **Help** key over the current element.
- ONKEYDOWN specifies that the referred-to script runs when a user presses and holds a key down over the span section.
- ONKEYPRESS specifies that the referred-to script runs when a user presses and releases a key over the span section.
- ONKEYUP specifies that the referred-to script runs when a user releases a key over the span section.
- ONMOUSEDOWN specifies that the referred-to script runs when a user moves the mouse pointer or other pointing device over the span section and presses and holds down the device button.
- ONMOUSEMOVE specifies that the referred-to script runs when a user moves the mouse pointer or other pointing device over the span section.
- ONMOUSEOUT specifies that the referred-to script runs when a user moves the mouse pointer or other pointing device away from the span section.
- ONMOUSEOVER specifies that the referred-to script runs the first time a user moves the mouse pointer or other pointing device over the span section.

- ONMOUSEUP specifies that the referred-to script runs when a user moves the mouse pointer or other pointing device over the span section and releases a pressed-down device button.

- **Microsoft** ONSELECTSTART specifies that the referred-to script runs when a user starts selecting an object.

- STYLE sets styles for the span section.

- TITLE provides a title or title information about the span section.

- *span-text* represents the contents of the span section.

## Notes

This is an HTML 4.0 element.

The HTML 4.0 DTD categorizes this as an inline element.

You can use the SPAN element within other elements, such as paragraphs and list items.

You can use the SPAN element to apply styles to a particular section—even a single character or word—in a document. SPAN is particularly useful with style sheets and dynamic HTML.

## Example

```
<DIV ID="emp-bro070875">
<SPAN CLASS="last_name"><B>Last Name</B></SPAN> Bronk
<SPAN CLASS="first_name"><B>First Name</B></SPAN> Brad
<SPAN CLASS="hire_date"><B>Hire Date</B></SPAN>07-08-75
<SPAN CLASS="department"><B>Dept</B></SPAN> Purchasing
<SPAN CLASS="title"><B>Title</B></SPAN> Agent
<SPAN CLASS="extension"><B>Ext</B></SPAN> 3456
<SPAN CLASS="email"><B>Email</B></SPAN> bronk@xyzyx.com
```

## Related Element

DIV

## STRIKE      Strikethrough

See S|STRIKE.

| STRONG | Strong Emphasis |

## Purpose

Applies strong emphasis, usually boldface, to selected text.

## Syntax

```
<STRONG[ CLASS="class_name"][ DIR="LTR"|"RTL"][
ID="id_name"][ LANG="lang_code"][
LANGUAGE="JAVASCRIPT"|"JSCRIPT"|"VBS[CRIPT]"][
ONCLICK="cl_script_data"][ ONDBLCLICK="dc_script_data"][
ONHELP="hlp_script_data"][ ONKEYDOWN="kd_script_data"][
ONKEYPRESS="kp_script_data"][ ONKEYUP="ku_script_data"][
ONMOUSEDOWN="md_script_data"][
ONMOUSEMOVE="mm_script_data"][
ONMOUSEOUT="mo_script_data"][
ONMOUSEOVER="mov_script_data"][
ONMOUSEUP="mu_script_data"][
ONSELECTSTART="ss_script_data"][ STYLE="name_1: value_1"[;
"name_2: value_2"][...; "name_n: value_n"]][
TITLE="title"]>text</STRONG>
```

## Where

- CLASS specifies a class identification for the strongly emphasized text.
- DIR specifies the direction in which the strongly emphasized text is displayed: left-to-right or right-to-left.
- ID provides a unique identifier name for the strongly emphasized text.
- LANG provides the code representing the language used for the strongly emphasized text.
- [Microsoft] LANGUAGE declares the scripting language of the current script.
- ONCLICK specifies that the referred-to script runs when a user moves the mouse pointer or other pointing

device over the strongly emphasized text and clicks the device button.

- ONDBLCLICK specifies that the referred-to script runs when a user moves the mouse pointer or other pointing device over the strongly emphasized text and double-clicks the device button.

-  ONHELP specifies that the referred-to script runs when a user presses the **F1** or **Help** key over the current element.

- ONKEYDOWN specifies that the referred-to script runs when a user presses and holds a key down over the strongly emphasized text.

- ONKEYPRESS specifies that the referred-to script runs when a user presses and releases a key over the strongly emphasized text.

- ONKEYUP specifies that the referred-to script runs when a user releases a key over the strongly emphasized text.

- ONMOUSEDOWN specifies that the referred-to script runs when a user moves the mouse pointer or other pointing device over the strongly emphasized text and presses and holds down the device button.

- ONMOUSEMOVE specifies that the referred-to script runs when a user moves the mouse pointer or other pointing device over the strongly emphasized text.

- ONMOUSEOUT specifies that the referred-to script runs when a user moves the mouse pointer or other pointing device away from the strongly emphasized text.

- ONMOUSEOVER specifies that the referred-to script runs the first time a user moves the mouse pointer or other pointing device over the strongly emphasized text.

- ONMOUSEUP specifies that the referred-to script runs when a user moves the mouse pointer or other pointing device over the strongly emphasized text and releases a pressed-down device button.

195

-  ONSELECTSTART specifies that the referred-to script runs when a user starts selecting an object.
- STYLE sets styles for the strongly emphasized text.
- TITLE provides a title or title information about the strongly emphasized text.
- *text* represents one or more characters.

## Notes

This element originated in HTML 2.0.

STRONG is a logical element, in which particular browsers are programmed to apply a certain style to the selected text. This is in contrast to a physical element (such as B) in which you "code" the styles yourself.

The HTML 4.0 DTD categorizes this as an inline element.

## Example

```
This is <STRONG>strong</STRONG> text.
```

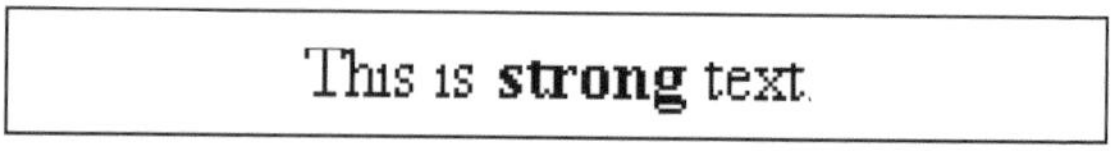

This is **strong** text.

*Figure 4.50 A sample of strongly emphasized text.*

## Related Elements

B, BIG, EM, FONT, I, S, SMALL, STRIKE, SUB, SUP, U

| STYLE | Style |
|-------|-------|

## Purpose

Encloses style information and overrides a linked cascading style sheet.

## Syntax

```
<STYLE TYPE="style_sheet_language"[ DIR="LTR"|"RTL"][ DIS-
ABLED][ LANG="lang_code"][
MEDIA=["screen"][,]["print"][,]["projection"][,]["braille"
][,]["speech"][,]["all"]][ TITLE="title"]>text</STYLE>
```

## Where

- TYPE specifies a language (that is, the Internet Media Type) for the current style.
- DIR specifies the direction in which the current text is displayed: left-to-right or right-to-left.
- **Microsoft** DISABLED prevents the element from receiving the focus.
- LANG provides the code representing the language used for the style.
- MEDIA indicates the type of destination for the document.
- TITLE provides a title or title information about the style.
- *text* represents one or more words or lines of text.

## Notes

This element originated in HTML 3.2.

Embed the STYLE element within the HEAD elements.

For detailed information about *properties* (that is, styles) and style sheets, see Part 5: Cascading Style Sheets.

## Examples

Part 5: Cascading Style Sheets includes many examples of styles.

| SUB | Subscript |
| --- | --- |

## Purpose

Moves the selected characters below the base line on which other characters sit and applies a smaller font.

## Syntax

```
<SUB[ CLASS="class_name"][ DIR="LTR"|"RTL"][
ID="id_name"][ LANG="lang_code"][
LANGUAGE="JAVASCRIPT"|"JSCRIPT"|"VBS[CRIPT]"][
ONCLICK="cl_script_data"][ ONDBLCLICK="dc_script_data"][
ONHELP="hlp_script_data"][ ONKEYDOWN="kd_script_data"][
ONKEYPRESS="kp_script_data"][ ONKEYUP="ku_script_data"][
ONMOUSEDOWN="md_script_data"][
ONMOUSEMOVE="mm_script_data"][
ONMOUSEOUT="mo_script_data"][
ONMOUSEOVER="mov_script_data"][
ONMOUSEUP="mu_script_data"][
ONSELECTSTART="ss_script_data"][ STYLE="name_1: value_1"[;
"name_2: value_2"][...; "name_n: value_n"]][
TITLE="title"]>characters</SUB>
```

## Where

- CLASS specifies a class identification for the subscript characters.
- DIR specifies the direction in which the subscript characters is displayed: left-to-right or right-to-left.
- ID provides a unique identifier name for the subscript characters.
- LANG provides the code representing the language used for the subscript characters.
- **Microsoft** LANGUAGE declares the scripting language of the current script.
- ONCLICK specifies that the referred-to script runs when a user moves the mouse pointer or other pointing

device over the subscript characters and clicks the device button.

- ONDBLCLICK specifies that the referred-to script runs when a user moves the mouse pointer or other pointing device over the subscript characters and double-clicks the device button.

- **Microsoft** ONHELP specifies that the referred-to script runs when a user presses the **F1** or **Help** key over the current element.

- ONKEYDOWN specifies that the referred-to script runs when a user presses and holds a key down over the subscript characters.

- ONKEYPRESS specifies that the referred-to script runs when a user presses and releases a key over the subscript characters.

- ONKEYUP specifies that the referred-to script runs when a user releases a key over the subscript characters.

- ONMOUSEDOWN specifies that the referred-to script runs when a user moves the mouse pointer or other pointing device over the subscript characters and presses and holds down the device button.

- ONMOUSEMOVE specifies that the referred-to script runs when a user moves the mouse pointer or other pointing device over the subscript characters.

- ONMOUSEOUT specifies that the referred-to script runs when a user moves the mouse pointer or other pointing device away from the subscript characters.

- ONMOUSEOVER specifies that the referred-to script runs the first time a user moves the mouse pointer or other pointing device over the subscript characters.

- ONMOUSEUP specifies that the referred-to script runs when a user moves the mouse pointer or other pointing device over the subscript characters and releases a pressed-down device button.

- **Microsoft** ONSELECTSTART specifies that the referred-to script runs when a user starts selecting an object.

- STYLE sets styles for the subscript characters.

- TITLE provides a title or title information about the subscript characters.
- *characters* represents one or more characters.

## Notes

This element originated in HTML 3.2.
    The HTML 4.0 DTD categorizes this as an inline element.

## Example

H<SUB>2</SUB>O

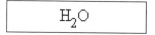

*Figure 4.51 The SUB element for the thirsty.*

## Related Elements

BIG, FONT, SMALL, SUP

| SUP | Superscript |
|-----|-------------|

## Purpose

Moves the selected characters above the baseline on which other characters sit and applies a smaller font.

## Syntax

```
<SUP[ CLASS="class_name"][ DIR="LTR"|"RTL"][
ID="id_name"][ LANG="lang_code"][
LANGUAGE="JAVASCRIPT"|"JSCRIPT"|"VBS[CRIPT]"][
ONCLICK="cl_script_data"][ ONDBLCLICK="dc_script_data"][
ONHELP="hlp_script_data"][ ONKEYDOWN="kd_script_data"][
ONKEYPRESS="kp_script_data"][ ONKEYUP="ku_script_data"][
ONMOUSEDOWN="md_script_data"][
ONMOUSEMOVE="mm_script_data"][
ONMOUSEOUT="mo_script_data"][
ONMOUSEOVER="mov_script_data"][
ONMOUSEUP="mu_script_data"][
ONSELECTSTART="ss_script_data"][ STYLE="name_1: value_1"[;
"name_2: value_2"][...; "name_n: value_n"]][
TITLE="title"]>characters</SUP>
```

## Where

- CLASS specifies a class identification for the super-script characters.
- DIR specifies the direction in which the superscript characters is displayed: left-to-right or right-to-left.
- ID provides a unique identifier name for the superscript characters.
- LANG provides the code representing the language used for the superscript characters.
- **Microsoft** LANGUAGE declares the scripting language of the current script.
- ONCLICK specifies that the referred-to script runs when a user moves the mouse pointer or other pointing

device over the superscript characters and clicks the device button.

- ONDBLCLICK specifies that the referred-to script runs when a user moves the mouse pointer or other pointing device over the superscript characters and double-clicks the device button.

- **Microsoft** ONHELP specifies that the referred-to script runs when a user presses the **F1** or **Help** key over the current element.

- ONKEYDOWN specifies that the referred-to script runs when a user presses and holds a key down over the superscript characters.

- ONKEYPRESS specifies that the referred-to script runs when a user presses and releases a key over the superscript characters.

- ONKEYUP specifies that the referred-to script runs when a user releases a key over the superscript characters.

- ONMOUSEDOWN specifies that the referred-to script runs when a user moves the mouse pointer or other pointing device over the superscript characters and presses and holds down the device button.

- ONMOUSEMOVE specifies that the referred-to script runs when a user moves the mouse pointer or other pointing device over the superscript characters.

- ONMOUSEOUT specifies that the referred-to script runs when a user moves the mouse pointer or other pointing device away from the superscript characters.

- ONMOUSEOVER specifies that the referred-to script runs the first time a user moves the mouse pointer or other pointing device over the superscript characters.

- ONMOUSEUP specifies that the referred-to script runs when a user moves the mouse pointer or other pointing device over the superscript characters and releases a pressed-down device button.

- **Microsoft** ONSELECTSTART specifies that the referred-to script runs when a user starts selecting an object.

- STYLE sets styles for the superscript characters.

- TITLE provides a title or title information about the superscript characters.
- *characters* represents one or more characters.

## Notes

This element originated in HTML 3.2.
The HTML 4.0 DTD categorizes this as an inline element.

## Example

x<SUP>2</SUP>+y<SUP>2</SUP>

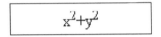

*Figure 4.52 Math the SUP way.*

## Related Elements

BIG, FONT, SMALL, SUB

203

| TITLE | Document Title |
|---|---|

## Purpose

Specifies a title for the current HTML document.

## Syntax

```
<TITLE[ DIR="LTR"|"RTL"][ LANG="lang_code"]>title-
text</TITLE>
```

## Where

- DIR specifies the direction in which the title text is displayed: left-to-right or right-to-left.
- LANG provides the code representing the language used for the title.
- *title-text* represents one or more characters making up the title.

## Notes

This element originated in HTML 2.0.

There can be only one title in an HTML document.

Titles can contain characters but not HTML elements or tags.

The TITLE element is valid only within the HEAD section.

Limit a title to 64 characters and spaces, so that it fits within a browser's title bar.

Use a meaningful title to describe the content of the document.

The TITLE attribute is related to the TITLE element. The TITLE element refers to an entire document; the TITLE attribute refers to a particular element.

Netscape Navigator also displays Netscape on the title bar.

## Example

```
<TITLE>The Eddy Group Home Page</TITLE>
```

The Eddy Group Home Page - Netscape

*Figure 4.53 An HTML document title in the title bar.*

| TT | Teletype Text |
|---|---|

## Purpose

Applies a teletype (monospace) font to selected text.

## Syntax

```
<TT[ CLASS="class_name"][ DIR="LTR"|"RTL"][ ID="id_name"][
LANG="lang_code"][
LANGUAGE="JAVASCRIPT"|"JSCRIPT"|"VBS[CRIPT]"][
ONCLICK="cl_script_data"][ ONDBLCLICK="dc_script_data"][
ONHELP="hlp_script_data"][ ONKEYDOWN="kd_script_data"][
ONKEYPRESS="kp_script_data"][ ONKEYUP="ku_script_data"][
ONMOUSEDOWN="md_script_data"][
ONMOUSEMOVE="mm_script_data"][
ONMOUSEOUT="mo_script_data"][
ONMOUSEOVER="mov_script_data"][
ONMOUSEUP="mu_script_data"][
ONSELECTSTART="ss_script_data"][ STYLE="name_1: value_1"[;
"name_2: value_2"][...; "name_n: value_n"]][
TITLE="title"]>text</TT>
```

## Where

- CLASS specifies a class identification for the teletype text.
- DIR specifies the direction in which the teletype text is displayed: left-to-right or right-to-left.
- ID provides a unique identifier name for the teletype text.
- LANG provides the code representing the language used for the teletype text.
- **Microsoft** LANGUAGE declares the scripting language of the current script.
- ONCLICK specifies that the referred-to script runs when a user moves the mouse pointer or other pointing

device over the teletype text and clicks the device button.

- ONDBLCLICK specifies that the referred-to script runs when a user moves the mouse pointer or other pointing device over the teletype text and double-clicks the device button.

-  ONHELP specifies that the referred-to script runs when a user presses the **F1** or **Help** key over the current element.

- ONKEYDOWN specifies that the referred-to script runs when a user presses and holds a key down over the teletype text.

- ONKEYPRESS specifies that the referred-to script runs when a user presses and releases a key over the teletype text.

- ONKEYUP specifies that the referred-to script runs when a user releases a key over the teletype text.

- ONMOUSEDOWN specifies that the referred-to script runs when a user moves the mouse pointer or other pointing device over the teletype text and presses and holds down the device button.

- ONMOUSEMOVE specifies that the referred-to script runs when a user moves the mouse pointer or other pointing device over the teletype text.

- ONMOUSEOUT specifies that the referred-to script runs when a user moves the mouse pointer or other pointing device away from the teletype text.

- ONMOUSEOVER specifies that the referred-to script runs the first time a user moves the mouse pointer or other pointing device over the teletype text.

- ONMOUSEUP specifies that the referred-to script runs when a user moves the mouse pointer or other pointing device over the teletype text and releases a pressed-down device button.

-  ONSELECTSTART specifies that the referred-to script runs when a user starts selecting an object.

- STYLE sets styles for the teletype text.

- TITLE provides a title or title information about the teletype text.
- *text* represents one or more characters.

## Notes

This element originated in HTML 2.0.

The HTML 4.0 DTD categorizes this as an inline element.

The TT element is a physical element in which you "code" the styles yourself. This is in contrast with logical elements, in which particular browsers are programmed to apply a certain style to the selected text.

Many browsers use the same font for the CODE, KBD, PRE, SAMP, and TT elements.

To display two or more lines of preformatted text, use the PRE element.

## Example

```
This is <TT>teletype</TT> text.
```

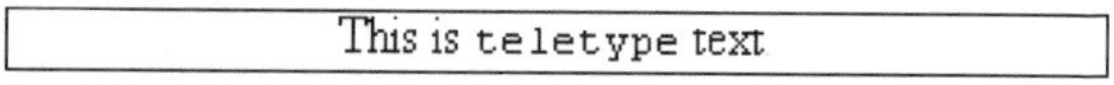

This is teletype text

*Figure 4.54 A sample of teletype text.*

## Related Elements

CODE, KBD, PRE, SAMP

| U | Underlined |
|---|---|

## Purpose

Underlines selected text.

## Syntax

```
<U[ CLASS="class_name"][ DIR="LTR"|"RTL"][ ID="id_name"][
LANG="lang_code"][
LANGUAGE="JAVASCRIPT"|"JSCRIPT"|"VBS[CRIPT]"][
ONCLICK="cl_script_data"][ ONDBLCLICK="dc_script_data"][
ONHELP="hlp_script_data"][ ONKEYDOWN="kd_script_data"][
ONKEYPRESS="kp_script_data"][ ONKEYUP="ku_script_data"][
ONMOUSEDOWN="md_script_data"][
ONMOUSEMOVE="mm_script_data"][
ONMOUSEOUT="mo_script_data"][
ONMOUSEOVER="mov_script_data"][
ONMOUSEUP="mu_script_data"][
ONSELECTSTART="ss_script_data"][ STYLE="name_1: value_1"[;
"name_2: value_2"][...; "name_n: value_n"]][
TITLE="title"]>text</U>
```

## Where

- CLASS specifies a class identification for the under-lined text.
- DIR specifies the direction in which the underlined text is displayed: left-to-right or right-to-left.
- ID provides a unique identifier name for the underlined text.
- LANG provides the code representing the language used for the underlined text.
- <br>Microsoft<br> LANGUAGE declares the scripting language of the current script.
- ONCLICK specifies that the referred-to script runs when a user moves the mouse pointer or other pointing

device over the underlined text and clicks the device button.

- ONDBLCLICK specifies that the referred-to script runs when a user moves the mouse pointer or other pointing device over the underlined text and double-clicks the device button.

- **Microsoft** ONHELP specifies that the referred-to script runs when a user presses the **F1** or **Help** key over the current element.

- ONKEYDOWN specifies that the referred-to script runs when a user presses and holds a key down over the underlined text.

- ONKEYPRESS specifies that the referred-to script runs when a user presses and releases a key over the underlined text.

- ONKEYUP specifies that the referred-to script runs when a user releases a key over the underlined text.

- ONMOUSEDOWN specifies that the referred-to script runs when a user moves the mouse pointer or other pointing device over the underlined text and presses and holds down the device button.

- ONMOUSEMOVE specifies that the referred-to script runs when a user moves the mouse pointer or other pointing device over the underlined text.

- ONMOUSEOUT specifies that the referred-to script runs when a user moves the mouse pointer or other pointing device away from the underlined text.

- ONMOUSEOVER specifies that the referred-to script runs the first time a user moves the mouse pointer or other pointing device over the underlined text.

- ONMOUSEUP specifies that the referred-to script runs when a user moves the mouse pointer or other pointing device over the underlined text and releases a pressed-down device button.

- **Microsoft** ONSELECTSTART specifies that the referred-to script runs when a user starts selecting an object.

- STYLE sets styles for the underlined text.

- TITLE provides a title or title information about the underlined text.
- *text* represents one or more characters.

## Notes

This element originated in HTML 2.0.

The HTML 4.0 DTD categorizes this as an inline element.

Although U is supported by HTML 4.0, it has been deprecated; that is, it will eventually be obsolete.

It's best not to use underlined text because users may confuse it with links.

## Example

```
This is <U>underlined</U> text.
```

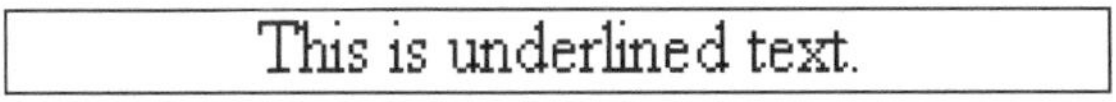

| This is underlined text. |
| --- |

*Figure 4.55 Text underlined using the U element.*

## Related Elements

```
B, BIG, I, EM, FONT, SMALL, STRIKE, STRONG, SUB, SUP
```

| UL | Unordered List |
|---|---|

## Purpose

Starts an unordered (bulleted) list.

## Syntax

```
<UL[ CLASS="class_name"][ COMPACT][ DIR="LTR"|"RTL"][
ID="id_name"][ LANG="lang_code"][
LANGUAGE="JAVASCRIPT"|"JSCRIPT"|"VBS[CRIPT]"][
ONCLICK="cl_script_data"][ ONDBLCLICK="dc_script_data"][
ONHELP="hlp_script_data"][ ONKEYDOWN="kd_script_data"][
ONKEYPRESS="kp_script_data"][ ONKEYUP="ku_script_data"][
ONMOUSEDOWN="md_script_data"][
ONMOUSEMOVE="mm_script_data"][
ONMOUSEOUT="mo_script_data"][
ONMOUSEOVER="mov_script_data"][
ONMOUSEUP="mu_script_data"][
ONSELECTSTART="ss_script_data"][ STYLE="name_1: value_1"[;
"name_2: value_2"][...; "name_n: value_n"]][
TITLE="title"][ TYPE="disc"|"square"|"circle"]>unordered-
list-items</UL>
```

## Where

- CLASS specifies a class identification for the unordered list.
- COMPACT indicates that a browser might decrease the size of the space between the bullet and the list item.
- DIR specifies the direction in which the unordered list text is displayed: left-to-right or right-to-left.
- ID provides a unique identifier name for the unordered list.
- LANG provides the code representing the language used for the unordered list text.
- **Microsoft** LANGUAGE declares the scripting language of the current script.

- ONCLICK specifies that the referred-to script runs when a user moves the mouse pointer or other pointing device over the unordered list and clicks the device button.

- ONDBLCLICK specifies that the referred-to script runs when a user moves the mouse pointer or other pointing device over the unordered list and double-clicks the device button.

- **[Microsoft]** ONHELP specifies that the referred-to script runs when a user presses the **F1** or **Help** key over the current element.

- ONKEYDOWN specifies that the referred-to script runs when a user presses and holds a key down over the unordered list.

- ONKEYPRESS specifies that the referred-to script runs when a user presses and releases a key over the unordered list.

- ONKEYUP specifies that the referred-to script runs when a user releases a key over the unordered list.

- ONMOUSEDOWN specifies that the referred-to script runs when a user moves the mouse pointer or other pointing device over the unordered list and presses and holds down the device button.

- ONMOUSEMOVE specifies that the referred-to script runs when a user moves the mouse pointer or other pointing device over the unordered list.

- ONMOUSEOUT specifies that the referred-to script runs when a user moves the mouse pointer or other pointing device away from the unordered list.

- ONMOUSEOVER specifies that the referred-to script runs the first time a user moves the mouse pointer or other pointing device over the unordered list.

- ONMOUSEUP specifies that the referred-to script runs when a user moves the mouse pointer or other pointing device over the unordered list and releases a pressed-down device button.

- **[Microsoft]** ONSELECTSTART specifies that the referred-to script runs when a user starts selecting an object.

- STYLE sets styles for the unordered list.
- TITLE provides a title or title information about the unordered list.
- TYPE sets a bullet style.
- *unordered-list-items* represents one or more entries for the list.

## Notes

This is an HTML 2.0 element, and the TYPE attribute is an HTML 3.2 feature.

The HTML 4.0 DTD categorizes this as a block-level element.

The COMPACT attribute does not work in all browsers.

If you nest an unordered list, it's a good idea to indent each level of lists in the HTML document to ensure that each of the start and end tags are on the same level. Indenting levels is not required.

When you nest unordered lists, there are three automatic levels of bullets: solid disk (the highest), circle, and square (the lowest). However, different browsers display different levels of bullets.

LI elements are embedded within UL elements.

## Examples

Example 1 (Figure 4.56)

```
<UL>
<LI>World Wide Web
<LI>Gopher
<LI>FTP
<LI>Telnet
</UL>
```

- World Wide Web
- Gopher
- FTP
- Telnet

*Figure 4.56 A default unordered list.*

## Example 2 (Figure 4.57)

```
<UL TYPE="square">
<LI>World Wide Web
<LI>Gopher
<LI>FTP
<LI>Telnet
</UL>
```

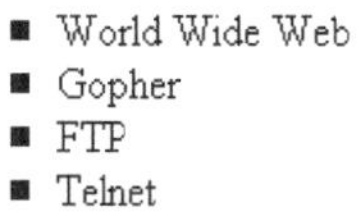

- World Wide Web
- Gopher
- FTP
- Telnet

*Figure 4.57 An unordered list with square bullets.*

## Example 3 (Figure 4.58)

```
<UL>
    <LI>Computers
        <UL>
            <LI>Desktop
            <LI>Notebooks
        </UL>
    <LI>Printers
        <UL>
            <LI>Laser
                <UL>
                    <LI>Color
                    <LI>Black & White
```

**215**

```
    </UL>
<LI>Inkjet
  <UL>
     <LI>Color
     <LI>Black & White
  </UL>
  </UL>
  <LI>Modems
</UL>
```

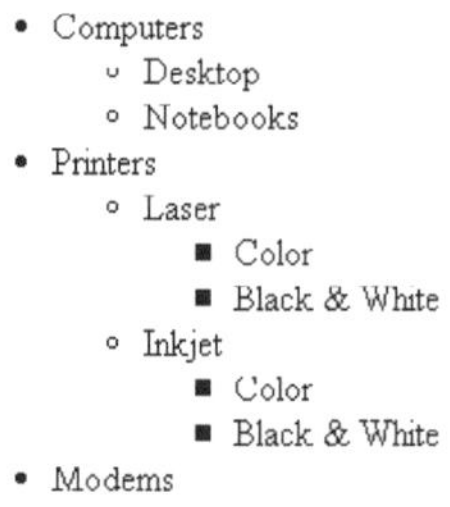

- Computers
  - Desktop
  - Notebooks
- Printers
  - Laser
    - Color
    - Black & White
  - Inkjet
    - Color
    - Black & White
- Modems

*Figure 4.58 Unordered lists nested in three levels.*

## Related Elements

DIR, MENU, OL

| VAR | Variable |
|-----|----------|

## Purpose

Indicates variable text by emphasizing it, usually with italics.

## Syntax

```
<VAR[ CLASS="class_name"][ DIR="LTR"|"RTL"][
ID="id_name"][ LANG="lang_code"][
LANGUAGE="JAVASCRIPT"|"JSCRIPT"|"VBS[CRIPT]"][
ONCLICK="cl_script_data"][ ONDBLCLICK="dc_script_data"][
ONHELP="hlp_script_data"][ ONKEYDOWN="kd_script_data"][
ONKEYPRESS="kp_script_data"][ ONKEYUP="ku_script_data"][
ONMOUSEDOWN="md_script_data"][
ONMOUSEMOVE="mm_script_data"][
ONMOUSEOUT="mo_script_data"][
ONMOUSEOVER="mov_script_data"][
ONMOUSEUP="mu_script_data"][
ONSELECTSTART="ss_script_data"][ STYLE="name_1: value_1"[;
"name_2: value_2"][...; "name_n: value_n"]][
TITLE="title"]>text</VAR>
```

## Where

- CLASS specifies a class identification for the variable.
- DIR specifies the direction in which the variable text is displayed: left-to-right or right-to-left.
- ID provides a unique identifier name for the variable.
- LANG provides the code representing the language used for the variable text.
- **Microsoft** LANGUAGE declares the scripting language of the current script.
- ONCLICK specifies that the referred-to script runs when a user moves the mouse pointer or other pointing device over the variable and clicks the device button.
- ONDBLCLICK specifies that the referred-to script runs when a user moves the mouse pointer or other

pointing device over the variable and double-clicks the device button.

-  ONHELP specifies that the referred-to script runs when a user presses the **F1** or **Help** key over the current element.

- ONKEYDOWN specifies that the referred-to script runs when a user presses and holds a key down over the variable.

- ONKEYPRESS specifies that the referred-to script runs when a user presses and releases a key over the variable.

- ONKEYUP specifies that the referred-to script runs when a user releases a key over the variable.

- ONMOUSEDOWN specifies that the referred-to script runs when a user moves the mouse pointer or other pointing device over the variable and presses and holds down the device button.

- ONMOUSEMOVE specifies that the referred-to script runs when a user moves the mouse pointer or other pointing device over the variable.

- ONMOUSEOUT specifies that the referred-to script runs when a user moves the mouse pointer or other pointing device away from the variable.

- ONMOUSEOVER specifies that the referred-to script runs the first time a user moves the mouse pointer or other pointing device over the variable.

- ONMOUSEUP specifies that the referred-to script runs when a user moves the mouse pointer or other pointing device over the variable and releases a pressed-down device button.

-  ONSELECTSTART specifies that the referred-to script runs when a user starts selecting an object.

- STYLE sets styles for the variable.

- TITLE provides a title or title information about the variable.

- *text* represents one or more characters.

## Notes

This element originated in HTML 2.0.

VAR is a logical element, in which particular browsers are programmed to apply a certain style to the selected text. This is in contrast to a physical element in which you "code" the styles yourself.

Many browsers use the same enhancement for the I, CITE, EM, and VAR elements.

The HTML 4.0 DTD categorizes this as an inline element.

## Example

Use the <VAR>VAR</VAR> element to highlight variables that you are introducing in a document.

Use the *VAR* element to highlight variables that you are introducing in a document.

*Figure 4.59 The VAR element highlights new terms.*

## Related Elements

B, BIG, CITE, EM, FONT, I, SMALL, STRONG, SUB, SUP, U

| XMP | Example |
| --- | --- |

This element is obsolete; that is, it is no longer part of the HTML standard. Use the PRE element instead.

# 2

# Special Characters

These special characters allow you to embed symbols and "nonkeyboard" characters in a document. Most browsers recognize all the special characters listed here. This section consists of three tables (Tables 4.2, 4.3, and 4.4) with these column headings:

| | |
|---|---|
| **Entity** | This column lists entities supported by the HTML 4.0 standard. The Universal Character Set (UCS), which is equivalent to Unicode 2.0, is the standard for HTML 4.0. |
| **Entity Name** | This column contains the approved syntax for the entities listed in the first column. In most cases, you should use this syntax instead of the numeric entity reference, which is listed in the next column. |
| **Numeric Entity Reference** | This column contains numeric code counter parts to the HTML entity names. |
| **Description** | This column contains brief descriptions and examples within parentheses. |

*Table 4.2 HTMLlat1 Character Set*

| ENTITY | ENTITY NAME | NUMERIC ENTRY REFERENCE | DESCRIPTION |
|--------|-------------|------------------------|-------------|
| Aacute | &Aacute; | &#193; | Acute accent A (Á) |
| aacute | &aacute; | &#225; | Acute accent a (á) |
| Acirc | &Acirc; | &#194; | Circumflex A (Â) |
| acirc | &acirc; | &#226; | Circumflex a (â) |
| acute | &acute; | &#180; | Acute accent (´) |
| AElig | &AElig; | &#198; | Ligature AE (Æ) |
| aelig | &aelig; | &#230; | Ligature ae (æ) |
| Agrave | &Agrave; | &#192; | Grave accent A (À) |
| agrave | &agrave; | &#224; | Grave accent a (à) |
| Aring | &Aring; | &#197; | Ring A (Å) |
| aring | &aring; | &#229; | Ring a (å) |
| Atilde | &Atilde; | &#195; | Tilde A (Ã) |
| atilde | &atilde; | &#227; | Tilde a (ã) |
| Auml | &Auml; | &#196; | Umlaut A (Ä) |
| auml | &auml; | &#228; | Umlaut a (ä) |
| brvbar | &brvbar; | &#166; | Broken bar (¦) |
| Ccedil | &Ccedil; | &#199; | Cedilla C (Ç) |
| ccedil | &ccedil; | &#231; | Cedilla c (ç) |
| cedil | &cedil; | &#184; | Cedilla (¸) |
| cent | &cent; | &#162; | Cent sign (¢) |
| copy | &copy; | &#169; | Copyright (©) |
| curren | &curren; | &#164; | General currency (¤) |
| deg | &deg; | &#176; | Degree (°) |
| divide | &divide; | &#247; | Division sign (÷) |
| Eacute | &Eacute; | &#201; | Acute accent E (É) |
| eacute | &eacute; | &#233; | Acute accent e (é) |
| Ecirc | &Ecirc; | &#202; | Circumflex E (Ê) |
| ecirc | &ecirc; | &#234; | Circumflex e (ê) |

*Table 4.2 HTMLlatl Character Set (continued)*

| Entity | Entity Name | Numeric Entry Reference | Description |
|---|---|---|---|
| Egrave | &Egrave; | &#200; | Grave accent E (È) |
| egrave | &egrave; | &#232; | Grave accent e (è) |
| ETH | &ETH; | &#208; | Icelandic Eth (Ð) |
| eth | &eth; | &#240; | Icelandic eth (ð) |
| Euml | &Euml; | &#203; | Umlaut E (Ë) |
| euml | &euml; | &#235; | Umlaut e (ë) |
| frac12 | &frac12; | &#189; | Fraction one-half (½) |
| frac14 | &frac14; | &#188; | Fraction one-quarter (¼) |
| frac34 | &frac34; | &#190; | Fraction three-quarters (¾) |
| Iacute | &Iacute; | &#205; | Acute accent I (Í) |
| iacute | &iacute; | &#237; | Acute accent i (í) |
| Icirc | &Icirc; | &#206; | Circumflex I (Î) |
| icirc | &icirc; | &#238; | Circumflex i (î) |
| iexcl | &iexcl; | &#161; | Inverted exclamation mark (¡) |
| Igrave | &Igrave; | &#204; | Grave accent I (Ì) |
| igrave | &igrave; | &#236; | Grave accent i (ì) |
| iquest | &iquest; | &#191; | Inverted question mark (¿) |
| Iuml | &Iuml; | &#207; | Umlaut I (Ï) |
| iuml | &iuml; | &#239; | Umlaut i (ï) |
| laquo | &laquo; | &#171; | Left angle quote («) |
| macr | &macr; | &#175; | Macron (¯) |
| micro | &micro; | &#181; | Micro (µ) |
| middot | &middot; | &#183; | Middle dot (·) |
| nbsp |   |   | Nonbreaking space |
| not | &not; | &#172; | Not (¬) |

*Table 4.2 HTMLlat1 Character Set (continued)*

| Entity | Entity Name | Numeric Entry Reference | Description |
|---|---|---|---|
| Ntilde | &Ntilde; | &#209; | Tilde N (Ñ) |
| ntilde | &ntilde; | &#241; | Tilde n (ñ) |
| Oacute | &Oacute; | &#211; | Acute accent O (Ó) |
| oacute | &oacute; | &#243; | Acute accent o (ó) |
| Ocirc | &Ocirc; | &#212; | Circumflex O (Ô) |
| ocirc | &ocirc; | &#244; | Circumflex o (ô) |
| Ograve | &Ograve; | &#210; | Grave accent O (Ò) |
| ograve | &ograve; | &#242; | Grave accent o (ò) |
| ordf | &ordf; | &#170; | Ordinal female ($^a$) |
| ordm | &ordm; | &#186; | Ordinal male ($^\circ$) |
| Oslash | &Oslash; | &#216; | Slash O (Ø) |
| oslash | &oslash; | &#248; | Slash o (ø) |
| Otilde | &Otilde; | &#213; | Tilde O (Õ) |
| otilde | &otilde; | &#245; | Tilde o (õ) |
| Ouml | &Ouml; | &#214; | Umlaut O (Ö) |
| ouml | &ouml; | &#246; | Umlaut o (ö) |
| para | &para; | &#182; | Paragraph mark (¶) |
| plusmn | &plusmn; | &#177; | Plus-minus (±) |
| pound | &pound; | &#163; | Pound sign (£) |
| raquo | &raquo; | &#187; | Right angle quote (») |
| reg | &reg; | &#174; | Registered trademark (®) |
| sect | &sect; | &#167; | Section sign (§) |
| shy | &shy; | &#173; | Soft hyphen (–) |
| sup1 | &sup1; | &#185; | Superscript 1([1]) |
| sup2 | &sup2; | &#178; | Superscript 2 ([2]) |
| sup3 | &sup3; | &#179; | Superscript 3 ([3]) |
| szlig | &szlig; | &#223; | Sharp s (ß) |
| THORN | &THORN; | &#222; | Icelandic Thorn (Þ) |

*Table 4.2 HTMLlat1 Character Set (continued)*

| ENTITY | ENTITY NAME | NUMERIC ENTRY REFERENCE | DESCRIPTION |
|--------|-------------|-------------------------|-------------|
| thorn | &thorn; | &#254; | Icelandic thorn (þ) |
| times | &times; | &#215; | Multiply sign (x) |
| Uacute | &Uacute; | &#218; | Acute accent U (Ú) |
| uacute | &uacute; | &#250; | Acute accent u (ú) |
| Ucirc | &Ucirc; | &#219; | Circumflex U (Û) |
| ucirc | &ucirc; | &#251; | Circumflex u (û) |
| Ugrave | &Ugrave; | &#217; | Grave accent U (Ù) |
| ugrave | &ugrave; | &#249; | Grave accent u (ù) |
| uml | &uml; | &#168; | Umlaut (¨) |
| Uuml | &Uuml; | &#220; | Umlaut U (Ü) |
| uuml | &uuml; | &#252; | Umlaut u (ü) |
| Yacute | &Yacute; | &#221; | Acute accent Y (Ý) |
| yacute | &yacute; | &#253; | Acute accent y (ý) |
| yen | &yen; | &#165; | Yen sign (¥) |
| Yuml | &Yuml; | &#376; | Umlaut Y (Ÿ) |
| yuml | &yuml; | &#255; | Umlaut y (ÿ) |

*Table 4.3 HTMLsymbol Mathematical, Greek and Symbolic Character Set*

| ENTITY | ENTITY NAME | NUMERIC ENTRY REFERENCE | DESCRIPTION |
|--------|-------------|-------------------------|-------------|
| alefsym | &alefsym; | &#8501; | aleph symbol (ℵ) |
| Alpha | &Alpha; | &#913; | Greek Alpha (A) |
| alpha | &alpha; | &#945; | Greek alpha (α) |
| and | &and; | &#8869; | Logical AND (∧) |
| ang | &ang; | &#8736; | Angle (∠) |
| asymp | &asymp; | &#8776; | Asymptotic to (≈) |
| Beta | &Beta; | &#914; | Greek Beta (B) |

*Table 4.3 HTMLsymbol Mathematical, Greek and Symbolic Character Set (continued)*

| ENTITY | ENTITY NAME | NUMERIC ENTRY REFERENCE | DESCRIPTION |
|---|---|---|---|
| beta | &beta; | &#946; | Greek beta (β) |
| bull | &bull; | &#8226; | Bullet (•) |
| cap | &cap; | &#8745; | Intersection, cap (∩) |
| Chi | &Chi; | &#935; | Greek Chi (X) |
| chi | &chi; | &#967; | Greek chi (χ) |
| clubs | &clubs; | &#9827; | Club, shamrock (♣) |
| cong | &cong; | &#8773; | Congruent ( ≅ ) |
| crarr | &crarr; | &#8629; | Carriage return (↵) |
| cup | &cup; | &#8746; | Union, cup (∪) |
| darr | &darr; | &#8595; | Down arrow (↓) |
| dArr | &dArr; | &#8659; | Down double arrow (⇓) |
| Delta | &Delta; | &#916; | Greek Delta (Δ) |
| delta | &delta; | &#948; | Greek delta (δ) |
| diams | &diams; | &#9830; | Diamond (♦) |
| empty | &empty; | &#8709; | Empty, null, set (∅) |
| Epsilon | &Epsilon; | &#917; | Greek Epsilon (E) |
| epsilon | &epsilon; | &#949; | Greek epsilon (ε) |
| equiv | &equiv; | &#8801; | Identical to (≡) |
| Eta | &Eta; | &#919; | Greek Eta (H) |
| eta | &eta; | &#951; | Greek eta (η) |
| exist | &exist; | &#8707; | There exists (∃) |
| forall | &forall; | &#8704; | For all (∀) |
| frasl | &frasl; | &#8260; | Fraction slash (/) |
| Gamma | &Gamma; | &#915; | Greek Gamma (Γ) |
| gamma | &gamma; | &#947; | Greek gamma (γ) |
| ge | &ge; | &#8805; | Greater-than or equal to (≥) |
| harr | &harr; | &#8596; | Left right arrow (↔) |

*Table 4.3 HTMLsymbol Mathematical, Greek and Symbolic Character Set (continued)*

| ENTITY | ENTITY NAME | NUMERIC ENTRY REFERENCE | DESCRIPTION |
|---|---|---|---|
| hArr | &hArr; | &#8660; | Left right double arrow (⇔) |
| hearts | &hearts; | &#9829; | Hearts, valentine (♥) |
| hellip | &hellip; | &#8230; | Horizontal ellipsis, three dot leader (...) |
| image | &image; | &#8465; | Blackletter I, imaginary part (ℑ) |
| infin | &infin; | &#8734; | Infinity (∞) |
| int | &int; | &#8747; | Integral (∫) |
| Iota | &Iota; | &#921; | Greek Iota (I) |
| iota | &iota; | &#953; | Greek iota (ι) |
| isin | &isin; | &#8712; | Element of (∈) |
| Kappa | &Kappa; | &#922; | Greek Kappa (K) |
| kappa | &kappa; | &#954; | Greek kappa (κ) |
| Lambda | &Lambda; | &#923; | Greek Lambda (Λ) |
| lambda | &lambda; | &#955; | Greek lambda (λ) |
| lang | &lang; | &#9001; | Left-pointing angle bracket (⟨) |
| larr | &larr; | &#8592; | Left arrow (←) |
| lArr | &lArr; | &#8656; | Left double arrow (⇐) |
| lceil | &lceil; | &#8968; | Left ceiling, apl upstile (⌈) |
| le | &le; | &#8804; | Less than or equal to (≤) |
| lfloor | &lfloor; | &#8970; | Left floor, apl downstile (⌊) |
| lowast | &lowast; | &#8727; | Asterisk operator (∗) |
| loz | &loz; | &#9674; | Lozenge (◊) |
| minus | &minus; | &#8722; | Minus sign (−) |
| Mu | &Mu; | &#924; | Greek Mu (M) |
| mu | &mu; | &#956; | Greek mu (μ) |

*Table 4.3 HTMLsymbol Mathematical, Greek and Symbolic Character Set (continued)*

| Entity | Entity Name | Numeric Entry Reference | Description |
|--------|-------------|-------------------------|-------------|
| nabla | &nabla; | &#8711; | Nabla, backward difference (∇) |
| ne | &ne; | &#8800; | Not equal to (≠) |
| ni | &ni; | &#8715; | Contains as member (∋) |
| notin | &notin; | &#8713; | Not an element of (∉) |
| nsub | &nsub; | &#8836; | Not a subset of (⊄) |
| Nu | &Nu; | &#925; | Greek Nu (N) |
| nu | &nu; | &#957; | Greek nu (ν) |
| oline | &oline; | &#8254; | Overline, spacing overscore (‾) |
| Omega | &Omega; | &#937; | Greek Omega (Ω) |
| omega | &omega; | &#969; | Greek omega (ω) |
| Omicron | &Omicron; | &#927; | Greek Omicron (O) |
| omicron | &omicron; | &#959; | Greek omicron (o) |
| oplus | &oplus; | &#8853; | Circled plus, direct sum (⊕) |
| or | &or; | &#8870; | Logical OR, vee (∨) |
| otimes | &otimes; | &#8855; | Circled times, vector product (⊗) |
| part | &part; | &#8706; | Partial differential (∂) |
| perp | &perp; | &#8869; | Up tack, orthogonal to, perpendicular (⊥) |
| Phi | &Phi; | &#934; | Greek Phi (Φ) |
| phi | &phi; | &#966; | Greek phi (φ) |
| Pi | &Pi; | &#928; | Greek Pi (Π) |
| pi | &pi; | &#960; | Greek pi (π) |
| piv | &piv; | &#982; | Greek pi symbol (ϖ) |
| prime | &prime; | &#8242; | Prime, minutes, feet (′) |

Table 4.3 HTMLsymbol Mathematical, Greek and Symbolic Character Set (continued)

| ENTITY | ENTITY NAME | NUMERIC ENTRY REFERENCE | DESCRIPTION |
|---|---|---|---|
| Prime | &Prime; | &#8243; | Double prime, seconds, inches (″) |
| prod | &prod; | &#8719; | N-ary product, product sign (Π) |
| prop | &prop; | &#8733; | Proportional to (∝) |
| Psi | &Psi; | &#936; | Greek Psi (Ψ) |
| psi | &psi; | &#968; | Greek psi, (ψ) |
| radic | &radic; | &#8730; | Radical sign, square root, (√) |
| rang | &rang; | &#9002; | Right-pointing angle bracket (⟩) |
| rarr | &rarr; | &#8594; | Right arrow (→) |
| rArr | &rArr; | &#8658; | Right double arrow (⇒) |
| rceil | &rceil; | &#8969; | Right ceiling (⌉) |
| real | &real; | &#8476; | Blackletter R, real part symbol (ℜ) |
| rfloor | &rfloor; | &#8971; | Right floor (⌋) |
| Rho | &Rho; | &#929; | Greek Rho (P) |
| rho | &rho; | &#961; | Greek rho (ρ) |
| sdot | &sdot; | &#8901; | Dot operator (.) |
| Sigma | &Sigma; | &#931; | Greek Sigma (Σ) |
| sigma | &sigma; | &#963; | Greek sigma (σ) |
| sigmaf | &sigmaf; | &#962; | Greek final sigma (S) |
| sim | &sim; | &#8764; | Tilde operator, varies with, similar to (~) |
| spades | &spades; | &#9824; | Spade (♠) |
| sub | &sub; | &#8756; | Subset of ( ⊂) |
| sube | &sube; | &#8838; | Subset of or equal to (⊆) |
| sum | &sum; | &#8721; | N-ary summation (Σ) |

*Table 4.3 HTMLsymbol Mathematical, Greek and Symbolic Character Set (continued)*

| Entity | Entity Name | Numeric Entry Reference | Description |
|---|---|---|---|
| Sup | &sup; | &#8835; | Superset of (⊃) |
| Supe | &supe; | &#8839; | Superset of or equal to (⊇) |
| Tau | &Tau; | &#932; | Greek Tau (T) |
| tau | &tau; | &#964; | Green tau (τ) |
| there4 | &there4; | &#8756; | Therefore (∴) |
| Theta | &Theta; | &#920; | Greek Theta (Θ) |
| theta | &theta; | &#952; | Greek theta (θ) |
| thetasym | &thetasym; | &#977; | Greek theta symbol (????) |
| trade | &trade; | &#8482; | Trade mark sign (™) |
| uarr | &uarr; | &#8593; | Up arrow (↑) |
| uArr | &uArr; | &#8657; | Up double arrow (⇑) |
| upsih | &upsih; | &#978; | Greek upsilon with hook symbol (ϒ) |
| Upsilon | &Upsilon; | &#933; | Greek Upsilon (Y) |
| upsilon | &upsilon; | &#965; | Greek upsilon (υ) |
| weierp | &weierp; | &#8472; | Script uppercase P, power set, Weierstrass p (℘) |
| Xi | &Xi; | &#926; | Greek Xi (Ξ) |
| xi | &xi; | &#958; | Greek xi (ξ) |
| Zeta | &Zeta; | &#918; | Greek Zeta (Z) |
| zeta | &zeta; | &#950; | Greek zeta (ζ) |

*Table 4.4  HTMLspecial Character Set*

| Entity | Entity Name | Numeric Entry Reference | Description |
|---|---|---|---|
| amp | &amp; | &#38; | Ampersand (&) |
| bdquo | &bdquo; | &#8222; | Double low-9 quotation mark („) |

*Table 4.4  HTMLspecial Character Set (continued)*

| Entity | Entity Name | Numeric Entry Reference | Description |
|---|---|---|---|
| circ | &circ; | &#710; | Modifier letter circumflex accent (ˆ) |
| dagger | &dagger; | &#8224; | Dagger (†) |
| Dagger | &Dagger; | &#8225; | Double dagger (‡) |
| emsp |   |   | Em space (  ) |
| ensp |   |   | En space ( ) |
| gt | &gt; | &#62; | Greater than sign (>) |
| ldquo | &ldquo; | &#8220; | Left double quotation mark (") |
| lrm | &lrm; | &#8206; | Left-to-right mark |
| lsaquo | &lsaquo; | &#8249; | Single left-pointing angle quotation mark (‹) |
| lsquo | &lsquo; | &#8216; | Left single quotation mark (') |
| lt | &lt; | &#60; | Less than sign (<) |
| mdash | &mdash; | &#8212; | Em dash (—) |
| ndash | &ndash; | &#8211; | En dash (–) |
| OElig | &OElig; | &#338; | Latin ligature OE (Œ) |
| oelig | &oelig; | &#339; | Latin ligature oe (œ) |
| permil | &permil; | &#8240; | Per mille sign (‰) |
| quot | &quot; | &#34; | Quotation mark, apl quote (") |
| rdquo | &rdquo; | &#8221; | Right double quotation mark (") |
| rlm | &rlm; | &#8207; | Right-to-left mark |
| rsaquo | &rsaquo; | &#8250; | Single right-pointing angle quotation (›) |
| rsquo | &rsquo; | &#8217; | Right single quotation mark (') |

*Table 4.4  HTML special Character Set (continued)*

| Entity | Entity Name | Numeric Entry Reference | Description |
|---|---|---|---|
| sbquo | &sbquo; | &#8218; | Single low-9 quotation mark (í) |
| Scaron | &Scaron; | &#352; | Latin S with caron |
| scaron | &scaron; | &#353; | Latin s with caron |
| thinsp |   |   | Thin space |
| tilde | &tilde; | &#732; | Small tilde |
| trade | &trade; | &#8482; | Registered trademark (™) |
| zwj | &zwj; | &#8205; | Zero width joiner |
| zwnj | &zwnj; | &#8204; | Zero width non-joiner |

# Table Elements

These elements enable you to create and format tables in HTML documents.

 Appendix B, "Attributes in Depth," describes all attributes in the HTML 4.0 standard and for the Netscape and Microsoft extensions. With each entry, you'll find valid values and usage notes.

## CAPTION | Caption

## Purpose

Adds a caption above or below a table.

## Syntax

```
<CAPTION[ ALIGN="top"|"bottom"|"left"|"right"|"center"][
CLASS="class_name"][ DIR="LTR"|"RTL"][ ID="id_name"][
LANG="lang_code"][
LANGUAGE="JAVASCRIPT"|"JSCRIPT"|"VBS[CRIPT]"][ ONAFTERUP-
DATE="au_script_data"][ ONBEFOREUPDATE="bu_script_data"][
ONBLUR="bl_script_data"][ ONCLICK="cl_script_data"][ OND-
BLCLICK="dc_script_data"][ ONDRAGSTART="ds_script_data"][
ONFOCUS="fc_script_data"][ ONHELP="hlp_script_data"][
ONKEYDOWN="kd_script_data"][ ONKEYPRESS="kp_script_data"][
ONKEYUP="ku_script_data"][ ONMOUSEDOWN="md_script_data"][
ONMOUSEMOVE="mm_script_data"][
ONMOUSEOUT="mo_script_data"][ONMOUSEOVER="mov_script_data"
][ ONMOUSEUP="mu_script_data"][
ONRESIZE="rsz_script_data"][ ONROWENTER="re_script_data"][
ONROWEXIT="rex_script_data"][ ONSCROLL="sc_script_data"][
ONSELECTSTART="ss_script_data"][ STYLE="name_1: value_1"[;
"name_2: value_2"][...; "name_n: value_n"]]][
TITLE="title"][ VALIGN="top"|"bottom"]>text</CAPTION>
```

## Where

- ALIGN indicates the alignment of the caption, above, below, to the left, or to the right of the table. Note that the center value is a Netscape-defined attribute.
- CLASS specifies a class identification for the caption.
- DIR specifies the direction in which the caption text is displayed: left-to-right or right-to-left.
- ID provides a unique identifier name for the caption.
- LANG provides the code representing the language used for the caption.

-  LANGUAGE declares the scripting language of the current script.

-  ONAFTERUPDATE specifies that the referred-to script runs after data has been transferred from the element to the data repository.

-  ONBEFOREUPDATE specifies that the referred-to script runs before data is transferred from the element to the data repository.

-  ONBLUR specifies that the referred-to script runs when the link loses focus (that is, it is no longer the active element).

- ONCLICK specifies that the referred-to script runs when a user moves the mouse pointer or other pointing device over the caption and clicks the device button.

- ONDBLCLICK specifies that the referred-to script runs when a user moves the mouse pointer or other pointing device over the caption and double-clicks the device button.

-  ONDRAGSTART specifies that the referred-to script runs when the user starts dragging a selection or element.

-  ONFOCUS specifies that the referred-to script runs when the current element receives focus (that is, is made active) by the mouse pointer or other pointing device.

-  ONHELP specifies that the referred-to script runs when a user presses the **F1** or **Help** key over the current element.

- ONKEYDOWN specifies that the referred-to script runs when a user presses and holds a key down over the caption.

- ONKEYPRESS specifies that the referred-to script runs when a user presses and releases a key over the caption.

- ONKEYUP specifies that the referred-to script runs when a user releases a key over the caption.

- ONMOUSEDOWN specifies that the referred-to script runs when a user moves the mouse pointer or other pointing device over the caption and presses and holds down the device button.
- ONMOUSEMOVE specifies that the referred-to script runs when a user moves the mouse pointer or other pointing device over the caption.
- ONMOUSEOUT specifies that the referred-to script runs when a user moves the mouse pointer or other pointing device away from the caption.
- ONMOUSEOVER specifies that the referred-to script runs the first time a user moves the mouse pointer or other pointing device over the caption.
- ONMOUSEUP specifies that the referred-to script runs when a user moves the mouse pointer or other pointing device over the caption and releases a pressed-down device button.
- **Microsoft** ONRESIZE specifies that the referred-to script runs when the user resizes the selected object.
- **Microsoft** ONROWENTER specifies that the referred-to script runs when the current row has been modified.
- **Microsoft** ONROWEXIT specifies that the referred-to script runs before the current row is modified.
- **Microsoft** ONSCROLL specifies that the referred-to script runs when a user moves the scroll box within the scroll bar.
- **Microsoft** ONSELECTSTART specifies that the referred-to script runs when a user starts selecting an object.
- STYLE sets styles for the caption.
- TITLE provides a title or title information about the caption.
- **Microsoft** VALIGN indicates the vertical alignment of the caption, above or below the table.
- *caption text* represents one or more required words.

## Notes

This element originated in HTML 3.2.
The HTML 4.0 DTD categorizes this as an inline element.
The CAPTION element must immediately follow the <TABLE> start tag within the table description.
Tables do not require captions.

## Examples

Example 1 (Figure 4.61)

```
<TABLE BORDER>
<CAPTION>A sample caption</CAPTION>
<TR><TH>Word
Processing</TH><TH>Spreadsheets</TH><TH>Databases</TH></TR>
<TR><TD>125</TD><TD>8</TD><TD>6</TD></TR>
</TABLE>
```

A sample caption

| Word Processing | Spreadsheets | Databases |
|-----------------|--------------|-----------|
| 125 | 8 | 6 |

*Figure 4.61 A table with its caption above (the default).*

Example 2 (Figure 4.62)

```
<TABLE BORDER>
<CAPTION ALIGN="bottom">A sample caption</CAPTION>
<TR><TH>Word
Processing</TH><TH>Spreadsheets</TH><TH>Databases</TH></TR>
<TR><TD>125</TD><TD>8</TD><TD>6</TD></TR>
</TABLE>
```

| Word Processing | Spreadsheets | Databases |
|---|---|---|
| 125 | 8 | 6 |

A sample caption

*Figure 4.62 A caption below a table.*

You'll find additional table examples throughout this chapter.

| COL | Column Properties |
|-----|-------------------|

## Purpose

Specifies alignment for one or more columns in a table.

## Syntax

```
<COL [ ALIGN="left"|"center"|"right"|"justify"|"char"][
CHAR="character"][ CHAROFF="offset"][ CLASS="class_name"][
DIR="LTR"|"RTL"][ ID="id_name"][ LANG="lang_code"][
ONCLICK="cl_script_data"][ ONDBLCLICK="dc_script_data"][
ONKEYDOWN="kd_script_data"][ ONKEYPRESS="kp_script_data"][
ONKEYUP="ku_script_data"][ ONMOUSEDOWN="md_script_data"][
ONMOUSEMOVE="mm_script_data"][
ONMOUSEOUT="mo_script_data"][
ONMOUSEOVER="mov_script_data"][
ONMOUSEUP="mu_script_data"][ SPAN="num_cols"|"1"|"0"][
STYLE="name_1: value_1"[; "name_2: value_2"][...; "name_n:
value_n"]][ TITLE="title"][ VALIGN="middle"|"top"|"bot-
tom"|"baseline"][ WIDTH="width_pix"|"width_%"|"0*"|"n*"]>
```

## Where

- ALIGN indicates the alignment of the text within the column: with the left or right margins, centered between the left and right margins, or aligned with a particular character.
- CHAR names a character from which column text is aligned in both directions.
- CHAROFF sets the horizontal distance between the left or right margin and the first occurrence of the CHAR character.
- CLASS specifies a class identification for the column.
- DIR specifies the direction in which the column contents are displayed: left-to-right or right-to-left.
- ID provides a unique identifier name for the column.
- LANG provides the code representing the language used for the column.

**239**

- ONCLICK specifies that the referred-to script runs when a user moves the mouse pointer or other pointing device over the column and clicks the device button.
- ONDBLCLICK specifies that the referred-to script runs when a user moves the mouse pointer or other pointing device over the column and double-clicks the device button.
- ONKEYDOWN specifies that the referred-to script runs when a user presses and holds a key down over the column.
- ONKEYPRESS specifies that the referred-to script runs when a user presses and releases a key over the column.
- ONKEYUP specifies that the referred-to script runs when a user releases a key over the column.
- ONMOUSEDOWN specifies that the referred-to script runs when a user moves the mouse pointer or other pointing device over the column and presses and holds down the device button.
- ONMOUSEMOVE specifies that the referred-to script runs when a user moves the mouse pointer or other pointing device over the column.
- ONMOUSEOUT specifies that the referred-to script runs when a user moves the mouse pointer or other pointing device away from the column.
- ONMOUSEOVER specifies that the referred-to script runs the first time a user moves the mouse pointer or other pointing device over the column.
- ONMOUSEUP specifies that the referred-to script runs when a user moves the mouse pointer or other pointing device over the column and releases a pressed-down device button.
- SPAN specifies the number of columns over which the COL attributes are set.
- STYLE sets styles for the column.
- TITLE provides a title or title information about the column.
- VALIGN indicates the vertical alignment of the column, from the top to the bottom.

- WIDTH indicates the absolute width of the column, in pixels or as a percentage of the full-screen width, or the relative width of the column to other columns in the current table.

## Notes

This is an HTML 4.0 element. Previously, it was a Microsoft extension.

Use COL to specify attributes for several columns in a column group.

The attributes set by the COL element override those set by the COLGROUP element.

A column group may or may not contain columns.

## Example

```
<TABLE BORDER=5 CELLSPACING=1 WIDTH="400" BGCOLOR="white">
<COL ALIGN="center" SPAN="3">
<THEAD>
<TR><TH></TH><TH>Income</TH><TH>Expenses</TH></TR>
</THEAD>
<TBODY>
<TR><TD><B>Quarter 1</B></TD><TD>800</TD><TD>784</TD></TR>
<TR><TD><B>Quarter
2</B></TD><TD>1000</TD><TD>1150</TD></TR>
<TR><TD><B>Quarter
3</B></TD><TD>1200</TD><TD>975</TD></TR>
<TR><TD><B>Quarter
4</B></TD><TD>1300</TD><TD>1230</TD></TR>
</TBODY>
```

| | Income | Expenses |
|---|---|---|
| Quarter 1 | 800 | 784 |
| Quarter 2 | 1000 | 1150 |
| Quarter 3 | 1200 | 975 |
| Quarter 4 | 1300 | 1230 |

*Figure 4.63 An example of the COL element.*

You'll find additional table examples throughout this chapter.

## Related Element

COLGROUP

## COLGROUP | Column Group

## Purpose

Groups and formats one or more columns in a table.

## Syntax

```
<COLGROUP [
ALIGN="left"|"center"|"right"|"justify"|"char"|"bleedleft"
|"bleedright"][ BACKGROUND="picture_url"][
CHAR="character"][ CHAROFF="offset"][ CLASS="class_name"][
DIR="LTR"|"RTL"][ HALIGN="center"|"left"|"right"][
ID="id_name"][ LANG="lang_code"][
ONCLICK="cl_script_data"][ ONDBLCLICK="dc_script_data"][
ONKEYDOWN="kd_script_data"][ ONKEYPRESS="kp_script_data"][
ONKEYUP="ku_script_data"][ ONMOUSEDOWN="md_script_data"][
ONMOUSEMOVE="mm_script_data"][
ONMOUSEOUT="mo_script_data"][
ONMOUSEOVER="mov_script_data"][
ONMOUSEUP="mu_script_data"][ SPAN="num_cols"|"1"|"0"][
STYLE="name_1: value_1"[; "name_2: value_2"][...; "name_n:
value_n"]][ TITLE="title"][ VALIGN="middle"|"top"|"bot-
tom"|"baseline"][
WIDTH="width_pix"|"width_%"|"0*"]>columns-contents[</COL-
GROUP>]
```

## Where

- ALIGN indicates the alignment of the text within the column group: with the left or right margins, centered between the left and right margins, or aligned with a particular character.
- **Microsoft** BACKGROUND specifies an image file that is displayed in the column group background.
- CHAR names a character from which text is aligned in both directions.

- CHAROFF sets the horizontal distance between the left or right margin and the first occurrence of the CHAR character.
- CLASS specifies a class identification for the column group.
- DIR specifies the direction in which the column group contents are displayed: left-to-right or right-to-left.
- | Netscape | HALIGN horizontally aligns the text within the cells in the column group.
- ID provides a unique identifier name for the column group.
- LANG provides the code representing the language used within the column group.
- ONCLICK specifies that the referred-to script runs when a user moves the mouse pointer or other pointing device over the column group and clicks the device button.
- ONDBLCLICK specifies that the referred-to script runs when a user moves the mouse pointer or other pointing device over the column group and double-clicks the device button.
- ONKEYDOWN specifies that the referred-to script runs when a user presses and holds a key down over the column group.
- ONKEYPRESS specifies that the referred-to script runs when a user presses and releases a key over the column group.
- ONKEYUP specifies that the referred-to script runs when a user releases a key over the column group.
- ONMOUSEDOWN specifies that the referred-to script runs when a user moves the mouse pointer or other pointing device over the column group and presses and holds down the device button.
- ONMOUSEMOVE specifies that the referred-to script runs when a user moves the mouse pointer or other pointing device over the column group.
- ONMOUSEOUT specifies that the referred-to script runs when a user moves the mouse pointer or other pointing device away from the column group.

- ONMOUSEOVER specifies that the referred-to script runs the first time a user moves the mouse pointer or other pointing device over the column group.
- ONMOUSEUP specifies that the referred-to script runs when a user moves the mouse pointer or other pointing device over the column group and releases a pressed-down device button.
- SPAN specifies the number of columns over which the COLGROUP attributes are set.
- STYLE sets styles for the column group.
- TITLE provides a title or title information about the column group.
- VALIGN indicates the vertical alignment of the column group, from the top to the bottom.
- WIDTH indicates the absolute width of the column group, in pixels or as a percentage of the full-screen width, or the relative width of the column group to other column groups in the current table.

## Notes

This is an HTML 4.0 element. Previously, it was a Microsoft extension.

The attributes set by the COL element override those set by the COLGROUP element.

You can embed the COLGROUP element within the TABLES elements.

## Example

```
<TABLE BORDER="3" WIDTH="300" BGCOLOR="white" BORDERCOL-
OR="teal"

BORDERCOLORLIGHT="yellow" BORDERCOLORDARK="maroon">

<COLGROUP ALIGN="left">

<COLGROUP SPAN="2 "ALIGN="right">

<THEAD>

<TR><TH></TH><TH>Income</TH><TH>Expenses</TH></TR>

</THEAD>
```

```
<TBODY>
<TR><TD><B>Quarter 1</B></TD><TD>800</TD><TD>784</TD></TR>
<TR><TD><B>Quarter
2</B></TD><TD>1000</TD><TD>1150</TD></TR>
<TR><TD><B>Quarter
3</B></TD><TD>1200</TD><TD>975</TD></TR>
<TR><TD><B>Quarter
4</B></TD><TD>1300</TD><TD>1230</TD></TR>
</TBODY>
</TABLE>
```

|  | Income | Expenses |
|---|---|---|
| **Quarter 1** | 800 | 784 |
| **Quarter 2** | 1000 | 1150 |
| **Quarter 3** | 1200 | 975 |
| **Quarter 4** | 1300 | 1230 |

*Figure 4.64 A* COLGROUP *example.*

You'll find additional table examples throughout this chapter.

## Related Element

COL

## TABLE | Table

## Purpose

Defines a table.

## Syntax

```
<TABLE[
ALIGN="left"|"center"|"right"|"bleedleft"|"bleedright"|"ju
stify"][ BACKGROUND="picture-url"][
BGCOLOR="#rrggbb"|"color"][ BORDER="border_pix"][ BORDER-
COLOR="#rrggbb"|"color"][
BORDERCOLORDARK="#rrggbb"|"color"][
BORDERCOLORLIGHT="#rrggbb"|"color"][
CELLPADDING="cell_pad"][ CELLSPACING="cell_space"][
CLASS="class_name"][CLEAR="left"|"right"|"all"|"no"][
COLS="num_cols"][ DATAPAGESIZE="num_records"][
DATASRC="ds_identifier"][ DIR="LTR"|"RTL"][
FRAME="void"|"above"|"below"|"hsides"|"vsides"|"lhs"|"rhs"
|"box"|"border"][ HEIGHT=height pix"|height%][
HSPACE="horiz_pix"][ ID="id_name"][ LANG="lang_code"][
LANGUAGE="JAVASCRIPT"|"JSCRIPT"|"VBS[CRIPT]"][ NOWRAP][
ONAFTERUPDATE="au_script_data"][
ONBEFOREUPDATE="bu_script_data"][
ONBLUR="bl_script_data"][ ONCLICK="cl_script_data"][ OND-
BLCLICK="dc_script_data"][ ONDRAGSTART="ds_script_data"][
ONFOCUS="fc_script_data"][ ONHELP="hlp_script_data"][
ONKEYDOWN="kd_script_data"][ ONKEYPRESS="kp_script_data"][
ONKEYUP="ku_script_data"][ ONMOUSEDOWN="md_script_data"][
ONMOUSEMOVE="mm_script_data"][
ONMOUSEOUT="mo_script_data"][
ONMOUSEOVER="mov_script_data"][
ONMOUSEUP="mu_script_data"][ ONRESIZE="rsz_script_data"][
ONROWENTER="re_script_data"][
ONROWEXIT="rex_script_data"][ ONSCROLL="sc_script_data"][
ONSELECTSTART="ss_script_data"][
RULES="none"|"groups"|"rows"|"cols"|"all"][ STYLE="name_1:
value_1"[; "name_2: value_2"][...; "name_n: value_n"] ][
TITLE="title"][VALIGN="middle"|"top"|"bottom"|"baseline"][
```

```
VSPACE="vert_pix"][ WIDTH="width_pix"|width_%]>table-con-
tents</TABLE>
```

## Where

- ALIGN indicates the horizontal alignment of the text within the table: with the left or right margins or centered between the left and right margins. BLEEDLEFT, BLEEDRIGHT, and JUSTIFY are Microsoft-defined values.

- **[Microsoft]** BACKGROUND specifies an image file that is displayed in the background of the table.

- BGCOLOR specifies the background color for the table.

- BORDER turns on a table border and sets the width, in pixels, of the table border.

- **[Microsoft]** BORDERCOLOR is the color of the table border.

- **[Microsoft]** BORDERCOLORDARK is the color of the table border shadow.

- **[Microsoft]** BORDERCOLORLIGHT is the color of the table border highlight.

- CELLPADDING sets spacing, in pixels or by percentage of the window width, between cell borders and the cell contents.

- CELLSPACING sets spacing, in pixels or by percentage of the window width, between the cells.

- CLASS specifies a class identification for the table.

- **[Microsoft]** CLEAR controls the alignment of text after the end of a table.

- COLS specifies the number of columns in the current table.

- **[Microsoft]** DATAPAGESIZE indicates the number of records included in a repeated table.

- **[Microsoft]** DATASRC specifies the identifier of the data source object.

- DIR specifies the direction in which the table contents are displayed: left-to-right or right-to-left.
- FRAME specifies the table borders that are displayed onscreen or are hidden.

 **The FRAME attribute refers to the border of the table and is not related to the FRAME element.**

NOTE

- HEIGHT specifies the height of the table, in pixels, or as a percentage of the entire height of the computer screen.

- HSPACE sets the vertical area, in pixels, in which the table will fit.

- ID provides a unique identifier name for the table.
- LANG provides the code representing the language used for the table contents.
- LANGUAGE declares the scripting language of the current script.

- NOWRAP disables word wrap within the current table.

- ONAFTERUPDATE specifies that the referred-to script runs after data has been transferred from the element to the data repository.

- ONBEFOREUPDATE specifies that the referred-to script runs before data is transferred from the element to the data repository.

- ONBLUR specifies that the referred-to script runs when the link loses focus (that is, it is no longer the active element).

- ONCLICK specifies that the referred-to script runs when a user moves the mouse pointer or other pointing device over the table and clicks the device button.

- ONDBLCLICK specifies that the referred-to script runs when a user moves the mouse pointer or other pointing device over the table and double-clicks the device button.

- **Microsoft** ONDRAGSTART specifies that the referred-to script runs when the user starts dragging a selection or element.

- **Microsoft** ONFOCUS specifies that the referred-to script runs when the current element receives focus (that is, is made active) by the mouse pointer or other pointing device.

- **Microsoft** ONHELP specifies that the referred-to script runs when a user presses the **F1** or **Help** key over the current element.

- ONKEYDOWN specifies that the referred-to script runs when a user presses and holds a key down over the table.

- ONKEYPRESS specifies that the referred-to script runs when a user presses and releases a key over the table.

- ONKEYUP specifies that the referred-to script runs when a user releases a key over the table.

- ONMOUSEDOWN specifies that the referred-to script runs when a user moves the mouse pointer or other pointing device over the table and presses and holds down the device button.

- ONMOUSEMOVE specifies that the referred-to script runs when a user moves the mouse pointer or other pointing device over the table.

- ONMOUSEOUT specifies that the referred-to script runs when a user moves the mouse pointer or other pointing device away from the table.

- ONMOUSEOVER specifies that the referred-to script runs the first time a user moves the mouse pointer or other pointing device over the table.

- ONMOUSEUP specifies that the referred-to script runs when a user moves the mouse pointer or other pointing device over the table and releases a pressed-down device button.

-  ONRESIZE specifies that the referred-to script runs when the user resizes the selected object.

-  ONROWENTER specifies that the referred-to script runs when the current row has been modified.

-  ONROWEXIT specifies that the referred-to script runs before the current row is modified.

-  ONSCROLL specifies that the referred-to script runs when a user moves the scroll box within the scroll bar.

-  ONSELECTSTART specifies that the referred-to script runs when a user starts selecting an object.

- RULES specifies the display of the inside table borders
- STYLE sets styles for the column group.
- TITLE provides a title or title information about the table.

-  VALIGN indicates the vertical alignment of the table, from the top to the bottom.

- VSPACE sets the vertical area, in pixels, in which the table will fit.

- WIDTH indicates the absolute width of the table, in pixels or as a percentage of the full-screen width.

- *table-contents* are the rows, columns, TH (table headings) elements, and TD (table data) elements within the table.

## Notes

This element originated in HTML 3.2.

The HTML DTD 4.0 categorizes this as a block-level element.

A table must contain at least one row.

A TFOOT element must precede a TBODY element within a table so that the browser can calculate the dimensions and contents of the footer.

The BGCOLOR value defined within the TABLE element is overridden by the BGCOLOR defined for table rows (TR), which in turn is overridden by the BGCOLOR defined for table headings (TH) and table data (TD).

BORDER=0 removes a border.

The BORDER attribute must be specified for the FRAME or RULES attribute to be used.

Using percentages for the HEIGHT and WIDTH can cause unexpected results. Of course, specifying actual heights and widths in pixels means that you must spend time measuring and calculating.

The RULES attribute is valid only if you use the TBODY, TFOOT, and THEAD elements.

You can embed the CAPTION, COL, COLGROUP, TBODY, TD, TFOOT, TH, THEAD, and TR elements within the TABLE start and end tags.

## Examples

Example 1 (Figure 4.65)

```
<TABLE>
<TR><TH>Word
Processing</TH><TH>Spreadsheets</TH><TH>Databases</TH></TR>
<TR><TD>125</TD><TD>8</TD><TD>6</TD></TR>
</TABLE>
```

**Word Processing Spreadsheets Databases**

125         8         6

*Figure 4.65 A table without borders.*

Example 2 (Figure 4.66)

```
<TABLE BORDER>
<TR><TH>Word
Processing</TH><TH>Spreadsheets</TH><TH>Databases</TH></TR>
<TR><TD>125</TD><TD>8</TD><TD>6</TD></TR>
</TABLE>
```

**252**

| Word Processing | Spreadsheets | Databases |
|---|---|---|
| 125 | 8 | 6 |

*Figure 4.66 A table with the default borders.*

## Example 3 (Figure 4.67)

```
<TABLE BORDER="8">
<TR><TH>Word
Processing</TH><TH>Spreadsheets</TH><TH>Databases</TH></TR>
<TR><TD>125</TD><TD>8</TD><TD>6</TD></TR>
</TABLE>
```

| Word Processing | Spreadsheets | Databases |
|---|---|---|
| 125 | 8 | 6 |

*Figure 4.67 A table with a three-dimensional eight-pixels border.*

## Example 4 (Figure 4.68)

```
<TABLE BORDER WIDTH="260" HEIGHT="120">
<TR><TH>Word
Processing</TH><TH>Spreadsheets</TH><TH>Databases</TH></TR>
<TR><TD>125</TD><TD>8</TD><TD>6</TD></TR>
</TABLE>
```

| Word Processing | Spreadsheets | Databases |
|---|---|---|
| 125 | 8 | 6 |

*Figure 4.68 A table showing a specified width and height.*

253

### Example 5 (Figure 4.69)

```
<TABLE BORDER CELLSPACING="8">
<TR><TH>Word
Processing</TH><TH>Spreadsheets</TH><TH>Databases</TH></TR>
<TR><TD>125</TD><TD>8</TD><TD>6</TD></TR>
</TABLE>
```

| Word Processing | Spreadsheets | Databases |
|-----------------|--------------|-----------|
| 125 | 8 | 6 |

*Figure 4.69 A table demonstrating the CELLSPACING attribute.*

### Example 6 (Figure 4.70)

```
<TABLE BORDER CELLPADDING="8">
<TR><TH>Word
Processing</TH><TH>Spreadsheets</TH><TH>Databases</TH></TR>
<TR><TD>125</TD><TD>8</TD><TD>6</TD></TR>
</TABLE>
```

| Word Processing | Spreadsheets | Databases |
|-----------------|--------------|-----------|
| 125 | 8 | 6 |

*Figure 4.70 The CELLPADDING attribute adds space within the cells.*

### Example 7 (Figure 4.71)

```
<TABLE BORDER="4" BGCOLOR="yellow">
<TR><TH>Word
Processing</TH><TH>Spreadsheets</TH><TH>Databases</TH></TR>
<TR><TD>125</TD><TD>8</TD><TD>6</TD></TR>
</TABLE>
```

| Word Processing | Spreadsheets | Databases |
|---|---|---|
| 125 | 8 | 6 |

*Figure 4.71 A yellow table with a slightly increased border.*

## Example 8 (Figure 4.72)

```
<BODY BGCOLOR="#ffffff">
<TABLE BORDER=0 HEIGHT="50">
<TR ALIGN="center">
<TD><A HREF="#a"><IMG SRC="a.gif"></TD>
<TD><A HREF="#b"><IMG SRC="b.gif"></TD>
<TD><A HREF="#c"><IMG SRC="c.gif"></TD>
<TD><A HREF="#d"><IMG SRC="d.gif"></TD>
</TR>
</TABLE>
<P>
<A NAME="a"><H2>A</H2>
Some text, graphics, and links
<A NAME="b"><H2>B</H2>
Some text, graphics, and links
<A NAME="c"><H2>C</H2>
Some text, graphics, and links
<A NAME="d"><H2>D</H2>
Some text, graphics, and links
```

**255**

A

Some text, graphics, and links

B

Some text, graphics, and links

C

Some text, graphics, and links

D

Some text, graphics, and links

*Figure 4.72 A borderless table with four embedded images and anchors.*

You'll find additional table examples throughout this chapter.

## TBODY | Table Body

### Purpose

Defines the body of a table and allows you to align the table body rows as a single unit.

### Syntax

```
[<TBODY[ ALIGN="left"|"center"|"right"|"justify"|"char][
BGCOLOR="#rrggbb"|"color"][ CHAR="character"][
CHAROFF="offset"][ CLASS="class_name"][ DIR="LTR"|"RTL"][
ID="id_name"][ LANG="lang_code"][
LANGUAGE="JAVASCRIPT"|"JSCRIPT"|"VBS[CRIPT]"][
ONCLICK="cl_script_data"][ ONDBLCLICK="dc_script_data"][
ONHELP="hlp_script_data"][ ONKEYDOWN="kd_script_data"][
ONKEYPRESS="kp_script_data"][ ONKEYUP="ku_script_data"][
ONMOUSEDOWN="md_script_data"][
ONMOUSEMOVE="mm_script_data"][
ONMOUSEOUT="mo_script_data"][
ONMOUSEOVER="mov_script_data"][
ONMOUSEUP="mu_script_data"][
ONSELECTSTART="ss_script_data"][ STYLE="name_1: value_1"[;
"name_2: value_2"][...; "name_n: value_n"] ][
TITLE="title"][ VALIGN="middle"|"top"|"bottom"|"base-
line"]>]table-body[</TBODY>]
```

### Where

- ALIGN indicates the horizontal alignment of the text within the table body: with the left or right margins, centered between the left and right margins, or aligned with a particular character.
- **Microsoft** BGCOLOR specifies the background color for the table body cells.
- CHAR names a character from which text is aligned in both directions.

257

- CHAROFF sets the horizontal distance between the left or right margin and the first occurrence of the CHAR character.
- CLASS specifies a class identification for the table body.
- DIR specifies the direction in which the table body contents are displayed: left-to-right or right-to-left.
- ID provides a unique identifier name for the table body.
- LANG provides the code representing the language used within the table body.
- **Microsoft** LANGUAGE declares the scripting language of the current script.
- ONCLICK specifies that the referred-to script runs when a user moves the mouse pointer or other pointing device over the table body and clicks the device button.
- ONDBLCLICK specifies that the referred-to script runs when a user moves the mouse pointer or other pointing device over the table body and double-clicks the device button.
- **Microsoft** ONHELP specifies that the referred-to script runs when a user presses the **F1** or **Help** key over the current element.
- ONKEYDOWN specifies that the referred-to script runs when a user presses and holds a key down over the table body.
- ONKEYPRESS specifies that the referred-to script runs when a user presses and releases a key over the table body.
- ONKEYUP specifies that the referred-to script runs when a user releases a key over the table body.
- ONMOUSEDOWN specifies that the referred-to script runs when a user moves the mouse pointer or other pointing device over the table body and presses and holds down the device button.
- ONMOUSEMOVE specifies that the referred-to script runs when a user moves the mouse pointer or other pointing device over the table body.

- ONMOUSEOUT specifies that the referred-to script runs when a user moves the mouse pointer or other pointing device away from the table body.
- ONMOUSEOVER specifies that the referred-to script runs the first time a user moves the mouse pointer or other pointing device over the table body.
- ONMOUSEUP specifies that the referred-to script runs when a user moves the mouse pointer or other pointing device over the table body and releases a pressed-down device button.
- **Microsoft** ONSELECTSTART specifies that the referred-to script runs when a user starts selecting an object.
- STYLE sets styles for the table body.
- TITLE provides a title or title information about the table body.
- VALIGN indicates the vertical alignment of the table body, from the top to the bottom.
- *table-body* indicates the rows that make up the body of a table.

## Notes

This is an HTML 4.0 element. Previously, it was a Microsoft extension.

A table can contain more than one table body.

A table group (that is, TBODY, TFOOT, or THEAD) must contain one or more rows.

A TFOOT element must precede a TBODY element within a table so that the browser can calculate the dimensions and contents of the foot.

When a table contains a body without THEAD or TFOOT sections, the TBODY start and end tags are optional.

## Examples

See the TFOOT element.

# Related Elements

TFOOT, THEAD

| TD | **Table Data** |
|---|---|

## Purpose

Defines the data in a table cell.

## Syntax

```
<TD[ ALIGN="left"|"center"|"right"|"justify"|"char][
AXES="row_ax_name","col_ax_name"][ AXIS="abbrev_name"][
BACKGROUND="picture_url"][ BGCOLOR="#rrggbb"|"color"][
BORDERCOLOR="#rrggbb"|"color"][ BORDERCOLORDARK="#rrgg-
bb"|"color"][ BORDERCOLORLIGHT="#rrggbb"|"color"][
CHAR="character"][ CHAROFF="offset"][ CLASS="class_name"][
COLSPAN="num_cols"|"1"|"0"][ DIR="LTR"|"RTL"][
ID="id_name"][ LANG="lang_code"][
LANGUAGE="JAVASCRIPT"|"JSCRIPT"|"VBS[CRIPT]"][ NOWRAP][
ONAFTERUPDATE="au_script_data"][
ONBEFOREUPDATE="bu_script_data"][
ONBLUR="bl_script_data"][ ONCLICK="cl_script_data"][ OND-
BLCLICK="dc_script_data"][ ONDRAGSTART="ds_script_data"][
ONFOCUS="fc_script_data"][ ONHELP="hlp_script_data"][
ONKEYDOWN="kd_script_data"][ ONKEYPRESS="kp_script_data"][
ONKEYUP="ku_script_data"][ ONMOUSEDOWN="md_script_data"][
ONMOUSEMOVE="mm_script_data"][
ONMOUSEOUT="mo_script_data"][
ONMOUSEOVER="mov_script_data"][
ONMOUSEUP="mu_script_data"][ ONRESIZE="rsz_script_data"][
ONROWENTER="re_script_data"][
ONROWEXIT="rex_script_data"][ ONSCROLL="sc_script_data"][
ONSELECTSTART="ss_script_data"][
ROWSPAN="num_rows"|"1"|"0"[ STYLE="name_1: value_1"[;
"name_2: value_2"][...; "name_n: value_n"]][
TITLE="title"][ VALIGN="middle"|"top"|"bottom"|"base-
line"][ WIDTH="width_pix"]>cell-contents[</TD>]
```

## Where

- ALIGN indicates the horizontal alignment of the text within the table cell: with the left or right margins, centered between the left and right margins, or aligned with a particular character.
- AXES is a list of one or more axis names, separated by commas, that specify the row and/or column headers of the current cell.
- AXIS specifies an abbreviated name for a cell in a table header.
- **[Microsoft]** BACKGROUND specifies an image file that is displayed in the background of the cell.
- BGCOLOR specifies the background color for the cell.
- **[Microsoft]** BORDERCOLOR is the color of the cell border.
- **[Microsoft]** BORDERCOLORDARK is the color of the cell border shadow.
- **[Microsoft]** BORDERCOLORLIGHT is the color of the cell border highlight.
- CHAR names a character from which text is aligned in both directions.
- CHAROFF sets the horizontal distance (offset) between the left or right margin and the first occurrence of the CHAR character.
- CLASS specifies a class identification for the cell.
- COLSPAN specifies the number of columns over which the current cell will extend.
- DIR specifies the direction in which the cell contents are displayed: left-to-right or right-to-left.
- ID provides a unique identifier name for the cell.
- LANG provides the code representing the language used within the cell.
- **[Microsoft]** LANGUAGE declares the scripting language of the current script.
- NOWRAP disables word wrap within the current cell.

-  ONAFTERUPDATE specifies that the referred-to script runs after data has been transferred from the element to the data repository.

-  ONBEFOREUPDATE specifies that the referred-to script runs before data is transferred from the element to the data repository.

-  ONBLUR specifies that the referred-to script runs when the link loses focus (that is, it is no longer the active element).

- ONCLICK specifies that the referred-to script runs when a user moves the mouse pointer or other pointing device over the cell and clicks the device button.

- ONDBLCLICK specifies that the referred-to script runs when a user moves the mouse pointer or other pointing device over the cell and double-clicks the device button.

-  ONDRAGSTART specifies that the referred-to script runs when the user starts dragging a selection or element.

-  ONFOCUS specifies that the referred-to script runs when the current element receives focus (that is, is made active) by the mouse pointer or other pointing device.

-  ONHELP specifies that the referred-to script runs when a user presses the **F1** or **Help** key over the current element.

- ONKEYDOWN specifies that the referred-to script runs when a user presses and holds a key down over the cell.

- ONKEYPRESS specifies that the referred-to script runs when a user presses and releases a key over the cell.

- ONKEYUP specifies that the referred-to script runs when a user releases a key over the cell.

- ONMOUSEDOWN specifies that the referred-to script runs when a user moves the mouse pointer or other pointing device over the cell and presses and holds down the device button.
- ONMOUSEMOVE specifies that the referred-to script runs when a user moves the mouse pointer or other pointing device over the cell.
- ONMOUSEOUT specifies that the referred-to script runs when a user moves the mouse pointer or other pointing device away from the cell.
- ONMOUSEOVER specifies that the referred-to script runs the first time a user moves the mouse pointer or other pointing device over the cell.
- ONMOUSEUP specifies that the referred-to script runs when a user moves the mouse pointer or other pointing device over the cell and releases a pressed-down device button.
- `Microsoft` ONRESIZE specifies that the referred-to script runs when the user resizes the selected object.
- `Microsoft` ONROWENTER specifies that the referred-to script runs when the current row has been modified.
- `Microsoft` ONROWEXIT specifies that the referred-to script runs before the current row is modified.
- `Microsoft` ONSCROLL specifies that the referred-to script runs when a user moves the scroll box within the scroll bar.
- `Microsoft` ONSELECTSTART specifies that the referred-to script runs when a user starts selecting an object.
- ROWSPAN specifies the number of rows down which the current cell will extend.
- STYLE sets styles for the cell.
- TITLE provides a title or title information about the cell.
- VALIGN indicates the vertical alignment of the cell contents, from the top to the bottom.
- `Microsoft` WIDTH specifies the width of the cell, in pixels.

- *cell-contents* are the data within the current cell.

## Notes

This element originated in HTML 3.2.

When you create long and complicated tables, consider indenting the TD and TH elements under the TR elements in the HTML document. This can help you to check for the accuracy of the elements and attributes that you select.

If a browser does not support ALIGN="justify", it may revert to ALIGN="left".

The BGCOLOR value defined within the TD element overrides the BGCOLOR defined for the row (TR) or the table (TABLE).

You can embed the TD element within the TR elements.

## Examples

Example 1 (Figure 4.73)

```
<TABLE BORDER WIDTH="120" HEIGHT="120">

<TR><TH>Word
Processing</TH><TH>Spreadsheets</TH><TH>Databases</TH></TR>

<TR><TD ALIGN="LEFT">125</TD>

<TD ALIGN="CENTER">8</TD>

<TD ALIGN="RIGHT">6</TD></TR>

</TABLE>
```

| Word Processing | Spreadsheets | Databases |
|---|---|---|
| 125 | 8 | 6 |

*Figure 4.73 A table illustrating three table data alignments.*

Example 2 (Figure 4.74)

```
<TABLE BORDER HEIGHT="180">
```

```
<TR><TH>Word
Processing</TH><TH>Spreadsheets</TH><TH>Databases</TH>
<TH>Presentations</TH></TR>
<TR><TD VALIGN="TOP">125</TD>
<TD VALIGN="MIDDLE">8</TD>
<TD VALIGN="BOTTOM">6</TD>
<TD VALIGN="BASELINE">12</TD></TR>
</TABLE>
```

| Word Processing | Spreadsheets | Databases | Presentations |
|---|---|---|---|
| 125 | 8 | 6 | 12 |

*Figure 4.74 Vertically aligned values in table data cells.*

## Example 3 (Figure 4.75)

```
<TABLE BORDER>
<TR>
    <TD BGCOLOR="#0000FF">#0000FF</TD>
    <TD BGCOLOR="#FFFFFF" COLSPAN="5">
    <TD BGCOLOR="#00FF00">#00FF00</TD>
</TR>
<TR>
    <TD BGCOLOR="#00868B">#00868B</TD>
    <TD BGCOLOR="#00C5CD">#00C5CD</TD>
    <TD BGCOLOR="#FFFFFF" COLSPAN="3"></TD>
    <TD BGCOLOR="#FFF68F">#FFF68F</TD>
    <TD BGCOLOR="#FFF8DC">#FFF8DC</TD>
</TR>
```

```
<TR>
    <TD BGCOLOR="#00757A">#004269</TD>
    <TD BGCOLOR="#00A3AB">#88A3AB</TD>
    <TD BGCOLOR="#FFDDDD">#FFDDDD</TD>
    <TD BGCOLOR="#FFFFFF"></TD>
    <TD BGCOLOR="#FFD46D">#FFD46D</TD>
    <TD BGCOLOR="#FFC46D">#FFC46D</TD>
    <TD BGCOLOR="#FFB46D">#FFB46D</TD>
</TR>
<TR>
    <TD BGCOLOR="#006460">#002047</TD>
    <TD BGCOLOR="#008190">#008190</TD>
    <TD BGCOLOR="#FFFFFF" COLSPAN="3"></TD>
    <TD BGCOLOR="#FFB24B">#FFB24B</TD>
    <TD BGCOLOR="#FFA24B">#FFA24B</TD>
</TR>
<TR>
    <TD BGCOLOR="#005359">#000825</TD>
    <TD BGCOLOR="#FFFFFF" COLSPAN="5">
    <TD BGCOLOR="#FF9029">#FF9029</TD>
</TR>
</TABLE>
```

*Figure 4.75 A multicolored table showing several COLSPAN attributes.*

## Example 4 (Figure 4.76)

```
<TABLE BGCOLOR="#FFFFFF" BORDER WIDTH=40%>
<TR>
    <TD BGCOLOR="#FF0000" ROWSPAN="2">1</TD>
    <TD>2</TD>
    <TD>3</TD>
    <TD>4</TD>
    <TD>5</TD>
    <TD>6</TD>
    <TD>7</TD>
    <TD>8</TD>
    <TD>9</TD>
    <TD>0</TD>
</TR>
<TR>
    <TD BGCOLOR="#FF0000" ROWSPAN="2">2</TD>
    <TD>3</TD>
    <TD>4</TD>
    <TD>5</TD>
    <TD>6</TD>
    <TD>7</TD>
    <TD>8</TD>
    <TD>9</TD>
    <TD>0</TD>
```

```
</TR>

<TR>

    <TD>1</TD>

    <TD BGCOLOR="#FF0000" ROWSPAN="2">3</TD>

    <TD>4</TD>

    <TD>5</TD>

    <TD>6</TD>

    <TD>7</TD>

    <TD>8</TD>

    <TD>9</TD>

    <TD>0</TD>

</TR>

<TR>

    <TD>1</TD>

    <TD>2</TD>

    <TD BGCOLOR="#FF0000" ROWSPAN="2">4</TD>

    <TD>5</TD>

    <TD>6</TD>

    <TD>7</TD>

    <TD>8</TD>

    <TD>9</TD>

    <TD>0</TD>

</TR>

<TR>

    <TD>1</TD>

    <TD>2</TD>

    <TD>3</TD>

    <TD>5</TD>

    <TD>6</TD>

    <TD>7</TD>

    <TD>8</TD>

    <TD>9</TD>
```

**269**

```
<TD>0</TD>
</TR>
</TABLE>
```

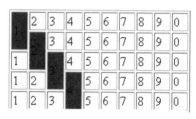

*Figure 4.76 A demonstration of the ROWSPAN attribute.*

You'll find additional table examples throughout this chapter.

## Related Element

TH

| TFOOT | Table Footer |
|-------|--------------|

## Purpose

Defines the footer rows at the bottom of a table and allows you to align the table footer rows as a single unit.

## Syntax

```
<TFOOT[ ALIGN="left"|"center"|"right"|"justify"|"char][
BGCOLOR="#rrggbb"|"color"][ CHAR="character"][
CHAROFF="offset"][ CLASS="class_name"][ DIR="LTR"|"RTL"][
ID="id_name"][ LANG="lang_code"][
LANGUAGE="JAVASCRIPT"|"JSCRIPT"|"VBS[CRIPT]"][
ONCLICK="cl_script_data"][ ONDBLCLICK="dc_script_data"][
ONHELP="hlp_script_data"][ ONKEYDOWN="kd_script_data"][
ONKEYPRESS="kp_script_data"][ ONKEYUP="ku_script_data"][
ONMOUSEDOWN="md_script_data"][
ONMOUSEMOVE="mm_script_data"][
ONMOUSEOUT="mo_script_data"][
ONMOUSEOVER="mov_script_data"][
ONMOUSEUP="mu_script_data"][
ONSELECTSTART="ss_script_data"][ STYLE="name_1: value_1"[;
"name_2: value_2"][...; "name_n: value_n"]]][
TITLE="title"][ VALIGN="middle"|"top"|"bottom"|"base-
line"]>table-footer-contents[</TFOOT>]
```

## Where

- ALIGN indicates the horizontal alignment of the text within the table footer: with the left or right margins, centered between the left and right margins, or aligned with a particular character.
- **Microsoft** BGCOLOR specifies the background color for the table footer cells.
- CHAR names a character from which text is aligned in both directions.

271

- CHAROFF sets the horizontal distance between the left or right margin and the first occurrence of the CHAR character.
- CLASS specifies a class identification for the table footer.
- DIR specifies the direction in which the table footer contents are displayed: left-to-right or right-to-left.
- ID provides a unique identifier name for the table footer.
- LANG provides the code representing the language used within the table footer.
- **Microsoft** LANGUAGE declares the scripting language of the current script.
- ONCLICK specifies that the referred-to script runs when a user moves the mouse pointer or other pointing device over the table footer and clicks the device button.
- ONDBLCLICK specifies that the referred-to script runs when a user moves the mouse pointer or other pointing device over the table footer and double-clicks the device button.
- **Microsoft** ONHELP specifies that the referred-to script runs when a user presses the **F1** or **Help** key over the current element.
- ONKEYDOWN specifies that the referred-to script runs when a user presses and holds a key down over the table footer.
- ONKEYPRESS specifies that the referred-to script runs when a user presses and releases a key over the table footer.
- ONKEYUP specifies that the referred-to script runs when a user releases a key over the table footer.
- ONMOUSEDOWN specifies that the referred-to script runs when a user moves the mouse pointer or other pointing device over the table footer and presses and holds down the device button.
- ONMOUSEMOVE specifies that the referred-to script runs when a user moves the mouse pointer or other pointing device over the table footer.

- ONMOUSEOUT specifies that the referred-to script runs when a user moves the mouse pointer or other pointing device away from the table footer.
- ONMOUSEOVER specifies that the referred-to script runs the first time a user moves the mouse pointer or other pointing device over the table footer.
- ONMOUSEUP specifies that the referred-to script runs when a user moves the mouse pointer or other pointing device over the table footer and releases a pressed-down device button.
- **Microsoft** ONSELECTSTART specifies that the referred-to script runs when a user starts selecting an object.
- STYLE sets styles for the table footer.
- TITLE provides a title or title information about the table footer.
- VALIGN indicates the vertical alignment of the table footer, from the top to the bottom.
- *table-footer* is the rows that make up the bottom of a table.

## Notes

This is an HTML 4.0 element. Previously, it was a Microsoft extension.

A table group (that is, TBODY, TFOOT, or THEAD) must contain one or more rows.

A TFOOT element must precede a TBODY element within a table so that the browser can calculate the dimensions and contents of the foot.

You are not required to use a TFOOT end tag if a TBODY or THEAD element follows a table footer.

## Example

```
<TABLE BORDER=1 BGCOLOR="white" WIDTH="550"

BORDERCOLORLIGHT="silver" BORDERCOLORDARK="teal">

<THEAD>

<TR><TH></TH><TH>Income</TH><TH>Expenses</TH></TR>
```

```
</THEAD>

<TBODY>

<COLGROUP ALIGN=left>

<COLGROUP SPAN=2 ALIGN=right>

<TR><TD><B>Quarter 1</B></TD><TD>800</TD><TD>784</TD></TR>

<TR><TD><B>Quarter
2</B></TD><TD>1000</TD><TD>1150</TD></TR>

<TR><TD><B>Quarter
3</B></TD><TD>1200</TD><TD>975</TD></TR>

<TR><TD><B>Quarter
4</B></TD><TD>1300</TD><TD>1230</TD></TR>

</TBODY>

<TFOOT>

<COL ALIGN=center>

<TR><TD></TD><TD><FONT SIZE=2><I>These are preliminary fig-
ures.</I></FONT></TD></TR>

</TFOOT>

</TABLE>
```

| | Income | Expenses |
|---|---|---|
| Quarter 1 | 800 | 784 |
| Quarter 2 | 1000 | 1150 |
| Quarter 3 | 1200 | 975 |
| Quarter 4 | 1300 | 1230 |
| | *These are preliminary figures.* | |

*Figure 4.77 A table with header, body, and footer rows.*

## Related Elements

TBODY, THEAD

## TH | Table Heading

## Purpose

Defines a heading in a table cell and shows it by applying emphasis, such as boldface.

## Syntax

```
<TH[ ALIGN="left"|"center"|"right"|"justify"|"char][
AXES="row_ax_name","col_ax_name"][ AXIS="abbrev_name"][
BACKGROUND="picture-url"][ BGCOLOR="#rrggbb"|"color"][
BORDERCOLOR="#rrggbb"|"color"][ BORDERCOLORDARK="#rrgg-
bb"|"color"][ BORDERCOLORLIGHT="#rrggbb"|"color"][
CHAR="character"][ CHAROFF="offset"][ CLASS="class_name"][
COLSPAN="num_cols"|"1"|"0"][ DIR="LTR"|"RTL"][
ID="id_name"][ LANG="lang_code"][
LANGUAGE="JAVASCRIPT"|"JSCRIPT"|"VBS[CRIPT]"][ NOWRAP][
ONCLICK="cl_script_data"][ ONDBLCLICK="dc_script_data"][
ONHELP="hlp_script_data"][ ONKEYDOWN="kd_script_data"][
ONKEYPRESS="kp_script_data"][ ONKEYUP="ku_script_data"][
ONMOUSEDOWN="md_script_data"][
ONMOUSEMOVE="mm_script_data"][
ONMOUSEOUT="mo_script_data"][
ONMOUSEOVER="mov_script_data"][
ONMOUSEUP="mu_script_data"][ ONSCROLL="sc_script_data"][
ONSELECTSTART="ss_script_data"][
ROWSPAN="num_rows"|"1"|"0"][ STYLE="name_1: value_1"[;
"name_2: value_2"][...; "name_n: value_n"]][
TITLE="title"][ VALIGN="middle"|"top"|"bottom"|"base-
line"][ WIDTH="width_pix"]>cell-contents[</TH>]
```

## Where

- ALIGN indicates the horizontal alignment of the text within the heading cell: with the left or right margins, centered between the left and right margins, or aligned with a particular character.

- AXES is a list of one or more axis names, separated by commas, that specify the row and/or column headers of the current cell.
- AXIS specifies an abbreviated name for a cell in a table header.
- **[Microsoft]** BACKGROUND specifies an image file that is displayed in the background of the cell.
- BGCOLOR specifies the background color for the cell.
- **[Microsoft]** BORDERCOLOR is the color of the cell border.
- **[Microsoft]** BORDERCOLORDARK is the color of the cell border shadow.
- **[Microsoft]** BORDERCOLORLIGHT is the color of the cell border highlight.
- CHAR names a character from which text is aligned in both directions.
- CHAROFF sets the horizontal distance between the left or right margin and the first occurrence of the CHAR character.
- CLASS specifies a class identification for the cell.
- COLSPAN specifies the number of columns over which the current cell will extend.
- DIR specifies the direction in which the cell contents are displayed: left-to-right or right-to-left.
- ID provides a unique identifier name for the cell.
- LANG provides the code representing the language used within the cell.
- **[Microsoft]** LANGUAGE declares the scripting language of the current script.
- NOWRAP disables word wrap within the current cell.
- ONCLICK specifies that the referred-to script runs when a user moves the mouse pointer or other pointing device over the cell and clicks the device button.
- ONDBLCLICK specifies that the referred-to script runs when a user moves the mouse pointer or other pointing device over the cell and double-clicks the device button.

-  ONHELP specifies that the referred-to script runs when a user presses the **F1** or **Help** key over the current element.
- ONKEYDOWN specifies that the referred-to script runs when a user presses and holds a key down over the cell.
- ONKEYPRESS specifies that the referred-to script runs when a user presses and releases a key over the cell.
- ONKEYUP specifies that the referred-to script runs when a user releases a key over the cell.
- ONMOUSEDOWN specifies that the referred-to script runs when a user moves the mouse pointer or other pointing device over the cell and presses and holds down the device button.
- ONMOUSEMOVE specifies that the referred-to script runs when a user moves the mouse pointer or other pointing device over the cell.
- ONMOUSEOUT specifies that the referred-to script runs when a user moves the mouse pointer or other pointing device away from the cell.
- ONMOUSEOVER specifies that the referred-to script runs the first time a user moves the mouse pointer or other pointing device over the cell.
- ONMOUSEUP specifies that the referred-to script runs when a user moves the mouse pointer or other pointing device over the cell and releases a pressed-down device button.
-  ONSCROLL specifies that the referred-to script runs when a user moves the scroll box within the scroll bar.
-  ONSELECTSTART specifies that the referred-to script runs when a user starts selecting an object.
- ROWSPAN specifies the number of rows down which the current cell will extend.
- STYLE sets styles for the cell.
- TITLE provides a title or title information about the cell.

- VALIGN indicates the vertical alignment of the cell contents, from the top to the bottom.
- **Microsoft** WIDTH specifies the width of the cell, in pixels.
- *cell-contents* are the data within the current cell.

## Notes

This element originated in HTML 3.2.

When you create long and complicated tables, consider indenting the TD and TH elements under the TR elements. This can help you to check for the accuracy of the elements and attributes that you select.

If a browser does not support ALIGN="justify", it may revert to ALIGN="left".

The BGCOLOR value defined within the TH element overrides the BGCOLOR defined for the row (TR) or the table (TABLE).

You can embed the TH element within the TR elements.

## Examples

Example 1 (Figure 4.78)

```
<TABLE BORDER>
<TR><TH COLSPAN=3>Files</TH></TR>
<TR><TH>Word
Processing</TH><TH>Spreadsheets</TH><TH>Databases</TH></TR>
<TR>
     <TD ALIGN="right">125</TD>
     <TD ALIGN="right">8</TD>
     <TD ALIGN="right">6</TD>
</TABLE>
```

| Files | | |
|---|---|---|
| Word Processing | Spreadsheets | Databases |
| 125 | 8 | 6 |

*Figure 4.78 A table title in a cell extending three cells in width.*

## Example 2 (Figure 4.79)

```
<TABLE BORDER>

<TR>

    <TH ROWSPAN=3>Files</TH>

    <TH ALIGN="left">Word Processing</TH>

    <TD ALIGN="right">125</TD>

</TR>

<TR>

    <TH ALIGN="left">Spreadsheets</TH>

    <TD ALIGN="right">8</TD>

</TR>

<TR>

    <TH ALIGN="left">Databases</TH>

    <TD ALIGN="right">6</TD>

</TR>

</TABLE>
```

| | Word Processing | 125 |
|---|---|---|
| Files | Spreadsheets | 8 |
| | Databases | 6 |

*Figure 4.79 A table title in a cell extending three rows.*

Example 3 (Figure 4.80)

```
<TABLE BGCOLOR="#FFFFFF" BORDER>
<TR>
    <TH BGCOLOR=#FE9B36">Word Processing</TH>
    <TH>Spreadsheets</TH>
    <TH>Databases</TH></TR>
<TR>
    <TD BGCOLOR="#FFFE8B" ALIGN="right">125</TD>
    <TD ALIGN="right">8</TD>
    <TD ALIGN="right">6</TD>
</TR>
</TABLE>
```

| Word Processing | Spreadsheets | Databases |
|---|---|---|
| 125 | 8 | 6 |

*Figure 4.80 The hierarchy of the BGCOLOR attribute for TABLE, TH, and TD elements.*

You'll find additional table examples throughout this chapter.

## Related Element

TD

| THEAD | Table Header |
|-------|--------------|

## Purpose

Defines the header rows at the top of a table and allows you to align the table header rows as a single unit.

## Syntax

```
<THEAD[ ALIGN="left"|"center"|"right"|"justify"|"char][
BGCOLOR="#rrggbb"|"color"][ CHAR="character"][
CHAROFF="offset"][ CLASS="class_name"][ DIR="LTR"|"RTL"][
ID="id_name"][ LANG="lang_code"][
LANGUAGE="JAVASCRIPT"|"JSCRIPT"|"VBS[CRIPT]"][
ONCLICK="cl_script_data"][ ONDBLCLICK="dc_script_data"][
ONHELP="hlp_script_data"][ ONKEYDOWN="kd_script_data"][
ONKEYPRESS="kp_script_data"][ ONKEYUP="ku_script_data"][
ONMOUSEDOWN="md_script_data"][
ONMOUSEMOVE="mm_script_data"][
ONMOUSEOUT="mo_script_data"][
ONMOUSEOVER="mov_script_data"][
ONMOUSEUP="mu_script_data"][
ONSELECTSTART="ss_script_data"][ STYLE="name_1: value_1"[;
"name_2: value_2"][...; "name_n: value_n"] ][
TITLE="title"][ VALIGN="middle"|"top"|"bottom"|"base-
line"]>table-header[</THEAD>]
```

## Where

- ALIGN indicates the horizontal alignment of the text within the table header: with the left or right margins, centered between the left and right margins, or aligned with a particular character.
- **Microsoft** BGCOLOR specifies the background color for the table header.
- CHAR names a character from which text is aligned in both directions.

281

- CHAROFF sets the horizontal distance between the left or right margin and the first occurrence of the CHAR character.
- CLASS specifies a class identification for the table header.
- DIR specifies the direction in which the table header contents are displayed: left-to-right or right-to-left.
- ID provides a unique identifier name for the table header.
- LANG provides the code representing the language used within the table header.
- **Microsoft** LANGUAGE declares the scripting language of the current script.
- ONCLICK specifies that the referred-to script runs when a user moves the mouse pointer or other pointing device over the table header and clicks the device button.
- ONDBLCLICK specifies that the referred-to script runs when a user moves the mouse pointer or other pointing device over the table header and double-clicks the device button.
- **Microsoft** ONHELP specifies that the referred-to script runs when a user presses the **F1** or **Help** key over the current element.
- ONKEYDOWN specifies that the referred-to script runs when a user presses and holds a key down over the table header.
- ONKEYPRESS specifies that the referred-to script runs when a user presses and releases a key over the table header.
- ONKEYUP specifies that the referred-to script runs when a user releases a key over the table header.
- ONMOUSEDOWN specifies that the referred-to script runs when a user moves the mouse pointer or other pointing device over the table header and presses and holds down the device button.
- ONMOUSEMOVE specifies that the referred-to script runs when a user moves the mouse pointer or other pointing device over the table header.

- ONMOUSEOUT specifies that the referred-to script runs when a user moves the mouse pointer or other pointing device away from the table header.
- ONMOUSEOVER specifies that the referred-to script runs the first time a user moves the mouse pointer or other pointing device over the table header.
- ONMOUSEUP specifies that the referred-to script runs when a user moves the mouse pointer or other pointing device over the table header and releases a pressed-down device button.
- **Microsoft** ONSELECTSTART specifies that the referred-to script runs when a user starts selecting an object.
- STYLE sets styles for the table header.
- TITLE provides a title or title information about the table header.
- VALIGN indicates the vertical alignment of the table header, from the top to the bottom.
- *table-header* is the rows that make up the top of a table.

## Notes

This is an HTML 4.0 element. Previously, it was a Microsoft extension.

A table group (that is, TBODY, TFOOT, or THEAD) must contain one or more rows.

When you include a header in a table, you must use the THEAD start tag.

If a TBODY or TFOOT element follows after a table header, you can omit the THEAD end tag.

## Examples

See the COLS, COLGROUP, and TFOOT elements.

## Related Elements

TBODY, TFOOT

| TR | **Table Row** |

## Purpose

Defines a table row.

## Syntax

```
<TR[ ALIGN="left"|"center"|"right"|"justify"|"char][
BGCOLOR="#rrggbb"|"color"][
BORDERCOLOR="#rrggbb"|"color"][ BORDERCOLORDARK="#rrgg-
bb"|"color"][ BORDERCOLORLIGHT="#rrggbb"|"color"][
CHAR="character"][ CHAROFF="offset"][ CLASS="class_name"][
DIR="LTR"|"RTL"][ ID="id_name"][ LANG="lang_code"][ LAN-
GUAGE="JAVASCRIPT"|"JSCRIPT"|"VBS[CRIPT]"][ NOWRAP][
ONAFTERUPDATE="au_script_data"][
ONBEFOREUPDATE="bu_script_data"][
ONBLUR="bl_script_data"][ ONCLICK="cl_script_data"][ OND-
BLCLICK="dc_script_data"][ ONDRAGSTART="ds_script_data"][
ONFOCUS="fc_script_data"][ ONHELP="hlp_script_data"][
ONKEYDOWN="kd_script_data"][ ONKEYPRESS="kp_script_data"][
ONKEYUP="ku_script_data"][ ONMOUSEDOWN="md_script_data"][
ONMOUSEMOVE="mm_script_data"][
ONMOUSEOUT="mo_script_data"][
ONMOUSEOVER="mov_script_data"][
ONMOUSEUP="mu_script_data"][ ONRESIZE="rsz_script_data"][
ONROWENTER="re_script_data"][
ONROWEXIT="rex_script_data"][
ONSELECTSTART="ss_script_data"][ STYLE="name_1: value_1"[;
"name_2: value_2"][...; "name_n: value_n"] ][
TITLE="title"][ VALIGN="middle"|"top"|"bottom"|"base-
line"]>row-contents[</TR>]
```

## Where

- ALIGN indicates the horizontal alignment of the text within the table row: with the left or right margins, centered between the left and right margins, or aligned with a particular character.

- BGCOLOR specifies the background color for the row.
- ▐Microsoft▌ BORDERCOLOR is the color of the border around all the cells in the row.
- ▐Microsoft▌ BORDERCOLORDARK is the color of the row border shadow.
- ▐Microsoft▌ BORDERCOLORLIGHT is the color of the row border highlight.
- CHAR names a character from which text is aligned in both directions.
- CHAROFF sets the horizontal distance between the left or right margin and the first occurrence of the CHAR character.
- CLASS specifies a class identification for the row.
- DIR specifies the direction in which the row contents are displayed: left-to-right or right-to-left.
- ID provides a unique identifier name for the row.
- LANG provides the code representing the language used within the row.
- ▐Microsoft▌ LANGUAGE declares the scripting language of the current script.
- ▐Microsoft▌ NOWRAP disables word wrap within the row.
- ▐Microsoft▌ ONAFTERUPDATE specifies that the referred-to script runs after data has been transferred from the element to the data repository.
- ▐Microsoft▌ ONBEFOREUPDATE specifies that the referred-to script runs before data is transferred from the element to the data repository.
- ▐Microsoft▌ ONBLUR specifies that the referred-to script runs when the link loses focus (that is, it is no longer the active element).
- ONCLICK specifies that the referred-to script runs when a user moves the mouse pointer or other pointing device over the row and clicks the device button.

- ONDBLCLICK specifies that the referred-to script runs when a user moves the mouse pointer or other pointing device over the row and double-clicks the device button.

- [Microsoft] ONDRAGSTART specifies that the referred-to script runs when the user starts dragging a selection or element.

- [Microsoft] ONFOCUS specifies that the referred-to script runs when the current element receives focus (that is, is made active) by the mouse pointer or other pointing device.

- [Microsoft] ONHELP specifies that the referred-to script runs when a user presses the F1 or Help key over the current element.

- ONKEYDOWN specifies that the referred-to script runs when a user presses and holds a key down over the row.

- ONKEYPRESS specifies that the referred-to script runs when a user presses and releases a key over the row.

- ONKEYUP specifies that the referred-to script runs when a user releases a key over the row.

- ONMOUSEDOWN specifies that the referred-to script runs when a user moves the mouse pointer or other pointing device over the row and presses and holds down the device button.

- ONMOUSEMOVE specifies that the referred-to script runs when a user moves the mouse pointer or other pointing device over the row.

- ONMOUSEOUT specifies that the referred-to script runs when a user moves the mouse pointer or other pointing device away from the row.

- ONMOUSEOVER specifies that the referred-to script runs the first time a user moves the mouse pointer or other pointing device over the row.

- ONMOUSEUP specifies that the referred-to script runs when a user moves the mouse pointer or other pointing device over the row and releases a pressed-down device button.

-  ONRESIZE specifies that the referred-to script runs when the user resizes the selected object.

-  ONROWENTER specifies that the referred-to script runs when the current row has been modified.

-  ONROWEXIT specifies that the referred-to script runs before the current row is modified.

-  ONSELECTSTART specifies that the referred-to script runs when a user starts selecting an object.

- STYLE sets styles for the row.
- TITLE provides a title or title information about the row.
- VALIGN indicates the vertical alignment of the row contents, from the top to the bottom.
- *row-contents* are contents, TH (table headings) elements, and TD (table data) elements of the current row.

## Notes

This element originated in HTML 3.2.

When you create long and complicated tables, consider indenting the TD and TH elements under the TR elements in the HTML document. This can help you to check for the accuracy of the elements and attributes that you select.

The BGCOLOR value defined within the TR element overrides the BGCOLOR defined for the table (TABLE) but is overridden by the BGCOLOR defined for table headings (TH) and table data (TD).

You can embed the TD and TH elements within the TR elements.

You can embed the TR element within the TABLE elements.

## Example

```
<TABLE BORDER="5">

<TR BGCOLOR="silver">
```

**287**

```
    <TH>Word Processing</TH>

    <TH>Spreadsheets</TH>

    <TH>Databases</TH>

</TR>

<TR>

    <TD ALIGN="right">125</TD>

    <TD ALIGN="right">8</TD>

    <TD ALIGN="right">6</TD>

</TR>

</TABLE>
```

| Word Processing | Spreadsheets | Databases |
|---|---|---|
| 125 | 8 | 6 |

*Figure 4.81 A table with its heading row highlighted.*

You'll find additional table examples throughout this chapter.

# Form Elements

These elements enable you to create forms for users to fill in and submit to an HTTP server.

 Appendix B, "Attributes in Depth," describes all attributes in the HTML 4.0 standard and for Netscape and Microsoft extensions. With each entry, you'll find valid values and usage notes.

NOTE

| **BUTTON** | **Push Button** |

## Purpose

Creates a script-operated button.

## Syntax

```
<BUTTON[ ACCESSKEY="shortcut_key"][ CLASS="class_name"][
DATAFLD="ds_col_name"][ DATAFORMATAS="HTML"|"TEXT"][
DATASRC="ds_identifier"][ DIR="LTR"|"RTL"][ ID="id_name"][
DISABLED][ LANG="lang_code"][
LANGUAGE="JAVASCRIPT"|"JSCRIPT"|"VBS[CRIPT]"][ NAME="but-
ton_name"][ ONAFTERUPDATE="au_script_data"][ ONBEFOREUP-
DATE="bu_script_data"][ ONBLUR="bl_script_data"][
ONCLICK="cl_script_data"][ ONDBLCLICK="dc_script_data"][
ONDRAGSTART="ds_script_data"][ ONFOCUS="fc_script_data"][
ONHELP="hlp_script_data"][ ONKEYDOWN="kd_script_data"][
ONKEYPRESS="kp_script_data"][ ONKEYUP="ku_script_data"][
ONMOUSEDOWN="md_script_data"][
ONMOUSEMOVE="mm_script_data"][
ONMOUSEOUT="mo_script_data"][
ONMOUSEOVER="mov_script_data"][
ONMOUSEUP="mu_script_data"][ ONRESIZE="rsz_script_data"][
ONROWENTER="re_script_data"][
ONROWEXIT="rex_script_data"][ ONSCROLL="sc_script_data"][
ONSELECTSTART="ss_script_data"][ STYLE="name_1: value_1"[;
name_2: value_2][...; name_n: value_n]]][ TABINDEX="posi-
tion_number"][ TITLE="title"][
TYPE="submit"|"button"|"reset""][
VALUE="button_value"]>input_data</BUTTON>
```

## Where

- ![Microsoft] ACCESSKEY assigns a shortcut key to the button in order to focus on it.
- CLASS specifies a class identification for the button.
- ![Microsoft] DATAFLD specifies the column name from the file that provides the data source object.

-  **DATAFORMATAS** indicates whether the data for this element is formatted as plain text (that is, unformatted ASCII) or HTML.

-  **DATASRC** specifies the identifier of the data source object.

- **DIR** specifies the direction in which the button text is displayed: left-to-right or right-to-left.

- **DISABLED** prevents a user from clicking on the button.

- **ID** provides a unique identifier name for the button.

- **LANG** provides the code representing the language used for the button text.

- **LANGUAGE** declares the scripting language of the current script.

- **NAME** names the button.

- **ONAFTERUPDATE** specifies that the referred-to script runs after data has been transferred from the element to the data repository.

- **ONBEFOREUPDATE** specifies that the referred-to script runs before data is transferred from the element to the data repository.

- **ONBLUR** specifies that the referred-to script runs when the button loses focus.

- **ONCLICK** specifies that the referred-to script runs when a user moves the mouse pointer or other pointing device over the button and clicks the device button.

- **ONDBLCLICK** specifies that the referred-to script runs when a user moves the mouse pointer or other pointing device over the button and double-clicks the device button.

- **ONDRAGSTART** specifies that the referred-to script runs when the user starts dragging a selection or element.

- **ONFOCUS** specifies that the referred-to script runs when the button receives focus by the mouse pointer or other pointing device.

-  ONHELP specifies that the referred-to script runs when a user presses the **F1** or **Help** key over the current element.

- ONKEYDOWN specifies that the referred-to script runs when a user presses and holds a key down over the button.

- ONKEYPRESS specifies that the referred-to script runs when a user presses and releases a key over the button.

- ONKEYUP specifies that the referred-to script runs when a user releases a key over the button.

- ONMOUSEDOWN specifies that the referred-to script runs when a user moves the mouse pointer or other pointing device over the button and presses and holds down the device button.

- ONMOUSEMOVE specifies that the referred-to script runs when a user moves the mouse pointer or other pointing device over the button.

- ONMOUSEOUT specifies that the referred-to script runs when a user moves the mouse pointer or other pointing device away from the button.

- ONMOUSEOVER specifies that the referred-to script runs the first time a user moves the mouse pointer or other pointing device over the button.

- ONMOUSEUP specifies that the referred-to script runs when a user moves the mouse pointer or other pointing device over the button and releases a pressed-down device button.

-  ONRESIZE specifies that the referred-to script runs when the user resizes the selected object.

-  ONROWENTER specifies that the referred-to script runs when the current row has been modified.

-  ONROWEXIT specifies that the referred-to script runs before the current row is modified.

292

-  ONSCROLL specifies that the referred-to script runs when a user moves the scroll box within the scroll bar.

-  ONSELECTSTART specifies that the referred-to script runs when a user starts selecting an object.

- STYLE sets styles for the button.
- TABINDEX defines the position of the button in all the elements that a user can navigate using a Tab or Shift+Tab key.
- TITLE provides a title or title information about the button.
- TYPE specifies the type of button.
- VALUE sets the initial value for a button.
- *input_data* is the data submitted when the button is clicked on.

## Notes

This is an HTML 4.0 element.

The HTML 4.0 DTD categorizes this as both a block-level element and inline element.

A browser should display the button as three-dimensional with a potential of appearing to be pressed down when clicked on.

Do not use an image map with an IMG embedded within a BUTTON element.

HTML automatically labels buttons created by BUTTON. Most browsers label buttons using the value of the VALUE attribute.

## Example

See INPUT.

## Related Elements

INPUT

| FIELDSET | Grouped Controls |
|----------|------------------|

## Purpose

Groups related input controls.

## Syntax

```
<FIELDSET[ CLASS="class_name"][ DIR="LTR"|"RTL"][
ID="id_name"][ LANG="lang_code"][
LANGUAGE="JAVASCRIPT"|"JSCRIPT"|"VBS[CRIPT]"][
ONCLICK="cl_script_data"][ ONDBLCLICK="dc_script_data"][
ONHELP="hlp_script_data"][ ONKEYDOWN="kd_script_data"][
ONKEYPRESS="kp_script_data"][ ONKEYUP="ku_script_data"][
ONMOUSEDOWN="md_script_data"][
ONMOUSEMOVE="mm_script_data"[
ONMOUSEOUT="mo_script_data"][
ONMOUSEOVER="mov_script_data"][
ONMOUSEUP="mu_script_data"][ STYLE="name_1: value_1"[;
name_2: value_2"][...; name_n: value_n"]][
TITLE="title"]>controls_group</FIELDSET>
```

## Where

- CLASS specifies a class identification for the controls group.
- DIR specifies the direction in which the controls text is displayed: left-to-right or right-to-left.
- ID provides a unique identifier name for the controls group.
- LANG provides the code representing the language used for the controls text.
- **Microsoft** LANGUAGE declares the scripting language of the current script.
- ONCLICK specifies that the referred-to script runs when a user moves the mouse pointer or other pointing device over the controls group and clicks the device button.

- ONDBLCLICK specifies that the referred-to script runs when a user moves the mouse pointer or other pointing device over the controls group and double-clicks the device button.

- **Microsoft** ONHELP specifies that the referred-to script runs when a user presses the **F1** or **Help** key over the current element.

- ONKEYDOWN specifies that the referred-to script runs when a user presses and holds a key down over the controls group.

- ONKEYPRESS specifies that the referred-to script runs when a user presses and releases a key over the controls group.

- ONKEYUP specifies that the referred-to script runs when a user releases a key over the controls group.

- ONMOUSEDOWN specifies that the referred-to script runs when a user moves the mouse pointer or other pointing device over the controls group and presses and holds down the device button.

- ONMOUSEMOVE specifies that the referred-to script runs when a user moves the mouse pointer or other pointing device over the controls group.

- ONMOUSEOUT specifies that the referred-to script runs when a user moves the mouse pointer or other pointing device away from the controls group.

- ONMOUSEOVER specifies that the referred-to script runs the first time a user moves the mouse pointer or other pointing device over the controls group.

- ONMOUSEUP specifies that the referred-to script runs when a user moves the mouse pointer or other pointing device over the controls group and releases a pressed-down device button.

- STYLE sets styles for the controls group.

- TITLE provides a title or title information about the controls group.

- *controls_group* represents a group of input controls.

## Notes

This is an HTML 4.0 element.

**295**

A FIELDSET is analogous to a division (DIV) or section (SPAN) of a document.

The HTML 4.0 DTD categorizes this as a block-level element.

Use the LEGEND element to add a caption to a FIELDSET.

## Example

See INPUT.

## Related Elements

LEGEND

| FORM | **Form** |
|------|----------|

## Purpose

Produces a fill-in form that will be processed by an HTTP server.

## Syntax

```
<FORM ACTION="submit_url"[ACCEPT-
CHARSET=["UNKNOWN"]|[["charset_1"][{ |,}"charset_2"][...{
|,}"charset_n"]]][ CLASS="class_name"][ DIR="LTR"|"RTL"][
ENCTYPE="Internet_Media_Type"][ ID="id_name"][
LANG="lang_code"][
LANGUAGE="JAVASCRIPT"|"JSCRIPT"|"VBS[CRIPT]"][
METHOD="GET"|"POST"][ NAME="form_name"][
ONCLICK="cl_script_data"][ ONDBLCLICK="dc_script_data"][
ONHELP="hlp_script_data"][ ONKEYDOWN="kd_script_data"][
ONKEYPRESS="kp_script_data"][ ONKEYUP="ku_script_data"][
ONMOUSEDOWN="md_script_data"][
ONMOUSEMOVE="mm_script_data"][
ONMOUSEOUT="mo_script_data"][
ONMOUSEOVER="mov_script_data"][
ONMOUSEUP="mu_script_data"][ ONRESET='rs_script_data"][
ONSELECTSTART="ss_script_data"][
ONSUBMIT="su_script_data"][ STYLE="name_1: value_1"[;
name_2: value_2][...; name_n: value_n"]]][ TARGET="win-
dow"|"_blank"|"_parent"|"_self"|"_top"][
TITLE="title"]>fill-in-form</FORM>
```

## Where

- ACTION sends the filled-in information to a cgi-bin program, or HTTP script.
- ACCEPT-CHARSET lists one or more charsets supported by the server processing the submitted forms.
- CLASS specifies a class identification for the form.
- DIR specifies the direction in which the form text is displayed: left-to-right or right-to-left.

**297**

- ENCTYPE specifies an Internet Media Type for encoding user responses to be submitted to the server.
- ID provides a unique identifier name for the form.
- LANG provides the code representing the language used for the form.
- **Microsoft** LANGUAGE declares the scripting language of the current script.
- METHOD specifies the HTTP method used to send the form to the server.
- **Netscape** NAME names the form.

- ONCLICK specifies that the referred-to script runs when a user moves the mouse pointer or other pointing device over the form and clicks the device button.
- ONDBLCLICK specifies that the referred-to script runs when a user moves the mouse pointer or other pointing device over the form and double-clicks the device button.
- **Microsoft** ONHELP specifies that the referred-to script runs when a user presses the F1 or Help key over the current element.
- ONKEYDOWN specifies that the referred-to script runs when a user presses and holds a key down over the form.
- ONKEYPRESS specifies that the referred-to script runs when a user presses and releases a key over the form.
- ONKEYUP specifies that the referred-to script runs when a user releases a key over the form.
- ONMOUSEDOWN specifies that the referred-to script runs when a user moves the mouse pointer or other pointing device over the form and presses and holds down the device button.
- ONMOUSEMOVE specifies that the referred-to script runs when a user moves the mouse pointer or other pointing device over the form.
- ONMOUSEOUT specifies that the referred-to script runs when a user moves the mouse pointer or other pointing device away from the form.

- ONMOUSEOVER specifies that the referred-to script runs the first time a user moves the mouse pointer or other pointing device over the form.

- ONMOUSEUP specifies that the referred-to script runs when a user moves the mouse pointer or other pointing device over the form and releases a pressed-down device button.

- ONRESET specifies that the referred-to script runs when a user clicks on the Reset button to clear the form.

-  ONSELECTSTART specifies that the referred-to script runs when a user starts selecting an object.

- ONSUBMIT specifies that the referred-to script runs when a user clicks on the Submit button to submit the current form.

- STYLE sets styles for the form.

- TARGET loads a linked and named document in a particular window or frame.

- TITLE provides a title or title information about the form.

- *fill-in-form* represents a form, which includes its INPUT, SELECT, and TEXTAREA elements, other embedded elements, text, and graphics.

**For more information about HTML, forms, GET, POST, and CGI programming, refer to Part 7, "Webliography."**

NOTE

## Notes

This element originated in HTML 2.0.

The FORM element contains all the form *controls* (that is, the parts of the form with which the user interacts).

The FORM element controls the form layout.

The HTML 4.0 DTD categorizes this as a block-level element.

When a user submits a form, it is sent to a user or to a form-processing program.

You cannot nest forms within forms.

The default ACTION attribute is the base address of the document.

## Example

```
<FORM ACTION="/cgi-bin/form-example" METHOD="post">
<INPUT TYPE="text" NAME="name-1" SIZE="60"><B><FONT
SIZE="-1">Line 1<BR>
<INPUT TYPE="text" NAME="name-2" SIZE="60">Line 2<BR>
<INPUT TYPE="text" NAME="name-3" SIZE="60">Line
3</FONT></B>
<P><INPUT TYPE="submit"><INPUT TYPE="reset">
</FORM>
```

*Figure 4.82  A simple three-line form.*

You'll find additional form examples under the INPUT, SELECT, and TEXTAREA elements.

## Related Elements

ISINDEX

| INPUT | Input Form Field |

## Purpose

Provides a way to accept various forms of input, using text boxes, check boxes, radio buttons, images, command buttons, or image maps.

## Syntax (Text Box)

```
<INPUT NAME="input_name"[
ACCEPT="MIME_type_1"[,MIME_type_2][...,MIME_type_n]][
ACCESSKEY="shortcut_key"][ ALIGN="top"|"middle"|"bot-
tom"|"left"|"right"][ ALT="alternate_name"][
CLASS="class_name"][ DIR="LTR"|"RTL"][ DISABLED][
ID="id_name"][ LANG="lang_code"][
LANGUAGE="JAVASCRIPT"|"JSCRIPT"|"VBS[CRIPT]"][
MAXLENGTH="maximum-length"][ NOTAB][
ONAFTERUPDATE="au_script_data"][
ONBEFOREUPDATE="bu_script_data"][
ONBLUR="bl_script_data"][ ONCHANGE="ch_script_data"][
ONCLICK="cl_script_data"][ ONDBLCLICK="dc_script_data"][
ONDRAGSTART="ds_script_data"][ ONFOCUS="fc_script_data"][
ONHELP="hlp_script_data"][ ONKEYDOWN="kd_script_data"][
ONKEYPRESS="kp_script_data"][ ONKEYUP="ku_script_data"][
ONMOUSEDOWN="md_script_data"][
ONMOUSEMOVE="mm_script_data"][
ONMOUSEOUT="mo_script_data"][
ONMOUSEOVER="mov_script_data"][
ONMOUSEUP="mu_script_data"][ ONSELECT="sl_script_data"][
ONSELECTSTART="ss_script_data"][ READONLY][
SIZE="input_control_size"][ STYLE="name_1: value_1"[;
name_2: value_2][...; name_n: value_n]]][ TABINDEX="posi-
tion_number"][ TITLE="title"][ TYPE="TEXT"][ VALUE="ini-
tial_value"]
```

## Syntax (Button)

```
<INPUT NAME="input_name"[
```

**301**

```
ACCEPT="MIME_type_1"[,MIME_type_2][...,MIME_type_n]][
ACCESSKEY="shortcut_key"][ ALIGN="top"|"middle"|"bot-
tom"|"left"|"right"][ ALT="alternate_name"][
CLASS="class_name"][ DIR="LTR"|"RTL"][ DISABLED][
ID="id_name"][ LANG="lang_code"][
LANGUAGE="JAVASCRIPT"|"JSCRIPT"|"VBS[CRIPT]"][ NOTAB][
ONAFTERUPDATE="au_script_data"][
ONBEFOREUPDATE="bu_script_data"][
ONBLUR="bl_script_data"][ ONCHANGE="ch_script_data"][
ONCLICK="cl_script_data"][ ONDBLCLICK="dc_script_data"][
ONDRAGSTART="ds_script_data"][ ONFOCUS="fc_script_data"][
ONHELP="hlp_script_data"][ ONKEYDOWN="kd_script_data"][
ONKEYPRESS="kp_script_data"][ ONKEYUP="ku_script_data"][
ONMOUSEDOWN="md_script_data"][
ONMOUSEMOVE="mm_script_data"][
ONMOUSEOUT="mo_script_data"][
ONMOUSEOVER="mov_script_data"][
ONMOUSEUP="mu_script_data"][ ONSELECT="sl_script_data"][
ONSELECTSTART="ss_script_data"][
SIZE="input_control_size"][ STYLE="name_1: value_1"[;
name_2: value_2"][...; name_n: value_n"]][ TABINDEX="posi-
tion_number"][ TITLE="title"][ TYPE="BUTTON"][ VALUE="ini-
tial_value"]
```

## Syntax (Check Box)

```
<INPUT NAME="input_name" VALUE="initial_value"[
ACCEPT="MIME_type_1"[,MIME_type_2][...,MIME_type_n]][
ACCESSKEY="shortcut_key"][ ALIGN="top"|"middle"|"bot-
tom"|"left"|"right"][ ALT="alternate_name"][ CHECKED][
CLASS="class_name"][ DIR="LTR"|"RTL"][ DISABLED][
ID="id_name"][ LANG="lang_code"][
LANGUAGE="JAVASCRIPT"|"JSCRIPT"|"VBS[CRIPT]"][ NOTAB][
ONAFTERUPDATE="au_script_data"][
ONBEFOREUPDATE="bu_script_data"][
ONBLUR="bl_script_data"][ ONCHANGE="ch_script_data"][
ONCLICK="cl_script_data"][ ONDBLCLICK="dc_script_data"][
ONDRAGSTART="ds_script_data"][ ONFOCUS="fc_script_data"][
ONHELP="hlp_script_data"][ ONKEYDOWN="kd_script_data"][
```

```
ONKEYPRESS="kp_script_data"][ ONKEYUP="ku_script_data"][
ONMOUSEDOWN="md_script_data"][
ONMOUSEMOVE="mm_script_data"][
ONMOUSEOUT="mo_script_data"][
ONMOUSEOVER="mov_script_data"][
ONMOUSEUP="mu_script_data"][ ONSELECT="sl_script_data"][
ONSELECTSTART="ss_script_data"][
SIZE="input_control_size"][ STYLE="name_1: value_1"[;
name_2: value_2"][...; name_n: value_n"]][ TABINDEX="posi-
tion_number"][ TITLE="title"][ TYPE="CHECKBOX"]
```

## Syntax (File)

```
<INPUT NAME="input_name"[
ACCEPT="MIME_type_1"[,MIME_type_2][...,MIME_type_n]][
ACCESSKEY="shortcut_key"][ ALIGN="top"|"middle"|"bot-
tom"|"left"|"right"][ ALT="alternate_name"][
CLASS="class_name"][ DIR="LTR"|"RTL"][ DISABLED][
ID="id_name"][ LANG="lang_code"][
LANGUAGE="JAVASCRIPT"|"JSCRIPT"|"VBS[CRIPT]"][ NOTAB][
ONAFTERUPDATE="au_script_data"][
ONBEFOREUPDATE="bu_script_data"][
ONBLUR="bl_script_data"][ ONCHANGE="ch_script_data"][
ONCLICK="cl_script_data"][ ONDBLCLICK="dc_script_data"][
ONDRAGSTART="ds_script_data"][ ONFOCUS="fc_script_data"][
ONHELP="hlp_script_data"][ ONKEYDOWN="kd_script_data"][
ONKEYPRESS="kp_script_data"][ ONKEYUP="ku_script_data"][
ONMOUSEDOWN="md_script_data"][
ONMOUSEMOVE="mm_script_data"][
ONMOUSEOUT="mo_script_data"][
ONMOUSEOVER="mov_script_data"][
ONMOUSEUP="mu_script_data"][ ONSELECT="sl_script_data"][
ONSELECTSTART="ss_script_data"][
SIZE="input_control_size"][ STYLE="name_1: value_1"[;
name_2: value_2"][...; name_n: value_n"]][ TABINDEX="posi-
tion_number"][ TITLE="title"][ TYPE="FILE"][ VALUE="ini-
tial_value"]
```

## Syntax (Hidden)

```
<INPUT NAME="input_name"[
ACCEPT="MIME_type_1"[,MIME_type_2][...,MIME_type_n]][
ALIGN="top"|"middle"|"bottom"|"left"|"right"][ ALT="alter-
nate_name"][ CLASS="class_name"][ DIR="LTR"|"RTL"][ DIS-
ABLED][ ID="id_name"][ LANG="lang_code"][
LANGUAGE="JAVASCRIPT"|"JSCRIPT"|"VBS[CRIPT]"][ NOTAB][
ONAFTERUPDATE="au_script_data"][
ONBEFOREUPDATE="bu_script_data"][
ONBLUR="bl_script_data"][ ONCHANGE="ch_script_data"][
ONCLICK="cl_script_data"][ ONDBLCLICK="dc_script_data"][
ONDRAGSTART="ds_script_data"][ ONFOCUS="fc_script_data"][
ONHELP="hlp_script_data"][ ONKEYDOWN="kd_script_data"][
ONKEYPRESS="kp_script_data"][ ONKEYUP="ku_script_data"][
ONMOUSEDOWN="md_script_data"][
ONMOUSEMOVE="mm_script_data"][
ONMOUSEOUT="mo_script_data"][
ONMOUSEOVER="mov_script_data"][
ONMOUSEUP="mu_script_data"][ ONSELECT="sl_script_data"][
ONSELECTSTART="ss_script_data"][
SIZE="input_control_size"][ STYLE="name_1: value_1"[;
name_2: value_2"][...; name_n: value_n"]][ TABINDEX="posi-
tion_number"][ TITLE="title"][ TYPE="HIDDEN"][ VALUE="ini-
tial_value"]
```

## Syntax (Image)

```
<INPUT NAME="input_name"[
ACCEPT="MIME_type_1"[,MIME_type_2][...,MIME_type_n]][
ALIGN="top"|"middle"|"bottom"|"left"|"right"|"absbot-
tom"|"absmiddle"|"baseline"|"texttop"][
ALT="alternate_name"][ CLASS="class_name"][
DIR="LTR"|"RTL"][ DISABLED][ ID="id_name"][
LANG="lang_code"][
LANGUAGE="JAVASCRIPT"|"JSCRIPT"|"VBS[CRIPT]"][ NOTAB][
ONAFTERUPDATE="au_script_data"][
ONBEFOREUPDATE="bu_script_data"][
ONBLUR="bl_script_data"][ ONCHANGE="ch_script_data"][
```

```
ONCLICK="cl_script_data"][ ONDBLCLICK="dc_script_data"][
ONDRAGSTART="ds_script_data"][ ONFOCUS="fc_script_data"][
ONHELP="hlp_script_data"][ ONKEYDOWN="kd_script_data"][
ONKEYPRESS="kp_script_data"][ ONKEYUP="ku_script_data"][
ONMOUSEDOWN="md_script_data"][
ONMOUSEMOVE="mm_script_data"][
ONMOUSEOUT="mo_script_data"][
ONMOUSEOVER="mov_script_data"][
ONMOUSEUP="mu_script_data"][ ONSELECT="sl_script_data"][
ONSELECTSTART="ss_script_data"][
SIZE="input_control_size"][ SRC="image_url"][
STYLE="name_1: value_1"[; name_2: value_2"][...; name_n:
value_n"]][ TABINDEX="position_number"][ TITLE="title"][
TYPE="IMAGE"][ USEMAP="map_url"][ VALUE="initial_value"]
```

## Syntax (Password)

```
<INPUT NAME="input_name"[
ACCEPT="MIME_type_1"[,MIME_type_2][...,MIME_type_n]][
ACCESSKEY="shortcut_key"][ ALIGN="top"|"middle"|"bot-
tom"|"left"|"right"][ ALT="alternate_name"][
CLASS="class_name"][ DIR="LTR"|"RTL"][ DISABLED][
ID="id_name"][ LANG="lang_code"][
LANGUAGE="JAVASCRIPT"|"JSCRIPT"|"VBS[CRIPT]"][
MAXLENGTH="maximum-length"][ NOTAB][
ONAFTERUPDATE="au_script_data"][
ONBEFOREUPDATE="bu_script_data"][
ONBLUR="bl_script_data"][ ONCHANGE="ch_script_data"][
ONCLICK="cl_script_data"][ ONDBLCLICK="dc_script_data"][
ONDRAGSTART="ds_script_data"][ ONFOCUS="fc_script_data"][
ONHELP="hlp_script_data"][ ONKEYDOWN="kd_script_data"][
ONKEYPRESS="kp_script_data"][ ONKEYUP="ku_script_data"][
ONMOUSEDOWN="md_script_data"][
ONMOUSEMOVE="mm_script_data"][
ONMOUSEOUT="mo_script_data"][
ONMOUSEOVER="mov_script_data"][
ONMOUSEUP="mu_script_data"][ ONSELECT="sl_script_data"][
ONSELECTSTART="ss_script_data"][ READONLY][
SIZE="input_control_size"][ STYLE="name_1: value_1"[;
```

**305**

```
name_2: value_2"][...; name_n: value_n"]][ TABINDEX="posi-
tion_number"][ TITLE="title"][ TYPE="PASSWORD"][
VALUE="initial_value"]
```

## Syntax (Radio Buttons)

```
<INPUT NAME="input_name" VALUE="initial_value"[
ACCEPT="MIME_type_1"[,MIME_type_2][...,MIME_type_n]][
ACCESSKEY="shortcut_key"][ ALIGN="top"|"middle"|"bot-
tom"|"left"|"right"][ ALT="alternate_name"][ CHECKED][
CLASS="class_name"][ DIR="LTR"|"RTL"][ DISABLED][
ID="id_name"][ LANG="lang_code"][
LANGUAGE="JAVASCRIPT"|"JSCRIPT"|"VBS[CRIPT]"][ NOTAB][
ONAFTERUPDATE="au_script_data"][
ONBEFOREUPDATE="bu_script_data"][
ONBLUR="bl_script_data"][ ONCHANGE="ch_script_data"][
ONCLICK="cl_script_data"][ ONDRAGSTART="ds_script_data"][
ONDBLCLICK="dc_script_data"][ ONFOCUS="fc_script_data"][
ONHELP="hlp_script_data"][ ONKEYDOWN="kd_script_data"][
ONKEYPRESS="kp_script_data"][ ONKEYUP="ku_script_data"][
ONMOUSEDOWN="md_script_data"][
ONMOUSEMOVE="mm_script_data"][
ONMOUSEOUT="mo_script_data"][
ONMOUSEOVER="mov_script_data"][
ONMOUSEUP="mu_script_data"][ ONSELECT="sl_script_data"][
ONSELECTSTART="ss_script_data"][
SIZE="input_control_size"][ STYLE="name_1: value_1"[;
name_2: value_2"][...; name_n: value_n"]][ TABINDEX="posi-
tion_number"][ TITLE="title"][ TYPE="RADIO"]
```

## Syntax (Reset Button)

```
<INPUT[
ACCEPT="MIME_type_1"[,MIME_type_2][...,MIME_type_n]][
ACCESSKEY="shortcut_key"][ ALIGN="top"|"middle"|"bot-
tom"|"left"|"right"][ ALT="alternate_name"][
CLASS="class_name"][ DIR="LTR"|"RTL"][ DISABLED][
ID="id_name"][ LANG="lang_code"][
LANGUAGE="JAVASCRIPT"|"JSCRIPT"|"VBS[CRIPT]"][
```

```
NAME="input_name"][ NOTAB][
ONAFTERUPDATE="au_script_data"][
ONBEFOREUPDATE="bu_script_data"][
ONBLUR="bl_script_data"][ ONCHANGE="ch_script_data"][
ONCLICK="cl_script_data"][ ONDBLCLICK="dc_script_data"][
ONDRAGSTART="ds_script_data"][ ONFOCUS="fc_script_data"][
ONHELP="hlp_script_data"][ ONKEYDOWN="kd_script_data"][
ONKEYPRESS="kp_script_data"][ ONKEYUP="ku_script_data"][
ONMOUSEDOWN="md_script_data"][
ONMOUSEMOVE="mm_script_data"][
ONMOUSEOUT="mo_script_data"][
ONMOUSEOVER="mov_script_data"][
ONMOUSEUP="mu_script_data"][ ONSELECT="sl_script_data"][
ONSELECTSTART="ss_script_data"][
SIZE="input_control_size"][ STYLE="name_1: value_1"[;
name_2: value_2][...; name_n: value_n]]][ TABINDEX="posi-
tion_number"][ TITLE="title"][ TYPE="RESET"][ VALUE="ini-
tial_value"]
```

## Syntax (Submit Button)

```
<INPUT[
ACCEPT="MIME_type_1"[,MIME_type_2][...,MIME_type_n]][
ACCESSKEY="shortcut_key"][ ALIGN="top"|"middle"|"bot-
tom"|"left"|"right"][ ALT="alternate_name"][
CLASS="class_name"][ DIR="LTR"|"RTL"][ DISABLED][
ID="id_name"][ LANG="lang_code"][
LANGUAGE="JAVASCRIPT"|"JSCRIPT"|"VBS[CRIPT]"]
NAME="input_name"][ NOTAB][
ONAFTERUPDATE="au_script_data"][
ONBEFOREUPDATE="bu_script_data"][
ONBLUR="bl_script_data"][ ONCHANGE="ch_script_data"][
ONCLICK="cl_script_data"][ ONDBLCLICK="dc_script_data"][
ONDRAGSTART="ds_script_data"][ ONFOCUS="fc_script_data"][
ONHELP="hlp_script_data"][ ONKEYDOWN="kd_script_data"][
ONKEYPRESS="kp_script_data"][ ONKEYUP="ku_script_data"][
ONMOUSEDOWN="md_script_data"][
ONMOUSEMOVE="mm_script_data"][
ONMOUSEOUT="mo_script_data"][
```

ONMOUSEOVER="*mov_script_data*"][

ONMOUSEUP="*mu_script_data*"][ ONSELECT="*sl_script_data*"][

ONSELECTSTART="*ss_script_data*"][

SIZE="*input_control_size*"][ STYLE="*name_1: value_1*"[;

*name_2: value_2*][...; *name_n: value_n*"]][ TABINDEX="*position_number*"][ TITLE="*title*"][ TYPE="SUBMIT"][ VALUE="*initial_value*"]

## Where

- ACCEPT is a list of one or more Internet Media Types that this part of the form and the form-processing server will accept.
- ┃Microsoft┃ ACCESSKEY assigns a shortcut key to the element in order to focus on it.
- ALIGN indicates the alignment of the input control.
- ALT describes an image for text-only browsers.
- CHECKED sets the initial value of a check box or radio button to on (that is, checked or filled in).
- CLASS specifies a class identification for the input control.
- DIR specifies the direction in which the input control text is displayed: left-to-right or right-to-left.
- DISABLED prevents user input in the input control.
- ID provides a unique identifier name for the input control.
- LANG provides the code representing the language used for the input control text.
- ┃Microsoft┃ LANGUAGE declares the scripting language of the current script.
- MAXLENGTH sets a maximum number of characters for a text box or password text box on the current form.
- NAME names the current input control.
- ┃Microsoft┃ NOTAB removes the input control from the tabbing order.
- ┃Microsoft┃ ONAFTERUPDATE specifies that the referred-to script runs after data has been

transferred from the element to the data repository.

-  ONBEFOREUPDATE specifies that the referred-to script runs before data is transferred from the element to the data repository.

- ONBLUR specifies that the referred-to script runs when the input control loses focus.

- ONCHANGE specifies that the referred-to script runs when a input control loses focus after it has gained focus and has had a value change.

- ONCLICK specifies that the referred-to script runs when a user moves the mouse pointer or other pointing device over the input control and clicks the device button.

- ONDBLCLICK specifies that the referred-to script runs when a user moves the mouse pointer or other pointing device over the input control and double-clicks the device button.

-  ONDRAGSTART specifies that the referred-to script runs when the user starts dragging a selection or element.

- ONFOCUS specifies that the referred-to script runs when the input control receives focus by the mouse pointer or other pointing device.

-  ONHELP specifies that the referred-to script runs when a user presses the **F1** or **Help** key over the current element.

- ONKEYDOWN specifies that the referred-to script runs when a user presses and holds a key down over the input control.

- ONKEYPRESS specifies that the referred-to script runs when a user presses and releases a key over the input control.

- ONKEYUP specifies that the referred-to script runs when a user releases a key over the input control.

- ONMOUSEDOWN specifies that the referred-to script runs when a user moves the mouse pointer or other

**309**

pointing device over the input control and presses and holds down the device button.

- ONMOUSEMOVE specifies that the referred-to script runs when a user moves the mouse pointer or other pointing device over the input control.

- ONMOUSEOUT specifies that the referred-to script runs when a user moves the mouse pointer or other pointing device away from the input control.

- ONMOUSEOVER specifies that the referred-to script runs the first time a user moves the mouse pointer or other pointing device over the input control.

- ONMOUSEUP specifies that the referred-to script runs when a user moves the mouse pointer or other pointing device over the input control and releases a pressed-down device button.

- ONSELECT specifies that the referred-to script runs when a user selects some text in the input control.

- **Microsoft** ONSELECTSTART specifies that the referred-to script runs when a user starts selecting an object.

- READONLY does not allow a user to change the current value of the input control.

- SIZE is the maximum size of the current text box or password text box.

- SRC specifies an image file that is displayed on a graphical Submit button (that is, TYPE="IMAGE").

- STYLE sets styles for the input control.

- TABINDEX defines the position of the input control in all the elements that a user can navigate using a Tab or Shift+Tab key.

- TITLE provides a title or title information about the input control.

- TYPE is the type of input control.

- In the future, USEMAP may specify a client-side image map that is displayed in a form. It is not currently supported.

- VALUE sets the initial value for the input control.

## Notes

This element originated in HTML 2.0.

The HTML 4.0 DTD categorizes this as an inline element.

HTML automatically labels buttons created by INPUT. Most browsers label input buttons using the value of the VALUE attribute.

When you click on an image, the browser acts as though you have clicked on a **SUBMIT** or **RESET** button.

## Examples

Example 1 (Figure 4.83)

```
<FORM ACTION="/cgi-bin/form-example" METHOD="post">

Type your name:<BR>

<INPUT TYPE="text" NAME="name" SIZE="40">

<P>Type your email address:<BR>

<INPUT TYPE="text" NAME="email" SIZE="30">

<P>Type your password:<BR>

<INPUT TYPE="password" NAME="pswd" SIZE="10"
MAXLENGTH="8">

<P><INPUT TYPE="submit"><INPUT TYPE="reset">

</FORM>
```

*Figure 4.83 A sample of a form with a filled-in password box.*

## Example 2 (Figure 4.84)

```
<FORM ACTION="/cgi-bin/form-example" METHOD="post">
<FIELDSET>
<LEGEND ALIGN="top"><B><FONT SIZE="+1">Name
Information</FONT></B></LEGEND>
First Name:<INPUT TYPE="text" NAME="name1"
SIZE="28">  
Last Name:<INPUT TYPE="text" NAME="name2"
SIZE="29"><BR></FIELDSET>
<P><FIELDSET>
<LEGEND ALIGN="top"><B><FONT SIZE="+1">Address
Information</FONT></B></LEGEND>
Address:<INPUT TYPE="text" NAME="address1" SIZE="72"><BR>
         &nbs
p;  
<INPUT TYPE="text" NAME="address2" SIZE="72"><BR>
City:
    
<INPUT TYPE="text" NAME="city" SIZE="40">
State:
<INPUT TYPE="text" NAME="state" SIZE="2">
Zip:<INPUT TYPE="text" NAME="zip" SIZE="9"><BR>
</FIELDSET>
<P>
<INPUT TYPE="submit">
<INPUT TYPE="reset">
</FORM>
```

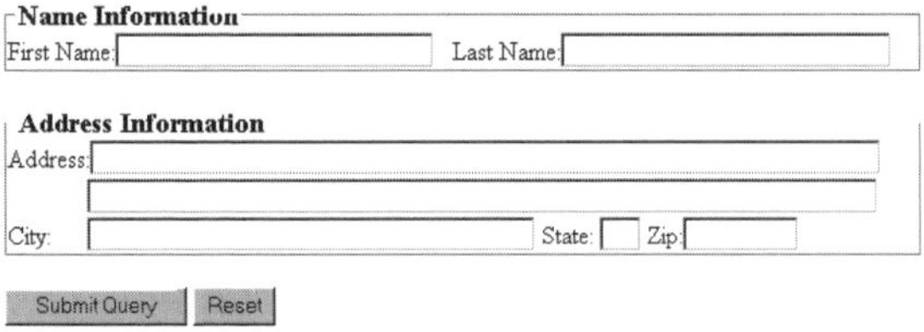

*Figure 4.84 A form with nonbreaking spaces between the command buttons.*

Example 3 (Figure 4.85)

```
<FORM ACTION="/cgi-bin/form-example" METHOD="post">
<FONT FACE="Courier New" SIZE="-1">
First Name:<INPUT TYPE="text" NAME="first" SIZE="28">
Last Name:<INPUT TYPE="text" NAME="last" SIZE="28"><BR>
Address:   <INPUT TYPE="text"
NAME="address1" SIZE="70"><BR>
         &nbs
p; <INPUT TYPE="text" NAME="address2" SIZE="70"><BR>
City:      <INPUT
TYPE="text" NAME="city" SIZE="42">
State:<INPUT TYPE="text" NAME="state" SIZE="2">Zip:</FONT>
<INPUT TYPE="text" NAME="zip" SIZE="9">
<P><INPUT TYPE="submit">   <INPUT
TYPE="reset">
</FORM>
```

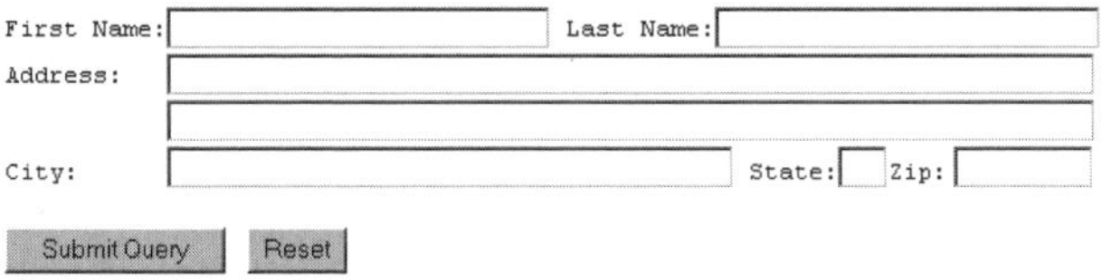

*Figure 4.85 A form using the monospace font Courier New for better alignment.*

**313**

## Example 4 (Figure 4.86)

```
<FORM ACTION="/cgi-bin/form-example" METHOD="post">
<INPUT TYPE="checkbox" NAME="chb01" CHECKED>WWW<BR>
<INPUT TYPE="checkbox" NAME="chb02" CHECKED>Gopher<BR>
<INPUT TYPE="checkbox" NAME="chb03">FTP<BR>
<INPUT TYPE="checkbox" NAME="chb04">Telnet
<P><INPUT TYPE="submit"><INPUT TYPE="reset">
</FORM>
```

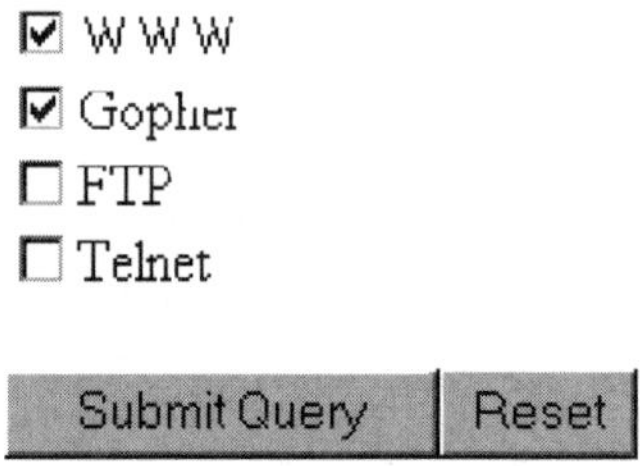

☑ WWW
☑ Gopher
☐ FTP
☐ Telnet

Submit Query    Reset

*Figure 4.86  A form with two checked and two cleared checkboxes.*

## Example 5 (Figure 4.87)

```
<FORM ACTION="/cgi-bin/form-example" METHOD="post">
<LABEL FOR="rbuttons" ID="rbuttons"><B><I>Choose a
path:</I></B></LABEL>
<P><INPUT TYPE="radio" NAME="radio1" CHECKED><B><FONT
FACE="Century Schoolbook" SIZE="-1">Nature Path<BR>
<INPUT TYPE="radio" NAME="radio2">Railroad Bed<BR>
<INPUT TYPE="radio" NAME="radio3">Lakeside Path<BR>
<INPUT TYPE="radio" NAME="radio4">Hillcrest
Path</FONT></B>
<P><INPUT TYPE="image" NAME="graphic" SRC="bike.gif"><BR>
<B><I>After selecting, click on<BR>
the &quot;bicycle&quot; button.</FONT></I></B>
<P><INPUT TYPE="reset">
</FORM>
```

*Choose a path:*

⊙ Nature Path
○ Railroad Bed
○ Lakeside Path
○ Hillcrest Path

*After selecting, click on
the "bicycle" button.*

[ Reset ]

*Figure 4.87  A form with radio buttons and a clickable submit graphic.*

## Example 6 (Figure 4.88)

```
<FORM ACTION="/cgi-bin/form-example" METHOD="post">
<B><FONT FACE="Century Schoolbook" SIZE="-1">
<INPUT TYPE="radio" NAME="radio1" CHECKED>Nature Path<BR>
<INPUT TYPE="radio" NAME="radio2">Railroad Bed<BR>
<INPUT TYPE="radio" NAME="radio3">Lakeside Path<BR>
<INPUT TYPE="radio" NAME="radio4">Hillcrest
Path</FONT></B>
<P><INPUT TYPE="submit" VALUE="Send Data">
<INPUT TYPE="reset" VALUE="Clear">
</FORM>
```

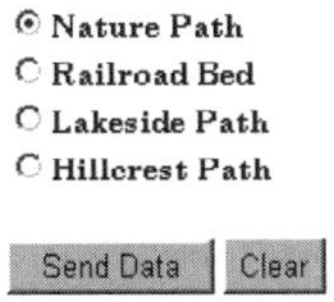

⊙ Nature Path
○ Railroad Bed
○ Lakeside Path
○ Hillcrest Path

[ Send Data ] [ Clear ]

*Figure 4.88  A form with radio buttons andnamed Subnit and Resubmit
buttons.*

## Example 7 (Figure 4.89)

```
<FORM ACTION="/cgi-bin/form-example" METHOD="post">
<P><INPUT TYPE="hidden" NAME="HIDE"
```

**315**

```
VALUE="eddygrp@sover.net">
<P><FONT FACE="Century Schoolbook" SIZE="-1">
The space above this line contains hidden<BR>information
that can be passed to a server.</FONT>
<P><INPUT TYPE="submit"><INPUT TYPE="reset">
</FORM>
```

The space above this line contains hidden
information that can be passed to a server

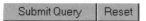

*Figure 4.89 A form that "illustrates" hidden items in a form.*

You'll find additional form examples under the FORM, SELECT, and TEXTAREA elements.

| ISINDEX | Searchable Index |
|---------|------------------|

## Purpose

States that this document is an index with a single text input field.

## Syntax

```
<ISINDEX[ ACTION="submit_url"][ CLASS="class_name"][
DIR="LTR"|"RTL"][ ID="id_name"][ LANG="lang_code"][
PROMPT="prompt-text"][ STYLE="name_1: value_1"[; name_2:
value_2"][...; name_n: value_n"]][ TITLE="title"]>
```

## Where

- ![Microsoft] ACTION sends the filled-in form to an HTTP or email URL.

- CLASS specifies a class identification for the index.

- DIR specifies the direction in which the index text is displayed: left-to-right or right-to-left.

- ID provides a unique identifier name for the index.

- LANG provides the code representing the language used for the index text.

- PROMPT issues a message prompting the user for a one-length response with an unlimited number of characters.

- STYLE sets styles for the index.

- TITLE provides a title or title information about the index.

## Notes

This element originated in HTML 2.0.

Place ISINDEX within the HEAD start and end tags.

The ISINDEX element creates elementary HTML forms.

The HTML 4.0 DTD categorizes this as a block-level element.

This element is deprecated. Because it will eventually be obsolete, it is best to use INPUT instead.

If you don't supply prompt-text, the default prompt is: "This is a searchable index. Enter search keywords:"

The user response to the prompt should be from the Latin-1 character set only.

## Related Element

FORM

| LABEL | Control Label |
|-------|---------------|

## Purpose

Includes information with an input control.

## Syntax

```
<LABEL[ ACCESSKEY="shortcut_key"][ CLASS="class_name"][
DATAFLD="ds_col_name"][ DATAFORMATAS="HTML"|"TEXT"][
DATASRC="ds_identifier"][ DIR="LTR"|"RTL"][ DISABLED][
FOR="id_name"][ ID="id_name"][ LANG="lang_code"][ LAN-
GUAGE="JAVASCRIPT"|"JSCRIPT"|"VBS[CRIPT]"][
ONBLUR="bl_script_data"][ ONCLICK="cl_script_data"][ OND-
BLCLICK="dc_script_data"][ ONFOCUS="fc_script_data"][
ONHELP="hlp_script_data"][ ONKEYDOWN="kd_script_data"][
ONKEYPRESS="kp_script_data"][ ONKEYUP="ku_script_data"][
ONMOUSEDOWN="md_script_data"][
ONMOUSEMOVE="mm_script_data"][
ONMOUSEOUT="mo_script_data"][
ONMOUSEOVER="mov_script_data"][
ONMOUSEUP="mu_script_data"][
ONSELECTSTART="ss_script_data"][ STYLE="name_1: value_1"[;
name_2: value_2"][...; name_n: value_n"]][
TITLE="title"]>label_text</LABEL>
```

## Where

- ACCESSKEY assigns a shortcut key to the label in order to focus on it.
- CLASS specifies a class identification for the label.
- **Microsoft** DATAFLD specifies the column name from the file that provides the data source object.
- **Microsoft** DATAFORMATAS indicates whether the data for this element is formatted as plain text (that is, unformatted ASCII) or HTML.
- **Microsoft** DATASRC specifies the identifier of the data source object.

**319**

- DIR specifies the direction in which the label text is displayed: left-to-right or right-to-left.
- DISABLED prevents user input associated with the label.
- FOR names the control with which the current label is associated.
- ID provides a unique identifier name for the label.
- LANG provides the code representing the language used for the label text.
- **Microsoft** LANGUAGE declares the scripting language of the current script.
- ONBLUR specifies that the referred-to script runs when the label loses focus.
- ONCLICK specifies that the referred-to script runs when a user moves the mouse pointer or other pointing device over the label and clicks the device button.
- ONDBLCLICK specifies that the referred-to script runs when a user moves the mouse pointer or other pointing device over the label and double-clicks the device button.
- ONFOCUS specifies that the referred-to script runs when the label receives focus by the mouse pointer or other pointing device.
- **Microsoft** ONHELP specifies that the referred-to script runs when a user presses the **F1** or **Help** key over the current element.
- ONKEYDOWN specifies that the referred-to script runs when a user presses and holds a key down over the label.
- ONKEYPRESS specifies that the referred-to script runs when a user presses and releases a key over the label.
- ONKEYUP specifies that the referred-to script runs when a user releases a key over the label.
- ONMOUSEDOWN specifies that the referred-to script runs when a user moves the mouse pointer or other pointing device over the label and presses and holds down the device button.

- ONMOUSEMOVE specifies that the referred-to script runs when a user moves the mouse pointer or other pointing device over the label.
- ONMOUSEOUT specifies that the referred-to script runs when a user moves the mouse pointer or other pointing device away from the label.
- ONMOUSEOVER specifies that the referred-to script runs the first time a user moves the mouse pointer or other pointing device over the label.
- ONMOUSEUP specifies that the referred-to script runs when a user moves the mouse pointer or other pointing device over the label and releases a pressed-down device button.
- **Microsoft** ONSELECTSTART specifies that the referred-to script runs when a user starts selecting an object.
- STYLE sets styles for the label.
- TITLE provides a title or title information about the label.
- *label_text* is the label information.

## Notes

This is an HTML 4.0 element.

The HTML 4.0 DTD categorizes this as an inline element.

When LABEL is made active, it causes the input control with which it is associated to become active.

## Example

See INPUT.

| **LEGEND** | **Fieldset Caption** |

## Purpose

Adds a caption to a group of controls (that is, FIELDSET).

## Syntax

```
<LEGEND[ ACCESSKEY="shortcut_key"][ ALIGN="top"|"bot-
tom"|"left"|"right"][ CLASS="class_name"][
DIR="LTR"|"RTL"][ ID="id_name"][ LANG="lang_code"][ LAN-
GUAGE="JAVASCRIPT"|"JSCRIPT"|"VBS[CRIPT]"][
ONCLICK="cl_script_data"][ ONDBLCLICK="dc_script_data"][
ONHELP="hlp_script_data"][ ONKEYDOWN="kd_script_data"][
ONKEYPRESS="kp_script_data"][ ONKEYUP="ku_script_data"][
ONMOUSEDOWN="md_script_data"][
ONMOUSEMOVE="mm_script_data"][
ONMOUSEOUT="mo_script_data"][
ONMOUSEOVER="mov_script_data"][
ONMOUSEUP="mu_script_data"][ STYLE="name_1: value_1"[;
name_2: value_2"][...; name_n: value_n"]][ TITLE="title"][
VALIGN="top"|"bottom"]>text</LEGEND>
```

## Where

- ACCESSKEY assigns a shortcut key to the fieldset caption in order to focus on it.
- ALIGN aligns the caption with the current fieldset.
- CLASS specifies a class identification for the fieldset caption.
- DIR specifies the direction in which the caption text is displayed: left-to-right or right-to-left.
- ID provides a unique identifier name for the fieldset caption.
- LANG provides the code representing the language used for the fieldset caption.
- Microsoft LANGUAGE declares the scripting language of the current script.

- ONCLICK specifies that the referred-to script runs when a user moves the mouse pointer or other pointing device over the caption and clicks the device button.

- ONDBLCLICK specifies that the referred-to script runs when a user moves the mouse pointer or other pointing device over the caption and double-clicks the device button.

- [Microsoft] ONHELP specifies that the referred-to script runs when a user presses the **F1** or **Help** key over the current element.

- ONKEYDOWN specifies that the referred-to script runs when a user presses and holds a key down over the caption.

- ONKEYPRESS specifies that the referred-to script runs when a user presses and releases a key over the caption.

- ONKEYUP specifies that the referred-to script runs when a user releases a key over the caption.

- ONMOUSEDOWN specifies that the referred-to script runs when a user moves the mouse pointer or other pointing device over the caption and presses and holds down the device button.

- ONMOUSEMOVE specifies that the referred-to script runs when a user moves the mouse pointer or other pointing device over the caption.

- ONMOUSEOUT specifies that the referred-to script runs when a user moves the mouse pointer or other pointing device away from the caption.

- ONMOUSEOVER specifies that the referred-to script runs the first time a user moves the mouse pointer or other pointing device over the caption.

- ONMOUSEUP specifies that the referred-to script runs when a user moves the mouse pointer or other pointing device over the caption and releases a pressed-down device button.

- STYLE sets styles for the caption.

- TITLE provides a title or title information about the caption.

- **Microsoft** VALIGN indicates the vertical alignment of the legend, above or below the table.

- *caption_text* represents one or more words.

## Notes

This is an HTML 4.0 element.

## Example

See INPUT.

## Related Element

FIELDSET

| OPTION | List Option |
|--------|-------------|

## Purpose

Inserts a single option in a list box or drop-down list.

## Syntax

```
<OPTION[ CLASS="class_name"][ DIR="LTR"|"RTL"][ DISABLED][
ID="id_name"][ LANG="lang_code"][
LANGUAGE="JAVASCRIPT"|"JSCRIPT"|"VBSCRIPT"][
ONCLICK="cl_script_data"][ ONDBLCLICK="dc_script_data"][
ONKEYDOWN="kd_script_data"][ ONKEYPRESS="kp_script_data"][
ONKEYUP="ku_script_data"][ ONMOUSEDOWN="md_script_data"][
ONMOUSEMOVE="mm_script_data"][
ONMOUSEOUT="mo_script_data"][
ONMOUSEOVER="mov_script_data"][
ONMOUSEUP="mu_script_data"][
ONSELECTSTART="ss_script_data"][ SELECTED][ STYLE="name_1:
value_1"[; name_2: value_2"][...; name_n: value_n"]][
TITLE="title"][ VALUE="submitted_value"]>text[</OPTION>]
```

## Where

- CLASS specifies a class identification for the option.
- DIR specifies the direction in which the option text is displayed: left-to-right or right-to-left.
- DISABLED prevents user input associated with the option.
- ID provides a unique identifier name for the option.
- LANG provides the code representing the language used for the option text.
- **Microsoft** LANGUAGE declares the scripting language of the current script.
- ONCLICK specifies that the referred-to script runs when a user moves the mouse pointer or other pointing device over the option and clicks the device button.

**325**

- ONDBLCLICK specifies that the referred-to script runs when a user moves the mouse pointer or other pointing device over the option and double-clicks the device button.
- ONKEYDOWN specifies that the referred-to script runs when a user presses and holds a key down over the option.
- ONKEYPRESS specifies that the referred-to script runs when a user presses and releases a key over the option.
- ONKEYUP specifies that the referred-to script runs when a user releases a key over the option.
- ONMOUSEDOWN specifies that the referred-to script runs when a user moves the mouse pointer or other pointing device over the option and presses and holds down the device button.
- ONMOUSEMOVE specifies that the referred-to script runs when a user moves the mouse pointer or other pointing device over the option.
- ONMOUSEOUT specifies that the referred-to script runs when a user moves the mouse pointer or other pointing device away from the option.
- ONMOUSEOVER specifies that the referred-to script runs the first time a user moves the mouse pointer or other pointing device over the option.
- ONMOUSEUP specifies that the referred-to script runs when a user moves the mouse pointer or other pointing device over the option and releases a pressed-down device button.
- Microsoft ONSELECTSTART specifies that the referred-to script runs when a user starts selecting an object.
- SELECTED indicates that this option is highlighted when the menu opens and is the default.
- STYLE sets styles for the option.
- TITLE provides a title or title information about the option.
- VALUE specifies the submitted value for this option.
- *text* represents one or more words.

## Notes

This element originated in HTML 2.0.

You can embed the OPTION tag within SELECT tags.

## Examples

You'll find examples of the OPTION tag under the SELECT tag and other form examples under the INPUT and TEXTAREA tags.

| SELECT | Selection List |
|--------|----------------|

## Purpose

Inserts a drop-down list or a list box in a form.

## Syntax

```
<SELECT NAME="element_name" [ ACCESSKEY="shortcut_key"] [
ALIGN="bottom" | "middle" | "top" | "left" | "right" | "absmid-
dle" | "absbottom" | "texttop" | "baseline" ] [
CLASS="class_name"] [ DATAFLD="ds_col_name"] [
DATASRC="ds_identifier"] [ DIR="LTR" | "RTL"] [ DISABLED] [
ID="id_name"] [ LANG="lang_code"] [
LANGUAGE="JAVASCRIPT" | "JSCRIPT" | "VBS[CRIPT]"] [ MULTIPLE] [
ONAFTERUPDATE="au_script_data"] [
ONBEFOREUPDATE="bu_script_data"] [
ONBLUR="bl_script_data"] [ ONCHANGE="ch_script_data"] [
ONCLICK="cl_script_data"] [ ONDBLCLICK="dc_script_data"] [
ONDRAGSTART="ds_script_data"] [ ONFOCUS="fc_script_data"] [
ONHELP="hlp_script_data"] [ ONKEYDOWN="kd_script_data"] [
ONKEYPRESS="kp_script_data"] [ ONKEYUP="ku_script_data"] [
ONMOUSEDOWN="md_script_data"] [
ONMOUSEMOVE="mm_script_data"] [
ONMOUSEOUT="mo_script_data"] [
ONMOUSEOVER="mov_script_data"] [
ONMOUSEUP="mu_script_data"] [ ONRESIZE="rsz_script_data"] [
ONROWENTER="re_script_data"] [
ONROWEXIT="rex_script_data"] [ ONSELECT="sl_script_data"] [
ONSELECTSTART="ss_script_data"] [ SIZE="no_of_rows"] [
STYLE="name_1: value_1" [; name_2: value_2"] [...; name_n:
value_n"]] [ TABINDEX="position_number"] [
TITLE="title"]>list-contents</SELECT>
```

## Where

- NAME names the current drop-down list or list box.
- **Microsoft** ACCESSKEY assigns a shortcut key to the element in order to focus on it.

-  ALIGN aligns the list box or drop-down list with the surrounding area of the HTML document.

- CLASS specifies a class identification for the selection list.

-  DATAFLD specifies the column name from the file that provides the data source object.

- DATASRC specifies the identifier of the data source object.

- DIR specifies the direction in which the selection list text is displayed: left-to-right or right-to-left.

- DISABLED prevents user input associated with the selection list.

- ID provides a unique identifier name for the selection list.

- LANG provides the code representing the language used for the selection list text.

- LANGUAGE declares the scripting language of the current script.

- MULTIPLE allows a user to select more than one item from a selection list.

- ONAFTERUPDATE specifies that the referred-to script runs after data has been transferred from the element to the data repository.

- ONBEFOREUPDATE specifies that the referred-to script runs before data is transferred from the element to the data repository.

- ONBLUR specifies that the referred-to script runs when the selection list loses focus.

- ONCHANGE specifies that the referred-to script runs when the selection list loses focus after it has gained focus and has had a value change.

- ONCLICK specifies that the referred-to script runs when a user moves the mouse pointer or other pointing device over the selection list and clicks the device button.

**329**

- ONDBLCLICK specifies that the referred-to script runs when a user moves the mouse pointer or other pointing device over the selection list and double-clicks the device button.

- **Microsoft** ONDRAGSTART specifies that the referred-to script runs when the user starts dragging a selection or element.

- ONFOCUS specifies that the referred-to script runs when the selection list receives focus by the mouse pointer or other pointing device.

- **Microsoft** ONHELP specifies that the referred-to script runs when a user presses the **F1** or **Help** key over the current element.

- ONKEYDOWN specifies that the referred-to script runs when a user presses and holds a key down over the selection list.

- ONKEYPRESS specifies that the referred-to script runs when a user presses and releases a key over the selection list.

- ONKEYUP specifies that the referred-to script runs when a user releases a key over the selection list.

- ONMOUSEDOWN specifies that the referred-to script runs when a user moves the mouse pointer or other pointing device over the selection list and presses and holds down the device button.

- ONMOUSEMOVE specifies that the referred-to script runs when a user moves the mouse pointer or other pointing device over the selection list.

- ONMOUSEOUT specifies that the referred-to script runs when a user moves the mouse pointer or other pointing device away from the selection list.

- ONMOUSEOVER specifies that the referred-to script runs the first time a user moves the mouse pointer or other pointing device over the selection list.

- ONMOUSEUP specifies that the referred-to script runs when a user moves the mouse pointer or other pointing device over the selection list and releases a pressed-down device button.

-  ONRESIZE specifies that the referred-to script runs when the user resizes the selected object.

-  ONROWENTER specifies that the referred-to script runs when the current row has been modified.

-  ONROWEXIT specifies that the referred-to script runs before the current row is modified.

- ONSELECT specifies that the referred-to script runs when a user selects some text in the selection list.

- ONSELECTSTART specifies that the referred-to script runs when a user starts selecting an object.

- SIZE specifies the maximum number of rows (that is, items) in the selection list.

- STYLE sets styles for the selection list.

- TABINDEX defines the position of the selection list in all the elements that a user can navigate using a Tab or Shift+Tab key.

- TITLE provides a title or title information about the selection list.

- *list-contents* is the items on the list, each preceded by an OPTION element.

## Notes

This element originated in HTML 2.0.

The HTML 4.0 DTD categorizes this as an inline element.

## Examples

Example 1 (Figures 4.90 and 4.91)

```
<FORM ACTION="/cgi-bin/form-example" METHOD="post">

<SELECT NAME="CHOICES">

<OPTION>Accounts Payable

<OPTION>Accounts Receivable

<OPTION>General Ledger

</SELECT>
```

```
<P><INPUT TYPE="submit"><INPUT TYPE="reset">
</FORM>
```

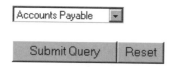

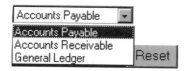

*Figure 4.90  A closed drop-down list box.*

*Figure 4.91  The same list box in an open state.*

Example 2 (Figure 4.92)

```
<FORM ACTION="/cgi-bin/form-example" METHOD="post">
<SELECT NAME="CHOICES" SIZE="3">
    <OPTION>red
    <OPTION SELECTED>orange
    <OPTION VALUE="something">yellow
    <OPTION>green
    <OPTION>blue
    <OPTION>indigo
    <OPTION>violet
</SELECT>
<P><INPUT TYPE="submit"><INPUT TYPE="reset">
</FORM>
```

Figure 4.92 *A list box with three of its seven attributes revealed.*

Example 3 (Figure 4.93)

```
<FORM ACTION="/cgi-bin/form-example" METHOD="post">
<SELECT NAME="CHOICES" SIZE="3" MULTIPLE>
<OPTION>red
<OPTION SELECTED>orange
<OPTION VALUE="something">yellow
</SELECT>
<P><INPUT TYPE="submit"><INPUT TYPE="reset">
</FORM>
```

Figure 4.93 *With all three list attributes displayed, there is no need for a scroll bar.*

You'll find additional form examples under the FORM, INPUT, and TEXTAREA elements.

## TEXTAREA | Multiline Text Input

## Purpose

Inserts a multiline area for text input.

## Syntax

```
<TEXTAREA COLS="number_of_columns" NAME="element_name"
ROWS="number_of_rows"[ ACCESSKEY="shortcut_key"][
ALIGN="bottom"|"middle"|"top"|"left"|"right"|"absmid-
dle"|"absbottom"|"texttop"|"baseline"][
CLASS="class_name"][ DATAFLD="ds_col_name"][
DATASRC="ds_identifier"][ DIR="LTR"|"RTL"][ DISABLED][
ID="id_name"][ LANG="lang_code"]][
LANGUAGE="JAVASCRIPT"|"JSCRIPT"|"VBS[CRIPT]"][ ONAFTERUP-
DATE="au_script_data"][ ONBEFOREUPDATE="bu_script_data"][
ONBLUR="bl_script_data"][ ONCHANGE="ch_script_data"][
ONCLICK="cl_script_data"][ ONDBLCLICK="dc_script_data"][
ONDRAGSTART="ds_script_data"][ ONFOCUS="fc_script_data"][
ONHELP="hlp_script_data"][ ONKEYDOWN="kd_script_data"][
ONKEYPRESS="kp_script_data"][ ONKEYUP="ku_script_data"][
ONMOUSEDOWN="md_script_data"][
ONMOUSEMOVE="mm_script_data"][
ONMOUSEOUT="mo_script_data"][
ONMOUSEOVER="mov_script_data"][
ONMOUSEUP="mu_script_data"][ONRESIZE="rsz_script_data"][
ONROWENTER="re_script_data"][
ONROWEXIT="rex_script_data"][ ONSCROLL="sc_script_data"][
ONSELECT="sl_script_data"][
ONSELECTSTART="ss_script_data"][
ONSTART="st_script_data"][ READONLY][ STYLE="name_1:
value_1"[; name_2: value_2"][...; name_n: value_n"]]][
TABINDEX="position_number"][ TITLE="title"][
WRAP="OFF"|"HARD"|"SOFT""PHYSICAL"|"VIRTUAL"]>text-
lines</TEXTAREA>
```

## Where

- COLS indicates the width of the text input area, by the number of columns, one per character.
- NAME specifies the name of this text input area.
- ROWS indicates the height of the text input area, the number of text lines, one row per line of text.
- **Microsoft** ACCESSKEY assigns a shortcut key to the element in order to focus on it.
- **Microsoft** ALIGN aligns the text area with the surrounding area of the HTML document.
- CLASS specifies a class identification for the input area.
- **Microsoft** DATAFLD specifies the column name from the file that provides the data source object.
- **Microsoft** DATASRC specifies the identifier of the data source object.
- DIR specifies the direction in which the input area text is displayed: left-to-right or right-to-left.
- DISABLED prevents user input in the text area.
- ID provides a unique identifier name for the input area.
- LANG provides the code representing the language used for the input area text.
- **Microsoft** LANGUAGE declares the scripting language of the current script.
- **Microsoft** ONAFTERUPDATE specifies that the referred-to script runs after data has been transferred from the element to the data repository.
- **Microsoft** ONBEFOREUPDATE specifies that the referred-to script runs before data is transferred from the element to the data repository.
- ONBLUR specifies that the referred-to script runs when the input area loses focus.
- ONCHANGE specifies that the referred-to script runs when a input area loses focus after it has gained focus and has had a value change.

335

- ONCLICK specifies that the referred-to script runs when a user moves the mouse pointer or other pointing device over the input area and clicks the device button.
- ONDBLCLICK specifies that the referred-to script runs when a user moves the mouse pointer or other pointing device over the input area and double-clicks the device button.
- **Microsoft** ONDRAGSTART specifies that the referred-to script runs when the user starts dragging a selection or element.
- ONFOCUS specifies that the referred-to script runs when the input area receives focus by the mouse pointer or other pointing device.
- **Microsoft** ONHELP specifies that the referred-to script runs when a user presses the **F1** or **Help** key over the current element.
- ONKEYDOWN specifies that the referred-to script runs when a user presses and holds a key down over the input area.
- ONKEYPRESS specifies that the referred-to script runs when a user presses and releases a key over the input area.
- ONKEYUP specifies that the referred-to script runs when a user releases a key over the input area.
- ONMOUSEDOWN specifies that the referred-to script runs when a user moves the mouse pointer or other pointing device over the input area and presses and holds down the device button.
- ONMOUSEMOVE specifies that the referred-to script runs when a user moves the mouse pointer or other pointing device over the input area.
- ONMOUSEOUT specifies that the referred-to script runs when a user moves the mouse pointer or other pointing device away from the input area.
- ONMOUSEOVER specifies that the referred-to script runs the first time a user moves the mouse pointer or other pointing device over the input area.
- ONMOUSEUP specifies that the referred-to script runs when a user moves the mouse pointer or other pointing

device over the input area and releases a pressed-down device button.

-  ONRESIZE specifies that the referred-to script runs when the user resizes the selected object.

-  ONROWENTER specifies that the referred-to script runs when the current row has been modified.

-  ONROWEXIT specifies that the referred-to script runs before the current row is modified.

-  ONSCROLL specifies that the referred-to script runs when a user moves the scroll box within the scroll bar.

- ONSELECT specifies that the referred-to script runs when a user selects some text in the input area.

-  ONSELECTSTART specifies that the referred-to script runs when a user starts selecting an object.

-  ONSTART specifies that the referred-to script runs when a loop begins.

- READONLY does not allow a user to change the current value of the input area.

- STYLE sets styles for the input area.

- TABINDEX defines the position of the input area in all the elements that a user can navigate using a Tab or Shift+Tab key.

- TITLE provides a title or title information about the input area.

-   WRAP indicates whether the text wraps when it reaches the right margin of the text box.

- *text-lines* is the default text in the text input area.

## Notes

This element originated in HTML 2.0.

The HTML 4.0 DTD categorizes this as an inline element.

In a text input area, you can type more characters that will be displayed at any time. You can use the vertical and horizontal scroll bars to scroll around the text in a text input area.

## Examples

Example 1 (Figure 4.94)

```
<FORM ACTION="/cgi-bin/form-example" METHOD="post">
<TEXTAREA NAME="TAREA1">This is initial text.
</TEXTAREA>
<P><INPUT TYPE="submit"><INPUT TYPE="reset">
</FORM>
```

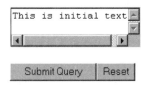

*Figure 4.94  A text input area with the default rows and columns.*

Example 2 (Figure 4.95)

```
<FORM ACTION="/cgi-bin/form-example" METHOD="post">
<TEXTAREA NAME="BIGTEXT" ROWS="8" COLS="50">
</TEXTAREA>
<P><INPUT TYPE="submit"><INPUT TYPE="reset">
</FORM>
```

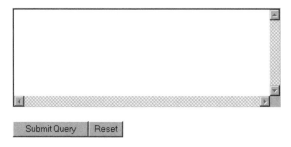

*Figure 4.95  A text input area containing an insertion point.*

You'll find additional form examples under the FORM, INPUT, and SELECT elements.

## Related Element

INPUT

# 5

# Frames Elements

These elements enable you to create and format frames in HTML documents.

**NOTE** Appendix B, "Attributes in Depth," describes all attributes in the HTML 4.0 standard and for Netscape and Microsoft extensions. With each entry, you'll find valid values and usage notes. In Part 1, "Overview," you will find more information about creating frames.

**FRAME** | **Frame**

## Purpose

Defines one pane within the computer desktop.

## Syntax

```
<FRAME[ ALIGN="left"|"center"|"right"|"top"|"bottom"][
BORDERCOLOR=#rrggbb"|"color] ][ CLASS="class_name"][
DATAFLD="ds_col_name"][ FRAMEBORDER="1"|"0"|"yes"|"no"][
HEIGHT="height_pix"|height_%][ ID="id_name"][
LANG="lang_code"][
LANGUAGE="JAVASCRIPT"|"JSCRIPT"|"VBS[CRIPT]"][ MARGIN-
HEIGHT="height_pix"][ MARGINWIDTH="width_pix"][
NAME="frame_name"|"_blank"|"_parent"|"_self"|"_top"][
NORESIZE[|RESIZE]][
ONREADYSTATECHANGE="rsc_script_data"][
SCROLLING="auto"|"yes"|"no"][ SRC="source_url"][
TITLE="title"][ WIDTH="width_pix"|width_%]>
```

## Where

-  ALIGN aligns the frame or the surrounding text.

-  BORDERCOLOR specifies the color for the borders of the current frame.

-  CLASS specifies a class identification for the element.

-  DATAFLD specifies the column name from the file that provides the data source object.

- FRAMEBORDER specifies whether the current frame will have a border.

-  HEIGHT specifies the height, in pixels or as a percentage of the entire height of the computer screen, of a frame.

-  ID provides a unique identifier name for the element.

- **Microsoft** LANG provides the code representing the language used for the element.

- **Microsoft** LANGUAGE declares the scripting language of the current script.

- MARGINHEIGHT is the space, in pixels, between the top and bottom margins of the frame and the contents of the frame.

- MARGINWIDTH is the space, in pixels, between the left and right margins of the frame and the contents of the frame.

- NAME specifies a name for the current frame. Microsoft supports the use of the _blank, _parent, _self, and _top reserved words.

- NORESIZE freezes the current frame at its current height and width.

- **Microsoft** ONREADYSTATECHANGE specifies that the referred-to script runs when an element is ready to be loaded.

- SCROLLING specifies whether the current frame contains scrollbars.

- SRC specifies the source file displayed within the current frame.

- **Microsoft** TITLE provides a title or title information about the element.

- **Microsoft** WIDTH specifies the width, in pixels or as a percentage of the entire height of the computer screen, of a frame.

## Notes

This HTML 4.0 element was formerly a Netscape extension and a Microsoft extension.

Embed the FRAME element within the FRAMESET elements.

A frame's contents cannot be within the same document as the frame's definition.

## Examples

Example 1 (Figure 4.96)

```
<!DOCTYPE HTML PUBLIC "-//W3C//DTD HTML 4.0//EN">
<HTML>
<HEAD>
    <TITLE>Chapter 5 Example</TITLE>
    <META NAME="GENERATOR" CONTENT="Mozilla/3.0b6Gold
(Win95; I) [Netscape]">
</HEAD>
<FRAMESET COLS=30%,20%,50%>
<FRAME SRC="FRAME1.HTM">
<FRAME SRC="FRAME2.HTM">
<FRAME SRC="FRAME3.HTM">
</FRAMESET>
</HTML>
```

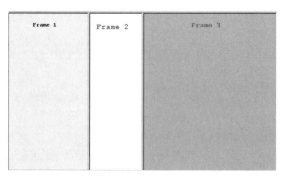

*Figure 4.96 Three frames, arranged in three columns.*

## Example 2 (Figure 4.97)

```
<!DOCTYPE HTML PUBLIC "-//W3C//DTD HTML 4.0//EN">
<HTML>
<HEAD>
    <TITLE>Chapter 5 Example</TITLE>
    <META NAME="GENERATOR" CONTENT="Mozilla/3.0b6Gold
(Win95; I) [Netscape]">
</HEAD>
```

```
<FRAMESET ROWS=40%,30%,30%>
<FRAME SRC="FRAME1.HTM">
<FRAME SRC="FRAME2.HTM">
<FRAME SRC="FRAME3.HTM">
</FRAMESET>
</HTML>
```

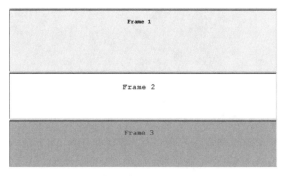

*Figure 4.97 Three frames arranged in rows.*

## Example 3 (Figure 4.98)

```
<!DOCTYPE HTML PUBLIC "-//W3C//DTD HTML 4.0//EN">
<HTML>
<HEAD>
    <TITLE>Chapter 5 Example</TITLE>
    <META NAME="GENERATOR" CONTENT="Mozilla/3.0b6Gold
(Win95; I) [Netscape]">
</HEAD>
<FRAMESET COLS=20%,*>
<FRAME SRC="FRAME1.HTM">
<FRAMESET ROWS=40%,*>
<FRAME SRC="FRAME2.HTM">
<FRAME SRC="FRAME3.HTM">
</FRAMESET>
</FRAMESET>
```

</HTML>

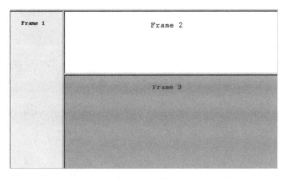

*Figure 4.98 One column and two rows of frames.*

## Example 4 (Figure 4.99)

```
<!DOCTYPE HTML PUBLIC "-//W3C//DTD HTML 4.0//EN">
<HTML>
<HEAD>
    <TITLE>Chapter 5 Example</TITLE>
    <META NAME="GENERATOR" CONTENT="Mozilla/3.0b6Gold
(Win95; I) [Netscape]">
</HEAD>
<FRAMESET COLS=20%,60%,*>
<FRAME SRC="FRAME1.HTM">
<FRAMESET ROWS=40%,*>
<FRAME SRC="FRAME2.HTM">
<FRAME SRC="FRAME3.HTM">
</FRAMESET><FRAMESET COLS=100%>
<FRAME SRC="FRAME4.HTM">
</FRAMESET>
</FRAMESET>
</HTML>
```

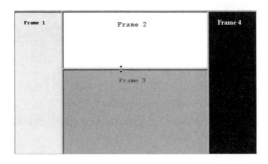

*Figure 4.99 Four frames and a sizing mouse pointer.*

## Example 5 (Figure 4.100)

```
<!DOCTYPE HTML PUBLIC "-//W3C//DTD HTML 4.0//EN">
<HTML>
<HEAD>
    <TITLE>Chapter 5 Example</TITLE>
    <META NAME="GENERATOR" CONTENT="Mozilla/3.0b6Gold
(Win95; I) [Netscape]">
</HEAD>
<FRAMESET ROWS=40%,60%>
<FRAME SRC="FRAME1.HTM" NORESIZE>
<FRAME SRC="FRAME2.HTM">
</FRAMESET>
</HTML>
```

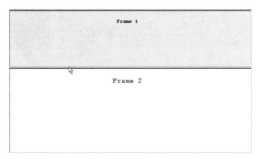

*Figure 4.100 The arrow mouse pointer showing no resizing possible.*

## Example 6 (Figure 4.101)

```
<!DOCTYPE HTML PUBLIC "-//W3C//DTD HTML 4.0//EN">
<HTML>
<HEAD>
    <TITLE>Chapter 5 Example</TITLE>
    <META NAME="GENERATOR" CONTENT="Mozilla/3.0b6Gold
(Win95; I) [Netscape]">
</HEAD>
<FRAMESET COLS=20%,60%,*>
<FRAME SRC="FRAME1.HTM">
<FRAMESET ROWS=40%,*>
<FRAME SRC="FRAME2.HTM">
<FRAME SRC="FRAME3.HTM" SCROLLING="yes">
</FRAMESET><FRAMESET COLS=100%>
<FRAME SRC="FRAME4.HTM">
</FRAMESET>
</FRAMESET>
</HTML>
```

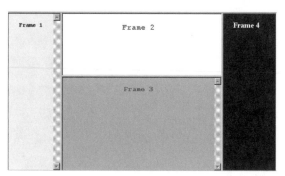

*Figure 4.101 Scroll bars in the first and third frame.*

## Example 7 (Figure 4.102)

This and the next three examples make a nonframes home page and a frameset comprised of a table of contents (in the leftmost "nonresizable" frame) and a main frame, which holds various parts of an online book. At the bottom of the table of contents and each document, you can click on the home image (or HOME text) to move back to the home page and end the frames.

```
<!DOCTYPE HTML PUBLIC "-//W3C//DTD HTML 4.0//EN">

<HTML>

<HEAD>

    <TITLE>The Eddy Group, Inc.</TITLE>

    <META NAME="keywords" CONTENT="HTML, HTML reference,
publishing, computer books, internet books">

</HEAD>

<BODY BGCOLOR="white" VLINK="blue" LINK="blue">

<FONT FACE="Letter Gothic" SIZE="3">

<CENTER>Welcome to The Eddy Group, Inc., home page.</CEN-
TER>

</FONT>

<P><FONT FACE="Letter Gothic" SIZE="1">

Sandra E. Eddy, co-founder of The Eddy Group, has written
several computer and Internet books, including reference
and tutorial books about computer applications, Windows,
and the Internet.

</FONT>

<P><FONT FACE="Letter Gothic" SIZE="2">

Some of the resources at our site—

<A HREF="fr_on1.htm" TARGET="_self">

<H5 ALIGN="center"><I>HTML in Plain English</I> - Online
Edition</H5></A>

<A HREF="fr_on2.htm" TARGET="_self">

<H5 ALIGN="center">Attributes in Depth - Reference
Pages</H5></A>

<A HREF="fr_on3.htm" TARGET="_self">

<H5 ALIGN="center"><I>The GIF Animator's Guide</I> -
Online Edition</H5></A>

<A HREF="fr_on4.htm" TARGET="_self">
```

```
<H5 ALIGN="center">GIF Animation and Downloads
Page</H5></A>

</FONT>

<FONT FACE="Letter Gothic" SIZE="2">

<P>To learn more about our company, visit our <A
HREF=about.htm>corporate information</A> page.

</FONT>

<FONT FACE="Letter Gothic" SIZE="1">

<P>Copyright &copy;1998 by The Eddy Group, Inc.

<BR><A
HREF="mailto:eddygrp@sover.net">eddygrp@sover.net</A>

</FONT>

</BODY>

</HTML>
```

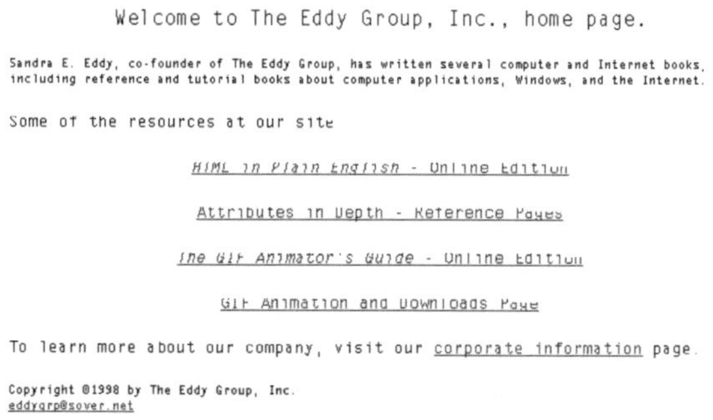

Welcome to The Eddy Group, Inc., home page.

Sandra E. Eddy, co-founder of The Eddy Group, has written several computer and Internet books,
including reference and tutorial books about computer applications, Windows, and the Internet.

Some of the resources at our site

HTML in Plain English - Online Edition

Attributes in Depth - Reference Pages

The GIF Animator's Guide - Online Edition

GIF Animation and Downloads Page

To learn more about our company, visit our corporate information page.

Copyright ©1998 by The Eddy Group, Inc.
eddygrp@sover.net

*Figure 4.102 A nonframes home page from which you can link to frames pages.*

Example 8 (Figure 4.103)

This example shows the frames page with two frames. On the left side is the table of contents, TOC.HTM, which never changes. On the right side is the introduction or the file linked to an entry in the table of contents.

The following HTML document produces and names the two frames. Other pages can then use the TARGET attribute to target the appropriate name to fill the frame whenever a user wants to view a new document.

```
<!DOCTYPE HTML PUBLIC "-//W3C//DTD HTML 4.0//EN">

<HTML>

<HEAD>

<TITLE>HTML in Plain English - Online Edition</TITLE>

<META NAME="GENERATOR" CONTENT="Mozilla/3.0b6Gold (Win95;
I) [Netscape]">

</HEAD>

<FRAMESET COLS=30%,70%>

<FRAME SRC="TOC.HTM" FRAMEBORDER="0" NORESIZE NAME="toc">

<FRAME SRC="INTRO.HTM" FRAMEBORDER="0" NAME="main">

</FRAMESET>

</HTML>
```

The following HTML document is the table of contents. Notice that each part (INTRO.HTM through APPC.HTM) of the book is targeted to the frame named MAIN. So, a user can click on a part of the book to display it in the rightmost frame. At the bottom of the table-of-contents document is a HOME image that, when clicked on, jumps to the top ("_TOP") page at the site, the home page. This action closes the frames.

```
<!DOCTYPE HTML PUBLIC "-//W3C//DTD HTML 4.0//EN">

<HTML>

<HEAD>

    <TITLE>Sample Document</TITLE>

    <META NAME="GENERATOR" CONTENT="Mozilla/3.0b6Gold
(Win95; I) [Netscape]">

</HEAD>

<BODY BGCOLOR="aqua">

<H2>Contents</H2>

<FONT FACE="book antigua" SIZE="2">

<A HREF="intro.htm" TARGET="main">Introduction
```

```
<BR><A HREF="pt01.htm" TARGET="main">1: Overview

<BR><A HREF="pt02.htm" TARGET="main">2: HTML in Plain
English

<BR><A HREF="pt03.htm" TARGET="main">3: HTML Elements A to
Z

<BR><A HREF="pt04.htm" TARGET="main">4: HTML Elements by
Group

<BR><A HREF="pt05.htm" TARGET="main">5: Cascading Style
Sheets

<BR><A HREF="pt06.htm" TARGET="main">6: Glossary

<BR><A HREF="pt07.htm" TARGET="main">7: Webliography

<BR><A HREF="appa.htm" TARGET="main">A: Elements by HTML
Version

<BR><A HREF="appb.htm" TARGET="main">B: Attributes in
Depth

<BR><A HREF="appc.htm" TARGET="main">C: HTML Editors

</FONT>

<P><A HREF="home.htm" TARGET="_top"><IMG
SRC="crazhome.gif">

<BR>HOME (no frames)

</BODY>

</HTML>
```

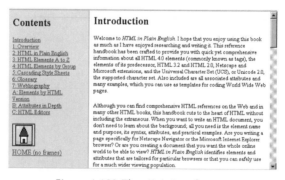

*Figure 4.103 The site's two frames.*

Example 9 (Figure 4.104)

You can add a third frame to the document to hold the title. Create a short new title document to hold a <H2> heading:

```
<!DOCTYPE HTML PUBLIC "-//W3C//DTD HTML 4.0//EN">

<HTML>

<HEAD>

<TITLE>HTML in Plain English - Online Edition</TITLE>

<META NAME="GENERATOR" CONTENT="Mozilla/3.0b6Gold (Win95;
I) [Netscape]">

</HEAD>

<BODY BGCOLOR="aqua">

<H2><I>HTML in Plain English - Online Edition</I></H2>

</BODY>

</HTML>
```

Then, change the frames document, making sure that a user cannot resize the new frame and that the only adjustable frame has a border.

```
<!DOCTYPE HTML PUBLIC "-//W3C//DTD HTML 4.0//EN">

<HTML>

<HEAD>

<TITLE>HTML in Plain English - Online Edition</TITLE>

<META NAME="GENERATOR" CONTENT="Mozilla/3.0b6Gold (Win95;
I) [Netscape]">

</HEAD>

<FRAMESET COLS=30%,70%>

<FRAME SRC="TOC.HTM" FRAMEBORDER="0" NORESIZE NAME="toc"
SCROLLING="no">

<FRAMESET ROWS=17%,*>

<FRAME SRC="TITLE.HTM" FRAMEBORDER="0" NORESIZE
SCROLLING="no">

<FRAME SRC="INTRO.HTM" FRAMEBORDER="1" NAME="main">

</FRAMESET>

</HTML>
```

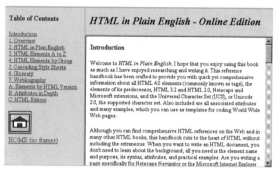

*Figure 4.104 A third frame holds the title.*

# Related Element

FRAMESET

| FRAMESET | Frame Set |
|----------|-----------|

## Purpose

Defines a set of frames making up the current document.

## Syntax

```
<FRAMESET[ BORDER="border_pix"][
BORDERCOLOR="#rrggbb"|"color"][ CLASS="class_name"][
COLS="col_value_1[, col_value_2[..., col_value_n]]"][
FRAMEBORDER="yes"|"no"|"1"|"0"][
FRAMESPACING="frame_space"][ ID="id_name"][
LANG="lang_code"][
LANGUAGE="JAVASCRIPT"|"JSCRIPT"|"VBS[CRIPT]"][
ONBLUR="bl_script_data"][ ONFOCUS="fc_script_data"][
ONLOAD="ol_script_data"][ ONUNLOAD="un_script_data"][
ROWS="row_value_1[, row_value_2[..., row_value_n]]"] [
TITLE="title"]>frames</FRAMESET>
```

## Where

- **Netscape** BORDER turns on a border and sets the width of the frameset.

- **Netscape** BORDERCOLOR specifies the color for the borders of the current frameset.

- **Microsoft** CLASS specifies a class identification for the element.

- COLS is a left-to-right measurement of the frameset.

- **Netscape** **Microsoft** FRAMEBORDER specifies whether frames in the frameset will have borders.

- **Microsoft** FRAMESPACING sets spacing, in pixels, between all the frames in a frameset.

- **Microsoft** ID provides a unique identifier name for the element.

**355**

-  LANG provides the code representing the language used for the element.

-  LANGUAGE declares the scripting language of the current script.

-  ONBLUR specifies that the referred-to script runs when the frameset loses focus.

-  ONFOCUS specifies that the referred-to script runs when the frameset receives focus by the mouse pointer or other pointing device.

- ONLOAD specifies that the referred-to script runs after the active browser has finished loading the frameset.

- ONUNLOAD specifies that the referred-to script runs after the active browser has removed a document from the frameset.

- ROWS is a top-to-bottom measurement of the frameset.

-  TITLE provides a title or title information about the element.

- *frames* are the frames within the frame set.

## Notes

This HTML 4.0 element was formerly a Netscape extension and a Microsoft extension.

In a document with frames, FRAMESET elements must precede BODY elements and elements that are usually embedded within a BODY. Improper placement of a BODY causes the FRAMESET to be disregarded.

Once you have defined a FRAMEBORDER, it is applied to other frames until you set new values for their borders.

A BODY following a FRAMESET is equivalent to a NOFRAMES section.

If you specify an absolute value for the ROWS and/or COLS in a frame set, you run the risk of setting widths and heights that are too large or small. It is best to use a combination of percentages and * values.

If you specify a percentage value for the ROWS and/or COLS in a frame set and the total is not 100%, the editor will scale the ROWS and/or COLS to reach 100%.

Once you have defined a FRAMEBORDER or FRAME-SPACING, its value is applied to other frames until you set a new value for their borders or spacing.

You can embed the following elements within the FRAMESET elements: FRAME, FRAMESET, and NOFRAMES.

## Examples

See the FRAME element.

## Related Elements

FRAME, NOFRAMES

| IFRAME | Inline Frame |
|--------|--------------|

## Purpose

Defines a floating frame within an HTML document.

## Syntax

```
<IFRAME[ ALIGN="left"|"center"|"right"|"top"|"bottom"
|"absbottom"|"absmiddle"|"baseline"|"middle"|"texttop"] [
BORDER="0"|"border_pix"][
BORDERCOLOR="#rrggbb"|"color"][ CLASS="class_name"][
DATAFLD="ds_col_name"][ DATASRC="ds_identifier"][
FRAMEBORDER="1"|"0] [ FRAMESPACING="frame_space"][
HEIGHT="height_pix"] [ HSPACE="horiz_pix"][
ID="id_name"][ LANG="lang_code"][
LANGUAGE="JAVASCRIPT"|"JSCRIPT"|"VBS[CRIPT]"][ MARGIN-
HEIGHT="height_pix"][ MARGINWIDTH="width_pix"][
NAME="frame-name" |"_blank"|"_parent"|"_self"|"_top"][
NORESIZE[|RESIZE]][ SCROLLING="auto"|"yes"|"no"][
SRC="source_url"] [ STYLE="name_1: value_1"[; "name_2:
value_2"][...; "name_n: value_n"]][ TITLE="title"][
WIDTH="width_pix"|"width_%"]> alternate_contents</IFRAME>
```

## Where

- **Microsoft** ALIGN aligns the frame or the surrounding text.

- **Microsoft** BORDER turns on a border and/or sets the width, in pixels, of the inline frame.

- **Microsoft** BORDERCOLOR specifies the color for the borders of the frame.

- **Microsoft** CLASS specifies a class identification for the element.

- **Microsoft** DATAFLD specifies the column name from the file that provides the data source object.

- **Microsoft** DATASRC specifies the identifier of the data source object.

- FRAMEBORDER specifies whether the current frame will have a border.
- **Microsoft** FRAMESPACING sets spacing, in pixels, between all the frames in a frameset.
- HEIGHT specifies the height of the current inline frame.
- **Microsoft** HSPACE is the horizontal area, in pixels, of the left and right sides of the frame and its contents.
- **Microsoft** ID provides a unique identifier name for the element.
- **Microsoft** LANG provides the code representing the language used for the element.
- **Microsoft** LANGUAGE declares the scripting language of the current script.
- MARGINHEIGHT is the space, in pixels, between the top and bottom margins of the frame and the contents of the frame.
- MARGINWIDTH is the space, in pixels, between the left and right margins of the frame and the contents of the frame.
- NAME specifies a name for the current frame. Microsoft supports the use of the _blank, _parent, _self, and _top reserved words.
- **Microsoft** NORESIZE freezes the current frame at its current height and width.
- SCROLLING specifies whether the current frame contains scrollbars.
- SRC specifies the source file displayed within the current frame.
- **Microsoft** STYLE sets styles for the element.
- **Microsoft** TITLE provides a title or title information about the element.
- WIDTH specifies the width of the current inline frame.
- *alternate_contents* represents text that will print if a browser does not support inline frames.

359

## Notes

This HTML 4.0 element was formerly a Microsoft extension.

The HTML 4.0 DTD categorizes this as both an inline and block-level element.

If a browser supports inline frames, the contents of the source file will appear within the frame. If a browser does not support inline frames, the text inserted between the start and end tags will appear in the HTML document.

According to the World Wide Web Consortium (W3C), "inserting an inline frame within a section of text is much like inserting an object via the OBJECT element; they both allow you to insert an HTML document in the middle of another, they may both be aligned with surrounding text, etc."

Use IFRAME to insert a frame within a block of text in the same way that you would insert a graphic.

## Related Elements

FRAME, OBJECT

| NOFRAMES | No Frames |
|---|---|

## Purpose

Presents alternative content with no frames for browsers that do not support frames.

## Syntax

```
<NOFRAMES[ ID="id_name"][ STYLE="name_1: value_1"[;
"name_2: value_2"][...; "name_n: value_n"]][
TITLE="title"]>non_frame_content</NOFRAMES>
```

## Where

- **Microsoft** ID provides a unique identifier name for the element.

- **Microsoft** STYLE sets styles for the element.

- **Microsoft** TITLE provides a title or title information about the element.

- *non_frame_content* represents characters, HTML elements, special characters, graphics, and/or links.

## Notes

This HTML 4.0 element was formerly a Netscape extension and a Microsoft extension.

You can insert the NOFRAMES element after the FRAMESET elements or in an HTML document with a BODY.

## Examples

```
<HTML>
<HEAD>
<TITLE>New York's CountyWeb</TITLE>
</HEAD>
<FRAMESET ROWS="*,65">
```

```
    <FRAME

        NAME="CountyWeb"

        SRC="top.html"

        MARGINHEIGHT="0"

        MARGINWIDTH="0"

        SCROLLING="yes"

        NORESIZE>

    <FRAME

        NAME="Footer"

        SRC="bot.html"

        MARGINHEIGHT="0"

        MARGINWIDTH="0"

        SCROLLING="no"

        TARGET="_top"

        NORESIZE>

</FRAMESET>

<NOFRAMES>

<BODY BGCOLOR="#FFFFFF">

<CENTER>

    <A HREF="/cgi-bin/imagemap/countyweb">

        <IMG WIDTH="590" HEIGHT="469" BORDER="0" SRC="coun-
tyweb.gif" ISMAP></A>

    <HR WIDTH="60%">

</CENTER>

<FONT SIZE="2"><I>Last Update: 2/9/96</I></FONT>

<FONT SIZE="2" COLOR="FFFF00">Optimized for Netscape
3.0</FONT><BR>

<A HREF="http://home.netscape.com/"><IMG
SRC="/images/now8.gif"></A></IMG>

</BODY>

</NOFRAMES>

</HTML>
```

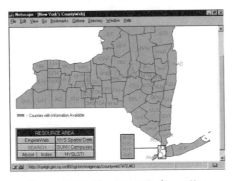

*Figure 4.105 The FRAME alternative.*

*Figure 4.106 The NOFRAMES alternative.*

Also see other examples under the FRAME element.

## Related Elements

FRAME, FRAMESET

# Multimedia and Special Effects Elements

These elements enable you to insert images, animations, sounds, and other special effects files into an HTML document.

**NOTE** Appendix B, "Attributes in Depth," describes all attributes in the HTML 4.0 standard and for Netscape and Microsoft extensions. With each entry, you'll find valid values and usage notes.

## APPLET | Applet

## Purpose

Indicates the start and end of a Java applet that is embedded in the current document.

## Syntax

```
<APPLET HEIGHT="height_pix"" WIDTH="%width_pix"[
ALIGN="bottom"|"middle"|"top"|"left"|"right"|"absmid-
dle"|"absbottom"|"texttop"|"baseline"|"center"][
ALT="alternate_name"][ ARCHIVE="preload_archive_1[, pre-
load_archive_2[..., preload_archive_n"][
CLASS="class_name"] [ CODE="subclass_resource_url"][
CODEBASE="base_url"][ DATAFLD="ds_col_name"][ DATAS-
RC="ds_identifier"] [ HSPACE="horiz_pix][ ID="id_name"] [
MAYSCRIPT][ NAME="applet_name"][ OBJECT="serial_resource"][
ONAFTERUPDATE="au_script_data"][
ONBEFOREUPDATE="bu_script_data"][
ONBLUR="bl_script_data"][ ONCLICK="cl_script_data"][ OND-
BLCLICK="dc_script_data"][
ONDRAGSTART="ds_script_data"][
ONFOCUS="fc_script_data"][ ONHELP="hlp_script_data"][
ONKEYDOWN="kd_script_data"][
ONKEYPRESS="kp_script_data"][ ONKEYUP="ku_script_data"][
ONLOAD="ol_script_data"][
ONMOUSEDOWN="md_script_data"][
ONMOUSEMOVE="mm_script_data"][
ONMOUSEOUT="mo_script_data"][
ONMOUSEOVER="mov_script_data"][
ONMOUSEUP="mu_script_data"][
ONREADYSTATECHANGE="rsc_script_data"][
ONRESIZE="rsz_script_data"][
ONROWENTER="re_script_data"][
ONROWEXIT="rex_script_data"][
ONSELECTSTART="ss_script_data"] [ SRC="object_url"][
STYLE="name_1: value_1"[ ; "name_2: value_2"][ ...;
"name_n: value_n"]] [ TITLE="title_text"][
VSPACE="vert_pix"]>applet</APPLET>
```

## Where

- HEIGHT specifies the height, in pixels, of the window in which the applet will run.
- WIDTH specifies the width, in pixels, of the window in which the applet will run.
- ALIGN aligns the applet window with the surrounding area of the HTML document.
- ALT specifies alternate text that will replace the Java applet if the browser does not support Java applets. Some browsers display alternate text as a tool tip.
- ARCHIVE names archives containing resources that will be loaded before the applet runs.
- **Microsoft** CLASS specifies a class identification for the element.
- CODE names the resource containing the compiled applet subclass for the applet.
- CODEBASE specifies the base URL of the applet.
- **Microsoft** DATAFLD specifies the column name from the file that provides the data source object.
- **Microsoft** DATASRC specifies the identifier of the data source object.
- HSPACE specifies a horizontal gutter, in pixels, between the left margin of the page and the left margin of the applet window.
- **Microsoft** ID provides a unique identifier name for the element.
- **Netscape** **Microsoft** MAYSCRIPT allows the applet to access JavaScript.
- NAME names the current applet.
- OBJECT names the resource containing a serialized version of the current applet.
- **Microsoft** ONAFTERUPDATE specifies that the referred-to script runs after data has been transferred from the element to the data repository.

- 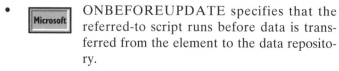 ONBEFOREUPDATE specifies that the referred-to script runs before data is transferred from the element to the data repository.

- ONBLUR specifies that the referred-to script runs when the link loses focus (that is, it is no longer the active element).

- ONCLICK specifies that the referred-to script runs when a user moves the mouse pointer or other pointing device over the applet and clicks the device button.

- ONDBLCLICK specifies that the referred-to script runs when a user moves the mouse pointer or other pointing device over the applet and double-clicks the device button.

- ONDRAGSTART specifies that the referred-to script runs when the user starts dragging a selection or element.

- ONFOCUS specifies that the referred-to script runs when the current element receives focus (that is, is made active) by the mouse pointer or other pointing device.

- ONHELP specifies that the referred-to script runs when a user presses the **F1** or **Help** key over the current element.

- ONKEYDOWN specifies that the referred-to script runs when a user presses and holds a key down over the applet.

- ONKEYPRESS specifies that the referred-to script runs when a user presses and releases a key over the applet.

- ONKEYUP specifies that the referred-to script runs when a user releases a key over the applet.

- 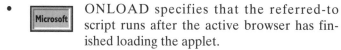 ONLOAD specifies that the referred-to script runs after the active browser has finished loading the applet.

- ONMOUSEDOWN specifies that the referred-to script runs when a user moves the mouse pointer or other pointing device over the applet and presses and holds down the device button.

- ONMOUSEMOVE specifies that the referred-to script runs when a user moves the mouse pointer or other pointing device over the applet.

- ONMOUSEOUT specifies that the referred-to script runs when a user moves the mouse pointer or other pointing device away from the applet.

- ONMOUSEOVER specifies that the referred-to script runs the first time a user moves the mouse pointer or other pointing device over the applet.

- ONMOUSEUP specifies that the referred-to script runs when a user moves the mouse pointer or other pointing device over the applet and releases a pressed-down device button.

- ONREADYSTATECHANGE specifies that the referred-to script runs when an element is ready to be loaded.

- ONRESIZE specifies that the referred-to script runs when the user resizes the selected object.

- ONROWENTER specifies that the referred-to script runs when the current row has been modified.

- ONROWEXIT specifies that the referred-to script runs before the current row is modified.

369

- **Microsoft** ONSELECTSTART specifies that the referred-to script runs when a user starts selecting an object.

- **Microsoft** SRC specifies an object, such as a sound or video file, embedded on the current page.

- **Microsoft** STYLE sets styles for the element.

- **Microsoft** TITLE inserts title information about the applet.

- VSPACE is the vertical area, in pixels, between the top margin of the page and the top margin of the applet window.

## Notes

This is an HTML 3.2 element.

The HTML 4.0 DTD categorizes this as an inline element.

Although APPLET is supported by HTML 4.0, it has been deprecated (that is, it will eventually be obsolete). Use the OBJECT element instead.

Embed the PARAM element within APPLET elements.

## Examples

Example 1 (Figures 4.107, 4.108, and 4.109)

```
<APPLET CODEBASE="Java/" CODE="MsgScroll" WIDTH="0"
HEIGHT="0">
   <PARAM NAME="line1" VALUE="This is an example....">
   <PARAM NAME="line2" VALUE="of the MsgScroll Java
Script">
   <PARAM NAME="line3" VALUE="Pretty nifty eh ?">
</APPLET>
```

This is an example....

*Figure 4.107 The first part of a Java task bar line.*

*Figure 4.108 The second part of a Java task bar line.*

*Figure 4.109 The last part of a Java task bar line.*

## Example 2 (Figure 4.110)

```
<!--Fireworks Display !-->
<!-------------->
<APPLET CODEBASE="Java/" CODE="fireworks.class" WIDTH="300"
HEIGHT="100"
<PARAM NAME="ROCKETS"      VALUE="10">
<PARAM NAME="POINTS"       VALUE="20">
<PARAM NAME="LIFELENGTH"   VALUE="30">
<PARAM NAME="GRAV"         VALUE="180">
<PARAM NAME="DELAY"        VALUE="20">
<PARAM NAME="POINTSIZE"    VALUE="2">
<PARAM NAME="TRAIL"        VALUE="4">
<PARAM NAME="HEIGHT"       VALUE="100">
<PARAM NAME="COLOR"        VALUE="3200AA">
</APPLET>
```

*Figure 4.110 Java fireworks.*

## Example 3 (Figure 4.111)

```
<APPLET CODE="Clock2.class" WIDTH="170"
HEIGHT="150"></APPLET>
```

*Figure 4.111 A Java clock.*

# Related Element

PARAM

## AREA | Area

## Purpose

Defines coordinates, actions, and shapes of clickable areas within client-side image maps.

## Syntax

```
<AREA ALT="alternate_name"[ CLASS="class_name"][
COORDS="coords_1, coords_2, coords_3[..., coords_n]"][
HREF="link_url"][ ID="id_name"][ LANG="lang_code"][ LAN-
GUAGE="JAVASCRIPT" |"JSCRIPT" |"VBS[CRIPT]"] [
NAME="map_name"][ NOHREF][ NOTAB][
ONBLUR="bl_script_data"][ ONCLICK="cl_script_data"][ OND-
BLCLICK="dc_script_data"][
ONDRAGSTART="ds_script_data"][
ONFOCUS="fc_script_data"][ ONHELP="hlp_script_data"][
ONKEYDOWN="kd_script_data"][
ONKEYPRESS="kp_script_data"][ ONKEYUP="ku_script_data"][
ONMOUSEDOWN="md_script_data"][
ONMOUSEMOVE="mm_script_data"] [
ONMOUSEOUT=mo_script_data][ ONMOUSEOVER=mov_script_data] [
ONMOUSEUP="mu_script_data"] [
SHAPE="RECT[ANGLE]" |"CIRC[LE]" |"POLY[GON]" |"DEFAULT"][
STYLE="name_1: value_1"[; "name_2: value_2"][...; "name_n:
value_n"]][ TABINDEX="position_number"][ TARGET="win-
dow" |"_blank" |"_parent" |"_self" |"_top"][
TITLE="title_text"]>image_map</AREA>
```

## Where

- ALT describes the image for text-only browsers, temporarily describes an image as it loads, or displays a tool tip.
- **Microsoft** CLASS specifies a class identification for the area.
- COORDS is a list containing the coordinates of a shape.

**373**

- HREF specifies a URL for a link.
- **Microsoft** ID provides a unique identifier name for the element.
- **Microsoft** LANG provides the code representing the language used for the element.
- **Microsoft** LANGUAGE declares the scripting language of the current script.
- **Netscape** NAME names the current area.
- NOHREF specifies that the area does not have a link associated with it.
- **Microsoft** NOTAB removes the element from the tabbing order.
- **Microsoft** ONBLUR specifies that the referred-to script runs when the link loses focus (that is, it is no longer the active element).
- **Microsoft** ONCLICK specifies that the referred-to script runs when a user moves the mouse pointer or other pointing device over the area and clicks the device button.
- **Microsoft** ONDBLCLICK specifies that the referred-to script runs when a user moves the mouse pointer or other pointing device over the area and double-clicks the device button.
- **Microsoft** ONDRAGSTART specifies that the referred-to script runs when the user starts dragging a selection or element.
- **Microsoft** ONFOCUS specifies that the referred-to script runs when the current element receives focus (that is, is made active) by the mouse pointer or other pointing device.
- **Microsoft** ONHELP specifies that the referred-to script runs when a user presses the **F1** or **Help** key over the current element.

-  ONKEYDOWN specifies that the referred-to script runs when a user presses and holds a key down over the area.

-  ONKEYPRESS specifies that the referred-to script runs when a user presses and releases a key over the area.

-  ONKEYUP specifies that the referred-to script runs when a user releases a key over the area.

-  ONMOUSEDOWN specifies that the referred-to script runs when a user moves the mouse pointer or other pointing device over the area and presses and holds down the device button.

-  ONMOUSEMOVE specifies that the referred-to script runs when a user moves the mouse pointer or other pointing device over the area.

-  ONMOUSEOUT specifies that the referred-to script runs when a user moves the mouse pointer or other pointing device away from the object.

-  ONMOUSEOVER specifies that the referred-to script runs the first time a user moves the mouse pointer or other pointing device over the object.

-  ONMOUSEUP specifies that the referred-to script runs when a user moves the mouse pointer or other pointing device over the area and releases a pressed-down device button.

- SHAPE is the shape of the area.
-  STYLE sets styles for the area.

- TABINDEX defines the position of the current element in all the elements that a user can navigate using a Tab or Shift+Tab key.

- TARGET loads a linked and named document in a particular window.

- **Microsoft**  TITLE inserts a balloon help title.

- *image_map* is the image map defined by the current AREA element.

## Notes

This element originated in HTML 3.2.

Most maps contain multiple AREA elements.

Embed the AREA element within the MAP elements.

## Example

```
<MAP NAME="Sample Image Map">

<AREA SHAPE="RECT" COORDS="9,148,168,209" HREF="rectan-
gle.htm">

<AREA SHAPE="CIRC" COORDS="86,45,19" HREF="circle.htm">

<AREA SHAPE="POLY"
COORDS="118,76,74,80,99,75,105,60,118,76"
HREF="polygon.htm">

<AREA SHAPE="DEFAULT" NOHREF>

</MAP>
```

## Related Elements

```
IMG, MAP
```

| IMG | Inline Image |
|-----|--------------|

## Purpose

Inserts an inline image in the document.

## Syntax

```
<IMG[
ALIGN="bottom"|"middle"|"top"|"left"|"right"|"absmid-
dle"|"absbottom"|"texttop"|"baseline"|"center"][
ALT="alternate_name"][ BORDER="border_pix"][
CLASS="class_name"][ CONTROLS] [ DATAFLD="ds_col_name"][
DATASRC="ds_identifier"][ DIR="LTR"|"RTL"][
DYNSRC="dynamic_url"][ HEIGHT="height_pix"][
HSPACE="horiz_pix"][ ID="id_name"][ ISMAP[="image"]][
LANG="lang_code"][
LANGUAGE="JAVASCRIPT"|"JSCRIPT"|"VBS[CRIPT]"] [
LOOP="number_of_plays"][ LOWSRC="low_res_url"][
NAME="image_name"][ ONABORT="oa_script_data"][ ONAFTERUP-
DATE="au_script_data"][
ONBEFOREUPDATE="bu_script_data"][
ONBLUR="bl_script_data"] [ ONCLICK="cl_script_data"][ OND-
BLCLICK="dc_script_data"][
ONDRAGSTART="ds_script_data"] [
ONERROR="oe_script_data"][ ONFOCUS="fc_script_data"][
ONHELP="hlp_script_data"] [ ONKEYDOWN="kd_script_data"][
ONKEYPRESS="kp_script_data"][ ONKEYUP="ku_script_data"][
ONLOAD="ol_script_data"][ ONMOUSEDOWN="md_script_data"][
ONMOUSEMOVE="mm_script_data"][
ONMOUSEOUT="mo_script_data"][
ONMOUSEOVER="mov_script_data"][
ONMOUSEUP="mu_script_data"][ ONRESIZE="rsz_script_data"][
ONROWENTER="re_script_data"][
ONROWEXIT="rex_script_data"][
ONSELECTSTART="ss_script_data"] [ SRC="image_url"][
STYLE="name_1: value_1"[; "name_2: value_2"][...; "name_n:
value_n"]][ TITLE="title"][ USEMAP="map_url"][
VSPACE="vert_pix"][ WIDTH="width_pix"]>
```

## Where

- ALIGN aligns the image with the surrounding area of the HTML document.
- ALT permanently describes the image for text-only browsers or temporarily describes an image as it loads. Some browsers display alternate text as a tool tip.
- BORDER turns on a border and sets the width, in pixels, of the image.
- CLASS specifies a class identification for the image.
- **Microsoft** CONTROLS adds a set of control buttons under an embedded video clip.
- **Microsoft** DATAFLD specifies the column name from the file that provides the data source object.
- **Microsoft** DATASRC specifies the identifier of the data source object.
- DIR specifies the direction in which the current text is displayed: left-to-right or right-to-left.
- **Microsoft** DYNSRC names the URL of a video clip or multimedia file to be inserted in an image.
- HEIGHT specifies the height, in pixels, of the window in which the image will be placed.
- HSPACE is the horizontal area, in pixels, between the left margin of the page and the left margin of the image.
- ID provides a unique identifier name for the image.
- ISMAP indicates that the image is a server-side image map. For Microsoft browsers, you can name the image.
- LANG provides the code representing the language used with text associated with the image.
- **Microsoft** LOOP indicates the number of times that an embedded video clip will play.
- **Netscape** **Microsoft** LOWSRC specifies the URL of a low-resolution graphic to be loaded in the same location as the image named with the SRC attribute.
- **Netscape** NAME is the name of the current image.

-   ONABORT specifies that the referred-to script runs when the user stops the current image from loading.

-  ONAFTERUPDATE specifies that the referred-to script runs after data has been transferred from the element to the data repository.

-  ONBEFOREUPDATE specifies that the referred-to script runs before data is transferred from the element to the data repository.

-  ONBLUR specifies that the referred-to script runs when the link loses focus (that is, it is no longer the active element).

- ONCLICK specifies that the referred-to script runs when a user moves the mouse pointer or other pointing device over the image and clicks the device button.

- ONDBLCLICK specifies that the referred-to script runs when a user moves the mouse pointer or other pointing device over the image and double-clicks the device button.

-  ONDRAGSTART specifies that the referred-to script runs when the user starts dragging a selection or element.

-   ONERROR specifies a script to run when the referred-to script experiences an error.

-  ONFOCUS specifies that the referred-to script runs when the current element receives focus (that is, is made active) by the mouse pointer or other pointing device.

-  ONHELP specifies that the referred-to script runs when a user presses the **F1** or **Help** key over the current element.

- ONKEYDOWN specifies that the referred-to script runs when a user presses and holds a key down over the image.
- ONKEYPRESS specifies that the referred-to script runs when a user presses and releases a key over the image.
- ONKEYUP specifies that the referred-to script runs when a user releases a key over the image.
-   ONLOAD specifies that the referred-to script runs after the active browser has finished loading an image.
- ONMOUSEDOWN specifies that the referred-to script runs when a user moves the mouse pointer or other pointing device over the image and presses and holds down the device button.
- ONMOUSEMOVE specifies that the referred-to script runs when a user moves the mouse pointer or other pointing device over the image.
- ONMOUSEOUT specifies that the referred-to script runs when a user moves the mouse pointer or other pointing device away from the image.
- ONMOUSEOVER specifies that the referred-to script runs the first time a user moves the mouse pointer or other pointing device over the image.
- ONMOUSEUP specifies that the referred-to script runs when a user moves the mouse pointer or other pointing device over the image and releases a pressed-down device button.
-  ONRESIZE specifies that the referred-to script runs when the user resizes the selected object.
-  ONROWENTER specifies that the referred-to script runs when the current row has been modified.
-  ONROWEXIT specifies that the referred-to script runs before the current row is modified.

-  ONSELECTSTART specifies that the referred-to script runs when a user starts selecting an object.
- SRC specifies the URL of an image file.
- STYLE sets styles for the image.
- TITLE provides a title or title information about the image.
- USEMAP specifies a client-side image map that is an embedded image within a document
- VSPACE is the vertical area, in pixels, between the top margin of the page and the top margin of the image.
- WIDTH specifies the width, in pixels, of the window in which the image will be placed.

## Notes

This element originated in HTML 2.0.

The HTML 4.0 DTD categorizes this as an inline element.

Consider displaying the file size next to an IMG element for a large graphic file, so that users can decide whether to wait for downloading.

As a rule, JPEG image files are smaller than GIF image files. This makes JPEG images load more quickly.

Netscape Navigator supports GIF, JPEG, XPM (X PixMap), and XBM (X BitMap) image files.

For a faster loading site, consider limited graphic images to 70 kilobytes or less and using fewer colors.

GIF animations are single GIF files with individual frames inserted within. For more information about GIF animations, refer to *The GIF Animator's Guide*, also written by Sandra E. Eddy and published by MIS:Press.

The ALIGN attribute is limited in its page formatting abilities. Use style sheets instead.

## Examples

Example 1 (Figure 4.112)

```
<IMG SRC="missing.gif">
```

*Figure 4.112 The icon representing a missing graphic file.*

## Example 2 (Figure 4.113)

```
<IMG SRC="scene.gif" ALIGN="top"> Top alignment
<P><IMG SRC="scene.gif" ALIGN="middle"> Middle alignment
<P><IMG SRC="scene.gif" ALIGN="bottom"> Bottom alignment
```

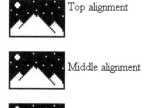

*Figure 4.113 Samples of text-to-graphic alignment.*

## Example 3 (Figure 4.114)

```
<IMG SRC="bike.gif" HEIGHT="90" WIDTH="100" BORDER="6">
```

*Figure 4.114 A demonstration of the HEIGHT, WIDTH, and BORDER attributes.*

## Example 4 (Figure 4.115)

```
<P><IMG SRC="scene.gif" HEIGHT="160" WIDTH="100">
```

*Figure 4.115 An elongated graphic.*

## Example 5 (Figure 4.116)

```
<IMG SRC="scene.gif" HSPACE="8">
<IMG SRC="scene.gif" HSPACE="480" VSPACE="-300">
```

*Figure 4.116 A demonstration of HSPACE values.*

## Example 6 (Figure 4.117)

```
<IMG SRC="scene.gif" VSPACE="10">
<IMG SRC="scene.gif" VSPACE="60" HSPACE="2">
```

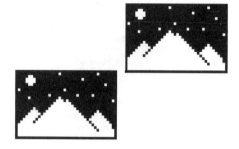

*Figure 4.117 A demonstration of VSPACE values.*

## Example 7 (Figure 4.118)

```
<IMG SRC="scene.gif" HEIGHT="180" WIDTH="200"
ALT="scene.gif">
```

*Figure 4.118 The ALT name for a graphic.*

## Example 8 (Figure 4.119)

```
<IMG SRC="scene.gif" ALIGN="TOP" WIDTH="80"
HEIGHT="52">This image is set for TOP alignment.
<P><IMG SRC="scene.gif" ALIGN="MIDDLE" WIDTH="80"
HEIGHT="52">This image shows MIDDLE alignment.
<P><IMG SRC="scene.gif" ALIGN="BOTTOM" WIDTH="80"
HEIGHT="52">This image is set for BOTTOM alignment.
<P ALIGN="LEFT">
    <IMG SRC="scene.gif" ALIGN="LEFT" WIDTH="80"
```

HEIGHT="52">This image and text are set for LEFT alignment.

<P ALIGN="RIGHT">

    <IMG SRC="scene.gif" ALIGN="RIGHT" WIDTH="80"
HEIGHT="52">This image and text are set for RIGHT alignment.

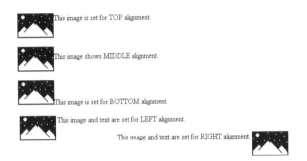

*Figure 4.119 Examples of image and text alignment.*

## Example 9 (Figure 4.120)

<P ALIGN="LEFT"><IMG SRC="scene.gif" ALIGN="LEFT"
WIDTH="80" HEIGHT="52">This image and text are set for
LEFT alignment. <BR>I typed this text after inserting a
break (BR). When you add more text, it behaves like this:
This image and text are set for LEFT alignment. This image
and text are set for LEFT alignment. This image and text
are set for LEFT alignment. This image and text are set
for LEFT alignment.

<P ALIGN="RIGHT"><IMG SRC="scene.gif" ALIGN="RIGHT"
WIDTH="80" HEIGHT="52">

This image and text are set for RIGHT alignment.<BR>I
typed this text after inserting a break (BR). This image
and text are set for RIGHT alignment. This image and text
are set for RIGHT alignment. This image and text are set
for RIGHT alignment. This image and text are set for RIGHT
alignment.

**385**

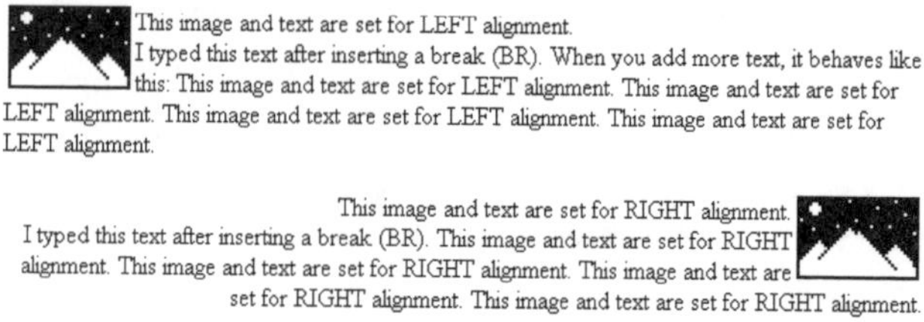

This image and text are set for LEFT alignment.
I typed this text after inserting a break (BR). When you add more text, it behaves like this: This image and text are set for LEFT alignment. This image and text are set for LEFT alignment. This image and text are set for LEFT alignment. This image and text are set for LEFT alignment.

This image and text are set for RIGHT alignment.
I typed this text after inserting a break (BR). This image and text are set for RIGHT alignment. This image and text are set for RIGHT alignment. This image and text are set for RIGHT alignment. This image and text are set for RIGHT alignment.

*Figure 4.120 Word wrap after inserting the BR element.*

# Related Elements

A, LINK

| MAP | Map |
|---|---|

## Purpose

Names a client-side image map.

## Syntax

```
<MAP[ CLASS="class_name"][ ID="id_name"] [
LANG=" lang_code"] [ NAME="map_name"][
ONCLICK=" cl_script_data"][ ONDBLCLICK=" dc_script_data"][
ONHELP=" hlp_script_data"][ ONKEYDOWN=" kd_script_data"][
ONKEYPRESS=" kp_script_data"][ ONKEYUP=" ku_script_data"][
ONMOUSEDOWN=" md_script_data"][
ONMOUSEMOVE=" mm_script_data"][
ONMOUSEOUT=" mo_script_data"][
ONMOUSEOVER=" mov_script_data"][
ONMOUSEUP=" mu_script_data"] [ STYLE="name_1: value_1"[;
"name_2: value_2"][...; "name_n: value_n"]][
TITLE= "title"]>map_contents</MAP>
```

## Where

- CLASS specifies a class identification for the image map.
- ID provides a unique identifier name for the image map.
- **Microsoft** LANG provides the code representing the language used for the element.
- NAME names the image map.
- **Microsoft** ONCLICK specifies that the referred-to script runs when a user moves the mouse pointer or other pointing device over the image map and clicks the device button.
- **Microsoft** ONDBLCLICK specifies that the referred-to script runs when a user moves the mouse

pointer or other pointing device over the image map and double-clicks the device button.

- [Microsoft] ONHELP specifies that the referred-to script runs when a user presses the **F1** or **Help** key over the current element.

- [Microsoft] ONKEYDOWN specifies that the referred-to script runs when a user presses and holds a key down over the image map.

- [Microsoft] ONKEYPRESS specifies that the referred-to script runs when a user presses and releases a key over the image map.

- [Microsoft] ONKEYUP specifies that the referred-to script runs when a user releases a key over the image map.

- [Microsoft] ONMOUSEDOWN specifies that the referred-to script runs when a user moves the mouse pointer or other pointing device over the image map and presses and holds down the device button.

- [Microsoft] ONMOUSEMOVE specifies that the referred-to script runs when a user moves the mouse pointer or other pointing device over the image map.

- [Microsoft] ONMOUSEOUT specifies that the referred-to script runs when a user moves the mouse pointer or other pointing device away from the image map.

- [Microsoft] ONMOUSEOVER specifies that the referred-to script runs the first time a user moves the mouse pointer or other pointing device over the image map.

- [Microsoft] ONMOUSEUP specifies that the referred-to script runs when a user moves the mouse pointer or other pointing device over the image map and releases a pressed-down device button.

- STYLE sets styles for the image map.
- TITLE provides a title or title information about the image map.
- *map_contents* is the contents of the image map, defined by one or more AREA elements.

## Notes

This element originated in HTML 3.2.

The HTML 4.0 DTD categorizes this as an inline element.

A client-side image map is stored in an HTML document; a server-side image map is processed by a browser program. You can use both types in the same map for browsers that do not support client-side image maps. Client-side image maps are rapidly taking the place of server-side image maps.

Embed AREA elements within the MAP elements.

## Examples

See the AREA element.

## Related Elements

AREA, IMG

## NOSCRIPT | Script Alternate

### Purpose

Presents alternative content for browsers that do not support scripts.

### Syntax

`<NOSCRIPT>`*alternate_content*`</NOSCRIPT>`

### Where

- *alternate_content* represents characters, HTML elements, special characters, graphics, and/or links.

### Notes

This is an HTML 4.0 element.

The HTML 4.0 DTD categorizes this as a block-level element.

Use NOSCRIPT to present alternate content for browsers that do not support or cannot run scripts.

### Related Element

SCRIPT

| OBJECT | Embed Object |

## Purpose

Embeds a multimedia object, such as an image, video file, or sound file, within the current document.

## Syntax

```
<OBJECT[ ACCESSKEY="shortcut_key"] [ ALIGN="texttop"|"mid-
dle"|"textmiddle"|"baseline"|"textbottom"|"left"|"cen-
ter"|"right" |
"absbottom"|"absmiddle"|bottom"|"top"][
BORDER="border_pix"|"border_%"][ CLASS="class_name"][
CLASSID="url_id"][ CODE="subclass_resource_url"][ CODE-
BASE="base_url"][ CODETYPE="Internet_Media_Type"][
DATA="data_url"][ DATAFLD="ds_col_name"][
DATASRC="ds_identifier"] [ DECLARE][ DIR="LTR"|"RTL"][
HEIGHT="height_pix"|"height_%"][
HSPACE="horiz_pix"|"horiz_%][ ID="id_name"][
LANG="lang_code"]
[ LANGUAGE="JAVASCRIPT"|"JSCRIPT"|"VBS[CRIPT]"] [
NAME="input_name"][ NOTAB][
ONAFTERUPDATE="au_script_data"][
ONBEFOREUPDATE="bu_script_data"][
ONBLUR="bl_script_data"] [ ONCLICK="cl_script_data"][ OND-
BLCLICK="dc_script_data"][
ONDRAGSTART="ds_script_data"][
ONFOCUS="fc_script_data"][ ONHELP="hlp_script_data"] [
ONKEYDOWN="kd_script_data"][ ONKEYPRESS="kp_script_data"][
ONKEYUP="ku_script_data"][ ONMOUSEDOWN="md_script_data"][
ONMOUSEMOVE="mm_script_data"][
ONMOUSEOUT="mo_script_data"][
ONMOUSEOVER="mov_script_data"][
ONMOUSEUP="mu_script_data"][
ONREADYSTATECHANGE="rsc_script_data"][
ONRESIZE="rsz_script_data"][
ONROWENTER="re_script_data"][
ONROWEXIT="rex_script_data"][
ONSELECTSTART="ss_script_data"] [ SHAPES][
```

**391**

```
STANDBY="message_text"][ STYLE="name_1: value_1"[;
"name_2: value_2"]][...; "name_n: value_n"][
TABINDEX="position_number"][ TITLE="title"][
TYPE="Internet_Media_Type"][ USEMAP="map_url"][
VSPACE="vert_pix"|"vert_%"][
WIDTH="width_pix"|"width_%"]>embedded_object</OBJECT>
```

## Where

- ![Microsoft] ACCESSKEY assigns a shortcut key to the element in order to focus on it.

- ALIGN horizontally or vertically aligns the object within its page. The absbottom, absmiddle, bottom, and top values are Microsoft-only values.

- BORDER turns on a border and sets the width, in pixels or as a percentage of the full-screen width, of the window surrounding the object.

- CLASS specifies a class identification for the object.

- CLASSID names an identifier for the object or class.

- ![Microsoft] CODE names the resource containing the compiled applet subclass for the current applet.

- CODEBASE specifies the base URL of the object.

- CODETYPE specifies a valid Internet Media Type (that is, MIMETYPE) used by the program that will produce the object.

- DATA specifies the URL of a document that includes object data to be embedded in the current document.

- ![Microsoft] DATAFLD specifies the column name from the file that provides the data source object.

- ![Microsoft] DATASRC specifies the identifier of the data source object.

- DECLARE indicates that you are declaring, but not *instantiating* (that is, creating and object in memory and enabling it to be addressed), the object, usually for cross-reference purposes.

- DIR specifies the direction in which the current text is displayed: left-to-right or right-to-left.

- HEIGHT specifies the height, in pixels or as a percentage of the full-screen, of the window in which the object will be placed.

- HSPACE is the horizontal area, in pixels or as a percentage of the full-screen, between the left margin of the page and the left margin of the applet window, image, or object.

- ID provides a unique identifier name for the current object.

- LANG provides the code representing the language used with the object's text.

- **Microsoft** LANGUAGE declares the scripting language of the current script.

- NAME names the object if it will be submitted as part of a form.

- **Microsoft** NOTAB removes the element from the tabbing order.

- **Microsoft** ONAFTERUPDATE specifies that the referred-to script runs after data has been transferred from the element to the data repository.

- **Microsoft** ONBEFOREUPDATE specifies that the referred-to script runs before data is transferred from the element to the data repository.

- **Microsoft** ONBLUR specifies that the referred-to script runs when the link loses focus (that is, it is no longer the active element).

- ONCLICK specifies that the referred-to script runs when a user moves the mouse pointer or other pointing device over the object and clicks the device button.

- ONDBLCLICK specifies that the referred-to script runs when a user moves the mouse pointer or other pointing device over the object and double-clicks the device button.

- **Microsoft** ONDRAGSTART specifies that the referred-to script runs when the user starts dragging a selection or element.

- **Microsoft** ONFOCUS specifies that the referred-to script runs when the current element receives focus (that is, is made active) by the mouse pointer or other pointing device.

- **Microsoft** ONHELP specifies that the referred-to script runs when a user presses the F1 or Help key over the current element.

- ONKEYDOWN specifies that the referred-to script runs when a user presses and holds a key down over the object.

- ONKEYPRESS specifies that the referred-to script runs when a user presses and releases a key over the object.

- ONKEYUP specifies that the referred-to script runs when a user releases a key over the object.

- ONMOUSEDOWN specifies that the referred-to script runs when a user moves the mouse pointer or other pointing device over the object and presses and holds down the device button.

- ONMOUSEMOVE specifies that the referred-to script runs when a user moves the mouse pointer or other pointing device over the object.

- ONMOUSEOUT specifies that the referred-to script runs when a user moves the mouse pointer or other pointing device away from the object.

- ONMOUSEOVER specifies that the referred-to script runs the first time a user moves the mouse pointer or other pointing device over the object.

- ONMOUSEUP specifies that the referred-to script runs when a user moves the mouse pointer or other pointing device over the object and releases a pressed-down device button.

- **Microsoft** ONREADYSTATECHANGE specifies that the referred-to script runs when an element is ready to be loaded.

- **Microsoft** ONRESIZE specifies that the referred-to script runs when the user resizes the selected object.

- **Microsoft** ONROWENTER specifies that the referred-to script runs when the current row has been modified.

- **Microsoft** ONROWEXIT specifies that the referred-to script runs before the current row is modified.

- SHAPES indicates that the current object is an image map.

- STANDBY displays a message while the object is loading onscreen.

- STYLE sets styles for the object.

- TABINDEX defines the position of the object in all the elements that a user can navigate using a Tab or Shift+Tab key.

- TITLE provides a title or title information about the object.

- TYPE specifies a valid Internet Media Type (that is, MIMETYPE) of the data embedded in the current document.

- USEMAP specifies a client-side image map that is an embedded object within a document

- VSPACE is the vertical area, in pixels or as a percentage of the full-screen, between the top margin of the page and the top margin of the applet window, image, or object.

- WIDTH specifies the width, in pixels or as a percentage of the full screen, of the window in which the object will be placed.

- *embedded_object* represents an object that is embedded in the HTML document.

## Notes

This is an HTML 4.0 element.

The HTML 4.0 DTD categorizes this as an inline element.

OBJECT may replace the IMG and APPLET elements in future versions of HTML.

# Example

```
<OBJECT DATA="grafbar.jpg" SHAPES>
<A HREF="toc.html" SHAPE="RECT" COORDS="0,0,100,30">Table
of Contents</A>
<A HREF="ch1.html" SHAPE="RECT"
COORDS="100,0,200,30">Chapter 1</A>
<A HREF="toc.html" SHAPE="RECT"
COORDS="200,0,300,30">Chapter 2</A>
<A HREF="appx.html" SHAPE="RECT"
COORDS="300,0,400,30">Appendix</A>
</OBJECT>
```

# Related Elements

A, APPLET, IMG

| PARAM | Parameter |
|-------|-----------|

## Purpose

Specifies parameters and run-time values in order to *render* (that is, produce) an object onscreen.

## Syntax

```
<PARAM NAME="parm_name" [ DATAFLD="ds_col_name"][
DATAFORMATAS="HTML" |"TEXT"] [
TYPE="Internet_Media_Type"][ VALUE="parm_value"][ VALUE-
TYPE="DATA" |"REF" |"OBJECT"]>
```

## Where

- NAME names a run-time parameter.
- **Microsoft** DATAFLD specifies the column name from the file that provides the data source object.
- **Microsoft** DATAFORMATAS indicates whether the data for this element is formatted as *plain text* (that is, unformatted ASCII) or HTML.
- TYPE specifies a valid Internet Media Type (that is, MIMETYPE) of the parameter.
- VALUE provides a value for the parameter defined by the NAME attribute.
- VALUETYPE specifies the type of the VALUE attribute: data string or URL.

## Notes

This element originated in HTML 3.2.

Embed the PARAM element within OBJECT or APPLET elements.

## Examples

```
<TITLE>Moving Ship Applet</TITLE>
<BODY>
```

```
<APPLET CODE=Ship.class WIDTH="400" HEIGHT="140">
<PARAM NAME="ImageSource" VALUE="Animator/images">
<PARAM NAME="BackGround" VALUE="back.gif">
<PARAM NAME="Ship" VALUE="ship.gif">
</APPLET>
<P>
<A HREF="Ship.java">View Source </A>
</BODY>
```

*Figure 4.121 An animated Java ship.*

See the APPLET element for other examples.

## Related Elements

APPLET

| SCRIPT | Script |
|---|---|

## Purpose

Includes a script in a document.

## Syntax

```
<SCRIPT[ CLASS="class_name"][ EVENT="event_name"][
FOR="element_name"][ ID="id_name"] [ LANGUAGE="script-
ing_language"][ SRC="ext_script_url"][ TITLE="title"] [
TYPE="Internet_Media_Type"]>script</SCRIPT>
```

## Where

- Microsoft   CLASS specifies a class identification for the element.

- Microsoft   EVENT names the event related to the current script.

- Microsoft   FOR names the element with which the current script is associated.

- Microsoft   ID provides a unique identifier name for the element.

- LANGUAGE declares the scripting language of the current script.

- SRC specifies a URL in which an external script to be run is stored.

- Microsoft   TITLE provides a title or title information about the element.

- TYPE specifies the scripting language, which must be a valid Internet Media Type.

- *script* is the current script.

## Notes

This element originated in HTML 3.2.
The HTML 4.0 DTD categorizes this as an inline element.

Use the TYPE attribute to specify a valid scripting language. The LANGUAGE attribute is deprecated.

For a list of valid Internet media types, see Table B.1 in Appendix B, "Attributes in Depth."

## Example

```
<HEAD>
<SCRIPT LANGUAGE="JavaScript">

<!- Beginning of JavaScript Applet ───────

.

.

.

// - End of JavaScript code ────────>
</SCRIPT>
```

## Related Element

```
NOSCRIPT
```

# 7

# Netscape and Microsoft Extensions

These elements are extensions designed and supported by Netscape Communications Corporation or Microsoft Corporation. These extensions have not been included in the current HTML standard, as of this writing. However, many of them will find their way into the next version of HTML. Keep in mind that Netscape and Microsoft extensions are supported by Netscape and Microsoft browsers, respectively. Very few other browsers support these extensions.

 **Appendix B, "Attributes in Depth," describes all attributes in the HTML 4.0 standard and for Netscape and Microsoft extensions. With each entry, you'll find valid values and usage notes.**

NOTE

| BGSOUND | Background Sound |
|---|---|

## Purpose

Defines a sound file, in .WAV, .AU, or .MID format, that plays when a user opens the page.

## Syntax

```
<BGSOUND SRC="sound_name"[ BALANCE="bal_num"][
CLASS="class_name"][ ID="id_name"][ LANG="lang_code"] [
LOOP="number_of_plays"|"INFINITE"][ TITLE="title"][
VOLUME="vol_num"] >[</BGSOUND>]
```

## Where

- **Microsoft** SRC specifies the name of the sound file.

- **Microsoft** BALANCE specifies the balance of volume for the left and right speakers.

- **Microsoft** CLASS specifies a class identification for the element.

- **Microsoft** ID provides a unique identifier name for the element.

- **Microsoft** LANG provides the code representing the language used for the element.

- **Microsoft** LOOP indicates the number of times that the sound file will play.

- **Microsoft** TITLE provides a title or title information about the element.

- **Microsoft** VOLUME specifies how loud or soft the background sound file will play.

## Notes

This is a Microsoft extension.

Most browsers do not support Microsoft extensions.

402

Place this element within the HEAD section of the document.

## Example

```
<BGSOUND SRC="tada.wav">
```

| **BLINK** | **Blink Text** |
| --- | --- |

## Purpose

Turns the display of a block of text on and off.

## Syntax

```
<BLINK>text</BLINK>
```

## Where

- **Netscape**   *text* represents one or more words.

## Notes

This is a Netscape extension.

Many browsers do not support Netscape extensions.

Use this element sparingly or not at all; many users dislike blinking text.

| EMBED | Embed Object |
|-------|--------------|

## Purpose

Embeds an object into an HTML document.

## Syntax

```
<EMBED {SRC="object_url"|TYPE="Internet_Media_Type"}|[
SRC="object_url"][
ALIGN="left"|"right"|"top"|"bottom"|"absbottom"|"absmi-
ddle"|"baseline"|"middle"|"texttop"][
ALT="alternate_name"][ BORDER="border_pix"][
CLASS="class_name"][ CODE="subclass_resource_url"][ CODE-
BASE="base_url"][ FRAMEBORDER="no"][
HEIGHT="height_pix"|"height_meas"][
HIDDEN="FALSE"|"TRUE"][ HSPACE="horiz_pix"][
ID="id_name"][ NAME="object_name"][ PALETTE="BACK-
GROUND"|"FOREGROUND"][ STYLE="name_1: value_1"[ ;
"name_2: value_2"][ ...; "name_n: value_n"]][ TITLE="title"][
VSPACE="vert_pix"][ WIDTH="width_pix"|"width_meas"]
```

## Where

- 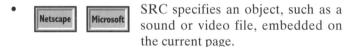 SRC specifies an object, such as a sound or video file, embedded on the current page.

- 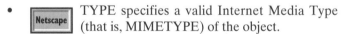 TYPE specifies a valid Internet Media Type (that is, MIMETYPE) of the object.

- 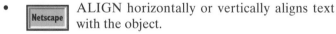 ALIGN horizontally or vertically aligns text with the object.

- 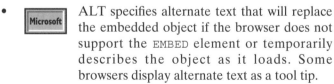 ALT specifies alternate text that will replace the embedded object if the browser does not support the EMBED element or temporarily describes the object as it loads. Some browsers display alternate text as a tool tip.

- BORDER sets the width, in pixels, of the object.

- **Microsoft** CLASS specifies a class identification for the element.

- **Microsoft** CODE names the resource containing the compiled object subclass for the applet.

- **Microsoft** CODEBASE specifies the base URL of the object.

- **Netscape** FRAMEBORDER turns off the border of the object.

- **Netscape** **Microsoft** HEIGHT specifies the height, in pixels or the unit of measure specified with the UNITS attribute (Microsoft), of the window in which the object is placed.

- **Netscape** HIDDEN indicates whether a plug-in application appears in the window.

- **Netscape** **Microsoft** HSPACE is the horizontal area, in pixels, of the left and right sides of the object and other text, graphics, and links on the current page.

- **Microsoft** ID provides a unique identifier name for the element.

- **Netscape** **Microsoft** NAME names the object.

- **Netscape** PALETTE specifies that the palette used by the plug-in object becomes the background or foreground palette for the current page.

- **Microsoft** STYLE sets styles for the element.

- **Microsoft** TITLE provides a title or title information about the element.

- **Netscape** VSPACE is the vertical area, in pixels, of the top and bottom of the object and other text, graphics, and links on the current page.

- **Netscape** **Microsoft** WIDTH specifies the width, in pixels or the unit of measure specified with the UNITS attribute (Microsoft), of the window in which the object is placed.

## Notes

This is a Netscape and Microsoft extension.

Many browsers do not support Netscape extensions or Microsoft extensions or attributes.

The OBJECT element serves the same purpose as EMBED. Therefore, it is preferable to use OBJECT rather than EMBED.

If you intend to use the EMBED element for Netscape browsers, the SRC attribute is required. If you intend to use the element for Microsoft browsers, either SRC or TYPE is required.

You can double-click on an embedded object to edit it in its original application or plug-in module.

## Examples

```
<EMBED SRC="scene.gif">

<EMBED SRC="tada.wav">
```

## Related Elements

IMG, OBJECT

| ILAYER | Inflow Layer |
|--------|--------------|

## Purpose

Defines opaque or transparent blocks of HTML content that overlap other content in the current document and are located as they occur in the document.

## Syntax

```
<ILAYER[ BACKGROUND="picture_url"][
BGCOLOR="#rrggbb"|"color"][
CLIP=[0|"l_pix,0|t_pix,]r_pix,b_pix"][
HEIGHT="height_pix"][ ID="id_name"][ LEFT="left_pos_pix"][
SRC="source_url"][ TOP="top_pos_pix"][ VISIBILITY="INHER-
IT"|"SHOW"|"HIDE"][ WIDTH="width_pix"[ Z-
INDEX="order_num"]></ILAYER>
```

## Where

- **Netscape** BACKGROUND specifies an image file that is displayed in the background of the current layer.

- **Netscape** BGCOLOR specifies the background color for the layer.

- **Netscape** CLIP specifies the dimensions of the layer window.

- **Netscape** HEIGHT specifies the height, in pixels, of the layer window.

- **Netscape** ID provides a unique identifier name for the layer.

- **Netscape** LEFT specifies the leftmost position, in pixels, of the left side of a layer window.

- **Netscape** SRC specifies a source file that contains the contents of a layer window.

- **Netscape** TOP specifies the topmost position, in pixels, of the top of a layer window.

-  WIDTH specifies the width, in pixels, of the layer window.

-  VISIBILITY specifies whether a layer is visible or hidden.

-  Z-INDEX specifies the numerical order of the current layer.

## Notes

This is a Netscape extension, which is supported only within Netscape Navigator 4.0 or greater.

Many browsers do not support Netscape extensions.

The LAYER element specifies the absolute position of a layer.

By default, a layer is transparent.

You can use layers to animate a page or to modify a page almost instantly.

You can stack multiple layers on a page, and you can nest layers.

Use JavaScript to move, hide, expand, contract, rearrange, and change color and image characteristics of layers.

## Related Elements

LAYER, NOLAYER

| **KEYGEN** | **Generate Key** |
|---|---|

## Purpose

Generates a public key in order to send a secure form.

## Syntax

```
<KEYGEN[ CHALLENGE="IA5STRONG"|"challenge_string"][
NAME="pair_name"]>
```

## Where

- **Netscape** CHALLENGE specifies a string that users will enter to verify the submission of a secure form.

- **Netscape** NAME names the name-value pair to be sent via a secure form.

## Notes

This is a Netscape extension.

Most browsers do not support Netscape extensions.

| LAYER | HTML Content Layer |
|-------|--------------------|

## Purpose

Defines opaque or transparent, positioned blocks of HTML content that overlap other content in the current document.

## Syntax

```
<LAYER[ ABOVE="top_layer_name"][
BACKGROUND="picture_url"][ BELOW="below_layer_name"][
BGCOLOR="#rrggbb"|"color"][
CLIP=[0|"l_pix,0|t_pix,]r_pix,b_pix"][
HEIGHT="height_pix"][ ID="id_name"][ LEFT="left_pos_pix"][
NAME="layer_name"][ ONBLUR="bl_script_data"][ ONFO-
CUS="fc_script_data"]ONLOAD="ol_script_data"[ ONMOUSE-
OUT="mo_script_data"][ ONMOUSEOVER="mov_script_data"][
PAGEX="horz_pos_pix"][ PAGEY="vert_pos_pix"][
SRC="source_url"][ TOP="top_pos_pix"][ VISIBILITY="INHER-
IT"|"SHOW"|"HIDE"][ WIDTH="width_pix"[ Z-
INDEX="order_num"]></LAYER>
```

## Where

- **Netscape** ABOVE names the layer that is the top layer in the stack of layers.

- **Netscape** BACKGROUND specifies an image file that is displayed in the background of the current layer.

- **Netscape** BELOW names the layer that is the immediately below the newest layer in the stack.

- **Netscape** BGCOLOR specifies the background color for the layer.

- **Netscape** CLIP specifies the dimensions of the layer window.

**411**

- **Netscape** HEIGHT specifies the height, in pixels, of the layer window.

- **Netscape** ID provides a unique identifier name for the layer.

- **Netscape** LEFT specifies the leftmost position, in pixels, of the left side of a layer window.

- **Netscape** NAME provides a unique identifier name for the layer. It is preferable to use ID instead.

- **Netscape** ONBLUR specifies that the referred-to script runs when the element loses focus (that is, it is no longer the active element).

- **Netscape** ONFOCUS specifies that the referred-to script runs when the current element receives focus (that is, is made active) by the mouse pointer or other pointing device.

- **Netscape** ONLOAD specifies that the referred-to script runs after the active browser has finished loading a layer.

- **Netscape** ONMOUSEOUT specifies that the referred-to script runs when a user moves the mouse pointer or other pointing device away from the layer.

- **Netscape** ONMOUSEOVER specifies that the referred-to script runs the first time a user moves the mouse pointer or other pointing device over the layer.

- **Netscape** PAGEX specifies the horizontal position, in pixels, of the top left corner of the layer window within the current HTML document.

- **Netscape** PAGEY specifies the vertical position, in pixels, of the top left corner of the layer window within the current HTML document.

- **Microsoft** SRC specifies a source file that contains the contents of a layer window.

- | Netscape | TOP specifies the topmost position, in pixels, of the top of a layer window.

- | Netscape | WIDTH specifies the width, in pixels, of the layer window.

- | Netscape | VISIBILITY specifies whether a layer is visible or hidden.

- | Microsoft | Z-INDEX specifies the numerical order of the current layer.

## Notes

This is a Netscape extension, which is supported only within Netscape Navigator 4.0 or greater.

Many browsers do not support Netscape extensions.

The LAYER element specifies the absolute position of a layer.

By default, a layer is transparent.

You can use layers to animate a page or to modify a page almost instantly.

You can stack multiple layers on a page, and you can nest layers.

Use JavaScript to move, hide, expand, contract, rearrange, and change color and image characteristics of layers.

## Related Elements

ILAYER, NOLAYER

413

| MARQUEE | Scrolling Marquee |
|---------|-------------------|

## Purpose

Creates a text marquee that scrolls within the current document.

## Syntax

```
<MARQUEE[ BEHAVIOR=scroll|slide|alternate][
BGCOLOR="#rrggbb"|"color"][ CLASS="class_name"][
DATAFLD="ds_col_name"][
DATAFORMATAS="HTML"|"TEXT"][ DATASRC="ds_identifi-
er"][ DIRECTION=left|right][ HEIGHT="height_pix"|height_%][
HSPACE="horiz_pix"][ ID="id_name"][ LANG="lang_code"][
LANGUAGE="JAVASCRIPT"|"JSCRIPT"|"VBS[CRIPT]"][
LOOP="number_of_plays"|"INFINITE"][
ONAFTERUPDATE="au_script_data"][
ONBLUR="bl_script_data"][ ONBOUNCE="bn_script_data"][
ONCLICK="cl_script_data"][ ONDBLCLICK="dc_script_data"][
ONDRAGSTART="ds_script_data"][
ONFINISH="fn_script_data"][ ONFOCUS="fc_script_data"][
ONHELP="hlp_script_data"][ ONKEYDOWN="kd_script_data"][
ONKEYPRESS="kp_script_data"][ ONKEYUP="ku_script_data"][
ONMOUSEDOWN="md_script_data"][
ONMOUSEMOVE="mm_script_data"][
ONMOUSEOUT="mo_script_data"][
ONMOUSEOVER="mov_script_data"][
ONMOUSEUP="mu_script_data"][
ONRESIZE="rsz_script_data"][
ONROWENTER="re_script_data"][
ONROWEXIT="rex_script_data"][
ONSELECTSTART="ss_script_data"][
ONSTART="st_script_data"][ SCROLLAMOUNT="gap_pix"][
SCROLLDELAY="millisecs"][ STYLE="name_1: value_1"[;
"name_2: value_2"][...; "name_n: value_n"]][ TITLE="title"][
TRUESPEED][ VSPACE="vert_pix"][
WIDTH="width_pix"|width_%]>marquee_text</MARQUEE>
```

## Where

- **Microsoft** BEHAVIOR specifies the way that the text within the marquee will scroll.

- **Microsoft** BGCOLOR specifies the background color for the marquee.

- **Microsoft** CLASS specifies a class identification for the element.

- **Microsoft** DIRECTION specifies the direction that the text scrolls within the marquee window.

- **Microsoft** HEIGHT specifies the height of the window in which the marquee will be placed.

- **Microsoft** HSPACE is the horizontal area, in pixels, of the left and right sides of the marquee window and text, graphics, and links on the current page.

- **Microsoft** ID provides a unique identifier name for the element.

- **Microsoft** LANG provides the code representing the language used for the element.

- **Microsoft** LANGUAGE declares the scripting language of the current script.

- **Microsoft** LOOP indicates the number of times that an embedded audio clip will play or marquee will scroll.

- **Microsoft** ONAFTERUPDATE specifies that the referred-to script runs after data has been transferred from the element to the data repository.

- **Microsoft** ONBLUR specifies that the referred-to script runs when the marquee loses focus (that is, it is no longer the active element).

- **Microsoft** ONBOUNCE specifies that the referred-to script runs when BEHAVIOR="alternate" and the marquee text reaches a side of the window in which it is scrolling.

415

-  ONCLICK specifies that the referred-to script runs when a user moves the mouse pointer or other pointing device over the emphasized text and clicks the device button.

-  ONDBLCLICK specifies that the referred-to script runs when a user moves the mouse pointer or other pointing device over the emphasized text and double-clicks the device button.

-  ONDRAGSTART specifies that the referred-to script runs when the user starts dragging a selection or element.

-  ONFINISH specifies that the referred-to script runs when the marquee text has stopped scrolling.

-  ONFOCUS specifies that the referred-to script runs when the current element receives focus (that is, is made active) by the mouse pointer or other pointing device.

-  ONHELP specifies that the referred-to script runs when a user presses the F1 or Help key over the current element.

-  ONKEYDOWN specifies that the referred-to script runs when a user presses and holds a key down over the marquee.

-  ONKEYPRESS specifies that the referred-to script runs when a user presses and releases a key over the marquee.

-  ONKEYUP specifies that the referred-to script runs when a user releases a key over the marquee.

-  ONMOUSEDOWN specifies that the referred-to script runs when a user moves the mouse pointer or other pointing device over the marquee and presses and holds down the device button.

- 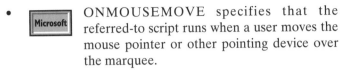 ONMOUSEMOVE specifies that the referred-to script runs when a user moves the mouse pointer or other pointing device over the marquee.

- ONMOUSEOUT specifies that the referred-to script runs when a user moves the mouse pointer or other pointing device away from the marquee.

- ONMOUSEOVER specifies that the referred-to script runs the first time a user moves the mouse pointer or other pointing device over the marquee.

- ONMOUSEUP specifies that the referred-to script runs when a user moves the mouse pointer or other pointing device over the marquee and releases a pressed-down device button.

- ONRESIZE specifies that the referred-to script runs when the user resizes the selected object.

- ONROWENTER specifies that the referred-to script runs when the current row has been modified.

- ONROWEXIT specifies that the referred-to script runs before the current row is modified.

- ONSELECTSTART specifies that the referred-to script runs when a user starts selecting an object.

- ONSTART specifies that the referred-to script runs when the loop starts.

- SCROLLAMOUNT specifies the gap, in pixels, from the end of the current marquee display and the beginning of the following display.

- **Microsoft** SCROLLDELAY specifies the time delay ,in milliseconds, from the end of the current marquee display and the beginning of the following display.

- **Microsoft** STYLE sets styles for the element.

- **Microsoft** TITLE provides a title or title information about the element.

- **Microsoft** TRUESPEED uses the SCROLLDELAY value as the speed of the scrolling text.

- **Microsoft** VSPACE is the vertical area, in pixels, of the top and bottom of the marquee window and other text, graphics, and links on the current page.

- **Microsoft** WIDTH specifies the width of the window in which the marquee will be placed.

- **Microsoft** *marquee_text* represents one or more characters.

## Notes

This is a Microsoft extension.

Most browsers do not support Microsoft extensions.

## Example

```
<MARQUEE BGCOLOR="silver" BEHAVIOR="alternate"
LOOP="3" HEIGHT="30" WIDTH="300"
DIRECTION="right">This is a scrolling marquee.</MAR-
QUEE>
```

This is a scrolling marquee.

*Figure 4.122 A sample of a marquee.*

| MULTICOL | Multiple Columns |
|---|---|

## Purpose

Applies a multiple-column format to a selected block of text, graphics, and/or links.

## Syntax

```
<MULTICOL[ COLS="num_cols"][ GUTTER="gutter_pix"][
WIDTH="width_pix"]>selected_area</MULTICOL>
```

## Where

- **Netscape** COLS specifies the number of columns in the selected area of the current document.

- **Netscape** GUTTER specifies the white space, in pixels, between columns.

- **Netscape** WIDTH specifies the width of all columns.

## Notes

This is a Netscape extension.

Most browsers do not support Netscape extensions.

The MULTICOL extension creates columns that are of equal width, separated by gutters of equal width.

| **NEXTID** | **Unique Identifier** |

## Purpose

Specifies a parameter that creates unique identifiers from within a text editor.

## Syntax

<NEXTID LANG=" *lang_code*"][ TITLE=" *title*"] >*parameter*[</NEX-TID>]

## Where

- **Microsoft** LANG provides the code representing the language used for the element.

- **Microsoft** TITLE provides a title or title information about the element.

- **Microsoft** *parameter* represents the parameter that leads to the unique identifier.

## Notes

This is a Microsoft extension.

Use NEXTID within the HEAD section of a document.

Many browsers do not support Microsoft extensions.

| NOBR | No Break |
| --- | --- |

## Purpose

Turns off automatic word wrap and line breaks except for those caused by the BR, P, or WBR elements.

## Syntax

<NOBR[ ID="*id_name*"][ STYLE="*name_1*: *value_1*"[ ; "*name_2*: *value_2*"][ ...; "*name_n*: *value_n*"]][ TITLE="*title*"] >*text*</NOBR>

## Where

- **Microsoft** ID provides a unique identifier name for the element.

- **Microsoft** STYLE sets styles for the element.

- **Microsoft** TITLE provides a title or title information about the element.

- **Netscape** **Microsoft** *text* represents one or more characters and spaces.

## Notes

This is a Netscape extension and a Microsoft extension.

Many browsers do not support Netscape and Microsoft extensions.

## Related Elements

BR, P, WBR

| **NOEMBED** | **Embed Alternate** |

## Purpose

Presents alternative content for browsers that do not support the use of the EMBED extension.

## Syntax

<NOEMBED>*alternate_content*</NOEMBED>

## Where

- **Netscape** *alternate_content* represents characters, HTML elements, special characters, graphics, and/or links.

## Notes

This is a Netscape extension.

Many browsers do not support Netscape extensions.

## Related Element

EMBED

| **NOLAYER** | **Layer Alternate** |

## Purpose

Presents alternative content for browsers that do not support the use of the LAYER extension.

## Syntax

<NOLAYER[SRC="*source_url*">*alternate_content*</NOLAYER>

## Where

- ![Netscape] SRC specifies a source file whose contents are displayed instead of a layer.

- ![Netscape] *alternate_content* represents characters, HTML elements, special characters, graphics, and/or links.

## Notes

This is a Netscape extension, which is supported only within Netscape Navigator 4.0 or greater.

Many browsers do not support Netscape extensions.

## Related Elements

ILAYER, LAYER

| SERVER | LiveWire Script |
|--------|-----------------|

## Purpose

Includes a JavaScript compiled by LiveWire in a document.

## Syntax

`<SERVER>LiveWire_script</SERVER>`

## Where

- **Netscape**    *LiveWire_script* is the current script.

## Notes

This is a Netscape extension.

SERVER is similar to the SCRIPT extension. However, it is interpreted at the server rather than the browser. For example, `<SERVER>write("Hello!")</SERVER>` would be run by the Netscape server and appear as Hello! on the client.

Many browsers do not support Netscape extensions.

## Related Element

SCRIPT

| SPACER | White Space |
|---|---|

## Purpose

Formats horizontal and/or vertical white space in an HTML document.

## Syntax

```
<SPACER[ ALIGN="left"|"right"|"top"|"absmiddle"|"abs-
bottom"|"texttop"|"middle"|"baseline"|"bottom"][
HEIGHT="height_pix"][ SIZE="size_pix"][ TYPE="horizon-
tal"|"vertical"|"block"][ WIDTH="width_pix"]>
```

## Where

- **Netscape** ALIGN aligns the white-space block with the surrounding text, graphics, and links.

- **Netscape** HEIGHT specifies the height of the white-space block (TYPE="block").

- **Netscape** SIZE specifies the width or height of the white space. (TYPE="horizontal" or TYPE="vertical")

- **Netscape** TYPE specifies the type of white-space area.

- **Netscape** WIDTH specifies the width of the white-space block (TYPE="block").

## Notes

This is a Netscape extension.

Many browsers do not support Netscape extensions.

You can use style sheets to add white space to a document. This is preferable to using the SPACER extension.

| **WBR** | **Word Break** |

## Purpose

Inserts a line break, if needed, within a no break (NOBR) line.

## Syntax

`<NOBR>text<WBR>text</NOBR>`

## Where

- **Netscape** *text* represents one or more characters.

## Notes

This is a Netscape extension.

Many browsers do not support Netscape extensions.

Embed the WBR element within the NOBR element.

## Related Elements

BR, NOBR, P

# PART 5

# Cascading Style Sheets

Those of us with considerable personal computer experience—especially using word processors—are familiar with *style sheets*, which we can use to define *rules* (that is, formats and enhancements) for selected text, paragraphs, or entire documents. Using an attached style sheet, a user can apply a rule by selecting part of a document and either choosing that rule from a drop-down list box or pressing a shortcut key or key combination—a considerable shortcut from making several menu or dialog box selections. For example, without a style sheet, changing selected text to a centered 18-point boldface heading with the Helvetica typeface requires four separate selections from menus or toolbars or, at the very least, opening a dialog box and making four choices. However, with a style sheet attached and a particular heading style defined, a user can make the same selections with the press of a single shortcut key or key combination.

 All word processing programs have a default style sheet (in Microsoft Word for Windows, it's called Normal), which automatically applies predefined formats to all new documents, their paragraphs, and text. For example, the Normal font in Word for Windows is Times New Roman, and the font size is 10 point. A default paragraph is left-aligned and single-spaced.

In addition to text formatting and enhancements, you can use style sheets to set document-wide margins, to add white space before and/or after a paragraph, to align paragraphs, and much more. A user can instantly change the look of a document by attaching a different style sheet. Or a single change in a style sheet can change one format for all the documents to which it is attached.

The World Wide Web Consortium (W3C) has announced the development of Cascading Style Sheets (CSS), which are sets of HTML document style sheets that enable HTML writers to change a document's format and look, just as they would a word processor document. At the time of this writing, some browsers, such as Microsoft Internet Explorer 3.0, Netscape Navigator, and W3C's Arena, support style sheets completely or in part; many others will support style sheets soon. We are still at the very beginning of the cascading style sheet era for HTML documents.

Part 7, "Webliography," includes a section titled "Cascading Style Sheets," which lists a number of online resources. You can also find up-to-date reference material and links to other style sheet resources at the W3C site.

## The Advantages of Using Style Sheets

By attaching a single style sheet to all its HTML documents, a business can ensure an identical format for an entire document and its elements—using the same colors, fonts, font sizes, white space, indentations, line spacing, and margins. Professional page designers can distribute style sheet templates with predefined table, heading, and body text formats and alignments, text enhancements, and page background colors. An HTML document writer can then attach the template and focus on a document's content; the formats and enhancements are already set.

 You can specify properties for an entire document by assigning properties for the BODY element because it is the element
NOTE that ultimately controls the contents of the document.

Those viewing an HTML document have the attribute of choosing from alternate rules by clicking on one of several rule links. For example, a visually impaired visitor could attach a sheet with large point sizes or, in a future cascading style sheet standard, the ability to pronounce the document's words through a computer sound system. Other visitors could attach sheets that would apply various colors to page and table backgrounds as well as fonts, point sizes, and enhancements to text. Before printing a document, a user could choose a completely different "printing-optimization" style sheet. Users can design and create their own style sheets.

**NOTE** It's important for those developing HTML documents to design style sheets that clash as little as possible with user-created style sheets and to realize that many browsers do not support style sheets. It's a good idea to look at your documents with and without style sheets attached.

A style sheet enables an HTML document writer to universally define formats for all like elements in a document. For example, all level-one headings (that is, paragraphs tagged with **H1**) should look the same. Using a style sheet, a writer can change the font, font size, and color, using a single rule. Without a style sheet, a writer can either stay with the defaults or redefine the look of every instance of a level-one heading.

## Associating a Cascading Style Sheet with a Document

You can associate a cascading style sheet in four ways:

- You can define styles for the document within STYLE elements in the HEAD section.
- You can link to a separate style sheet (a separate HTML document) using the LINK element, also placed in the HEAD section. This is preferable for developers working with large sites with many pages.
- Using the STYLE element, you can import an HTML document style sheet using a CSS @import notation.
- You can specify a style for a paragraph within the BODY section using the STYLE attribute.

## Defining Styles within a Document

For small documents or small sites, the easiest way to define rules is to include them in the HEAD section within STYLE elements. For example:

```
<HTML>

<HEAD>
```

```
<TITLE>Sample Document</TITLE>
<STYLE
<!—
BODY { BACKGROUND: silver }
H1 { FONT: 24pt "Arial"; FONT-WEIGHT: bold; COLOR: navy }
H2 { FONT: 20pt "Arial"; FONT-WEIGHT: bold; COLOR: maroon
}
H3 { FONT: 16pt "Arial"; FONT-WEIGHT: bold; COLOR: olive }
A:link { COLOR: red; FONT-SIZE: 12pt }
A:visited { COLOR: blue; FONT-SIZE: 12pt }
P { FONT: 12pt "Century Schoolbook" }
—>
</STYLE>
</HEAD>
<BODY>
body-content
</BODY>
</HTML>
```

A rule is composed of two parts. The *selector* is the element to
which the rule applies, and the *declaration* consists of the property and the value. For instance, in `P { FONT: 12pt "Century
Schoolbook" }`, the last style in the previous HTML example,
`P` is the selector, `FONT` is the property, and both `12pt` and
`"Century Schoolbook"` are values.

The previous set of rules specifies these formats:

- The page background color is silver, which is the same
  as specifying `<BODY BGCOLOR="silver">` in HTML.
- All level-one headings (`H1`) are Arial, 24 point, bold,
  and navy. In contrast, in an HTML document without
  this property, every level-one heading requires this
  statement: `<H1><B><FONT SIZE=2 COLOR="navy"
  FACE="Arial">`*heading-text*`</FONT></B></H1>`.

**NOTE** For these examples, the value of FONT SIZE is an approximation. For all headings, the font size would probably depend on the editor in which you created the heading and the browser with which you viewed the heading. In fact, many experienced style-sheet users recommend using relative, rather than absolute, font sizes.

- All level-two headings (H2) are Arial, 20 point, bold, and maroon. In an HTML document without this property, every level-two heading requires this statement: `<H2><B><FONT SIZE=2 COLOR="maroon" FACE="Arial"> heading-text</FONT></B></H2>`.

- All level-three headings (H3) are Arial, 16 point, bold, and olive. In an HTML document without this property, every level-three heading requires this statement: `<H3><B><FONT SIZE=1 COLOR="olive" FACE="Arial">heading-text< /FONT></B></H3>`.

- All active links are red with a point size of 12, which is the same as specifying `<BODY ALINK="red"><FONT SIZE=1>body-contents</FONT></BODY>` in HTML.

- All visited links are blue with a point size of 12, which is the same as specifying `<BODY ALINK="blue"><FONT SIZE=1>body-contents</FONT></BODY>` in HTML.

- All body text in a document appears in the Century Schoolbook font, with a point size of 12, which is the same as specifying `<P><FONT SIZE=1 FACE="Century Schoolbook">paragraph-text</FONT></P>` at the start of every paragraph following a paragraph with text defined as something other than Century Schoolbook 12 point.

## Linking to a Style Sheet File

To link an external style sheet, which is a separate HTML document, to an HTML document, add a LINK element statement in the HEAD section:

```
<HTML>
<HEAD>
```

```
<TITLE>Sample Document</TITLE>
<LINK REL="STYLESHEET" TYPE="text/css"
HREF="http://style.com/style_1/" TITLE="Style 1">
</HEAD>
<BODY>
```
*body-contents*
```
</BODY>
</HTML>
```

 **When uploading the HTML document and its associated files to a server, remember to also upload cascading style sheet** NOTE **files.**

## Importing a Style Sheet

The proposed syntax for importing a style sheet is:

```
<STYLE TYPE="text/css">
@IMPORT URL(http://style.com/style_1/)
</STYLE>
```

## Specifying a Paragraph Style

To specify a paragraph style, use the STYLE attribute within elements that define paragraphs (for example, P and heading elements). An example of a paragraph style follows:

```
P { color: red; font-family: Arial, "Century Gothic",
sans-serif; font-style: italic }
```

or

```
P {
   color: red;
   font-family: Arial, "Century Gothic", sans-serif;
   font-style: italic
}
```

This set of properties specifies that all text in this paragraph is red and Arial, Century Gothic, or another sans serif typeface (depending on the fonts installed on the computer), and italic. Because no point size (font-size) is specified, the browser uses the default size.

If you want to use the same rules for several elements, you can list the elements and the rules that apply. Perhaps the most common application for this is applying the same color to all the heading levels in a document: H1, H2, H3, H4 { color: red }. You can also define properties for elements embedded within other elements. For example, OL LI { font-style: Arial; font-size: small }. Notice that the headings on the same level are separated by commas, and the unlike elements that are separated by spaces.

If you want to add comments to a style sheet, enclose them within */; for example: UL { font-weight: demi-bold } */ All unordered lists */.

## Style Sheet Properties

This section is comprised of selected properties that are in effect for cascading style sheets, documented at the time of this writing. Each entry includes the syntax, a brief description, notes, and examples. To make sure that you have up-to-date information, refer to the "Cascading Style Sheets" section of *Part 7, Webliography*.

The syntax uses certain conventions:

> Required attributes are listed before optional attributes. Each type of attributes is arranged in alphabetical order.

[]   You can choose one or more of the attributes, values, or punctuation within the brackets.

|   A pipe symbol indicates an OR. Choose one attribute or value OR another. In other words, just choose one.

...   An ellipsis indicates a continuation of the preceding attribute and that the next attribute is the end of the series.

default  If an attribute or value is underlined, it is the default. In other words, if you do not use the attribute, your browser will automatically use the default attribute or value.

*Italics*  Italicized text represents a variable (such as a file name, path, color, number, URL, and so on) that you enter. Most times, enclose a variable within double quotes ("") or single quotes (''); do not mix double and single quotes.

| **BACKGROUND** | **Background Properties** |

## Purpose

Specifies up to five properties for the page background.

## Syntax

```
background: { background-attachment_value| background-
color_value| background-image_value| background-posi-
tion_value| background-repeat_value }
```

## Where

- *background-attachment_value* specifies the font size. For more information, see the BACKGROUND-ATTACHMENT property.
- *background-color_value* specifies the font family. For more information, see the BACKGROUND-COLOR property.
- *background-image_value* specifies the font style. For more information, see the BACKGROUND-IMAGE property.
- *background-position_value* specifies the font variant. For more information, see the BACKGROUND-POSI-TION property.
- *background-repeat_value* specifies the font weight. For more information, see the BACKGROUND-REPEAT property.

## Notes

This property specifies multiple properties for backgrounds in the same way that you can individually set rules for the BACK-GROUND-ATTACHMENT, BACKGROUND-COLOR, BACKGROUND-IMAGE, BACKGROUND-POSITION, and BACKGROUND-REPEAT properties.

You do not need to specify the property name. The browser should interpret the unique values for each property.

**437**

Table 4.1 contains selected hexadecimal color values.

This property can affect all elements.

For browsers that do not support background images, also define a background color.

The characteristics of this property are not inherited.

## Example

```
P.image {background: url(pattern.gif) silver repeat fixed }
```

## Related Elements

BODY (BACKGROUND and BGCOLOR attributes), BASEFONT, FONT

| BACKGROUND-ATTACHMENT | Attach Background Image |
|---|---|

## Purpose

Specifies whether the background image is fixed or scrolls in the background of the page.

## Syntax

```
background-attachment:{ scroll|fixed }
```

## Where

- scroll scrolls a background image as a user scrolls up or down the current page.
- fixed freezes the background image in place on the current page.

## Notes

This property can affect all elements.

For browsers that do not support background images, also define a background color.

Some browsers do not recognize this property.

The characteristics of this property are not inherited.

## Example

```
BODY { background-image: url(pattern.gif); background-color: silver; background-attachment: fixed }
```

## Related Element

BODY (BACKGROUND attribute)

| BACKGROUND-COLOR | Background Color |
| --- | --- |

## Purpose

Specifies a background color for the current document or document part.

## Syntax

```
background-color: { color-
name|#rgb|#rrggbb|rgb(rrr,ggg,bbb)|rgb(rrr%, ggg%,
bbb%)|transparent }
```

## Where

- *color-name* specifies a foreground color by valid name (that is, red, maroon, yellow, green, lime, teal, olive, aqua, blue, navy, purple, fuchsia, black, gray, silver, or white).
- *#rgb* is a three-digit hexadecimal color code, where *r* represents the red attributes, from 0 to F; *g* represents the green attributes, from 0 to F; and *b* represents the blue attributes, from 0 to F.
- *#rrggbb* is a six-digit hexadecimal color code, where *rr* represents the red attributes, from 00 to FF; *gg* represents the green attributes, from 00 to FF; and *bb* represents the blue attributes, from 00 to FF.
- rgb(*rrr,ggg,bbb*) represents absolute red-green-blue values, each ranging from 000 to 255.
- rgb(*rrr.d*%, *ggg.e*%, *bbb.f*%) represents the relative red-green-blue values, each ranging from 0.0% to 100.0%. Note that 0.0% is equivalent to an absolute value of 000, and 100.0% is equivalent to 255.
- transparent represents no background color.

## Notes

The initial color value is set within the user's browser.

Table 4.1 contains selected hexadecimal color values.
This property can affect all elements.
The characteristics of this property are not inherited.

## Example

```
BODY { background-color: silver }
```

## Related Elements

BODY (BGCOLOR attribute), BASEFONT, FONT

## BACKGROUND-IMAGE | Background Image

### Purpose

Specifies a background image for the current document or document part.

### Syntax

```
background-image: { url(url_name)|none }
```

### Where

- *url_name* names the URL of the image to be used for the background.
- none indicates no background image.

### Notes

This property can affect all elements.

For browsers that do not support background images, also define a background color.

The characteristics of this property are not inherited.

### Example

```
BODY { background-image: url(pattern.gif); background-
color: silver }
```

### Related Element

BODY (BACKGROUND attribute)

| **BACKGROUND-POSITION** | **Background Image Position** |
| --- | --- |

## Purpose

Specifies a starting position for a background image.

## Syntax

```
background-position:{ [+|-]percent%|[+|-]length
|{1,2}|[0%|[+|-]vert_pos]|[0%|[+|-]horiz_pos] }
```

## Where

- *percent* is a positive value that is relative to the size of the image. Follow *percent* with a percentage sign (%).
- *length* is a positive value followed by a two-letter abbreviation representing the unit of measure.
- 1,2 represent the coordinates of the upper left or lower right corner of the image.
- *vert_pos* represents the vertical position of the image onscreen. Valid values are top, center, and bottom.
- *horiz_pos* represents the horizontal position of the image onscreen. Valid values are left, center, and right.

## Notes

Valid relative units of measure are em (the height of the current font), ex (the height of the letter *x* in the current font), and px (pixels, relative to the size of the window). Valid absolute units of measure are in (inches), cm (centimeters), mm (millimeters), pt (points), and pc (picas).

If you specify one percentage or length, it determines the horizontal position of the image.

This property can affect block-level elements: ADDRESS, BLOCKQUOTE, BUTTON, CENTER, DIR, DIV, DL, FIELDSET, FORM, H1, H2, H3, H4, H5, H6, HR, ISINDEX, MENU, NOFRAMES, NOSCRIPT, OL, P, PRE, TABLE, and UL.

This property can affect *replaced elements* (that is, elements that are replaced with content such as images and user input): IMG, INPUT, OBJECT, SELECT, and TEXTAREA.

The default value of 0% 0% is equivalent to the values of top left and left top.

The value of 0% 50% is equivalent to left, left center, and center left.

The value of 50% 0% is equivalent to top, top center, and center top.

The value of 100% 0% is equivalent to right top and top right.

The value of 0% 100% is equivalent to left bottom and bottom left.

The value of 100% 100% is equivalent to bottom right and right bottom.

For browsers that do not support background images, also define a background color.

The characteristics of this property are not inherited.

## Example

```
BODY { background-image: url(pattern.gif); background-
position: 50% 50%; background-color: silver }
```

## BACKGROUND-REPEAT | Background Repeat

## Purpose

Repeats a background image onscreen a particular number of times.

## Syntax

```
background-repeat: { repeat|repeat-x|repeat-y|no-repeat }
```

## Where

- repeat fills the page completely with the image.
- repeat-x fills the page horizontally from the left edge to the right edge.
- repeat-y fills the page vertically from top to bottom.
- no-repeat does not repeat the image.

## Notes

This property can affect all elements.

For browsers that do not support background images, also define a background color.

The characteristics of this property are not inherited.

## Example

```
BODY { background-image: url(pattern.gif); background-
repeat: repeat-x; background-color: teal }
```

## Related Element

BODY (BACKGROUND attribute)

| BORDER | Border Properties |

## Purpose

Specifies the color, style, and/or width of all four borders.

## Syntax

```
border: {[ border-color_value]|[ border-style_value][
border-width_value] }
```

## Where

- *border-color_value* specifies the color of all four borders. For more information, see the BORDER-COLOR property.
- *border-style_value* specifies the style of all four borders. For more information, see the BORDER-STYLE property.
- *border-width_value* specifies the width of all four borders. For more information, see the BORDER-TOP-WIDTH property.

## Notes

This property specifies multiple properties for the four borders in the same way that you can individually set rules for the BORDER-COLOR, BORDER-STYLE, and BORDER-WIDTH properties.

You do not need to specify the property name. The browser should interpret the unique values for each property.

There is no initial value for this property.

This property can affect all elements.

The characteristics of this property are not inherited.

A BORDER is outside the content of the page but within the page edges and within the top, left, right, and bottom margins.

## Example

```
S { border: red double medium }
```

| **BORDER-BOTTOM** | **Bottom Border Properties** |
| --- | --- |

## Purpose

Specifies the color, style, and/or width of the bottom border.

## Syntax

```
border-bottom: {[ border-color_value]|[ border-
style_value][ border-bottom-width_value] }
```

## Where

- *border-color_value* specifies the border color. For more information, see the BORDER-COLOR property.
- *border-style_value* specifies the border style. For more information, see the BORDER-STYLE property.
- *border-bottom-width_value* specifies the border width. For more information, see the BORDER-BOTTOM-WIDTH property.

## Notes

This property specifies multiple properties for a bottom border in the same way that you can individually set rules for the BORDER-COLOR, BORDER-STYLE, and BORDER-BOTTOM-WIDTH properties.

You do not need to specify the property name. The browser should interpret the unique values for each property.

There is no initial value for this property.

This property can affect all elements.

The characteristics of this property are not inherited.

BORDER-BOTTOM accepts only one style, in contrast to BORDER-STYLE, which accepts as many as four.

A BORDER is outside the content of the page but within the page edges and within the top, left, right, and bottom margins.

## Example

```
IMG { border-bottom: black solid thick }
```

| BORDER-BOTTOM-WIDTH | Bottom Border Width |
|---|---|

## Purpose

Sets the width of the bottom border.

## Syntax

```
border-bottom-width:{ thin|medium|thick|length }
```

## Where

- thin is a narrower width than medium or thick.
- medium is wider than thin but narrower than thick.
- thick is wider than thin or medium.
- *length* is a positive value followed by a two-letter abbreviation representing the unit of measure.

## Notes

This property can affect any element.

A BORDER is outside the content of the page but within the page edges and within the top, left, right, and bottom margins.

The width of borders varies from browser to browser.

The characteristics of this property are not inherited.

## Example

```
TEXTAREA { border-bottom-width: thick }
```

| BORDER-COLOR | Border Color |
| --- | --- |

## Purpose

Sets colors of one, two, three, or four borders.

## Syntax

```
border-color: { [color-
name_t|#rgb_t|#rrggbb_t|rgb(rrr_t,ggg_t,bbb_t)|rgb(rrr
_t%, ggg_t%, bbb_t%)][color-
name_rt|#rgb_rt|#rrggbb_rt|rgb(rrr_rt,ggg_rt,bbb_rt)|rg
b(rrr_rt%, ggg_rt%, bbb_rt%)][color-
name_b|#rgb_b|#rrggbb_b|rgb(rrr_b,ggg_b,bbb_b)|rgb(rrr_
b%, ggg_b%, bbb_b%)][color-
name_l|#rgb_l|#rrggbb_l|rgb(rrr_l,ggg_l,bbb_l)|rgb(rrr_
l%, ggg_l%, bbb_l%)] }
```

## Where

- *color-name_t*, *color-name_rt*, *color-name_b*, and *color-name_l* specify border colors for the top, right, bottom, and left borders by valid name (that is, red, maroon, yellow, green, lime, teal, olive, aqua, blue, navy, purple, fuchsia, black, gray, silver, or white).
- *#rgb_t*, *#rgb_rt*, *#rgb_b*, and *#rgb_l* each represent a three-digit hexadecimal color code for the top, right, bottom, and left borders, where *r* represents the red attributes, from 0 to F; *g* represents the green attributes, from 0 to F; and *b* represents the blue attributes, from 0 to F.
- *#rrggbb_t*, *#rrggbb_rt*, *#rrggbb_b*, and *#rrggbb_l* each represent a six-digit hexadecimal color code for the top, right, bottom, and left borders, where *rr* represents the red attributes, from 00 to FF; *gg* represents the green attributes, from 00 to FF; and *bb* represents the blue attributes, from 00 to FF.

- rgb($rrr\_t,ggg\_t,bbb\_t$), rgb($rrr\_rt,ggg\_rt,bbb\_rt$), rgb($rrr\_b,ggg\_b,bbb\_b$), and rgb($rrr\_l,ggg\_l,bbb\_l$) each represent absolute red-green-blue values for the top, right, bottom, and left borders. Each of the values ranges from 000 to 255.

- rgb($rrr.d\_t\%$, $ggg.e\_t\%$, $bbb.f\_t\%$), rgb($rrr.d\_rt\%$, $ggg.e\_rt\%$, $bbb.f\_rt\%$), rgb($rrr.d\_b\%$, $ggg.e\_b\%$, $bbb.f\_b\%$), rgb($rrr.d\_l\%$, $ggg.e\_l\%$, $bbb.f\_l\%$) each represent the relative red-green-blue values, each ranging from 0.0% to 100.0%. Note that 0.0% is equivalent to an absolute value of 000, and 100.0% is equivalent to 255.

## Notes

The initial border color value is set within the user's browser.

Table 4.1 contains selected hexadecimal color values.

The characteristics of this property are inherited.

This property can affect any element.

A BORDER is outside the content of the page but within the page edges and within the top, left, right, and bottom margins.

## Example

```
H4 { border-color: blue; border-width: thin }
```

## Related Attribute

COLOR

| BORDER-LEFT | Left Border Properties |
|---|---|

## Purpose

Specifies the color, style, and/or width of the left border.

## Syntax

```
border-left: {[ border-color_value]|[ border-
style_value][ border-left-width_value] }
```

## Where

- *border-color_value* specifies the border color. For more information, see the BORDER-COLOR property.
- *border-style_value* specifies the border style. For more information, see the BORDER-STYLE property.
- *border-left-width_value* specifies the border width. For more information, see the BORDER-LEFT-WIDTH property.

## Notes

This property specifies multiple properties for borders in the same way that you can individually set rules for the BORDER-COLOR, BORDER-STYLE, and BORDER-LEFT-WIDTH properties.

You do not need to specify the property name. The browser should interpret the unique values for each property.

There is no initial value for this property.

This property can affect all elements.

The characteristics of this property are not inherited.

BORDER-LEFT accepts only one style, in contrast to BORDER-STYLE, which accepts as many as four.

A BORDER is outside the content of the page but within the page edges and within the top, left, right, and bottom margins.

## Example

```
INS { border-left: blue solid thin }
```

**451**

| BORDER-LEFT-WIDTH | Left Border Width |

## Purpose

Sets the width of the left border.

## Syntax

```
border-left-width:{ thin|medium|thick|length }
```

## Where

- thin is a narrower width than medium or thick.
- medium is wider than thin but narrower than thick.
- thick is wider than thin or medium.
- *length* is a positive value followed by a two-letter abbreviation representing the unit of measure.

## Notes

This property can affect any element.

A BORDER is outside the content of the page but within the page edges and within the top, left, right, and bottom margins.

The width of borders varies from browser to browser.

The characteristics of this property are not inherited.

## Example

```
H1 { border-left-width: 0.25in }
```

| BORDER-RIGHT | Right Border Properties |
|---|---|

## Purpose

Specifies the color, style, and/or width of the right border.

## Syntax

```
border-right: {[ border-color_value]|[ border-
style_value][ border-right-width_value] }
```

## Where

- *border-color_value* specifies the border color. For more information, see the BORDER-COLOR property.
- *border-style_value* specifies the border style. For more information, see the BORDER-STYLE property.
- *border-right-width_value* specifies the border width. For more information, see the BORDER-RIGHT-WIDTH property.

## Notes

This property specifies multiple properties for borders in the same way that you can individually set rules for the BORDER-COLOR, BORDER-STYLE, and BORDER-RIGHT-WIDTH properties.

You do not need to specify the property name. The browser should interpret the unique values for each property.

There is no initial value for this property.

This property can affect all elements.

The characteristics of this property are not inherited.

BORDER-RIGHT accepts only one style, in contrast to BORDER-STYLE, which accepts as many as four.

A BORDER is outside the content of the page but within the page edges and within the top, left, right, and bottom margins.

## Example

```
SPAN { border-right: teal dotted medium }
```

## BORDER-RIGHT-WIDTH | Right Border Width

### Purpose

Sets the width of the right border.

### Syntax

```
border-right-width:{ thin|medium|thick|length }
```

### Where

- thin is a narrower width than medium or thick.
- medium is wider than thin but narrower than thick.
- thick is wider than thin or medium.
- *length* is a positive value followed by a two-letter abbreviation representing the unit of measure.

### Notes

This property can affect any element.

A BORDER is outside the content of the page but within the page edges and within the top, left, right, and bottom margins.

The width of borders varies from browser to browser.

The characteristics of this property are not inherited.

### Example

```
BLOCKQUOTE { border-right-width: 2pt }
```

| BORDER-STYLE | Border Style |

## Purpose

Formats one, two, three, or four borders.

## Syntax

```
border:{ [
none|dotted|dashed|solid|double|groove|ridge|inset|out
set][
none|dotted|dashed|solid|double|groove|ridge|inset|out
set][
none|dotted|dashed|solid|double|groove|ridge|inset|out
set][
none|dotted|dashed|solid|double|groove|ridge|inset|out
set] }
```

## Where

- *none* omits a border. This overrides any BORDER-WIDTH value.
- *dotted* draws a dotted-line border over the element background.
- *dashed* draws a dashed-line border over the element background.
- *solid* draws a solid-line border over the element background.
- *double* draws a double-solid-line border over the element background.
- *groove* draws a three-dimensional grooved border over the element background using the BORDER-COLOR value.
- *ridge* draws a three-dimensional ridged border over the element background using the BORDER-COLOR value.
- *inset* draws a three-dimensional inset over the element background using the BORDER-COLOR value.

- *outset* draws a three-dimensional outset over the element background using the BORDER-COLOR value.

## Notes

This property can affect any element.

Some browsers that cannot interpret most BORDER-STYLE values will draw a solid line instead.

The characteristics of this property are not inherited.

A BORDER is outside the content of the page but within the page edges and within the top, left, right, and bottom margins.

If you supply one style, all borders are set to that style.

If you supply two or three styles, the browser supplies styles from the opposite side of the element. Elements are paired as follows: top and bottom, left and right.

## Example

```
H1 { border-style: inset outset }
```

| BORDER-TOP | Top Border Properties |

## Purpose

Specifies the color, style, and/or width of the top border.

## Syntax

```
border-top: { border-color_value| border-style_value|
border-top-width_value }
```

## Where

- *border-color_value* specifies the border color. For more information, see the BORDER-COLOR property.
- *border-style_value* specifies the border style. For more information, see the BORDER-STYLE property.
- *border-top-width_value* specifies the border width. For more information, see the BORDER-TOP-WIDTH property.

## Notes

This property specifies multiple properties for borders in the same way that you can individually set rules for the BORDER-COLOR, BORDER-STYLE, and BORDER-TOP-WIDTH properties.

You do not need to specify the property name. The browser should interpret the unique values for each property.

There is no initial value for this property.

This property can affect all elements.

The characteristics of this property are not inherited.

BORDER-TOP accepts only one style, in contrast to BORDER-STYLE, which accepts as many as four.

A BORDER is outside the content of the page but within the page edges and within the top, left, right, and bottom margins.

## Example

```
P.intro { border-top: red dotted thin }
```

**457**

| **BORDER-TOP-WIDTH** | **Top Border Width** |

## Purpose

Sets the width of the top border.

## Syntax

```
border-top-width:{ thin|medium|thick|length }
```

## Where

- thin is a narrower width than *medium* or *thick*.
- medium is wider than *thin* but narrower than *thick*.
- thick is wider than *thin* or *medium*.
- *length* is a positive value followed by a two-letter abbreviation representing the unit of measure.

## Notes

This property can affect any element.

A BORDER is outside the content of the page but within the page edges and within the top, left, right, and bottom margins.

The width of borders varies from browser to browser.

The characteristics of this property are not inherited.

## Example

```
BLOCKQUOTE { border-top-width: thin }
```

| BORDER-WIDTH | Border Width |

## Purpose

Sets the width of one, two, three, or four borders.

## Syntax

```
border-width:{
[thin|medium|thick|length] [thin|medium|thick|length] [thin|
medium|thick|length] [thin|medium|thick|length] }
```

## Where

- *thin* is a narrower width than *medium* or *thick*.
- *medium* is wider than *thin* but narrower than *thick*.
- *thick* is wider than *thin* or *medium*.
- *length* is a positive value followed by a two-letter abbreviation representing the unit of measure.

## Notes

This property can affect any element.

A BORDER is outside the content of the page but within the page edges and within the top, left, right, and bottom margins.

BORDER-WIDTH is the equivalent of BORDER-WIDTH-TOP, BORDER-WIDTH-RIGHT, BORDER-WIDTH-BOTTOM, and/or BORDER-WIDTH-LEFT, in that order.

If you supply one width, all borders are set to that width.

If you supply two or three widths, the browser supplies widths from the opposite side of the element. Elements are paired as follows: top and bottom, left and right.

The width of borders varies from browser to browser.

The characteristics of this property are not inherited.

## Example

```
UL { border-width: thin }
```

| CLEAR | Clear Element |

## Purpose

Displays a floating element next to or below the current element.

## Syntax

```
clear: { none|left|right|both }
```

## Where

- none does not wait for the margins to be clear; the element floats at the current alignment setting.
- left floats an element after the left margin is clear.
- right floats an element after the right margin is clear.
- both floats an element after both the left and right margins are clear.

## Notes

This property can affect any element, especially images.
    The characteristics of this property are not inherited.

## Example

```
IMG.float.gif { float: left }
```

## Related Attribute

ALIGN

| COLOR | Foreground Color |
|-------|------------------|

## Purpose

Specifies a foreground color for the current document or document part.

## Syntax

```
color: { color-
name|#rgb|#rrggbb|rgb(rrr,ggg,bbb)|rgb(rrr%, ggg%, bbb%) }
```

## Where

- *color-name* specifies a foreground color by valid name (that is, red, maroon, yellow, green, lime, teal, olive, aqua, blue, navy, purple, fuchsia, black, gray, silver, or white).
- *#rgb* is a three-digit hexadecimal color code, where *r* represents the red attributes, from 0 to F; *g* represents the green attributes, from 0 to F; and *b* represents the blue attributes, from 0 to F.
- *#rrggbb* is a six-digit hexadecimal color code, where *rr* represents the red attributes, from 00 to FF; *gg* represents the green attributes, from 00 to FF; and *bb* represents the blue attributes, from 00 to FF.
- rgb(*rrr,ggg,bbb*) represents absolute red-green-blue values, each ranging from 000 to 255.
- rgb(*rrr.d%, ggg.e%, bbb.f%*) represents the relative red-green-blue values, each ranging from 0.0% to 100.0%. Note that 0.0% is equivalent to an absolute value of 000, and 100.0% is equivalent to 255.

## Notes

The initial color value is set within the user's browser.

Table 4.1 contains selected hexadecimal color values.

The characteristics of this property are inherited.

# Example

```
P.intro { color: teal; font-size: 10pt; font-style: italic
}
```

# Related Elements

BODY, BASEFONT, FONT

| DISPLAY | Display Element |
|---------|-----------------|

## Purpose

Displays the current element in a particular way onscreen or in a printed format.

## Syntax

```
display: { inline|block|list-item|none }
```

## Where

- inline displays an inline box on the same line as the element that was most recently displayed.
- block creates a box in which to display the current element.
- list-item creates a box in which to display the current element and adds a list-item marker.
- none does not display the element, its child elements, and the box.

## Notes

An inline box is large enough to hold the content of the element. If the content is longer than one line, a new box is created for each line.

Some browsers will have initial values for all HTML elements. These values override the default value of block. Other browsers may completely ignore the DISPLAY property.

The characteristics of this property are not inherited.

## Example

```
Q { display: block }
```

| FLOAT | Float Element |
|-------|---------------|

## Purpose

Floats or inserts the element in the document.

## Syntax

```
float: { left|right|none }
```

## Where

- left floats the element on the left side and wraps text on its right side.
- right floats the element on the right side and wraps text on its left side.
- none displays the element as inserted on the page.

## Notes

This property can affect any element, especially images.
   The characteristics of this property are not inherited.

## Example

```
IMG.float.gif { float: left }
```

## Related Attribute

ALIGN

| **FONT** | **Font Properties** |
|----------|---------------------|

## Purpose

Specifies up to six properties for fonts.

## Syntax

```
font: { font-size_value |font-family_value|[[ font-
style_value ]|[ font-variant_value ]|[ font-
weight_value ]]|[/line-height_value ]}
```

## Where

- *font-size_value* specifies the font size. For more information, see the FONT-SIZE property.
- *font-family_value* specifies the font family. For more information, see the FONT-FAMILY property.
- *font-style_value* specifies the font style. For more information, see the FONT-STYLE property.
- *font-variant_value* specifies the font variant. For more information, see the FONT-VARIANT property.
- *font-weight_value* specifies the font weight. For more information, see the FONT-WEIGHT property.
- *line-height_value* specifies the line height. For more information, see the LINE-HEIGHT property.

## Notes

This property specifies multiple properties for fonts in the same way that you can individually set rules for the FONT-SIZE, FONT-STYLE, FONT-VARIANT, FONT-WEIGHT, and LINE-HEIGHT properties.

You do not need to specify the property name. The browser should interpret the unique values for each property.

If you do not specify a particular value, the browser uses the initial value.

By default, the value of LINE-HEIGHT is the height of one line of text.

There is no initial value for this property.

You can set percentage values for FONT-SIZE and LINE-HEIGHT only.

This property can affect all elements.

The characteristics of this property are inherited.

## Example

```
P {FONT: small-caps/90% "times new roman", serif }
```

## Related Elements

*BASEFONT, FONT*

| FONT-FAMILY | Font Family |
|---|---|

## Purpose

Specifies a font by name, font family, or both.

## Syntax

```
font-family:{ ["]family_name_1["]| serif|sans-serif|cur-
sive|fantasy|monospace }[, ["]family_name_2["]|
serif|sans-serif|cursive|fantasy|monospace][..., ["]fami-
ly_name_n["]| serif|sans-serif|cursive|fantasy|monospace]
```

## Where

- *family-name* is the name of a specific typeface.
- serif, sans-serif, cursive, fantasy, and monospace are the names of generic typefaces that might match one or more family names on a particular computer.

## Notes

This property specifies a font by name and/or font family.

You can specify multiple font families.

It is a good idea to end a list of font families with at least one generic typeface. This ensures that a font family will be defined.

The initial FONT-FAMILY value is set by the user's browser.

Use quotation marks to enclose family names of two or more words separated by spaces (for example, "Courier New" or "Bookman Old Style".

The characteristics of this property are inherited.

## Example

```
BODY { FONT-FAMILY: "Times New Roman", "Book Antigua",
serif }
```

## Related Elements

```
BASEFONT, FONT
```

| FONT-SIZE | Font Size |
|-----------|-----------|

## Purpose

Specifies an absolute or relative font size.

## Syntax

```
font-size: { length|percent%|absolute_size|relative_size }
```

## Where

- *length* is a positive value followed by a two-letter abbreviation representing the unit of measure.
- *percent* is a positive value that is relative to the font of the element immediately above the current element. Follow *percent* with a percentage sign (%).
- *absolute_size* is a set of font sizes that are determined by the user's browser. Valid values are xx-small, x-small, small, medium, large, x-large, xx-large.
- *relative_size* is larger than (larger) or smaller than (smaller) the font of the element immediately above the current element.

## Notes

Valid relative units of measure are em (the height of the current font), ex (the height of the letter x in the current font), and px (pixels, relative to the size of the window). Valid absolute units of measure are in (inches), cm (centimeters), mm (millimeters), pt (points), and pc (picas).

The characteristics of this property are inherited.

## Example

```
H4 { FONT-SIZE: 14pt }
H5 { FONT-SIZE: 125% }
H6 { FONT-SIZE: larger }
```

## Related Elements

```
BASEFONT, FONT
```

| FONT-STYLE | Font Style |
|---|---|

## Purpose

Specifies one or more text enhancements.

## Syntax

```
font-style: { normal|italic|oblique }
```

## Where

- normal is unitalicized text.
- italic is italicized text.
- oblique is usually slightly italicized text.

## Notes

This property specifies the degree of slant for text.

If you choose italic and the current typeface does not offer italics, text may be oblique instead.

Synonyms for oblique include slanted and incline. A synonym for italic is cursive.

The characteristics of this property are inherited.

## Example

```
H2, H4 { FONT-STYLE: italic; FONT-WEIGHT: bold}
```

## Related Elements

BASEFONT, FONT

| FONT-VARIANT | Font Variations |
|---|---|

## Purpose

Specifies one or more text variations.

## Syntax

```
font-style: { normal|small-caps }
```

## Where

- normal is any variation that is not small caps.
- small-caps is a variation that is all uppercase characters that are smaller than the usual uppercase characters in a typeface.

## Notes

This property specifies the case of text.

If a typeface does not include smaller uppercase characters, standard uppercase characters may be scaled down or may replace small caps.

The characteristics of this property are inherited.

## Example

```
P.note { font-variant: small-caps; font-weight: bolder }
```

## Related Elements

```
BASEFONT, FONT
```

| FONT-WEIGHT | Bold Font |

## Purpose

Specifies the degree of boldness or lightness of text.

## Syntax

```
font-weight: {
normal|bold|bolder|lighter|100|200|300|400|500|600|700|800
|900 }
```

## Where

- normal is the standard non-bold, non-light weight of text.
- bold is the standard boldface text.
- bolder is bolder than standard boldface. It can be the equivalent of Ultra Bold or Heavy text. This is a relative value.
- lighter is the equivalent of light text. This is a relative value.
- 100 is the lightest weight.
- 200 and 300 are somewhere between light and normal weight.
- 400 is the equivalent of normal weight.
- 500 and 600 are somewhere between normal and bold weight. 500 is the equivalent of a Medium weight.
- 700 is the equivalent of bold weight.
- 800 and 900 are bolder than bold weight.

## Notes

This property specifies the boldness or lightness of the font, in an absolute or relative value.

The characteristics of this property are inherited.

# Example

```
P.warning { font-weight: 800 }
```

# Related Elements

```
BASEFONT, FONT
```

| HEIGHT | Element Height |

## Purpose

Specifies the height of the selected element.

## Syntax

```
height: { length|auto }
```

## Where

- *length* is a positive value followed by a two-letter abbreviation representing the unit of measure.
- auto is a value automatically calculated by the user's browser.

## Notes

This property sets the height of the selected element, in pixels, or by calculating its height automatically, scaled proportionately with the width.

Valid relative units of measure are em (the height of the current font), ex (the height of the letter x in the current font), and px (pixels, relative to the size of the window). Valid absolute units of measure are in (inches), cm (centimeters), mm (millimeters), pt (points), and pc (picas).

This property can affect block-level elements: ADDRESS, BLOCKQUOTE, BUTTON, CENTER, DIR, DIV, DL, FIELDSET, FORM, H1, H2, H3, H4, H5, H6, HR, ISINDEX, MENU, NOFRAMES, NOSCRIPT, OL, P, PRE, TABLE, and UL.

This property can affect replaced elements: IMG, INPUT, OBJECT, SELECT, and TEXTAREA. Some browsers may ignore the HEIGHT property if the affected element is not a replaced element.

If the height of the element is equal to auto, the *aspect ratio* (that is, the current proportions of the element) is maintained.

If both the height and width of the element are equal to auto, the browser does not change the element's dimensions.

The characteristics of this property are not inherited.

## Example

```
IMG.bigpics { height: 400px; width: 250px }
```

## Related Element

IMG

## Related Property

WIDTH

| **IMPORTANT** | **Important Declaration** |
|---|---|

## Purpose

States that the current declaration is more important than others.

## Syntax

```
!important;
```

## Notes

Add `!important;` to the end of a declaration to specify that the declaration overrides other declarations.

An author-defined declaration that is not important overrides a user-defined declaration that is not important.

A user-defined important declaration overrides an author declaration that is not important.

An author-defined important declaration overrides a user-defined important declaration.

| **LETTER-SPACING** | **Character Spacing** |

## Purpose

Sets spacing between characters.

## Syntax

```
letter-spacing: { normal|[+|-]length }
```

## Where

- normal represents the normal spacing between characters.
- *length* is a positive value followed by a two-letter abbreviation representing the unit of measure. *length* is usually an increase in the spacing between characters but can be a decrease (a negative value).

## Notes

Valid relative units of measure are em (the height of the current font), ex (the height of the letter x in the current font), and px (pixels, relative to the size of the window). Valid absolute units of measure are in (inches), cm (centimeters), mm (millimeters), pt (points), and pc (picas).

This property can affect all elements.

The characteristics of this property are inherited.

## Example

```
P.emphasis { letter-spacing: 4mm; font-weight: bolder }
```

## Related Property

```
word-spacing
```

| **LINE-HEIGHT** | **Baseline Height** |
|---|---|

## Purpose

Specifies the height of the line from baseline to baseline.

## Syntax

```
line-height: { normal|number|length|percent% }
```

## Where

- normal is the parent element's line height. The suggested numeric value for normal should range between 1.0 and 1.2.
- *number* is a number by which the current font size is multiplied to result in a new line height.
- *length* is a positive value followed by a two-letter abbreviation representing the unit of measure.
- *percent* is a positive value that is relative to the size of the line height. Follow *percent* with a percentage sign (%).

## Notes

This property specifies the height from baseline to baseline, in a number multiplied by the present font size, the length (in the default unit of measure), or a percentage of the present font size.

Valid relative units of measure are em (the height of the current font), ex (the height of the letter x in the current font), and px (pixels, relative to the size of the window). Valid absolute units of measure are in (inches), cm (centimeters), mm (millimeters), pt (points), and pc (picas).

Negative values are not valid.

This property can affect all elements.

The initial LINE-HEIGHT value is set by the user's browser.

The characteristics of this property are inherited.

## Example

```
SPAN { line-height: 110%; font-size: 12pt }
```

| **LIST-STYLE** | **List Style Properties** |
|---|---|

## Purpose

Specifies up to three properties for lists.

## Syntax

```
list-style: { list-style-image_value| list-style-posi-
tion_value| list-style-type_value }
```

## Where

- *list-style-image_value* specifies the list-item image. For more information, see the LIST-STYLE-IMAGE property.
- *list-style-position_value* specifies the list-item position. For more information, see the LIST-STYLE-POSITION property.
- *list-style-type_value* specifies the list-style-type. For more information, see the LIST-STYLE-TYPE property.

## Notes

This property specifies multiple properties for list-item markers in the same way that you can individually set rules for the LIST-STYLE-IMAGE, LIST-STYLE-POSITION, and LIST-STYLE-TYPE properties.

You do not need to specify the property name. The browser should interpret the unique values for each property.

## Example

```
UL { list-style: url(button.gif) circle outside}
```

## Related Attribute

TYPE

## LIST-STYLE-IMAGE | List Style Image

### Purpose

Specifies the image preceding items on an ordered or unordered list.

### Syntax

```
list-style-image: { url(url_name)|none }
```

### Where

- *url_name* names the URL of the image to be used for the list-item marker.
- none indicates no background image.

### Notes

This property applies to list elements: DIR, MENU, OL, and UL.
    The characteristics of this property are inherited.

### Example

```
UL { list-style-image: url(button.gif) }
```

### Related Attribute

TYPE

| LIST-STYLE-POSITION | List Style Position |
|---|---|

## Purpose

Specifies the position of an ordered or unordered list.

## Syntax

```
list-style-position: { inside|outside }
```

## Where

- inside aligns the second line of the list-item text with the left margin (that is, under the list-item marker).
- outside displays the second line of the list-item text under the first line (that is, it creates a hanging indent).

## Notes

This property applies to list elements: DIR, MENU, OL, and UL.
The characteristics of this property are inherited.

## Example

```
UL { list-style-position: outside }
```

## Related Attribute

```
TYPE
```

| LIST-STYLE-TYPE | List Style Type |
|---|---|

## Purpose

Specifies the number or bullet type preceding items on an ordered or unordered list.

## Syntax

```
list-style-type: { disc|circle|square|decimal|lower-
roman|upper-roman|lower-alpha|upper-alpha|none }
```

## Where

- disc uses filled bullets.
- circle uses unfilled circles.
- square uses filled square bullets.
- decimal uses Arabic numerals (1, 2, 3)
- lower-roman uses small Roman numerals (i, ii, iii).
- upper-roman uses large Roman numerals (I, II, III).
- lower-alpha uses lowercase alphabetic letters (a, b, c).
- upper-alpha uses uppercase alphabetic letters (A, B, C).
- none uses no bullets or numbers.

## Notes

This property applies to list elements: DIR, MENU, OL, and UL.
The characteristics of this property are inherited.

## Example

```
UL { list-style-type: square }
```

## Related Attribute

TYPE

| **MARGIN** | **Margins Characteristics** |
|------------|------------------------------|

## Purpose

Turns on or off one, two, three, or four margins or sets margin size.

## Syntax

```
margin: {
[length_top|percent_top%|auto][length_right|percent_rig
ht%|auto][length_bottom|percent_bottom%|auto][length_le
ft|percent_left%|auto] }
```

## Where

- *length_top*, *length_right*, *length_bottom*, and *length_left* are positive or negative values followed by a two-letter abbreviation representing the unit of measure.
- *percent_top*, *percent_right*, *percent_bottom*, *and percent_left* are positive values that are relative to the parent element's selected margins. Follow a percent value with a percentage sign (%).
- auto are top-margin, right-margin, bottom-margin, and left-margin values automatically calculated by the user's browser.

## Notes

This property turns one, two, three, or four margins on or off, or sets margin size (in the default unit of measure) as a percentage of the current width, or automatically by calculating a minimum amount.

Valid relative units of measure are em (the height of the current font), ex (the height of the letter x in the current font), and px (pixels, relative to the size of the window). Valid absolute units of measure are in (inches), cm (centimeters), mm (millimeters), pt (points), and pc (picas).

This property can set margin characteristics for all HTML elements.

If you supply one value, all margins are set to that value.

If you supply two or three values, the browser supplies values from the opposite side of the element. Elements are paired as follows: top and bottom, left and right.

A MARGIN is above the content of the page, borders, and padding but within the page edges.

The characteristics of this property are not inherited.

## Example

```
BODY {margin: 1in 1in 0.5in}
```

## Related Attributes

HSPACE, MARGINHEIGHT, MARGINWIDTH , TOPMARGIN (Microsoft-defined attribute), VSPACE

| **MARGIN-BOTTOM** | **Bottom Margin** |

## Purpose

Turns on or off bottom margin and/or specifies bottom-margin size.

## Syntax

```
{ margin-bottom: 0|length|percent%|auto }
```

## Where

- *0* represents the parent element's current bottom margin.
- *percent* is a positive value that is relative to the parent element's bottom margin. Follow percent with a percentage sign (%).
- *length* is a positive or negative value followed by a two-letter abbreviation representing the unit of measure.
- auto is a value automatically calculated by the user's browser.

## Notes

This property turns bottom margins on or off, or sets a margin size (in the default unit of measure) as a percentage of the current height, or automatically by calculating a minimum amount.

Valid relative units of measure are em (the height of the current font), ex (the height of the letter x in the current font), and px (pixels, relative to the size of the window). Valid absolute units of measure are in (inches), cm (centimeters), mm (millimeters), pt (points), and pc (picas).

This property can set bottom-margin characteristics for all HTML elements.

A MARGIN is above the content of the page, borders, and padding but within the page edges.

The characteristics of this property are not inherited.

## Example

```
BODY { margin-bottom: 18pt }
```

## Related Attributes

MARGINHEIGHT, VSPACE

| **MARGIN-LEFT** | **Left Margin** |
|---|---|

## Purpose

Turns on or off left margins or sets left-margin size.

## Syntax

```
{ margin-left: 0|length|percent%|auto }
```

## Where

- 0 represents the parent element's current left margin.
- *percent* is a positive value that is relative to the parent element's left margin. Follow percent with a percentage sign (%).
- *length* is a positive or negative value followed by a two-letter abbreviation representing the unit of measure.
- auto is a value automatically calculated by the user's browser.

## Notes

This property turns the left margin on or off and/or sets the left margin size (in the default unit of measure) as a percentage of the current width, or automatically by calculating a minimum amount.

Valid relative units of measure are em (the width of the current font), ex (the width of the letter x in the current font), and px (pixels, relative to the size of the window). Valid absolute units of measure are in (inches), cm (centimeters), mm (millimeters), pt (points), and pc (picas).

This property can set left-margin characteristics for all HTML elements.

A MARGIN is above the content of the page, borders, and padding but within the page edges.

The characteristics of this property are not inherited.

## Example

```
BODY { margin-right: 0.5in; margin-top: 1.0in; margin-
bottom: 1.0in; margin-left: 0.5in }
```

## Related Attributes

HSPACE, MARGINWIDTH

| **MARGIN-RIGHT** | **Right Margin** |

## Purpose

Turns on or off the right margin and/or sets the right-margin size.

## Syntax

```
{ margin-right: 0|length|percent%|auto }
```

## Where

- *0* represents the parent element's current right margin.
- *percent* is a positive value that is relative to the parent element's right margin. Follow percent with a percentage sign (%).
- *length* is a positive or negative value followed by a two-letter abbreviation representing the unit of measure.
- auto is a value automatically calculated by the user's browser.

## Notes

This property turns right margins on or off, or sets the margin size (in the default unit of measure) as a percentage of the current width, or automatically by calculating a minimum amount.

Valid relative units of measure are em (the width of the current font), ex (the width of the letter x in the current font), and px (pixels, relative to the size of the window). Valid absolute units of measure are in (inches), cm (centimeters), mm (millimeters), pt (points), and pc (picas).

This property can set right-margin characteristics for all HTML elements.

A MARGIN is above the content of the page, borders, and padding but within the page edges.

The characteristics of this property are not inherited.

## Example

```
BODY { margin-right: 18pt; margin-top: 36pt; margin-
bottom: 18pt; margin-left: 18pt }
```

## Related Attributes

HSPACE, MARGINWIDTH

| **MARGIN-TOP** | **Top Margin** |

## Purpose

Turns on or off top margins or sets top-margin size.

## Syntax

```
{ margin-top: 0|length|percent%|auto }
```

## Where

- 0 represents the parent element's current top margin.
- *percent* is a positive value that is relative to the parent element's top margin. Follow percent with a percentage sign (%).
- *length* is a positive or negative value followed by a two-letter abbreviation representing the unit of measure.
- auto is a value automatically calculated by the user's browser.

## Notes

This property turns top margins on or off, or sets a margin size (in the default unit of measure) as a percentage of the current height, or automatically by calculating a minimum amount.

Valid relative units of measure are em (the height of the current font), ex (the height of the letter x in the current font), and px (pixels, relative to the size of the window). Valid absolute units of measure are in (inches), cm (centimeters), mm (millimeters), pt (points), and pc (picas).

This property can set top-margin characteristics for all HTML elements.

A MARGIN is above the content of the page, borders, and padding but within the page edges.

The characteristics of this property are not inherited.

## Example

```
BODY { margin-top: 36pt }
```

## Related Attributes

MARGINHEIGHT, TOPMARGIN (Microsoft-defined attribute), VSPACE

| PADDING | Padding Characteristics |
|---------|-------------------------|

## Purpose

Turns on or off one, two, three, or four paddings or sets padding size.

## Syntax

```
padding: { [length_top|percent_top%] [length_right|per-
cent_right%] [length_bottom|percent_bottom%] [length_lef
t|percent_left%] }
```

## Where

- *length_top*, *length_right*, *length_bottom*, and *length_left* are positive or negative values followed by a two-letter abbreviation representing the unit of measure.
- *percent_top*, *percent_right*, *percent_bottom*, *and percent_left* are positive values that are relative to the parent element's selected paddings. Follow percent with a percentage sign (%).

## Notes

Padding is space between the border and content. This property turns one, two, three, or four paddings on or off, or sets padding size (in the default unit of measure) as a percentage of the current width, or automatically by calculating a minimum amount.

Valid relative units of measure are em (the height of the current font), ex (the height of the letter x in the current font), and px (pixels, relative to the size of the window). Valid absolute units of measure are in (inches), cm (centimeters), mm (millimeters), pt (points), and pc (picas).

This property can set padding characteristics for all HTML elements.

If you supply one value, all paddings are set to that value.

If you supply two or three values, the browser supplies values from the opposite side of the element. Elements are paired as follows: top and bottom, left and right.

The characteristics of this property are not inherited.

## Example

```
P.special { padding: 6pt 4pt }
```

| PADDING-BOTTOM | Bottom Padding |
|----------------|----------------|

## Purpose

Turns on or off bottom padding and/or specifies bottom-padding size.

## Syntax

```
{ padding-bottom: 0|length|percent% }
```

## Where

- 0 represents the parent element's current bottom padding.
- *percent* is a positive value that is relative to the parent element's bottom padding. Follow percent with a percentage sign (%).
- *length* is a positive value followed by a two-letter abbreviation representing the unit of measure.

## Notes

This property turns bottom padding on or off, or sets a padding size (in the default unit of measure) as a percentage of the current height, or automatically by calculating a minimum amount.

Valid relative units of measure are em (the height of the current font), ex (the height of the letter x in the current font), and px (pixels, relative to the size of the window). Valid absolute units of measure are in (inches), cm (centimeters), mm (millimeters), pt (points), and pc (picas).

This property can set bottom-padding characteristics for all HTML elements.

Padding is above the content of the page, within the page edges, and below margins and borders.

The characteristics of this property are not inherited.

## Example

```
BODY { padding-bottom: 8pt }
```

**495**

## PADDING-LEFT | Left Padding

## Purpose

Turns on or off left padding or sets left-padding size.

## Syntax

```
{ padding-left: 0|length|percent% }
```

## Where

- 0 represents the parent element's current left padding.
- *percent* is a positive value that is relative to the parent element's left padding. Follow percent with a percentage sign (%).
- *length* is a positive value followed by a two-letter abbreviation representing the unit of measure.

## Notes

This property turns the left padding on or off and/or sets the left padding size (in the default unit of measure) as a percentage of the current width, or automatically by calculating a minimum amount.

Valid relative units of measure are em (the width of the current font), ex (the width of the letter x in the current font), and px (pixels, relative to the size of the window). Valid absolute units of measure are in (inches), cm (centimeters), mm (millimeters), pt (points), and pc (picas).

This property can set left-margin characteristics for all HTML elements.

Padding is above the content of the page, within the page edges, and below margins and borders.

The characteristics of this property are not inherited.

## Example

```
BODY { padding-right: 0.5in; padding-top: 0.25in; padding-
bottom: 0.5in; padding-left: 0.5in }
```

| **PADDING-RIGHT** | **Right Padding** |

## Purpose

Turns on or off the right padding and/or sets the right-padding size.

## Syntax

```
{ padding-right: 0|length|percent% }
```

## Where

- 0 represents the parent element's current right padding.
- *percent* is a positive value that is relative to the parent element's right padding. Follow percent with a percentage sign (%).
- *length* is a positive value followed by a two-letter abbreviation representing the unit of measure.

## Notes

This property turns right padding on or off, or sets the padding size (in the default unit of measure) as a percentage of the current width, or automatically by calculating a minimum amount.

Valid relative units of measure are em (the width of the current font), ex (the width of the letter x in the current font), and px (pixels, relative to the size of the window). Valid absolute units of measure are in (inches), cm (centimeters), mm (millimeters), pt (points), and pc (picas).

This property can set right-padding characteristics for all HTML elements.

Padding is above the content of the page, within the page edges, and below margins and borders.

The characteristics of this property are not inherited.

## Example

```
BODY { padding-right: 8pt; padding-top: 6pt; padding-bot-
tom: 4pt; padding-left: 8pt }
```

## PADDING-TOP | Top Padding

## Purpose

Turns on or off top padding or sets top-padding size.

## Syntax

```
{ padding-top: 0|length|percent% }
```

## Where

- 0 represents the parent element's current top padding.
- *percent* is a positive value that is relative to the parent element's top padding. Follow percent with a percentage sign (%).
- *length* is a positive value followed by a two-letter abbreviation representing the unit of measure.

## Notes

This property turns top padding on or off, or sets a padding size (in the default unit of measure) as a percentage of the current height, or automatically by calculating a minimum amount.

Valid relative units of measure are em (the height of the current font), ex (the height of the letter x in the current font), and px (pixels, relative to the size of the window). Valid absolute units of measure are in (inches), cm (centimeters), mm (millimeters), pt (points), and pc (picas).

This property can set top-padding characteristics for all HTML elements.

Padding is above the content of the page, within the page edges, and below margins and borders.

The characteristics of this property are not inherited.

## Example

```
BODY { padding-top: 6pt }
```

| **TEXT-ALIGN** | **Horizontal Alignment** |
| --- | --- |

## Purpose

Sets horizontal alignment of selected text.

## Syntax

```
text-align: { left|right|justify|center }
```

## Where

- left aligns text within the element with the left margin.
- right aligns text within the element with the right margin.
- justify aligns text within the element with the both the left and right margins.
- center centers text within the element between the left and right margins.

## Notes

This property specifies the alignment of text: with the left or right margin, with both left and right margins, or centered between the margins.

The initial alignment value depends on the user's browser and the direction in which the language is displayed.

The characteristics of this property are inherited.

This property can affect block-level elements: ADDRESS, BLOCKQUOTE, BUTTON, CENTER, DIR, DIV, DL, FIELDSET, FORM, H1, H2, H3, H4, H5, H6, HR, ISINDEX, MENU, NOFRAMES, NOSCRIPT, OL, P, PRE, TABLE, and UL.

## Example

```
P.FORMAL { text-align: justify }
```

# Related Property

VERTICAL-ALIGN

## Related Attribute

ALIGN

| **TEXT-DECORATION** | **Enhance Text** |

## Purpose

Enhances text with lines or blinking.

## Syntax

```
text-decoration: { none|[underline|overline|line-
through|blink] }
```

## Where

- none does not decorate the selected text.
- underline underlines the selected text.
- overline draws a line over the selected text.
- line-through strikes through the selected text.
- blink turns the display of selected text on and off.

## Notes

This property can affect all elements.

The characteristics of this property are not inherited. However, the children of the current elements should have the same TEXT-DECORATION properties.

Although browsers should recognize blink, they may not "blink" the selected text.

## Example

```
P.MESSAGE { TEXT-DECORATION: underline; TEXT-DECORATION:
overline }
```

## Related Elements

BLINK (Netscape extension), S, STRIKE, U

| TEXT-INDENT | First-Line Indention |
|---|---|

## Purpose

Indents the first line of text.

## Syntax

```
text-indent: { length|percent% }
```

## Where

- *length* is a positive value followed by a two-letter abbreviation representing the unit of measure.
- *percent* is a positive value that is relative to the width of the parent element. Follow *percent* with a percentage sign (%).

## Notes

This property specifies the first-line indention of the text, measured from the left margin (in the default unit of measure) or as a percentage of change from the original indent.

Valid relative units of measure are em (the height of the current font), ex (the height of the letter x in the current font), and px (pixels, relative to the size of the window). Valid absolute units of measure are in (inches), cm (centimeters), mm (millimeters), pt (points), and pc (picas).

This property can affect block-level elements: ADDRESS, BLOCKQUOTE, BUTTON, CENTER, DIR, DIV, DL, FIELDSET, FORM, H1, H2, H3, H4, H5, H6, HR, ISINDEX, MENU, NOFRAMES, NOSCRIPT, OL, P, PRE, TABLE, and UL.

The characteristics of this property are inherited.

## Example

```
P { text-indent: 0.5in }
```

| TEXT-TRANSFORM | Change Case |
| --- | --- |

## Purpose

Changes case of the selected text.

## Syntax

```
text-transform: { capitalize|uppercase|lowercase|none }
```

## Where

- capitalize applies initial uppercase to the selected text.
- uppercase applies all uppercase to the selected text.
- lowercase applies all lowercase to the selected text.
- none turns off the value inherited from the parent.

## Notes

This property transforms text to initial uppercase, all uppercase, all lowercase, or unchanged for its current case.

This property can apply to all elements.

The characteristics of this property are inherited.

## Example

```
P.warning { text-transform: uppercase; font-weight: 900 }
```

| VERTICAL-ALIGN | Vertical Alignment |
|---|---|

## Purpose

Sets vertical alignment of the element.

## Syntax

```
vertical-align: { baseline|sub|super|top|text-
top|middle|bottom|text-bottom|percent% }
```

## Where

- baseline vertically aligns the element with the baseline of the current element or the parent element if the current element has no baseline.
- sub makes the element a subscript.
- super makes the element a superscript.
- top vertically aligns the top of the element with the top of the highest element on the current line.
- text-top vertically aligns the element with the top of the parent element's typeface.
- middle vertically aligns the element with the middle of the element, computed by starting with the baseline and adding half the x-height of the parent element's typeface.
- bottom vertically aligns the bottom of the element with the lowest element on the current line.
- text-bottom vertically aligns the bottom of the element with the bottom of the parent element's typeface.
- *percent* is a positive value that is relative to the text line height. Follow percent with a percentage sign (%).

## Notes

This property specifies the vertical alignment of text with the baseline or font, or as a percentage above or below the baseline.

A percentage value is in relationship to the height of the affected element.

**504**

Using the top or bottom values may result in an inadvertent loop in the display of the element.

This property applies to inline elements.

The characteristics of this property are not inherited.

## Example

```
SUB { vertical-align: text-bottom; color: red }
```

## Related Property

```
TEXT-ALIGN
```

## Related Attribute

ALIGN

| **WHITE-SPACE** | **White Space** |

## Purpose

Turns on or off white space.

## Syntax

```
white-space: { normal|pre|nowrap }
```

## Where

- normal does not add white space to an element.
- pre treats the element as preformatted content in the same way that the PRE element works in HTML documents.
- nowrap does not wrap text. Use BR to insert line breaks.

## Notes

This property specifies whether white space is eliminated as in normal HTML documents or preformatted as in the PRE element.

This property can affect block-level elements: ADDRESS, BLOCKQUOTE, BUTTON, CENTER, DIR, DIV, DL, FIELDSET, FORM, H1, H2, H3, H4, H5, H6, HR, ISINDEX, MENU, NOFRAMES, NOSCRIPT, OL, P, PRE, TABLE, and UL.

The characteristics of this property are inherited.

## Example

```
H1 { white-space: pre }
```

## Related Elements

```
BR, PRE
```

## Related Attributes

GUTTER and SIZE (Netscape-defined attributes)

**506**

| **WIDTH** | **Element Width** |
|-----------|-------------------|

## Purpose

Specifies the width of the selected element.

## Syntax

```
width: { length|percent%|auto }
```

## Where

- *length* is a positive value followed by a two-letter abbreviation representing the unit of measure.
- *percent* is a positive value that is relative to the size of the image. Follow *percent* with a percentage sign (%).
- auto is a value automatically calculated by the user's browser.

## Notes

This property sets the width of the selected element, in pixels, as a percentage of the original size, or by calculating its width automatically, scaled proportionately with the height.

Valid relative units of measure are em (the height of the current font), ex (the height of the letter x in the current font), and px (pixels, relative to the size of the window). Valid absolute units of measure are in (inches), cm (centimeters), mm (millimeters), pt (points), and pc (picas).

This property can affect block-level elements: ADDRESS, BLOCKQUOTE, BUTTON, CENTER, DIR, DIV, DL, FIELDSET, FORM, H1, H2, H3, H4, H5, H6, HR, ISINDEX, MENU, NOFRAMES, NOSCRIPT, OL, P, PRE, TABLE, and UL.

This property can affect replaced elements: IMG, INPUT, OBJECT, SELECT, and TEXTAREA.

If the element is wider than the width, the browser will scale the element.

If the height of the element is equal to auto, the aspect ratio (proportions of the element) is maintained.

If both the height and width of the element are equal to auto, the browser does not change the element's dimensions.

This property can affect all elements.

The characteristics of this property are not inherited.

## Example

```
IMG.bigpics { width: 250px }
```

## Related Element

```
IMG
```

## Related Property

```
HEIGHT
```

| WORD-SPACING | Word Spacing |
|---|---|

## Purpose

Sets spacing between words.

## Syntax

```
word-spacing: { normal|[+|-]length }
```

## Where

- normal represents the normal spacing between words.
- *length* is a positive value followed by a two-letter abbreviation representing the unit of measure. *length* is usually an increase in the spacing between words but can be a decrease (a negative value).

## Notes

Valid relative units of measure are em (the height of the current font), ex (the height of the letter x in the current font), and px (pixels, relative to the size of the window). Valid absolute units of measure are in (inches), cm (centimeters), mm (millimeters), pt (points), and pc (picas). Valid absolute units of measure are in (inches), cm (centimeters), mm (millimeters), pt (points), and pc (picas).
    This property can affect all elements.
    The characteristics of this property are inherited.

## Example

```
H1 { word-spacing: 2pt }
```

## Related Property

```
letter-spacing
```

## Pseudo-Elements

Cascading style sheets allow you to specify particular styles for a first line or first letter of a paragraph.

| FIRST-LINE | First Line |
|---|---|

## Purpose

Styles the first line of a paragraph.

## Syntax

`<P:first-line>`*first_line_text*`</P:first-line>`

## Where

- *first_line_text* represents the contents of the first line.

## Notes

For FIRST-LINE, you can use the following properties: BACK-GROUND-ATTACHMENT, BACKGROUND-COLOR, BACKGROUND-IMAGE, BACKGROUND-POSITION, BACKGROUND-REPEAT, CLEAR, COLOR, FONT, FONT-FAMILY, FONT-SIZE, FONT-STYLE, FONT-VARI-ANT, FONT-WEIGHT, LETTER-SPACING, LINE-HEIGHT, TEXT-DECORATION, TEXT-TRANSFORM, VERTICAL-ALIGN, and WORD-SPACING.

You can use the CLASS attribute to specify first-line rules for all paragraphs in a particular class.

| **FIRST-LETTER** | **First Letter** |
|---|---|

## Purpose

Styles the first letter of a paragraph.

## Syntax

```
<P:first-letter>first_character</P:first-letter>
```

## Where

- *first_character* represents the first character in a paragraph.

## Notes

For FIRST-LINE, you can use the following properties: BACK-GROUND-ATTACHMENT, BACKGROUND-COLOR, BACKGROUND-IMAGE, BACKGROUND-POSITION, BACKGROUND-REPEAT, BORDER, BORDER-BOTTOM, BORDER-BOTTOM-WIDTH, BORDER-COLOR, BORDER-LEFT, BORDER-LEFT-WIDTH, BORDER-RIGHT, BORDER-RIGHT-WIDTH, BORDER-STYLE, BORDER-TOP, BORDER-TOP-WIDTH, BORDER-WIDTH, CLEAR, COLOR, FLOAT, FONT, FONT-FAMILY, FONT-SIZE, FONT-STYLE, FONT-VARIANT, FONT-WEIGHT, LINE-HEIGHT, MARGIN, MARGIN-BOTTOM, MARGIN-LEFT, MARGIN-RIGHT, MARGIN-TOP, PADDING, PADDING-BOTTOM, PADDING-LEFT, PADDING-RIGHT, PADDING-TOP, TEXT-DECORATION, TEXT-TRANSFORM, VERTICAL-ALIGN (if float is none), and WORD-SPACING.

You can use the CLASS attribute to specify first-letter rules for all paragraphs in a particular class.

# PART 6

# Glossary

## absolute link

A link to another document using the complete URL or address, including the transfer protocol, the computer or network name, the directory or folder, and a filename (for example, http://www.mispress.com/index.html). See *relative link*.

## address

An electronic location to which e-mail is sent; an electronic location on the Internet or on a network.

## agent

Robot. A search index that finds information from all or part of the Internet or a network, sometimes at a regular time or date or when page content changes. Another definition of agent is anything (such as a browser) that processes user request. See *search index* and *search tool*.

## American National Standards Institute

See *ANSI*.

## American Standard Code for Information Interchange

See *ASCII*.

## anchor

The starting link that refers to another location within the current document or within another document; the ending link to which a starting link refers.

## Anonymous FTP

See *FTP*.

### ANSI

American National Standards Institute. A U.S. affiliate of the International Organization for Standardization (ISO), an organization that formulates many international standards for characters, numbers, and symbols; computing; telecommunicating; and so on. See *ISO*.

### archive

A collection of information, usually from the past but sometimes from the present.

### ASCII

American Standard Code for Information Interchange. A coding standard for characters, numbers, and symbols that is the same as the first 128 characters of the ASCII character set but differs from the remaining characters. See also *ASCII file*.

### ASCII file

A text file or a text-only file. A file format that can be read by almost any word processor or text editor, allowing for transfer and viewing between individuals with dissimilar computers, operating systems, and programs. ASCII files contain characters, spaces, punctuation, end-of-line marks, and some formats. See also *ASCII*.

### attributes

A World Wide Web Consortium (W3C) term for options, which are settings that affect formats, alignments, text enhancements, paragraphs, or other parts of an HTML document.

### AU

A UNIX-based sound file format.

### AVI

Audio Video Interleave; a popular Windows-based video file format.

### base

See *absolute link*.

## bit

Binary digit. The smallest unit of computer information, represented by a 1 (which represents *yes* or *on*) or 0 (representing *no* or *off*).

## bit map

A graphic image made up of pixels (also known as "pels" in some circles). Bit map file formats include BMP, GIF, and JPEG.

## block elements

Elements that affect blocks of text, such as paragraphs and lists. Many block elements affect text in much the same way as paragraph formatting in a word processor.

## bookmarks

Hot lists. URLs of sites that you regularly visit and that you have had your browser save. When you want to visit a bookmarked site, just select it from your browser's bookmark list.

## browser

A program (such as Netscape Navigator, Microsoft Internet Explorer, or Mosaic) with which you can surf the World Wide Web as well as Gopher and FTP sites. Some browsers also provide e-mail and Telnet utilities. Other browsers are part of suites of Internet access programs.

## CGI

Common Gateway Interface. A protocol that enables developers to write programs that create HTML in response to user requests; frequently used to connect databases to the World Wide Web.

## client

A program (such as a browser) that is programmed to communicate with and ask for information from a server program (such as a World Wide Web or Gopher server), usually on a remote computer. See *browser* and *server*.

## client pull

The automatic loading or reloading of a document at a specific time or time interval by a browser. You can either use the META element or write a CGI program to incorporate client pull features. See also *server push*.

## Common Gateway Interface

See *CGI*.

## declaration

A statement that defines the elements and attributes in a document without telling the computer how to use them. In HTML, an attribute (such as color) and its value (for example, blue) are declarations. In a cascading style sheet, a declaration specifies a property (for example, font style) and its value (for example, italic).

## deprecated

An outdated element or attribute. Although it is still supported in the current HTML standard, it will eventually be obsolete. When you create or edit HTML documents, replace deprecated elements or attributes with fully supported elements or attributes. Deprecated elements in HTML 4.0 are APPLET, BASE-FONT, CENTER, DIR, FONT, ISINDEX, MENU, S, STRIKE, and U. See also *obsolete*.

## dialup

A temporary network connection, made by dialing a telephone number with a modem and logging in with a user identifier (ID) and a password. This is the typical way that an individual gains access to the Internet. Since the dialup is not a dedicated (or permanent) connection, the individual can use the telephone line for other purposes.

## Document Type Definition

See *DTD*.

## domain

The two- or three-character codes for organizations (COM, EDU, INT, NET, GOV, MIL, NET) and for regions or countries (for example, the United States is US) in which the organization is located. At the time of this writing, new domains are under consideration.

## domain name

The name for a site (for example, psu, which represents Pennsylvania State University, or lotus, which represents Lotus Development Corporation) and its domain. A typical domain name is psu.edu or lotus.com.

## Domain Name System

DNS. The system by which Internet sites are named; for example, www.lotus.com or eddygrp@sover.net.

## download

The transfer of a file from a remote computer to your computer. The standard protocol for downloading files from the Internet is anonymous FTP (file transfer protocol). See *FTP* and *upload.*

## DTD

Document Type Definition. A document, written in SGML, that specifies the elements (popularly known as *tags*), attributes (options), entities (special characters), and rules for creating documents using a particular HTML version or other SGML-related markup language. The !DOCTYPE comment, which names the DTD with which a document has been created, enables HTML validators to properly check a document. XML also uses DTDs.

## dynamic HTML

A proposed standard that allows the appearance and content of an HTML document to change whenever a user interacts with it. Interactions that trigger document updating include moving the mouse, clicking, double-clicking, and pressing keys.

## electronic mail

See *e-mail.*

## element

The proper name for what is popularly known as a *tag*, one unit of a markup language. A command with which you define part of an HTML document. An element usually starts with a start tag, *<tagname>*, includes an element name, may contain attributes with which you vary the results of the element, and may end with an end tag, *</tagname>*. See *end tag* and *start tag*.

## e-mail

Electronic mail. Messages (which may have files attached) sent from an individual to one or more individuals on a network or remote computer.

## e-mail address

The electronic mailing address of an individual, group, or organization. For example, my e-mail address is `eddygrp@sover.net` (where "eddygrp" is the user ID, the @ (at) sign is a separator symbol, and "sover.net" is the name of the computer to which my e-mail address is identified). My e-mail address is pronounced "Eddy Group at sover dot net."

## end tag

The part of an HTML statement that indicates the end of an element and its attributes. The format of an end tag is *</elementname>*, in contrast to the start tag format, *<elementname>*. Sometimes, an end tag is either an optional or forbidden (that is, it must not be used) part of a statement. See *element* and *start tag*.

## entity

A special character; a single unit or item.

## extension

(1). An element that is not part of the current approved standard version of HTML. Netscape and Microsoft extensions are the best known. (2). Two or three characters (for example, DOC, TXT, HTM, GIF, PS, and so on) that identify a file type or format.

## FAQ

Frequently Asked Questions. Documents that list commonly asked questions and their answers about almost any topic, including computing and the Internet. FAQs are designed to save those in the know the bother of responding to questions asked and answered many times before. First-time visitors to a newsgroup or a support site should always read the FAQ (if one is provided) before asking questions.

## File Transfer Protocol

See *FTP*.

## firewall

A combination of a security program and hardware that creates a virtual wall between unwanted visitors and specified parts of a network.

## fixed-width typeface

See *monospaced typeface*.

## freeware

Public-domain programs. Programs you can download and use without making any payment to the software publisher. See also *shareware*.

## Frequently Asked Questions

See *FAQ*.

## FTP

File Transfer Protocol. A protocol, or set of rules, that allows the access, reading, and/or downloading of files from a remote computer. You can either log on to a remote computer using an assigned user identifier (ID) and password, or use anonymous FTP, which uses the word "anonymous" as the user ID, and the user's e-mail address as the password. With the growth of the World Wide Web, FTP login is becoming *transparent* to the user; that is, login is automatically enabled by the user clicking on a link in an HTML document.

## GIF

Graphics Interchange Format. A format for graphics files used within World Wide Web documents. GIF files are larger than graphics files with the JPEG format. See also *JPEG*.

### glyph

A graphic that represents a character, particularly in a typeface.

### home page

The top hypertext document at a World Wide Web site or the document to which a user first goes when visiting a site. Typically, the home page provides an introduction to the site as well as links to the site's other pages. Most browsers are programmed to automatically go to a particular home page after your computer connects to the Internet.

### host

A server. A computer that hosts other computers and provides information and services to client programs. See *client* and *server*.

### HTML

HyperText Markup Language. A subset of SGML (Standard Generalized Markup Language); the language with which you typically mark up (or create) documents, with hypertext links, for the World Wide Web. HTML 4.0 is the current version. See *hypertext, link, SGML,* and *World Wide Web*.

### HTML document

A document created using elements and attributes from HTML (HyperText Markup Language).

### HTTP

HyperText Transport Protocol. The rules and standards that client programs use to read hypertext files on host computers. See *client, host, hypertext,* and *World Wide Web*.

### hyperlink

See *link*.

### hypermedia

See *multimedia*.

## hypertext

A variety of media in a document. Hypertext includes links to other documents or sections of documents, text, graphics, audio, and video. See *link*, *multimedia*, and *World Wide Web*.

## icon

A small button or graphic on which you click or double-click to open a folder, document, or file; to perform an action or issue a command, usually avoiding multiple steps; or to start a program.

## IETF

Internet Engineering Task Force. An organization that evaluates and sets most standards for the Internet.

## inline elements

Elements that affect characters. These elements affect text in much the same way as font or character formatting in a word processor. Most inline elements do not cause line breaks. One obvious exception is the inline element BR.

## inline image

A graphic within an HTML document.

## International Organization for Standardization

See *ISO*.

## internet

Two or more networks connected into a single network.

## Internet

The largest internet of all, comprised of networks connecting government agencies, private and public organizations, educational institutions, laboratories, and individuals.

## Internet Engineering Task Force

See *IETF*.

## Internet media type

IMEDIA. See *media type*.

## Internet provider

An organization that provides user access to the Internet. Also known as *Internet access provider* and *Internet service provider*.

## ISO

International Organization for Standardization. An international standards-setting organization. ISO sets standards for computing, telecommunicating, and so on. ANSI, the American National Standards Institute, is the U.S. affiliate. See *ANSI*.

## JPEG

Joint Photographic Expert Group. A graphics file format with a JPG extension. JPEG graphics are usually smaller than GIF graphics. See also *GIF*.

## keyword

A word or phrase stored in a META tag statement. Search indexes use keywords to compile and optionally rank lists of HTML documents. See *search index* and *search tool*.

## link

A highlighted and/or underlined word or phrase or a graphic coded into an A element. Click on a link to go to another document or section of the current document. See *hypertext* and *World Wide Web*.

## log in

Typing a user identifier (ID) and, optionally, a password to gain access to a file, program, computer, or network.

## mailing list

An electronic mail distribution list for members of a discussion group.

## man

Manual pages. Documentation for a program, such as UNIX.

## markup

A document that includes commands to define attributes, such as formats and enhancements, and to describe the document. In an HTML document, the commands with which the document is marked up are known as *elements*. The term *markup* refers to the marks that editors make on manuscripts to be revised.

## media type

The type of file and its contents, formatted as *file type/file format*. Examples include text/html and video/mpeg.

## MIDI

Musical Instrumental Digital Interface. An audio standard for communications among computers, musical instruments, and synthesizers. MIDI files are commonly used to transfer musical information in a compact format.

## MIME

Multipurpose Internet Mail Extensions or Multiple Internet Mail Extensions. A standard for sending and receiving messages that contain text, graphics, audio files, video files, and other multimedia files.

## monospaced typeface

A font in which every character is a fixed width. A letter as wide as *w* or as narrow as *i* is the same width. Monospaced text, which often represents computer code and keyboard entries, is ideal for spacing table columns.

## MPEG

Moving Pictures Experts Group. A standard for both video and audio files.

## multimedia

Multiple media. A file composed of text, links, graphics, video files, and/or audio components.

## Multiple Internet Mail Extensions

See *MIME*.

## Multipurpose Internet Mail Extensions
See *MIME*.

## Musical Instrumental Digital Interface
See *MIDI*.

## National Center for Supercomputing Applications
NCSA. A center for computing and telecommunications at the University of Illinois; the developer of the pioneer Mosaic graphical browser.

## nested
A command line (including attributes) that is inserted completely within another command line. For example, an IMG line, referring to an image used as a link, can be nested within the A line, which specifies the destination of the link.

## newsgroup
A group devoted to discussing a particular topic, using mailing lists and other messages.

## obsolete
An element or attribute that is no longer supported by the current HTML standard. Elements from the HTML 3.2 standard that are now obsolete in HTML 4.0 are LISTING, PLAINTEXT, and XMP. See also *deprecated*.

## options
See *attributes*.

## password
A hidden combination of characters and special symbols that a user types or that is automatically entered to gain access to a secure file, computer, directory, folder, or network.

## pixel
Picture element; pel. A dot that represents the smallest part of an image displayed on a computer monitor or printed on paper.

**post**

Send a message electronically; add an HTML document to a server.

**PostScript**

A page description language developed by Adobe Systems; a standard for some Internet documents. If a document has a PS extension, it is a PostScript document.

**protocol**

Standards or rules that control the way in which a program and computer, two computers, a computer and network, two networks, and so on, communicate.

**provider**

See *Internet provider.*

**rank**

A score assigned to an entry in a list of results from a search index. A high rank indicates that several keywords or other attributes in the entry closely fit the keywords and other criteria that a user typed. A low rank indicates very few matches. See *search index* and *search tool.*

**relative link**

A link to a resource within the current document, directory or folder, or computer or network, using a partial URL or address (for example, /index.html). If your browser reads a partial URL or address, it will attempt to go to a relative link. See *absolute link.*

**RFC**

Request for Comments. Official standards developed by the Internet Engineering Task Force (IETF). See *IETF.*

**search index**

Search engine. A fill-out form in which you type one or more keywords, select or click on checkboxes and/or option buttons, optionally select other parameters for an Internet search, and click on a button to start the search. Examples of search indexes are Alta Vista, Excite, Lycos, and Savvy Search. See *search tool*.

### search tool

A search index (such as Savvy Search, Alta Vista, Excite, Lycos, and many more) with which you search for Internet sites that closely match one or more keywords and other attributes that you select, or a master list or directory (such as Yahoo, the InterNIC Directory of Directories, or one of the World Wide Web Virtual Libraries), through which you can browse for Internet sites that you might want to visit. See *search index*.

### selector

A string that identifies an element to which a declaration applies. For example, in HTML, the FONT element is a selector on which the SIZE, COLOR, and FACE attributes and their values can apply. Or, the H2 tag is a selector that can be defined by other elements, their attributes, and values. See *declaration*.

### server

A program (such as a World Wide Web or Gopher server) or computer that is programmed to communicate with and provide information to a client program (such as a browser). See *browser* and *client*.

### server push

The automatic loading or reloading of a document or data at a specific time or time interval by a server. You can write a CGI program to incorporate server push features. See also *client pull*.

### SGML

Standard Generalized Markup Language. An internationally accepted text-processing language. HTML is a subset of SGML. See *HTML*.

### shareware

A complete or partial version of a program that you can download and try out before buying it for a small fee. If the downloaded program is not a complete version, the author will send you a complete version, a manual, and sometimes additional programs when you license it. See *freeware*.

### site

A home page and its linked pages, all of which are located at a particular Internet address. See *home page*.

### Standard Generalized Markup Language

See *SGML*.

### start tag

The part of an HTML statement that indicates the start of an element and its attributes. The format of a start tag is *<element-name>*, in contrast to the end tag format, *</elementname>*. Occasionally, the start tag is an optional part of a statement. See *element* and *end tag*.

### tag

See *element*. See also *end tag* and *start tag*.

### Unicode

A standards organization that develops the Unicode Worldwide Character Standard, which supports characters comprising the principal written languages of the world as well as symbols either within or outside character sets.

### Uniform Resource Identifier

See *URI*.

### Uniform Resource Locator

See *URL*.

### upload

The transfer of a file from your computer to a remote computer. The standard protocol for uploading files is anonymous FTP (file transfer protocol). See *download* and *FTP*.

## URI

Uniform Resource Identifier. The Internet address of an anchor. A URI can either be a URL (absolute link) or a partial address (relative link). See *URL*.

## URL

Uniform Resource Locator. An Internet address composed of the protocol type (such as http:, ftp:, gopher:, and so on), the name of the server to be contacted (such as www.w3.org), the directories or folders (such as /pub/WWW/Provider/), and the optional filename (for example, contents.html or homepage.htm).

### user agent

See *agent*.

## W3C

World Wide Web Consortium. The organization that develops standards for the World Wide Web and contributes to HTML standards.

## WAV

A Windows-supported sound file format.

### World Wide Web

WWW, W3, or the Web. A hypertext-based information system that supports the use of multimedia, including text, links, graphics, video files, and sound files. The Web was developed at the European Laboratory for Particle Physics (CERN) in Switzerland.

## XML

Extensible Markup Language; a "child" of SGML and a language that will coexist with both SGML and HTML. XML will enable complex hyperlinks, support long documents, and allow custom tag statements.

# PART 7

# Webliography

With the obvious exception of this edition of *HTML in Plain English* (and its future editions), you'll never have to buy another HTML book. You can get all the HTML information you need online.

During the writing of this book, I visited many Web sites—corporate, academic, and individual—all over the world. In every session, I struck new veins of HTML gold. This "Webliography" lists and briefly describes many of the best HTML sites on the World Wide Web.

# HTML History and Standards

Tracing HTML back to its SGML roots is an interesting endeavor. In this section are resources covering SGML, various HTML versions (both alive and dead), and Netscape and Microsoft extensions.

## SGML

SGML is the parent of HTML and the language used to code DTDs (Document Type Definitions). This section provides information about SGML standards, documents of all types, organizations, tools, forums, and more.

**Overview of SGML Resources** (http://www.w3.org/MarkUp/SGML/), by Dan Connolly of the World Wide Web Consortium (W3C) is a list of links organized under the following headings, *Learning and Using SGML*; *Specs, Drafts, and Reports*; *Groups and Discussion Forums*; and *Research Notebook*.

**SGML, XML, and Structured Document Interchange** (http://www.w3.org/XML/Activity), by Dan Connolly and Jon Bosak of the World Wide Web Consortium (W3C) is an activity report on SGML and another "child," XML. Links to new papers, standards, and organizations are included.

**A Gentle Introduction to SGML** (http://www-tei.uic.edu/ orgs/tei/sgml/teip3sg/index.html), by C. M. Sperberg-McQueen and Lou Burnard, is an academic document in HTML format. The table of contents contains 11 chapters.

**An Introduction to SGML** (http://www.pineapplesoft .com/reports/sgml/index.html), by Benoît Marchal, is an entry point to an HTML document on SGML. Links include an *Executive Summary, Preface, Background on Generalized Markup, Basic SGML*, and *References.*

**A Little Bit of SGML** (http://www.ozemail.com.au/~dkgsoft /html/sgml.html), by Dianne Gorman, summarizes selected SGML rules and interprets parts of the HTML 2.0 DTD (Document Type Definition), which was written in SGML.

**SGML Syntax Summary Index** (http://www.tiac.net/ users/bingham/sgmlsyn/index.htm), by Harvey Bingham, contains a list of links to SGML-related documents, including terminal variables and constants and **SGML Syntax Summary** (http://www.tiac.net/users/bingham/sgmlsyn/sgmlsyn.htm), which is based on the ISO 8879-1986(E) SGML standard. You can download suites of these and related documents from the **Sources for DSSSL and SGML Syntax Summary Suites** page (http://www.tiac.net/users/bingham/sources/index.htm).

**SGML on the Web** (http://www.ncsa.uiuc.edu/SDG/ Software/Mosaic/WebSGML.html), sponsored by SoftQuad, provides links to SGML resources and to many samples of work coded in SGML. Also included is information about putting SGML online and links to downloadable documentation files from SoftQuad.

**The SGML Web Page** (http://www.sil.org/sgml/sgml.html), by Robin Cover, is well known in SGML circles. Its long table of contents contains links of all types, organized under 19 categories.

**1A List of SGML Reference Sites** (http://www.cdc.com/ DocSvc/sgmlref.htm) is an excellent resource that is billed as "the most comprehensive list of SGML reference sites on the Internet." At the time of this writing, this page included 42 links.

**SGML—Standard Generalized Markup Language** (http://www.cs.helsinki.fi/research/rati/sgml.html) is almost three pages of links to SGML resources organized under these headings: *General, SGML Databases, Tools, Converters/Transformers, Viewers, Frequently Asked Questions, Organizations, Commercial Sites, Varia,* and *SGML Archives.*

**Definitions of SGML-Related Terms** (http://csgrad.cs.vt.edu/~fdrake/cs5704/definitions.html), by Fred L. Drake, Jr., of Virginia Tech, is a glossary of SGML terms.

**SGML Assessment: SGML Acronyms Explained** (http://www.sil.org/sgml/exetacro.html) contains a long list of acronyms related to SGML, HTML, World Wide Web, and the Internet.

**SGML Open Home Page** (http://www.sgmlopen.org/) is "a non-profit, international consortium of suppliers whose products and services support" SGML. The pages at this site include **Standard Generalized Markup Language** (http://www.sgmlopen.org/sgml/docs/sgmldesc.htm), the history and use of SGML, and the **Library of SGML Resources** (http://www.sgmlopen.org/sgml/docs/library.htm), which includes links to SGML-related white papers (some downloadable) and other publications, the SGML Syntax Summary Index (cited earlier), Document Style Semantics and Specification Language (DSSSL), HyTime, CALS Table Model, and Miscellaneous SGML Subjects.

**Who Needs Industrial Strength SGML?** (http://www.arbor-text.com/needs.html) justifies using SGML as a solution for information publishers.

**HTML to the Max: A Manifesto for Adding SGML Intelligence to the World-Wide Web** (http://www.ncsa.uiuc.edu/SDG/IT94/Proceedings/Autools/sperberg-mcqueen/sperberg.html) is a paper by C. M. Sperberg-McQueen and Robert F. Goldstein. The authors propose development of SGML browsers to read HTML and other SGML-based documents, built-in style sheets, rules that are dynamically loaded into browsers, user-customized elements sets, and more.

**A Lexical Analyzer for HTML and Basic SGML** (http://www.w3.org/TR/WD-sgml-lex/) specifies a lexical analyzer that enables the better use of SGML within HTML documents.

**RFC Index** (http://ds.internic.net/ds/rfc-index.html) presents links to Requests for Comments (RFC), Internet standards documents, arranged in numerical order from the newest to the oldest. This document lists titles, authors, date, page count, and format for RFCs 2200 and newer. Links to older RFCs are presented in numerical groups, without additional information.

## HTML Versions and Standards

In a very few years, HTML has gone through quite a few transitions. In this section, you'll get about information and resources for all HTML versions.

### HTML 2.0

HTML 2.0 provides the set of elements that is the foundation of HTML 4.0 and future versions. This section provides reference documents to HTML 2.0.

**HTML DTD Reference** (http://www.w3.org/MarkUp/html-spec/L2index.html) is a useful reference with links to all the elements in the HTML 2.0 element set. Each entry includes information about the element arranged under the headings *Required Parts*, *All Parts*, and *Allowed in Content of....*

**RFC 1866: Hypertext Markup Language—2.0** (ftp://ds.internic.net/rfc/rfc1866.txt) is a large (147K) text document of the Request for Comments (RF that specifies the HTML 2.0 standards. Written by Tim Berners-Lee, this long document completely describes the HTML 2.0 element set and places it in the context of Standard Generalized Markup Language (SGML).

### HTML 3.2

HTML 3.2 is the Web-document standard that is the immediate predecessor of HTML 4.0. This section lists several documents about HTML 3.2.

**Introducing HTML 3.2** (http://www.w3.org/MarkUp/Wilbur/) is a brief introduction, with many links, to HTML 3.2.

**The Structure of HTML 3.2 Documents** (http://www.w3.org/MarkUp/Wilbur/features.html), in six pages, briefly summarizes HTML 3.2 document.

**W3C Document Type Definition (DTD) for the HyperText Markup Language** (http://www.w3.org/MarkUp/Wilbur/ HTML32.dtd) is the working draft of the HTML 3.2 DTD. At first view, DTDs are difficult to understand. After you spend some time learning HTML elements and attributes, you will be able to interpret the contents of this document.

**All Elements in W3C Wilbur DTD** (http://www.webtechs .com/sgml/Wilbur/ALL-ELEM.html) provides a list of links to all the elements in the HTML 3.2 element set. Also included are links to the Top Elements (see the following entry) and a Tree of elements.

**W3C Wilbur DTD: Top Element Tree(s)** (http://www.webtechs .com/sgml/Wilbur/DTD-TREE.html) not only shows the hierarchy of HTML 3.2 elements but also includes links to all elements.

**The Hierarchy of the HTML 3.2 DTD** (http://www.ozemail .com.au/~dkgsoft/html/html32.html) presents HTML trees illustrating how particular elements and their attributes fit into the HTML 3.2 element set.

## Netscape Extensions

Most of the Netscape extensions given here are already part of HTML 4.0. However, some of these elements and some attributes have not yet made their way in. History shows that many, if not most, will eventually become standard elements of a future HTML element set.

**Index of Netscape Extensions** (http://www.willcam.com/ cmat/html/netscape.html) is a list of links to Netscape extensions and a very brief description of each.

## Microsoft Extensions

The document in this section includes Microsoft extensions, which are supported by the Microsoft Internet Explorer browser, and older extensions that are now part of HTML 4.0.

**DTD for Internet Explorer 2.0 HTML** (http://www.webtechs .com/html-tk/src/lib/iehtml.dtd) covers HTML and Microsoft extensions. At first view, DTDs are difficult to understand. After you spend some time learning HTML elements and attributes, you will be able to interpret the contents of this document.

## HTML 4.0

The current HTML standard is 4.0. The documents featured in this section enhance the information provided in this book.

**HTML 4.0 Working Draft Release** (http://www.w3.org/TR/WD-html40/) is the centerpiece of the W3C HTML 4.0 pages. From this page, you can download the working draft and link to the DTD.

The **HTML 4.0 DTD** (http://www.w3.org/TR/WD-html40/sgml/HTML4.dtd) is the working draft DTD (Document Type Definition) defining the current HTML standard.

**Inserting Objects into HTML** (http://www.w3.org/TR/WD-object.html) describes the element, which is used to embed multimedia files of all types in HTML documents.

## Special Characters (Entities)

Use special characters to enhance a document with symbols such as trademarks, umlauts, and non-breaking spaces. This section points to several documents that list special characters (that is, entities) supported by or proposed for HTML.

**8 Bit ASCII Codes** (http://www.w3.org/MarkUp/Wilbur/latin1.gif) is a chart of Latin-1 entities and their 0-255 ASCII code counterparts.

**HTML Special Character Entity Names** (http://www.sandia.gov/sci_compute/symbols.html), from Sandia Labs, lists character names for the Latin-1 special character set. Also included are suggestions for future special characters. HTML standards documents specify using character names rather than numeric entity names. Sandia also provides a list of **HTML Numeric Entity Names** (http://www.sandia.gov/sci_compute/iso_symbol.html).

**Additional Named Entities for HTML** (http://www.w3.org/TR/WD-entities) is a working draft discussing entities that might be included in HTML. This document also includes charts of entities.

**Mathematical, Greek and Symbolic Characters for HTML** and **Special Characters for HTML** (http://www.w3.org/MarkUp/Cougar/HTMLsym.ent and http://www.w3.org/MarkUp/Cougar/HTMLmisc.ent ) lists some of the new entities (that is, special characters) supported by HTML 4.0.

## INTERNATIONALIZATION

One of the main purposes of the HTML 4.0 standard is to "internationalize" Web documents. As such, the developers of HTML 4.0 must address issues such as bi-directional text (for example, English vs. Hebrew) and characters that make up particular alphabets.

The **Unicode Consortium** (http://www.unicode.org/) is responsible for the Unicode standard: compiling character groups, setting data standards, establishing character mappings, and so on. From this home page, you can read the Unicode Standard, learn about conferences, link to resources, and find out more about the consortium. Unicode has also compiled charts and names of special characters at this site.

**W3C Internationalization and Localization** (http://www.w3 .org/International/Overview.html) lists links related to the 11th International Unicode Conference. Links include *HTML, HTTP, URL, CSS* (cascading style sheets), *Fonts, Character sets*, and *LISA* (Localization Industry Standards Organization).

**Bi-Directional Text** (http://www.w3.org/International/O-HTML-bidi.html) is a short page with several links to information about bi-directional topics and standards.

**The Next Topics for WWW Internationalization** (http://www.w3.org/International/martin.duerst.html) discusses the future of internationalization, including the issues, internationalization of URLs, typography, and annotation of ideographic texts. **A World-Wide World Wide Web** (http://www.w3 .org/International/francois.yergeau.html) covers similar issues.

ISO/IEC 10646-1 will eventually include many language character sets. For a list of the current European Subset, go to **Minimum European Subset of ISO/IEC 10646-1** (http://www.indigo.ie/egt/standards/mes.html).

**Input Methods for 10646** (http://www-rocq.inria.fr/ ~deschamp/www/divers/ALB-WD.html) discusses how users may be able to enter characters from the ISO/IEC character set with a keyboard or other input device.

**HTML in Every Language** (http://babel.alis.com:8080/ web_ml/html/) is an article about the internationalization of HTML and the supported special characters.

# HTML EDITORS

When creating HTML documents, you have two choices: write element statements using a word processor or text editor, or use an editor to insert the elements for you. This section provides resources with lists of HTML editors, most of which can be downloaded to your personal computer. You can find a list of HTML editors and utilities in Appendix C.

**Mag's Big List of HTML Editors** (http://union.ncsa.uiuc.edu/HyperNews/get/www/html/editors.html), by Tom Magliery, is a home page from which you can link to HTML editing tools by platform: Amiga, DOS, Mac, NeXTstep, OS/2, UNIX, VMS, Windows, non-English, nonplatform, and The Mystery List. Each entry for a program contains the name, author, price, current version, a description, and a link to the home page of the software publisher. Also included on the home page are links to messages and replies about finding and using HTML programs as well as creating HTML documents.

**HTML Editors for Windows** (http://omni.cc.purdue.edu/%7Exniu/winsock/htmledit.htm) , by Xiaomu Niu, is a document with links of HTML editors and related programs under the following categories: *Freeware, Shareware, Commercial Demo*, and *HTML Authoring Tools*. A typical entry includes the version number and the release date, a link to the home page of the software and its publisher, program type (freeware, shareware, or commercial) and description, and a link on which you can click to download the program.

**Stroud's CWSApps List—HTML Editors** (http://cws.internet.com/32html.html and http://cws.internet.com/16html.html) presents HTML editors, each in a table. The information for each entry includes a link to a review, version number, date of release, rating (up to five stars), program size, location, description, status (freeware, shareware, or commercial), company, information, notes, and also available (other versions). In addition, from the home page (http://cws.internet.com/), you can link to other categories of software for Windows computers.

# CREATING HTML DOCUMENTS

The tutorials and how-tos in this section can answer almost all your HTML questions. Using these resources, you can learn how to create an HTML document, including the appropriate elements and information.

**Style Guide for Online Hypertext** (http://www.w3.org/Provider/Style/), by Tim Berners-Lee (the father of the World Wide Web), provides a common-sense method of creating workable HTML documents. Written in 1994, this document does not include recent events in HTML (for example, the HTML 3.2 and 4.0 standards).

**Web Etiquette** (http://www.w3.org/Provider/Style/Etiquette .html), written by Tim Berners-Lee, is a very short paper about Web conventions, especially for those who are Webmasters.

**HTML Language and Resource Guide** (http://tarzan .aoc.nrao.edu/aips++/docs/html/htm4aips.html), by Alan H. Bridle of the National Radio Astronomy Observatory, includes four chapters describing hypertext, HTML, how to generate it, and how to convert it to ASCII and PostScript formats. Throughout the document are valuable links: to HTML standards and versions; to manuals, tutorials, and style guides; to home pages for HTML editors; to HTML validation services; and to conversion utilities.

**Composing Good HTML** (http://www.cs.cmu.edu/~tilt/cgh/), by James Tilton, is a well-known and well-written comprehensive document about HTML authoring and proper usage. It even includes a section on style sheets.

**Survival Guide** (http://www.mcp.com/general/workshop/survival/guide.html), by Michael Hughes, is a basic, well-written primer on how to create a Web page using some of the most popular elements.

**NCSA—A Beginner's Guide to HTML** (http://www.ncsa .uiuc.edu/General/Internet/WWW/HTMLPrimer.html) is a popular guide that hits the highlights of page design and coding from the most basic to images, tables, and forms. Its troubleshooting section is particularly useful.

**Creating HTML—A Simple Guide** (http://www.netusa1.net/~jbornema/html.html), by Jason Borneman, is an overview of almost all HTML elements written for beginners. At the time of this writing, this document does not include HTML 3.2.

**Netscape Page Starter Site** (http://home.netscape.com/assist/net_sites/starter/index.html) is a list of links to creating Web pages from the Netscape point of view and using Netscape Communicator, the Gold Rush Tool Chest, and other tools.

**Yale Center for Advanced Instructional Media's (C/AIM) Web Style Guide** (http://info.med.yale.edu/caim/manual/index.html)is a long and comprehensive guide that tells how to design pages and how to optimize page performance (especially with graphics). Although this document is directed at those who are creating HTML documents for the Yale Center for Advanced Instructional Media, it is useful to the rest of us. This document also describes how pages fit into a site. To find out how to download the manual, go to http://info.med.yale.edu/caim/manual/misc/downloading.html.

**Elements of HTML Style** (http://www.book.uci.edu/Staff/StyleGuide.html), written by J. K. Cohen, is a popular link that provides tips on HTML style and formatting. Note that this document was written in 1994.

**Hints for Web Authors** (http://www.mcsr.olemiss.edu/~mudws/webhints.html), by Warren Steel, is a strong opinion piece about creating documents for the Web.

**Sun on the Net: Guide to Web Style** (http://www.sun.com/styleguide/tables/Printing_Version.html) is an elegant, very long (approximately 162K), illustrated guide to creating Web pages. It also addresses security, selling, and Java programming, and includes some technical notes.

**The Ten Commandments of HTML** (http://www.visdesigns.com/design/commandments.html), by Sean Howard, guides you to the best FAQs (frequently asked questions) and newsgroups, tells you the best ways of using particular elements, and provides his thoughts about learning and using HTML.

**World Wide Web FAQ** (http://www.shu.edu/about/WWWFaq/ and other mirror sites) provides links to answers to typical questions about the Web, organized under these categories: *Overview of the World Wide Web*; *Obtaining and Using Web Browsers*; *Establishing and Using Web Servers*; *Authoring*

*Web Pages, Images, and Scripts*; and *Other Resources about the Web*. You can download this document in several formats.

## Using Graphics and Multimedia

The proper use of graphics can make or break a Web page, and enhancing a page with animation, sound, and audio can attract Web surfers. This section lists selected graphic and multimedia resources.

 You can obtain information about GIF animation from *The GIF Animator's Guide,* also by Sandra E. Eddy and published by MIS:Press (1997).

**Creating High-Impact Documents** (http://home.netscape .com/assist/net_sites/impact_docs/index.html) discusses how to use graphics efficiently. Sections include using interlaced GIF images and JPEG images, specifying height and width of a graphic to load a document more quickly, and low-resolution and high-resolution graphic loading.

**Internet Explorer Multimedia Gallery** (http://www.microsoft .com/workshop/design/mmgallry/mmgallry.htm) provides links to a gallery of images, sounds, and video arranged in a table of themes. Download this collection to Windows 95 systems only.

**GIF Animation on the WWW** (http://member.aol.com/ royalef/gifanim.htm) is the definitive online GIF animation tutorial and reference guide. Visit this site before you go elsewhere.

**Yahoo Icons** (http://www.yahoo.com/Computers/World _Wide_Web/Programming/Icons/) contains over two pages of links to graphics libraries containing icons, buttons, bitmaps, backgrounds, horizontal rules, and other graphics-related resources.

**The WDVL: Images and Icons** (http://WWW.Stars.com/ Vlib/Providers/Images_and_Icons.html) contains 10 pages of graphics resources, including graphics libraries, instructions, background color charts, commercial services, and more. Each entry includes a link and a short description.

## Color and Backgrounds

In just a few months, HTML pages evolved from black text and blue links on a silver background to well-designed, multicolored pages. This section helps you choose colors for page and table backgrounds, text, and active and visited links.

**NOTE** Colors vary according to the graphics board and software installed in a computer, so it's best to view all colors and see how they work together before making a final color choice. Regardless of your color choice, there is a very good chance that some browsers will interpret your colors in a very strange way.

**Controlling Document Backgrounds** (http://home.netscape.com /assist/net_sites/bg/index.html) explains how to specify page backgrounds and set text and link attributes. Also included is an example of an HTML document with color settings.

**RGB Color Chart** (http://www.phoenix.net/~jacobson/ rgb.html) is an eight-column table showing color samples and equivalent hexadecimal values. Also included is a small hexadecimal-to-decimal conversion chart.

**The Color Specifier for Netscape** (http://www.users. interport.net/~giant/COLOR/hype_color.html) demonstrates page background colors. Links to colors are centered between the left and right margins. To the left of the color link is the three-digit RGB value; to the right is the hexadecimal code. Click on a link to see the background color. To return to the home page, click on the **Back** button.

**List of Colors** (http://www.imagitek.com/hex) is a text message that lists over eight pages of colors sorted by their hexadecimal codes.

**HTML Background Color Selector** (http://www.imagitek .com/bcs.html) allows you.to choose background, text, and link colors from drop-down list boxes. Then, click on the **Preview** button to see the results.

## Tables

Tables are an excellent way to present data or even format a document. Tables elements can be daunting to many HTML document writers. This section provides table-creation resources, including tutorials, standards, and proposals for the future.

**The Table Sampler** (http://home.netscape.com/assist/ net_sites/table_sample.html) is a "tutorial by example of tables." The examples demonstrate most table-creation elements.

**The HTML3 Table Model** (http://www.w3.org/TR/WD-tables-960123.html), written by Dave Raggett of the World Wide Web Consortium (W3C) is a working draft of the future of tables and tables elements, including rendering to braille or speech, transferring table data to databases and spreadsheets, and using style sheets to format tables.

## Image Maps

The newest versions of Web browsers allow your users to click on areas of images to jump to pages within or outside your Web site. In this section, you will find resources that help you create image maps and program them to work properly.

**Clickable Image Support in W3C httpd** (http://www.w3.org/ Daemon/User/CGI/HTImageDoc.html) describes the htimage program, which handles clicks on image maps. This document includes information on how to install htimage and how to create an HTML document with one or more clickable images.

**NCSA Imagemap Tutorial** (http://hoohoo.ncsa.uiuc.edu/ docs/tutorials/imagemapping.html) leads you through the image map creation process. You must be able to use NCSA HTTPd version 1.5 (or greater), for which there is a link on this page. At the end of the document, you'll find links to real-world examples.

**How to Do Imagemaps** (http://www2.ncsu.edu/bae/ people/faculty/walker/hotlist/imagemap.html) is a little over one page of information on creating image maps. Also included are links to image map editors, other image maps, and graphics resources.

**CERN Server Clickable Image Demo** (http://www.cern.ch/ Demo/Images/Dragons.html) is an image map and a link to instructions on how the map works.

**Imagemap Authoring Guide and Tutorial Sites** (http://www.cris.com/~automata/tutorial.shtml) is a valuable short directory of links to image map resources, including pages at this site (for example, **Introduction to Image Maps and Web**

**Hotspots**, a one-page explanation of image maps, at http://www.cris.com/~automata/maps.htm), source guides, and tutorials. Also included is a link to Web Hotspots, an image map editor.

**Imagemap Help Page** (http://www.ihip.com/) is a short but detailed tutorial on image maps. Also included are names of HTML authoring newsgroups and links to image map tools and other image map pages.

Sky Coyote has put together an easy-to-understand, detailed, and well-organized tutorial on **Advanced HTML Programming** (http://www.intergalact.com/hp/part2/part2.html), which contains links to the following pages:

- **What Is Imagemap?** (http://www.intergalact.com/ hp/part2/imagemap.html)
- **Creating an Image Map** (http://www.intergalact.com/ hp/part2/map.html)
- **Creating Imagemap and Target Pages** (http://www .intergalact.com/hp/part2/pages.html)
- **Putting It All Together** (http://www.intergalact.com/ hp/part2/together.html)

**Creating Image Maps with Web Hotspots** (http://www.cris .com/~automata/hotstuto.htm) includes two tutorials on using the Web Hotspots image map editor to create a client-side image map and a backward-compatible client-side image map, respectively. From this site, you can download a fully functional evaluation copy of Web Hotspots. You can read a brief explanation of client-side and server-side image maps at the **Varieties of Image Maps** page (http://www.cris.com/~automata/variety.htm).

The Web Communications HTML Guide (see the section "HTML Reference Guides" later in this Webliography) contains pages of image map information:

- **Creating Imagemaps** (http://www.webcom.com/ ~webcom/html/tutor/imagemaps.shtml), a short page of links to images, client side image maps, and server side image maps.
- **Images** (http://www.webcom.com/~webcom/html/tutor/ images.shtml), the entry point into the images tutorial.

- **Images Overview** (http://www.webcom.com/webcom/html/tutor/images_overview.shtml), an introduction to images and links to other pages at this site.
- **The Map File** (http://www.webcom.com/webcom/html/tutor/imap_map.shtml), a description of the map file that is used to create an image map.
- **Template and Syntax for an Imagemap** (http://www.webcom.com/webcom/html/tutor/imap_syntax.shtml), image map elements and attributes, including a detailed explanation of each.
- **Example Imagemap** (http://www.webcom.com/webcom/html/tutor/imap_example.shtml), an example of a horizontal bar image map.
- **A More Complex Example of an Imagemap** (http://www.webcom.com/webcom/html/tutor/imap_complex.shtml), an image map example.
- **Tools to Manipulate Images** (http://www.webcom.com/webcom/html/graphics.shtml), from which you can download image map and graphics editors. Note that the Mapedit home page is now at http://www.boutell.com/mapedit/.
- **Imagemap Editors** (http://www.webcom.com/webcom/html/mapedit.shtml), links to image map editors. Note that the Mapedit home page is now at http://www.boutell.com/mapedit/.
- **Tips for Including Images on Your Page** (http://www.webcom.com/webcom/html/tutor/images_tips.shtml), tips on image map creation.

## Testing a Page

Before posting an HTML document on the World Wide Web, it is very important to test it—not only to validate its elements and their attributes, but also to view it on a variety of browsers. These resources provide information about HTML testing and validation; some even enable you to test online.

**A Kinder, Gentler Validator** (http://ugweb.cs.ualberta.ca/~gerald/validate) validates an HTML document. This service can run Weblint (see the Weblint entry in this section), show source input and/or a document outline, and *parse* the document (break it into small chunks to analyze them piece by piece) against SGML DTDs. This site also includes links to other information about document validation.

**Webtechs HTML Validation Service** (http://www.webtechs .com/html-val-svc/) validates one or more HTML documents or pieces of documents. You can select a strict level of conformance to HTML 2.0, HTML 3.0, HTML 3.2, Mozilla (Netscape), SoftQuad, or Microsoft Internet Explorer. You can show input, parser output, and formatted output.

**Weblint** (http://www.cre.canon.co.uk/~neilb/weblint.html) checks HTML syntax and style (that is, picks lint off a document). This page includes links to information about Weblint, the Weblint ftp site, supported platforms, publications related to Weblint, and a list of HTML and validation resources.

## Registering a Domain Name

You can get your own domain name on the Internet through the InterNIC Registration Services. This section points you to resources through which you can register a domain name or learn more about the process.

**InterNIC Registration Services** (http://rs.internic.net/rs-internic.html) is the center for registering domain names. From this home page, you can learn about choosing a name, checking if anyone else has registered the name, registering, using registration tools and templates, and so on. Also included is more information about the InterNIC. Important pages at this site include:

- **About InterNIC Registration Services** (http://rs. internic.net/internic/about.html), which provides information about the organization that registers domains as well as an overview of the registration process.
- **Registration Services Policy Statements** (http://rs. internic.net/help/policy.html), which contains links to policy statements, draft policies, and supporting materials.
- **Registration and Renewal Fees: Fact Sheet** (http://rs.internic.net/fees/facts.html), which explains the registration process; specifies registration guide-

lines; and specifies registration fees, maintenance fees, and payment plans; and tells how the funds are dispersed.

- **Frequently Asked Questions** (http://rs.internic.net/help/index.html#faq) answers frequently asked questions about registration.

- **Whois** (http://rs.internic.net/cgi-bin/whois), which allows you to find out whether the name that you want to register is already in use. In the text box at the bottom of the page, type the complete name (for example, interstuff.com) and press **Enter**.

## Posting a Page

Internet providers, perhaps including your own, present information about posting a page to its servers. To learn more about the process, the resources in this section should help.

**N O T E**  Internet providers have created the following entries for their own clients. When you get to the point of uploading a page, remember to transfer it to your own provider's server. In fact, before uploading, see whether your provider can furnish instructions via a Web page, e-mail, or fax. If so, use those instructions rather than any information in this section.

**BuffNET: Your Homepage** (http://www.buffnet.net/~alyx1/tech/homepage.htm), composed of two sections, is a well-organized, comprehensive document on uploading pages to a server.

**The Forbin Project: Homepage HowTo** (http://www.forbin.com/homepages/) is an illustrated step-by-step tutorial on activating a home page using the WS_FTP utility.

**File Transfer to RTPnet** (http://www.rtpnet.org/rtpnet/provider/filetrans.html) provides links to file transfer instructions with various utilities: ISIS and Telix, ISIS with Zterm, Fetch, and Telnet and FTP. This page also includes instructions for selecting a directory, setting read-write permissions, and solving problems that you may encounter. RTPnet also provides **Maintaining Web Pages** (http://www.rtpnet.org/rtpnet/provider/maintenance.html), an online article on editing uploaded Web pages; and **Basic Unix Commands for**

**Maintaining Web Pages** (http://www.rtpnet.org/rtpnet/
provider/unix.html).

## Publicizing a Page

Once you have posted a page, all that's left is publicizing it and
maintaining it on a regular basis. The maintenance is up to you,
but you can use the services listed in this section to automatically add your URL to Web search indexes and directories.

**Submit It!** (http://www.submit-it.com/) is the home page with
perhaps the most well-known URL submission service, with
free and commercial versions. **Submit It!** submits your URL to
search engines and directories.

**WebCom Guide - Publicizing Your Web Site** (http://www
.webcom.com/html/publicize.shtml) includes vast amounts of
information arranged under these categories: *Quick Reference,
Direct Registration Services, Listings in Hierarchical Indexes,
Listings Submitted Through E-Mail, Other Sites of Interest,
Other Resources,* and *Unacceptable Web Site Promotion
Techniques.*

---

# HTML

While researching the chapters in Part 4, "HTML Elements
and Codes, Organized by Group," I used many of the sites in
this section as resources.

## HTML Directories

Directories are usually lists of links organized under a heading
or by category. This section contains valuable directories of
HTML resources.

**The HTML Writers Guild** (http://www.hwg.org/) is an international organization of World Wide Web page authors and
other Internet publishing professionals. From this home page,
you can learn about and join the organization, read a newsletter,
and access **HTML Resources** (http://www.hwg.org/resources/)
and **Mailing Lists** (http://www.hwg.org/lists/index.html).

**Guide to HTML and Web Authoring Resources**
(http://www.library.nwu.edu/resources/www/), from the
Northwestern University Library, presents pages of links orga-

nized under these major headings: *Issues of Style and Design, Tutorials on Web Authoring, HTML Editors & Other Tools, Web Development Resources, Technical Reference Resources, Media on the Web, Advanced Topics, Netscape Reference Sources, Microsoft Internet Explorer,* and *WWW Newsgroups.*

**Electronic PR Links** (http://www.utm.edu/~moo/PRlinks .shtml) provides links to many valuable HTML resources, arranged under these categories: *Internet, Email, Listservs, Usenet, FTP/GOPHER, WWW, Browsers, HTML, Design, Style, Publications, Validation, Low Memory Graphics, Color Palette, Hexadecimal Color, Background Patterns, Transparency, Typography, Alignment, Horizontal Rules, Bullets, Images, Image Maps, Tables, Frames, Web Animation, Forms, Music & Movies, Future Technologies,* and *Promote.*

**The WWW Help Page** (http://werbach.com/web/wwwhelp .html) is a directory of links arranged under these section headings: *General Reference, HTML, Colors, Style, CGI, Forms, Counters, Guestbooks, Imagemaps, Frames, Java, Graphics, GIF Animation, Sound, Javascript,* and *Publicizing.*

**The Web Wanderer's HTML Authoring Page** (http://www.xnet.com/~blatura/html.shtml) provides over two pages of links organized under these headings: *HTML Specifications*; *HTML Language Guides*; *HTML Style Guides*; *HTML Authoring Guides*; *HTML Editors*; *HTML Code Validators*; *Images and Icons*; *Scripts, CGI, and Forms*; *Imagemaps*; and *Servers and Configuration.* This page is copyrighted 1994, 1995.

**Willcam's List of HTML Resources on the Web** (http://www.willcam.com/res-html.html) is a directory of HTML-related links to HTML information, graphics images, HTML site submission services, counter utilities, and the comp.infosystems.www.authoring.html news group.

**The HTML Station** (http://www.december.com/html/ index.html) contains a table of resources, organized under these headings: *HTML Demonstrations*; *HTML Specifications*; *HTML Entities, Codes, and Types*; and *Techniques.* Also included in the table are *Introductory* and *Web Development Reference.*

**The WDVL: The Virtual Library of WWW Development** (http://WWW.Stars.com/Vlib/) is a library of hundreds of links

organized on one page, under these headings: *Authoring,
Internet, Location, Gallery, Multimedia, Reference*, and
*Software*. Other links are arranged along the bottom of the
home page.

**The Cossack's Home Page/HTML Creation Page**
(http://www.utoledo.edu/www/homepages/dechelb/html.html) is
a green page of both standard and unique links arranged under
*Beginner's Stuff, Style Manuals, Medium to High Level HTML,
Incorporating Video* (on making an MPEG movie), *Special
Characters, HTML Authoring Tools, Validate Your Pages,
Templates, Converters, Netscape*, and *Mac/Apple WebLinks*.
There are a few editorial comments along the way. The last
modification date on this page is October 2, 1995.

**Putting Information onto the Web** (http://www.w3.org/
Provider) provides links to publishing HTML documents
arranged under three headings: *Author, Webmaster*, and *System
Administrator*. This is a 1995 document.

**Creating Net Sites** (http://home.netscape.com/assist/
net_sites/) contains links organized under the following headings: *Authoring Documents, Adding Functionality*, and
*Developer Tools*.

**HTML Reference Pages** (http://www.cs.uct.ac.za/
HTMLdocs/) provides links to HTML resources: *HTML
Primer, URL Primer, HTML Forms, HTML Quick Reference,
HTML Spec* (for HTML 2.0), and *Composing Good HTML*.

**The WDVL: HTML** (http://WWW.Stars.com/Seminars/
HTML/) is a two-page document that describes and provides an
example of a small HTML document and also includes links to
HTML standards, types of HTML elements, and HTML draft
specifications. This document includes information about
HTML 4.0 and Dynamic HTML.

**Tw2's Web Resources Area** (http://www.tw2.com/
webresources/) provides a home page of links to pages of
HTML links, organized under the following categories: *HTML,
CGI Programming, Graphics, Webpage Scripting*, and *Resources
Home*.

## HTML Reference Guides

When you are learning about the entire HTML 4.0 element set or a element that you have never used before, these HTML reference guides can serve you well. Some of the following resources are standard reference guides, and others provide helpful examples that can help you to learn.

**The WDG Reference Section** (http://www.htmlhelp.com/reference/), by Arnoud "Galactus" Engelfriet, is a well-organized document that includes information about HTML 3.2, cascading style sheets, the Latin 1 character set, links, and a glossary.

The information in the **HTML 4.0 Working Draft Release** (http://www.w3.org/TR/WD-html40/) is the cornerstone of this book. This document, which is available in several formats for downloading or printing, is the HTML 4.0 bible.

Although the **HTML Reference Guide** (http://developer.netscape.com/library/documentation/htmlguid/intro.htm) does not include the latest HTML 4.0 elements, it is a valuable resource. Each element, including the latest Netscape extensions and attributes, is concisely described.

At the time of this writing, Microsoft's **HTML Reference** (http://www.microsoft.com/workshop/author/newhtml/default.htm) did not include HTML 4.0. However, this well-organized site is being updated with Microsoft attributes.

At the time of this writing, **HTML 4 Complete Reference** (http://www.december.com/html/4/) is a rough draft of HTML 4.0. It includes all elements, attributes, and data types.

**HTML Design Guide** (http://ncdesign.kyushu-id.ac.jp/html/Normal/html_design.html), written by Yuriko Ienaga, is the starting point for a set of documents, in normal (not a table and not with frames), table, and frame versions, featuring many examples illustrating almost every element and extension from HTML 2.0, Netscape extensions, and Microsoft extensions. This document was last updated on November 11, 1996. Documents include:

- **Page Elements** (http://ncdesign.kyushu-id.ac.jp/html/ Normal/page.html)
- **Font Elements** (http://ncdesign.kyushu-id.ac.jp/html/ Normal/font.html)
- **Text Style Elements** (http://ncdesign.kyushu-id.ac.jp/ html/Normal/text_style.html)
- **Image Elements** (http://ncdesign.kyushu-id.ac.jp/html/ Normal/image.html)
- **Form Elements** (http://ncdesign.kyushu-id.ac.jp/html/ Normal/form.html)
- **Table Elements** (http://ncdesign.kyushu-id.ac.jp/html/ Normal/table.html
- **Table Advanced** (http://ncdesign.kyushu-id.ac.jp/html/ Normal/table02.html)
- **Frames** (http://ncdesign.kyushu-id.ac.jp/html/ Normal/frame.html)
- **Marquee** (http://ncdesign.kyushu-id.ac.jp/html/ Normal/marquee.html)
- **Alternative Inline Elements** (http://ncdesign.kyushu-id. ac.jp/html/Normal/inline.html)

Also available is a **Tag Index** (http://ncdesign.kyushu-id.ac.jp/html/Normal/tag-index.html), which contains links to elements and attributes. Each entry includes syntax, element statements, an illustration, and sometimes an icon that shows the browser in which this element or attribute is supported. Occasionally, the examples show that the author is not completely experienced in English.

## MORE ON INDIVIDUAL HTML ELEMENTS

Some elements are more difficult to learn than others. When a element and associated programming help you interface with the outside world, your job can be even less arduous. The resources in this section should help you learn advanced concepts about selected elements.

### Forms, CGI Scripts, and PERL

Forms are a common way to communicate with those who reach your page. Using the forms elements and their attributes is the easy part of creating a form. To make a form work, you need to use CGI (Common Gateway Interface) scripts and a programming language, such as PERL. This section contains resources with which you can learn more about forms, CGI, and PERL.

**Instantaneous Introduction to CGI Scripts and HTML Forms** (http://kuhttp.cc.ukans.edu/info/forms/forms-intro.html) presents an illustrated paper on how Common Gateway Interface (CGI) works and how CGI scripts, browsers, servers, and the HTTP protocol process forms. This document includes examples and links to additional information.

**RFC 1867: Form-Based File Upload in HTML** (http://ds.internic.net/rfc/rfc1867.txt), written by E. Nebel and L. Masinter of Xerox Corporation, defines an experimental protocol that would provide a standard for uploading files.

**Using HTML Forms** (http://163.6.7.9/KNOWLTON/ LDSBC/FORMHELP.HTM) is a well-designed and illustrated reference of HTML forms and the attributes used to add certain elements to a form.

**HTML Forms** (http://www.lib.stthomas.edu/ireland/ htmintro/pages/forms.htm) completely explains how to use forms elements and attributes. Examples and HTML lines are included.

**Forms Element for Fill-Out Forms** (http://www.utoronto.ca/ webdocs/HTMLdocs/NewHTML/forms.html), by Ian Graham, provides information about how forms work, an example and illustration of a simple form, and an explanation of form attributes. Also included are links to a CGI page and to the NCSA Fill-Out Forms page. This page is copyrighted 1994-1995.

**A Simple Forms Page** (http://www.intergalact.com/hp/ part2/forms.html) is a short illustrated tutorial, which provides an easy-to-understand explanation of forms along with an example. At the end of the document are links to tutorials on imagemaps and forms.

**WWW Fill-Out Forms** (http://www.webcom.com/ ~webcom/html/tutor/forms/) is a short page of links to forms tutorials and a forms processor.

**HTML Forms and CGIs** (http://www.chin.gc.ca/~training/ html/forms.html) is a list of links—many found in this section— arranged under the headings *General References*, *Common Gateway Interfaces* (*CGI*), *PERL*, and *Examples*.

**NUL—Creating Forms for the Web** (http://www.library
.nwu.edu/resources/www/forms/) is an excellent document from
the Northwestern University Library. Here you will learn about
the basics and the attributes that you can use to create a form.
At the end of the document are links to Web programming,
forms, and CGI resources. Also included are many links to sample forms and scripts.

**An Interactive Introduction to HTML and CGI Scripts on
the WWW** (http://snowwhite.it.brighton.ac.uk/~mas/mas/
courses/html/html.html#FORM) is a list of links to basic HTML
elements, form filling, CGI scripts, new HTML, and system
programming (sample CGI scripts).

**HTML Form-Testing Home Page** (http://www.research.
digital.com/nsl/formtest/home.html), provided by Digital
Equipment Corporation, enables you to test your forms using
simulations of various browsers. Once you start the test, you will
go through a series of pages, each of which tests a form in some
way. Also included are links to test results, HTML documentation and pages, as well as a long list of links to browser home
pages.

**The Common Gateway Interface** (http://hoohoo.ncsa.uiuc
.edu/cgi/overview.html) starts a well-known and comprehensive
tutorial about CGI and forms processing. Be sure to explore the
many links for users of all levels.

**PERL—Practical Extraction and Report Language**
(http://www.cs.cmu.edu/afs/cs/usr/rgs/mosaic/perl.html) is a
comprehensive manual of the Perl language. You can find a
searchable version of this site at http://www-cgi.cs.cmu.edu/cgi-
bin/perl-man.

## The META Element

When you first hear about the META element, it doesn't seem
particularly important. However, if you want search engines to
find your site, use the element to define keywords to be used in
matching user keywords. Or, if you want to document when you
created or have modified a page, or who worked on it, and so
on, use the element. The resources in this section will help you
use the META element in the best possible way.

**HTML Metadata** (http://www.erin.gov.au/technical/management/metadata/metadata.html) is a three-page document that completely explains metadata and the  element and its future. Several examples of  statements are included.

**The META Element** (http://www.acl.lanl.gov/HTML_WG/html-wg-94q3.messages/0125.html) is a 1994 message by Roy T. Fielding, who invented the  element. In the message, he justifies its existence and argues for its inclusion in the HTML 2.0 element set.

**An Exploration of Dynamic Documents** (http://home.netscape.com/assist/net_sites/pushpull.html) is a long document that discusses "server push," in which a server sends a chunk of data to the client but keeps the connection open, and "client pull," in which the client obeys the server, dynamic documents of Netscape Navigator. The article contains a complete description and sample HTML code.

**META Builder** (http://vancouver-webpages.com/VWbot/mk-metas.html) is a form that you fill in to generate  statements. Also included are links to another META generator, robot-driven search engines, and a more complete description of how the  element works.

**How Search Engines (Say They) Work** (http://www.searchenginewatch.com/work.htm) is an article about how search engines work, how they rank found sites, and links to search engines and other articles. Other links are provided on this page—some for the general public and some for registered subscribers

## Frames

The frames elements, which are the target of user admiration or hatred, are in the HTML 4.0 standard. The resources in this section will help you create pages with frames.

**Frames: An Introduction** (http://home.netscape.com/assist/net_sites/frames.html) introduces HTML document developers to frames and includes links to other frame documents. **Frames—Syntax - General** (http://home.netscape.com/assist/net_sites/frame_syntax.html) and **Frame Syntax - Names, Targets, and Window Control** (http://home.netscape.com/eng/

mozilla/2.0/relnotes/demo/target.html) describe frame documents, the syntax of frame elements, and how to target windows, which is a very important HTML concept.

**The Frame Element: A Bit of a Bust, for Now** (http://www.webweek.com/96Jun03/news/frame.html), an article written by Whit Andrews, is critical of frames—especially for users with monitors of standard sizes.

## CASCADING STYLE SHEETS

Cascading style sheets are supported in HTML 4.0. In this section, you can get a head start to this relatively new part of the standard by reading these style sheet resources.

**Cascading Style Sheets, Level 1** (http://www.w3.org/TR/WD-css1) is the official and comprehensive (181K) working draft for the World Wide Web Consortium (W3C).

**HTML3 and Style Sheets** (http://www.w3.org/TR/WD-style) is a comprehensive working draft that describes associating HTML documents with style sheets. Also included are descriptions of elements, the default style sheet language, performance issues, and so on.

**Web Style Sheets** (http://www.w3.org/Style/) is an overview of the development of style sheets by the World Wide Web Consortium and other organizations. Also included are links to online articles, other style sheet standards, and other resources.

**Cascading Style Sheets** (http://www.w3.org/Style/css/) documents the progress and provides links about the development of cascading style sheets.

**Quick Reference to Cascading Style Sheets, Level 1** (http://www.w3.org/Style/css/css1-qr.html) is a short document covering cascading style sheet syntax, properties, and definitions.

**W3C Activity: Style Sheets** (http://www.w3.org/Style/Activity) is an activity report, which is updated frequently.

**The W3 Consortium Announces Web Style Sheets** (http://www.w3.org/Style/960305_News.html) is the May 1, 1995, press release announcing style sheets.

**Frame-Based Layout Via Style Sheets** (http://www.w3.org/TR/WD-layout.html) discusses how style sheets will be used to create frames in HTML documents.

# APPENDIX A

# Elements by Version and Activity

HTML 4.0 includes most HTML 3.2 and HTML 2.0 elements plus elements that have been added for this version by the member companies of the World Wide Web Consortium. In addition, companies and individuals have developed elements, known as *extensions*, which are not part of the HTML 4.0 standard.

This appendix lists all HTML 4.0 elements. Each entry includes a short description and, within parentheses, the version from which it originated:

- 4.0 represents HTML 4.0. In other words, this element is new or revived from a previously obsolete standard, such as HTML, HTML+, HTML 1.0, or HTML 3.0— but not HTML 3.2 or HTML 2.0.
- 3.2 and 2.0 represent HTML 3.2 and HTML 2.0, respectively. HTML 3.2, the previous standard, was made up of completely new elements, HTML 2.0 elements, and some extensions from the Netscape Communications Corporation and Microsoft Corporation.
- M indicates that this element was most recently a Microsoft extension.
- N indicates that this element was most recently a Netscape extension.

On the last pages of the appendix are four additional lists: current Netscape extensions, current Microsoft extensions, elements deprecated as of HTML 4.0, and elements now obsolete as of HTML 4.0.

# HTML 4.0

| !— | Comment (2.0) |
|---|---|
| !DOCTYPE | Document type (2.0) |
| A | Hypertext link (2.0) |
| ACRONYM | Acronym (4.0) |
| ADDRESS | Address (2.0) |
| APPLET | Applet (3.2) |
| AREA | Area (3.2) |
| B | Bold text (2.0) |
| BASE | Base URL (2.0) |
| BASEFONT | Base font (N, M) |
| BDO | Bidirectional (4.0) |
| BIG | Big text (3.2) |
| BLOCKQUOTE | Define quote (2.0) |
| BODY | Document body (2.0) |
| BR | Line break (2.0) |
| BUTTON | 3D form button (4.0) |
| CAPTION | Caption (3.2) |
| CENTER | Center text (3.2) |
| CITE | Citation (2.0) |
| CODE | Source code (2.0) |
| COL | Column properties (M) |
| COLGROUP | Column group (M) |
| DD | Definition description (2.0) |
| DEL | Deleted text (4.0) |
| DFN | Definition (3.2) |
| DIR | Directory list (2.0) |
| DIV | Division (3.2) |
| DL | Definition list (2.0) |
| DT | Definition term (2.0) |
| EM | Emphasis (2.0) |

| | |
|---|---|
| FIELDSET | Form fields set (4.0) |
| FONT | Font (3.2) |
| FORM | Form (2.0) |
| FRAME | Frame (N,M) |
| FRAMESET | Frame set (N, M) |
| H1 | Level one heading (2.0) |
| H2 | Level two heading (2.0) |
| H3 | Level three heading (2.0) |
| H4 | Level four heading (2.0) |
| H5 | Level five heading (2.0) |
| H6 | Level six heading (2.0) |
| HEAD | Document head (2.0) |
| HR | Horizontal rule (2.0) |
| HTML | HTML document (2.0) |
| I | Italic text (2.0) |
| IFRAME | Floating frame (M) |
| IMG | Inline image (2.0) |
| INPUT | Input form field (2.0) |
| INS | Inserted text (4.0) |
| ISINDEX | Searchable index (2.0) |
| KBD | Keyboard input (2.0) |
| LABEL | Form element label (4.0) |
| LEGEND | Fields set caption (4.0) |
| LI | List item (2.0) |
| LINK | Link (2.0) |
| MAP | Map (3.2) |
| MENU | Menu list (2.0) |
| META | Meta (2.0) |
| NOBR | No break (M) |
| NOFRAMES | No frames (N, M) |
| NOSCRIPT | No script (4.0) |
| OBJECT | Multimedia object (M) |

| OL | Ordered list (2.0) |
| OPTION | Menu option (3.2) |
| P | Paragraph (2.0) |
| PARAM | Parameter (3.2) |
| PRE | Preformatted text (2.0) |
| Q | Quote (4.0) |
| S | Strikethrough (4.0) |
| SAMP | Sample output (2.0) |
| SCRIPT | Script (N, M) |
| SELECT | Form selection list (2.0) |
| SMALL | Small text (3.2) |
| SPAN | Style text span (M) |
| STRIKE | Strikethrough (2.0) |
| STRONG | Strong (2.0) |
| STYLE | Style (3.2) |
| SUB | Subscript (3.2) |
| SUP | Superscript (3.2) |
| TABLE | Table (3.2) |
| TBODY | Table body (M) |
| TD | Table data (3.2) |
| TEXTAREA | Form text input (2.0) |
| TFOOT | Table footer (M) |
| TH | Table heading (3.2) |
| THEAD | Table header (M) |
| TITLE | Document title (2.0) |
| TR | Table row (3.2) |
| TT | Teletype text (2.0) |
| U | Underlined (2.0) |
| UL | Unordered list (2.0) |
| VAR | Variable (2.0) |

# NETSCAPE EXTENSIONS

| | |
|---|---|
| BLINK | Blink text |
| EMBED | Embed |
| ILAYER | Inflow layer |
| KEYGEN | Generate key |
| LAYER | Layer |
| MULTICOL | Multiple columns |
| NOEMBED | No embed |
| NOBR | No break |
| NOLAYER | No layer |
| SERVER | LiveWire script |
| SPACER | Insert space |
| WBR | Word break |

# MICROSOFT EXTENSIONS

| | |
|---|---|
| BGSOUND | Background sound |
| EMBED | Embed |
| MARQUEE | Marquee |
| NEXTID | Create identifers |

# Deprecated Elements

APPLET

BASEFONT

CENTER

DIR

FONT

ISINDEX

MENU

S

STRIKE

U

# Obsolete Elements

LISTING

PLAINTEXT

XMP

# APPENDIX B

# Attributes in Depth

This appendix contains an alphabetically arranged list of HTML 4.0 attributes. Each entry includes a brief description, usage notes, and the elements under which the attribute is used.

If an attribute is unique to Netscape or Microsoft browsers, look for the text *Netscape-only attribute* or *Microsoft-only attribute*, enclosed within parentheses. Netscape and Microsoft extensions are clearly marked, too.

**When you use Netscape or Microsoft extensions or attributes, be aware that most browsers do not support them. Use HTML 4.0 elements and attributes instead.**

ABOVE=*"top_layer_name"*

The ABOVE attribute names the layer that is the top layer in the stack of layers. This is a Microsoft-defined attribute.

- top_layer_name must be the same as the ID name.
- This attribute overrides the default stacking order of newest (on the top) to the oldest (at the bottom). The remaining layers in the stack remain in the default order.
- The layer being made the top layer must already exist.
- Nested layers are above their parents in the stack of layers.
- Most browsers do not support Microsoft-defined attributes.

## Associated Element

LAYER

ACCEPT CHARSET=[ "<u>UNKNOWN</u>" ] | [ [ "*charset_1*" ]
[ { | , } "*charset_2*" ] [ . . . { | , } "*charset_n*" ] ]

The ACCEPT-CHARSET attribute lists one or more character encodings (that is, charsets) supported by the server processing the submitted forms.

- The form-handling program must support the charset of the data in the submitted form.
- Charsets can include characters and/or special characters from the supported character set.
- Supported charsets are included in RFC 2045.

## Associated Element

FORM

ACCEPT=" *MIME_type_1* " [ , *MIME_type_2* ] [ . . . ,
*MIME_type_n* ]

The ACCEPT attribute is a list of one or more Internet Media Types that this part of the form and the form-processing server will accept.

- If INPUT TYPE="file", the ACCEPT attribute can eliminate files that do not match a supported Internet Media Type.
- For more information about Internet Media Types, refer to Multipurpose Internet Mail Extensions (MIME) Part One: Format of Internet Message Bodies (ftp://ds.internic.net/rfc/rfc2045.txt) and Multipurpose Internet Mail Extensions (MIME) Part Two: Media Types (ftp://ds.internic.net/rfc/rfc2046.txt).

## Associated Element

INPUT

ACCESSKEY=" *shortcut_key* "

The ACCESSKEY attribute assigns a shortcut key (such as the **Enter** key) to the current element in order to activate (that is, focus) it.

- *shortcut_key* is a single case-insensitive keyboard key.
- *shortcut_key* can include any character that the user's browser supports.
- A user may have to press another key before pressing the shortcut key. For example, Windows users may have to press **Alt** first, and Macintosh users may have to press **Cmd** first. Be sure to add that key to the descriptive text associated with the element.

**571**

## Associated Elements

A, BODY (Microsoft-only attribute), BUTTON (Microsoft-only attribute), INPUT (Microsoft-only attribute), LABEL, LEGEND, OBJECT (Microsoft-only attribute), SELECT (Microsoft-only attribute), TEXTAREA (Microsoft-only attribute)

---

ACTION="*submit_url*"

The ACTION attribute sends the filled-in form to an HTTP or email URL.

- The form-handling program must support the type of data in the submitted form.
- *submit_url* is an absolute or relative Universal Resource Locator.
- When you send the form to an HTTP URL, the form is submitted to a program, which can be processed by a cgi-bin program or an HTTP script, which is known as a server-side form handler.

## Associated Elements

FORM, ISINDEX (Microsoft-only attribute)

---

ALIGN is a popular attribute whose values and behavior vary, depending on the element with which it is associated at a particular time. In this appendix, you'll find several versions of ALIGN arranged alphabetically by element name.

```
ALIGN="bottom"|"middle"|"top"|"left"|"r
ight"|"absmiddle"|"absbottom"|
"texttop"|"baseline"
```

The ALIGN attribute aligns the applet window or image with the surrounding area of the HTML document. For the SELECT and TEXTAREA elements, this is a Microsoft-defined attribute.

- ALIGN="bottom" aligns the bottom of the applet window, list box, drop-down list, or text area with the baseline of the current line.

- ALIGN="middle" aligns the middle of the applet window, list box, drop-down list, or text area with the baseline of the current line.

- ALIGN="top" aligns the top of the applet window, list box, drop-down list, or text area with the top of the current line.

- ALIGN="left" floats the window, list box, drop-down list, or text area at the left margin. Text wraps around the window.

- ALIGN="right" floats the window, list box, drop-down list, or text area at the right margin. Text wraps around the window.

- ALIGN="absmiddle" aligns the middle of the image, list box, drop-down list, or text area with the middle of the text on the current line. This is a Netscape- and Microsoft-defined attribute.

- ALIGN="absbottom" aligns the bottom of the image, list box, drop-down list, or text area with the bottom of the text on the current line. This is a Netscape- and Microsoft-defined attribute.

- ALIGN="texttop" aligns the top of the image, list box, drop-down list, or text area with the top of the tallest character on the current line. This is a Netscape- and Microsoft-defined attribute.

- ALIGN="baseline" aligns the bottom of the image, list box, drop-down list, or text area with the current baseline. This is a Netscape- and Microsoft-defined attribute.

- The ALIGN attribute is deprecated. Use style sheets to set alignment.
- Most browsers do not recognize Netscape- and Microsoft-defined attributes.
- Different browsers can treat the ALIGN attribute slightly differently. Some don't recognize ALIGN="left" and ALIGN="right". Some evaluate a text line immediately before an element, and some evaluate text lines above and below an element.

## Associated Elements

APPLET, IMG, SELECT (Microsoft-only attribute), TEXTAREA (Microsoft-only attribute)

---

ALIGN="<u>top</u>" | "bottom" | "left" | "right" | "center"

The ALIGN attribute aligns the caption, above, below, to the left, or to the right of the table.

- ALIGN="top" moves the caption above the top border of the table.
- ALIGN="bottom" moves the caption below the bottom border of the table.
- ALIGN="left" aligns the caption with the left border of the table.
- ALIGN="right" aligns the caption with the right border of the table.
- ALIGN="center" centers the caption between the left and right margins. This is a Netscape-defined attribute.
- If you use the ALIGN attribute more than once within a table, the order in which the attribute is processed (that is, the order of precedence), from highest to lowest, is:
    1. Alignment of an element within a cell's contents.
    2. Alignment of a TH or TD cell.
    3. Alignment of a column (COL) or column group (COLGROUP).

4. Alignment of a row (TR) or group of rows (TBODY, TFOOT, or THEAD).

5. Alignment of a table.

6. The default alignment.

- The ALIGN attribute is deprecated. Use style sheets to set alignment.

- Different browsers can treat the ALIGN attribute slightly differently. Some don't recognize ALIGN="left" and ALIGN="right". Some evaluate a text line immediately before an element, and some evaluate text lines above and below an element.

## Associated Element

CAPTION

ALIGN="<u>left</u>" | "center" | "right" | "justi-fy" | "char

The ALIGN attribute horizontally aligns the contents of table cells or columns.

- ALIGN="left" aligns data with the left margin of the current cell or columns.

- ALIGN="center" centers data in the current cell or columns.

- ALIGN="right" aligns data with the right margin of the current cell or columns.

- ALIGN="justify" aligns data with both the left and right margins of the current cell or columns.

- ALIGN="char" aligns data on both sides of a particular character.

- The ALIGN attribute is deprecated. Use style sheets to set alignment.

- Different browsers can treat the ALIGN attribute slightly differently. Some don't recognize ALIGN="left" and ALIGN="right". Some evaluate a text line immediately before an element, and some evaluate text lines above and below an element.

## Associated Elements

COL, COLGROUP, TBODY, TD, TFOOT, TH, TR

---

ALIGN="left" | "center" | "right" | "justify"

The ALIGN attribute horizontally aligns the contents of a section of text.

- ALIGN="left" aligns text with the left margin.
- ALIGN="center" centers text between the left and right margins.
- ALIGN="right" aligns text with the right margin.
- ALIGN="justify" aligns text with both the left and right margins.
- The ALIGN attribute is deprecated. Use style sheets to set alignment.
- Different browsers can treat the ALIGN attribute slightly differently. Some don't recognize ALIGN="left" and ALIGN="right". Some evaluate a text line immediately before an element, and some evaluate text lines above and below an element.

## Associated Elements

DIV, H1, H2, H3, H4, H5, H6, P

---

ALIGN="<u>left</u>" | "right" | "top" | "bottom" | "ab sbottom" | "absmiddle" | "baseline" | "middle" | "texttop"

The ALIGN attribute horizontally or vertically aligns text with an embedded object. This is a Netscape- and Microsoft-defined attribute.

- ALIGN="left" places the text to the left of the object.
- ALIGN="right" places the text to the right of the object.
- ALIGN="top" places the text above the object.

- ALIGN="bottom" places the text below the object.
- ALIGN="absbottom" aligns the bottom of the object with the bottom of the text on the current line. This is a Microsoft-only attribute.
- ALIGN="absmiddle" aligns the middle of the object with the middle of the text on the current line. This is a Microsoft-only attribute.
- ALIGN="baseline" aligns the bottom of the object with the current baseline. This is a Microsoft-only attribute.
- ALIGN="texttop" aligns the top of the object with the top of the tallest character on the current line. This is a Microsoft-only attribute.
- ALIGN="middle" aligns the middle of the object with the baseline of the current line. This is a Microsoft-only attribute.
- The ALIGN attribute is deprecated. Use style sheets to set alignment.
- Most browsers do not support Netscape- and Microsoft-defined attributes.

## Associated Element

EMBED (Netscape and Microsoft extension)

---

ALIGN="left" | "center" | "right"

The ALIGN attribute horizontally aligns a horizontal rule.

- ALIGN="left" aligns the rule with the left margin.
- ALIGN="center" centers the rule between the left and right margins.
- ALIGN="right" aligns the rule with the right margin.
- The ALIGN attribute is deprecated. Use style sheets to set alignment.
- Different browsers can treat the ALIGN attribute slightly differently. Some don't recognize ALIGN="left" and ALIGN="right". Some evaluate a text line immediately before an element, and some evaluate text lines above and below an element.

- You cannot align a rule that is the full width of the window.

## Associated Element

HR

---

ALIGN="<u>left</u>" | "center" | "right" | "top" | "bo
ttom"

The ALIGN attribute aligns the frame or marquee with the surrounding text. This is a Microsoft-defined attribute.

- ALIGN="left" floats the frame or marquee at the left margin. Text wraps around the frame or marquee.
- ALIGN="center" aligns text with the center of the frame or marquee.
- ALIGN="right" floats the frame or marquee at the right margin. Text wraps around the frame or marquee.
- ALIGN="top"aligns text with the top of the frame or marquee.
- ALIGN="bottom" aligns text with the bottom of the frame or marquee.
- Most browsers do not support Microsoft-defined attributes.

## Associated Elements

IFRAME (Microsoft-only attribute), MARQUEE (Microsoft-only attribute)

---

ALIGN="top" | "middle" | "bottom" | "left" | "r
ight" | "absbottom" | "absmiddle" | "base-
line" | "texttop"

The ALIGN attribute horizontally or vertically aligns an input control.

- ALIGN="top" aligns the input control with the top of the form. Note that Netscape browsers interpret ALIGN="top" as aligning the top of the input control with the top of the tallest character in the current line.
- ALIGN="middle" centers the input control between the top and bottom of the form. Note that Netscape browsers interpret ALIGN="middle" as aligning the middle of the input control with the bottom of the text on the current line.
- ALIGN="bottom" aligns the input control with the bottom of the form. Note that Netscape browsers interpret ALIGN="bottom" as aligning the bottom of the input control with the current baseline. This is the Netscape default.
- ALIGN="left" aligns the input control with the left margin of the form.
- ALIGN="right" aligns the input control with the right margin of the form.
- ALIGN="absbottom" aligns the bottom of the input control with the bottom of the text on the current line. This is a Netscape-defined attribute.
- ALIGN="absmiddle" aligns the middle of the input control with the middle of the text on the current line. This is a Netscape-defined attribute.
- ALIGN="baseline" aligns the bottom of the input control with the current baseline. This is a Netscape-defined attribute.
- ALIGN="texttop" aligns the top of the input control with the top of the tallest character on the current line. This is a Netscape-defined attribute.
- The ALIGN attribute is deprecated. Use style sheets to set alignment.
- Different browsers can treat the ALIGN attribute slightly differently. Some don't recognize ALIGN="left" and ALIGN="right". Some evaluate a text line immediately before an element, and some evaluate text lines above and below an element.

## Associated Element

INPUT

---

ALIGN="top" | "bottom" | "left" | "right"

The ALIGN attribute horizontally or vertically aligns a fieldset caption.

- ALIGN="top" places the caption above the fieldset.
- ALIGN="bottom" places the caption below the fieldset.
- ALIGN="left" places the caption to the left of the fieldset.
- ALIGN="right" places the caption to the right of the fieldset.
- The ALIGN attribute is deprecated. Use style sheets to set alignment.
- Different browsers can treat the ALIGN attribute slightly differently. Some don't recognize ALIGN="left" and ALIGN="right". Some evaluate a text line immediately before an element, and some evaluate text lines above and below an element.

## Associated Element

LEGEND

---

ALIGN="texttop" | "middle" | "textmiddle" | "baseline" | "textbottom" | "left" | "center" | "right" | "absbottom" | "absmiddle" | bottom" | "top"

The ALIGN attribute horizontally or vertically aligns an embedded object within its page.

- ALIGN="texttop" aligns the top of the object with the top of the tallest character on the current line.
- ALIGN="middle" aligns the middle of the object with the baseline of the current line.

- ALIGN="textmiddle" aligns the middle of the object with the middle of the current line.
- ALIGN="baseline" aligns the bottom of the object with the baseline of the current line.
- ALIGN="textbottom" aligns the bottom of the object with the bottom of the current line.
- ALIGN="left" floats the object at the left margin. Text wraps around the object.
- ALIGN="center" floats the object in the center of the page. Text appears on both sides of the object.
- ALIGN="right" floats the object at the right margin. Text wraps around the object.
- ALIGN="absbottom" aligns the bottom of the object with the bottom of the text on the current line. This is a Microsoft-defined attribute.
- ALIGN="absmiddle" aligns the middle of the object with the middle of the text on the current line. This is a Microsoft-defined attribute.
- ALIGN="bottom" aligns the bottom of the object with the baseline of the current text line. This is a Microsoft-only attribute.
- ALIGN="top" aligns the top of the object with the top of the highest character on the current line. This is a Microsoft-only attribute.
- The ALIGN attribute is deprecated. Use style sheets to set alignment.

## Associated Element

OBJECT

---

ALIGN="<u>bottom</u>"|"middle"|"top"|"left"|"r
ight"|"absmiddle"|"absbottom"|"text-
top"|"baseline"

The ALIGN attribute aligns the white-space block with the surrounding text, graphics, and links in the current document. This is a Netscape-defined attribute.

- The ALIGN attribute is in effect only when TYPE="BLOCK".
- ALIGN="bottom" aligns the bottom of the white-space block with the baseline of the current text line.
- ALIGN="middle" aligns the middle of the white-space block with the baseline of the current text line.
- ALIGN="top" aligns the top of the white-space block with the top of the highest character on the current line.
- ALIGN="left" aligns the white-space block with the left margin.
- ALIGN="right" aligns the white-space block with the right margin.
- ALIGN="absmiddle" aligns the middle of the white-space block with the middle of the text on the current line.
- ALIGN="absbottom" aligns the bottom of the white-space block with the bottom of the lowest character on the current line.
- ALIGN="texttop" aligns the top of the white-space block with the top of the tallest character on the current line.
- ALIGN="baseline" aligns the bottom of the white-space block with the baseline of the current text line. This is the same as ALIGN="bottom".
- The ALIGN attribute is deprecated. Use style sheets to set alignment.
- Most browsers do not recognize Netscape-defined attributes.

## Associated Element

SPACER (Netscape extension)

---

```
ALIGN="left" | "center" | "right" | "bleedlef
t" | "bleedright" | "justify"
```

The ALIGN attribute horizontally aligns a table in the window in which it is contained.

- ALIGN="left" moves the table to the left margin of the window.
- ALIGN="center" aligns the table with the center of the window.
- ALIGN="right" moves the table to the right margin of the window.
- ALIGN="bleedleft" moves the table to the left edge of the window beyond the left margin. This is a Microsoft-defined attribute.
- ALIGN="bleedright" moves the table to the right edge of the window beyond the right margin. This is a Microsoft-defined attribute.
- ALIGN="justify" aligns the table with both the left and right margins. This is a Microsoft-defined attribute.
- The ALIGN attribute is deprecated. Use style sheets to set alignment.
- Different browsers can treat the ALIGN attribute slightly differently. Some don't recognize ALIGN="left" and ALIGN="right". Some evaluate a text line immediately before an element, and some evaluate text lines above and below an element.

## Associated Element

TABLE

---

ALIGN="left" | "center" | "right" |
"justify" | "char

The ALIGN attribute horizontally aligns the contents of table headers.

- ALIGN="left" aligns header text with the left margin of the current cell.
- ALIGN="center" centers header text in the current cell.
- ALIGN="right" aligns header text with the right margin of the current cell.
- ALIGN="justify" aligns header text with both the left and right margins of the current cell.

- ALIGN="char" aligns header text on both sides of a particular character.
- The ALIGN attribute is deprecated. Use style sheets to set alignment.
- Different browsers can treat the ALIGN attribute slightly differently. Some don't recognize ALIGN="left" and ALIGN="right". Some evaluate a text line immediately before an element, and some evaluate text lines above and below an element.

## Associated Element

THEAD

---

ALINK="#*rrggbb*" | "*color*"

The ALINK attribute defines the color of the text and graphics borders of the link that has just been clicked.

- When you click on a link, the ALINK attribute causes a momentary flash of a different color.
- *rrggbb* is the hexadecimal code of the color; *rr* represents the red attributes, from 00 to FF; *gg* represents the green attributes, from 00 to FF; and *bb* represents the blue attributes, from 00 to FF. Table 4.1 contains selected hexadecimal color values.
- *color* represents supported color names: red, maroon, yellow, green, lime, teal, olive, aqua, blue, navy, purple, fuchsia, black, gray, silver (the default), and white.
- Colors vary according to the graphics board and associated software installed in a computer, so it's best to view all colors and see how they work together before making a final color choice. Regardless of your color choice, there is a very good chance that some browser will interpret your colors in a very strange way.
- Both Netscape and Microsoft provide additional color names. Most browsers do not support Netscape and Microsoft attributes.
- This attribute is deprecated. Use a style sheet to specify the look of a document.

## Associated Element

BODY

---

## ALT="alternate_name"

The ALT attribute permanently describes an image for text-only browsers, specifies alternate text that will replace an applet for browsers that don't support the running of applets, temporarily describes an image as it loads, or displays a *tool tip*, a boxed message similar to toolbar bubble help.

- The ALT attribute allows users to learn about the content of an image without viewing it.
- *alternate_name* can include characters and/or special characters from the supported character set.
- Use the LANG attribute to specify the language for the alternate text.
- Use alternate text (for example, a filename) that carefully describes the image.
- If you are using an image to format a page, *alternate_name* should be empty (that is, "").
- When you omit the ALT attribute from an element, a browser might use the value of the NAME, TITLE, or TYPE attribute as alternate text.
- For special characters, use the following syntax: &#*D*; (where *D* is a decimal character) or &#x*H*; (where *H* is a hexadecimal character).
- Special characters are case-sensitive.

## Associated Elements

APPLET, AREA, EMBED (Microsoft-defined attribute), IMG, INPUT

ARCHIVE=*"preload_archive_1*[,
*preload_archive_2*[...,
preload_archive_n*"

The ARCHIVE attribute names archives containing resources that will be loaded before the applet runs.

- Preloading resources before loading an applet can improve the running performance of the applet.
- Classes are loaded using AppletClassLoader using the CODEBASE URL.

## Associated Element

APPLET

AXES=*"row_ax_name"*,*"col_ax_name"*

The AXES attribute is a list of one or more axis names, separated by commas, that specify the row and/or column headers of the current cell.

- *row_ax_name* and *col_ax_name* can include characters and/or special characters from the supported character set.
- For special characters, use the following syntax: &#*D*; (where *D* is a decimal character) or &#x*H*; (where *H* is a hexadecimal character).
- Special characters are case-sensitive.
- Browsers can use AXES names to name database fields when transferring the contents of a table to a database.
- Speech synthesizers can use AXES names to find a particular cell and its contents for processing.

## Associated Elements

TD, TH

AXIS="*abbrev_name*"

The AXIS attribute specifies an abbreviated name for a cell in a table header.

- If you do not specify a name, the default name is the contents of the cell.
- *abbrev_name* can include characters and/or special characters from the supported character set.
- For special characters, use the following syntax: &#*D*; (where *D* is a decimal character) or &#x*H*; (where *H* is a hexadecimal character).
- Special characters are case-sensitive.
- Browsers can use AXIS names to name database fields when transferring the contents of a table to a database.
- Speech synthesizers can use AXIS names to find a particular cell and its contents for processing.

## Associated Elements

TD, TH

BACKGROUND="*picture_url*"

The BACKGROUND attribute specifies an image file that is displayed in the background of each page of the current document, table (Microsoft-only attribute), or layer (Netscape-only attribute).

- *picture_url* is an absolute or relative Universal Resource Locator.
- If the dimensions of the image are smaller than the dimensions of the page, the browser will tile the image in the background.
- This attribute is deprecated. Use a style sheet to specify the look of a document.

## Associated Elements

BODY, COLGROUP (Microsoft-only attribute), ILAYER (Netscape-only attribute) LAYER (Netscape-only attribute) TABLE (Microsoft-only attribute), TD (Microsoft-only attribute), TH (Microsoft-only attribute)

---

BALANCE="*bal_num*"

The BALANCE attribute specifies the balance of volume for the left and right speakers. This is a Microsoft-defined attribute.

- Valid values range from -10,000 to +10,000.
- BALANCE="0" centers the balance between the left and right speakers.
- Most browsers do not support Microsoft-defined attributes.

## Associated Element

BGSOUND

---

BEHAVIOR="scroll"|"slide"|"alternate"

The BEHAVIOR attribute specifies the way that the text within the marquee will scroll. This is a Microsoft-defined attribute.

- BEHAVIOR="SCROLL" continuously scrolls the text from off the marquee window on one side to off the window on the other.
- BEHAVIOR="SLIDE" scrolls the text in from off the marquee window on one side and stop at the other side of the window.
- BEHAVIOR="ALTERNATE" causes the text to jump back and forth within the marquee window.
- Most browsers do not support Microsoft-defined attributes.

## Associated Element

MARQUEE (Microsoft extension)

BELOW=" *below_layer_name* "

The BELOW attribute names the layer that is the immediately below the newest layer in the stack. This is a Microsoft-defined attribute.

- *below_layer_name* must be the same as the ID name.
- This attribute overrides the default stacking order of newest (on the top) to the oldest (at the bottom). The remaining layers in the stack remain in the default order.
- The layer being made the below layer must already exist.
- Nested layers are above their parents in the stack of layers.
- Most browsers do not support Microsoft-defined attributes.

## Associated Element

LAYER

BGCOLOR=" *#rrggbb* " | " *color* "

The BGCOLOR attribute specifies the background color for document body, marquees (Microsoft-only), tables, table rows, table cells, or layers (Netscape-only).

- *rrggbb* is the hexadecimal code of the color; *rr* represents the red attributes, from 00 to FF; *gg* represents the green attributes, from 00 to FF; and *bb* represents the blue attributes, from 00 to FF. Table 4.1 contains selected hexadecimal color values.
- *color* represents supported color names: red, maroon, yellow, green, lime, teal, olive, aqua, blue, navy, purple, fuchsia, black, gray, silver (the default), and white.
- Colors vary according to the graphics board and associated software installed in a computer, so it's best to view all colors and see how they work together before

making a final color choice. Regardless of your color choice, there is a very good chance that some browser will interpret your colors in a very strange way.

- Both Netscape and Microsoft provide additional color names. Most browsers do not support Netscape and Microsoft attributes.

- This attribute is deprecated. Use a style sheet to specify the look of a document.

## Associated Elements

BODY, ILAYER (Netscape extension), LAYER (Netscape extension), MARQUEE (Microsoft extension), TABLE, TBODY (Microsoft-only attribute), TD, TFOOT (Microsoft-only attribute), TH, THEAD (Microsoft-only attribute), TR

---

BGPROPERTIES="FIXED"

The BGPROPERTIES attribute specifies that the background picture does not move when you scroll the document. This is a Microsoft-defined attribute.

- Most browsers do not support Microsoft-defined attributes.

## Associated Element

BODY

---

 BORDER is a popular attribute whose values and behavior vary, depending on the element with which it is associated at a particular time. In this appendix, you'll find several versions of BORDER arranged alphabetically by element name.

BORDER=*"border_pix"*

The BORDER attribute turns on a border and/or sets the width, in pixels, of an object, image, or a frameset. For EMBED and FRAMESET, this is a Netscape-defined attribute.

- Pixels is a value representing the number of pixels based on a 640x480 resolution.
- BORDER="0" specifies no border around any of the frames in the frameset.
- For the OBJECT element, use the FRAMEBORDER attribute to turn off the border of an embedded object.
- For framesets, the default BORDER setting is 5 pixels.
- The BORDER attribute only works for the outermost framesets in a set of nested framesets.
- Most browsers do not support Netscape-defined attributes.

## Associated Elements

EMBED (Netscape extension), FRAMESET (Netscape-only attribute), IMG

BORDER=*"0" | "border_pix"*

The BORDER attribute turns on a border and/or sets the width, in pixels, of an inline frame. This is a Microsoft-defined attribute.

- Pixels is a value representing the number of pixels based on a 640x480 resolution.
- BORDER="0" specifies no border around any of the frames in the frame.
- Most browsers do not support Microsoft-defined attributes.

## Associated Element

IFRAME

BORDER=" *border_pix*" | *border_%*

The BORDER attribute turns on a border and sets the width, in pixels or as a percentage of the full-screen width, of the window surrounding an object.

- Pixels is a value representing the number of pixels based on a 640x480 resolution.
- BORDER="0" removes a border.
- Do not enclose percentage values within quotation marks.
- Using the BORDER, HEIGHT, and/or WIDTH attributes to specify the actual size of the border, image height, and image width, respectively, can increase loading speed.
- This attribute is deprecated. Use a style sheet to specify the look of a document.

## Associated Element

OBJECT

BORDER=" *border_pix*"

The BORDER attribute turns on a border and sets the width, in pixels, of the table frame.

- Pixels is a value representing the number of pixels based on a 640x480 resolution.
- *border_pix* can include characters and/or special characters from the supported character set.
- If BORDER="0", then FRAME="void" and usually RULES="none".
- If the value of BORDER is greater than 0, FRAME="border" and usually RULES="all".

## Associated Element

TABLE

BORDERCOLOR=" #*rrggbb*" | "*color*"

The BORDERCOLOR attribute specifies the color for the borders of the current frameset or frame. This is a Netscape- and Microsoft-defined attribute.

- *rrggbb* is the hexadecimal code of the color; *rr* represents the red attributes, from 00 to FF; *gg* represents the green attributes, from 00 to FF; and *bb* represents the blue attributes, from 00 to FF. Table 4.1 contains selected hexadecimal color values.
- *color* represents supported color names: red, maroon, yellow, green, lime, teal, olive, aqua, blue, navy, purple, fuchsia, black, gray, silver (the default), and white.
- Colors vary according to the graphics board and associated software installed in a computer, so it's best to view all colors and see how they work together before making a final color choice. Regardless of your color choice, there is a very good chance that some browser will interpret your colors in a very strange way.
- Both Netscape and Microsoft provide additional color names. Most browsers do not support Netscape and Microsoft attributes.
- Most browsers do not support Netscape-defined attributes.
- If you specify different border colors for framesets and frames, a Netscape browser may attempt to define colors, in the following order, from high to low priority:
  1. The BORDERCOLOR of the current frame.
  2. The BORDERCOLOR of the current frameset.
  3. The BORDERCOLOR of the next frameset in a nested frameset.
  4. The BORDERCOLOR of the outermost frameset in a nested frameset.

## Associated Elements

FRAME (Netscape-only attribute), FRAMESET (Netscape-only attribute), IFRAME (Microsoft-only attribute)

BORDERCOLOR="#*rrggbb*" | "*color*"

The BORDERCOLOR attribute specifies the color for the border of the current table. This is a Microsoft-defined attribute.

- *rrggbb* is the hexadecimal code of the color; *rr* represents the red attributes, from 00 to FF; *gg* represents the green attributes, from 00 to FF; and *bb* represents the blue attributes, from 00 to FF. Table 4.1 contains selected hexadecimal color values.
- *color* represents supported color names: red, maroon, yellow, green, lime, teal, olive, aqua, blue, navy, purple, fuchsia, black, gray, silver (the default), and white.
- Colors vary according to the graphics board and associated software installed in a computer, so it's best to view all colors and see how they work together before making a final color choice. Regardless of your color choice, there is a very good chance that some browser will interpret your colors in a very strange way.
- Both Netscape and Microsoft provide additional color names. Most browsers do not support Netscape and Microsoft attributes.
- Most browsers do not support Microsoft-defined attributes.

## Associated Elements

TABLE, TD, TH, TR

BORDERCOLORDARK="#*rrggbb*" | "*color*"

The BORDERCOLORDARK attribute specifies the table border shadow. This is a Microsoft-defined attribute.

- *rrggbb* is the hexadecimal code of the color; *rr* represents the red attributes, from 00 to FF; *gg* represents the green attributes, from 00 to FF; and *bb* represents the blue attributes, from 00 to FF. Table 4.1 contains selected hexadecimal color values.

- *color* represents supported color names: red, maroon, yellow, green, lime, teal, olive, aqua, blue, navy, purple, fuchsia, black, gray, silver (the default), and white.
- Colors vary according to the graphics board and associated software installed in a computer, so it's best to view all colors and see how they work together before making a final color choice. Regardless of your color choice, there is a very good chance that some browser will interpret your colors in a very strange way.
- Both Netscape and Microsoft provide additional color names. Most browsers do not support Netscape and Microsoft attributes.
- Most browsers do not support Microsoft-defined attributes.

## Associated Elements

TABLE, TD, TH, TR

---

BORDERCOLORLIGHT="#*rrggbb*" | "*color*"

The BORDERCOLORLIGHT attribute specifies the color of the table border highlight. This is a Microsoft-defined attribute.

- *rrggbb* is the hexadecimal code of the color; *rr* represents the red attributes, from 00 to FF; *gg* represents the green attributes, from 00 to FF; and *bb* represents the blue attributes, from 00 to FF. Table 4.1 contains selected hexadecimal color values.
- *color* represents supported color names: red, maroon, yellow, green, lime, teal, olive, aqua, blue, navy, purple, fuchsia, black, gray, silver (the default), and white.
- Colors vary according to the graphics board and associated software installed in a computer, so it's best to view all colors and see how they work together before making a final color choice. Regardless of your color choice, there is a very good chance that some browser will interpret your colors in a very strange way.

- Both Netscape and Microsoft provide additional color names. Most browsers do not support Netscape and Microsoft attributes.
- Most browsers do not support Microsoft-defined attributes.

## Associated Elements

TABLE, TD, TH, TR

---

BOTTOMMARGIN=" *bot_mar_pix* "

The BOTTOMMARGIN attribute specifies the measurement, in pixels, of the bottom margin of the document (that is, the distance between the edge of the page and the contents of the page. This is a Microsoft-defined attribute.

- BOTTOMMARGIN="0" indicates that the bottom margin is located at the bottom edge of the page.
- Most browsers do not support Microsoft-defined attributes.

## Associated Element

BODY

---

CELLPADDING=" *cell_pad* "

The CELLPADDING attribute sets spacing, in pixels or as a percentage, between cell borders and the cell contents.

- CELLPADDING usually surrounds data in the cells with additional white space.
- It's a good idea to set CELLPADDING and/or CELLSPACING values before specifying the table or column width.
- Pixels is a value representing the number of pixels based on a 640x480 resolution.

## Associated Element

TABLE

---

CELLSPACING=*"cell_space"*

The CELLSPACING attribute sets spacing, in pixels or as a percentage, between the table frame and outer cell borders and between all other table cells.

- CELLSPACING usually makes the cell and table borders larger than the default.
- It's a good idea to set CELLPADDING and/or CELLSPACING values before specifying the table or column width.
- Pixels is a value representing the number of pixels based on a 640x480 resolution.

## Associated Element

TABLE

---

CHALLENGE="IA5STRONG" | *"challenge_string"*

The CHALLENGE attribute specifies a string that users will enter to verify the submission of a secure form. This is a Netscape-defined attribute.

- The CHALLENGE string is packaged with the public key.
- IA5STRONG has a zero length.
- Most browsers do not support Netscape-defined attributes.

## Associated Element

KEYGEN (Netscape extension)

CHAR="`character`"

The CHAR attribute names a character from which text is aligned in both directions. The default character is the decimal point character for the current language.

- *character* can include characters and/or special characters from the supported character set.
- For special characters, use the following syntax: &#*D*; (where *D* is a decimal character) or &#x*H*; (where *H* is a hexadecimal character).
- Special characters are case-sensitive.
- The CHAR attribute aligns characters in the same way as a decimal tab in a word processor.
- If you use the CHAR attribute more than once within a table, the order in which the attribute is processed (that is, the order of precedence), from highest to lowest, is:
  1. Alignment of an element within a cell's contents.
  2. Alignment of a TH or TD cell.
  3. Alignment of a column (COL) or column group (COLGROUP).
  4. Alignment of a row (TR) or group of rows (TBODY, TFOOT, or THEAD).
  5. Alignment of a table.
  6. The default alignment.

## Associated Elements

COL, COLGROUP, TBODY, TD, TFOOT, TH, THEAD, TR

CHAROFF="*offset*"

The CHAROFF attribute sets the *offset*, the horizontal distance between the left or right margin and the first occurrence of the CHAR alignment character.

- CHAROFF represents CHARacter OFFset.
- *offset* can include characters and/or special characters from the supported character set.

- For special characters, use the following syntax: &#$D$; (where $D$ is a decimal character) or &#x$H$; (where $H$ is a hexadecimal character).
- Special characters are case-sensitive.
- The current text direction set by the DIR attribute determines whether the left or right margin is the starting point of the offset. If the text direction is left-to-right, the default, the offset is measured from the left margin. If the text direction is right-to-left, the offset is measured from the right margin.
- If you use the CHAROFF attribute more than once within a table, the order in which the attribute is processed (that is, the order of precedence), from highest to lowest, is:
  1. Alignment of an element within a cell's contents.
  2. Alignment of a TH or TD cell.
  3. Alignment of a column (COL) or column group (THEAD).
  4. Alignment of a row (TR) or group of rows (TBODY, TFOOT, or THEAD).
  5. Alignment of a table.
  6. The default alignment.

## Associated Elements

COL, COLGROUP, TBODY, TD, TFOOT, TH, THEAD, TR

---

CHARSET=" ISO-8859-1 " | " *char_set* "

The CHARSET attribute names the source of the character set of the data referred to by the HREF attribute.

- The character set must be found in RFC 2045.

## Associated Element

A

CHARSET="*char_set*"

The CHARSET attribute names the source of the character set of the data in the current HTML document. This is a Microsoft-defined attribute.

- Most browsers do not support Microsoft-defined attributes.

## Associated Element

META

---

CHECKED

The CHECKED attribute sets the initial value of a check box (TYPE="CHECKBOX") or radio button (TYPE="RADIO") to on (that is, checked or filled in).

## Associated Element

INPUT

---

CITE="*cite_url*"

The CITE attribute provides a URL for a document or message that contains information about a BLOCKQUOTE or Q citation or the reason for a DEL or INS document change.

- *url* is an absolute or relative Universal Resource Locator.

## Associated Elements

BLOCKQUOTE, DEL, INS, Q

---

CLASS="*class_name*"

The CLASS attribute specifies one or more classifications for a particular element in the current document.

- *class_name* can include characters and/or special characters from the supported character set.

- For special characters, use the following syntax: &#$D$; (where $D$ is a decimal character) or &#x$H$; (where $H$ is a hexadecimal character).
- Special characters are case-sensitive.
- Use CLASS within a style sheet to specify a style to a particular classification of elements.
- Use CLASS to identify a field in a database or a document into which you are copying data from a document.

## Associated Elements

A, ACRONYM, ADDRESS, APPLET (Microsoft-only attribute), AREA (Microsoft-only attribute), B, BASE (Microsoft-only attribute), BASEFONT (Microsoft-only attribute), BIG, BLOCKQUOTE, BODY, BR, BUTTON, CAPTION, CENTER, CITE, CODE, COL, COLGROUP, DD, DEL, DFN, DIR, DIV, DL, DT, EM, EMBED (Microsoft-only attribute), FIELDSET, FONT (Microsoft-only attribute), FORM, FRAME, (Microsoft-only attribute), FRAMESET (Microsoft-only attribute), H1, H2, H3, H4, H5, H6, HEAD (Microsoft-only attribute), HR, I, IFRAME (Microsoft-only attribute), IMG, INPUT, INS, ISINDEX, KBD, LABEL, LEGEND, LI, LINK, MAP, MARQUEE (Microsoft-only attribute), MENU, OBJECT, OL, OPTION, P, OPTION, Q, S, SAMP, SCRIPT (Microsoft-only attribute), SELECT, SMALL, SPAN, STRIKE, STRONG, SUB, SUP, TABLE, TBODY, TD, TEXTAREA, TFOOT, TH, THEAD, TR, TT, U, UL, VAR

---

CLASSID="*url_id*"

The CLASSID attribute names an identifier for an object or class.

- *url_id* is an absolute or relative Universal Resource Locator.
- CLASSID helps the TYPE attribute to identify a valid media type the object to be inserted in a document.

## Associated Element

OBJECT

CLEAR="<u>none</u>" | "left" | "all" | "right"

CLEAR clears previous alignment settings when the left or right margin, both margins, or no margins are free from floating images in conjunction with a line break.

- CLEAR="none" does not wait for the margins to be clear; the "broken" text starts immediately at the current alignment setting.
- CLEAR="left" starts the text in the left margin after the left margin is clear from floating objects.
- CLEAR="right" starts the text in the right margin after the right margin is clear from floating objects.
- CLEAR="all" starts the text after both the left and right margins are clear from floating objects.
- It is best to use style sheets to control the flow of text rather than the CLEAR attribute.

## Associated Element

BR

CLEAR="<u>no</u>" | "left" | "right" | "all"

The CLEAR attribute controls the display of text after the end of a table. This is a Microsoft-defined attribute.

- CLEAR="no" does not clear the table; text immediately follows the table without a break.
- CLEAR="left" starts the text after the left margin is clear from the table.
- CLEAR="right" starts the text after the right margin is clear from the table.
- CLEAR="all" starts the text after both the left and right margins are clear from the table.
- Most browsers do not support Microsoft-defined attributes.
- It is best to use style sheets to control the flow of text rather than the CLEAR attribute.

## Associated Element

TABLE

---

CLIP=[0 | "*l_pix, 0 / t_pix, ] r_pix, b_pix*"

The CLIP attribute specifies the dimensions of the layer window. This is a Microsoft-defined attribute.

- You can either specify the left, top, right, and bottom dimensions, in pixels, or specify the right and bottom dimensions, in pixels.

- If you specify the right and bottom dimensions, the left and top dimensions are set to 0 by default.

- The left and right dimensions are measured from the left edge of the layer.

- The top and bottom dimensions are measured from the top edge of the layer.

- If you do not use CLIP, the layer dimensions are calculated as follows: *l_pix*="0", *t_pix*="0", *r_pix* is equal to the value of WIDTH, if provided, and *b_pix* is equal to the value of HEIGHT, if provided.

- If you do not use CLIP and WIDTH, the value of *r_pix* is what Netscape documentation says is "wrapping width."

- If you do not use CLIP and HEIGHT, the value of *t_pix* is equal to the height of the contents of the layer window.

- Most browsers do not support Microsoft-defined attributes.

## Associated Elements

ILAYER, LAYER

CODE=" *subclass_resource_url* "

The CODE attribute names the resource containing the compiled applet subclass for the current applet.

- *subclass_resource_url* must be a relative URL of the applet's base URL.

## Associated Element

APPLET, EMBED (Microsoft-only attribute), OBJECT (Microsoft-only attribute)

CODEBASE=" *base_url* "

The CODEBASE attribute specifies the base URL of the applet or the object.

- For the OBJECT element, CODEBASE completes relative URLs furnished by the CLASSID attribute.
- *base_url* is an absolute or relative URL.
- If you do not include the CODEBASE attribute, the default value is the base URL of the current HTML document.

## Associated Elements

APPLET, EMBED (Microsoft-only attribute) OBJECT

CODETYPE=" *Internet_Media_Type* "

The CODETYPE attribute specifies a valid Internet Media Type (that is, MIMETYPE) used by the program that will produce the object.

- Although CODETYPE is optional, add it to the OBJECT element if you use the CLASSID attribute.
- If you omit CODETYPE, the default is the value of the TYPE attribute.
- For more information about Internet Media Types, refer to Multipurpose Internet Mail Extensions

(MIME) Part One: Format of Internet Message Bodies (ftp://ds.internic.net/rfc/rfc2045.txt) and Multipurpose Internet Mail Extensions (MIME) Part Two: Media Types (ftp://ds.internic.net/rfc/rfc2046.txt).

## Associated Element

OBJECT

---

COLOR="#*rrggbb*" | "*color*"

The COLOR attribute defines the color of text or a horizontal rule.

- *rrggbb* is the hexadecimal code of the color; *rr* represents the red attributes, from 00 to FF; *gg* represents the green attributes, from 00 to FF; and *bb* represents the blue attributes, from 00 to FF. Table 4.1 contains selected hexadecimal color values.
- *color* represents supported color names: red, maroon, yellow, green, lime, teal, olive, aqua, blue, navy, purple, fuchsia, black, gray, silver (the default), and white.
- Colors vary according to the graphics board and associated software installed in a computer, so it's best to view all colors and see how they work together before making a final color choice. Regardless of your color choice, there is a very good chance that some browser will interpret your colors in a very strange way.
- Both Netscape and Microsoft provide additional color names. Most browsers do not support Netscape and Microsoft attributes.
- This attribute is deprecated. Use a style sheet to specify the look of a document.

## Associated Elements

BASEFONT, FONT, HR (Microsoft-only attribute)

COLS="*num_cols*"

The COLS attribute specifies the number of columns in the current table or selected area of a document (Netscape-only).

- The default value for COLS is 1.
- For the TABLE element, setting this attribute helps speed the loading of the table and other page contents because the browser will be able to calculate the approximate dimensions of the table and keep loading other page contents.
- Most browsers do not support Netscape-defined elements and attributes.

## Associated Elements

MULTICOL (Netscape extension), TABLE

COLS=*number_of_columns*

The COLS attribute sets the width of the text input area, by the number of columns, one per character.

- If a user enters a line that is longer than the text box width, the browser should insert a horizontal scroll bar or other means of scrolling or automatically wrap the text to the start of the following line.

## Associated Element

TEXTAREA

COLS="*col_value_1*[, *col_value_2*[...,
*col_value_n*]]"

The COLS attribute is a left-to-right measurement of the frameset.

- *col_value* can be an absolute number of pixels in the left-to-right measurement of the frameset.

- Pixels is a value representing the number of pixels based on a 640x480 resolution.
- *col_value* can be an absolute percentage of the frameset compared to the full width of the computer screen.
- *col_value* can be the relative height (*n\** or *\**) of the frameset to other framesets.
- *n\** is a multiplier of the default relative width, and *\** specifies a relative value of the rest of the available space in the width (for example, if the first frameset is 4* and the second frameset is *, the first frameset will be four times wider than the second).
- An * indicator implies a multiplier value of 1.
- Do not enclose * within quotation marks.
- Browsers set absolute widths first and relative widths after that.
- The default value of COLS is the full width of the computer screen.
- Netscape browsers require that you define COLS or ROWS.

## Associated Element

FRAMESET

COLSPAN="*num_cols*" | "1" | "0"

The COLSPAN attribute specifies the number of columns across which the current cell will extend.

- If COLSPAN="0", the span for the current column extends the remaining columns of the table.

## Associated Elements

TD, TH

COMPACT

The COMPACT attribute indicates that a browser might decrease the size of the space between a number or bullet and a list item or between a term and a description.

- Some browsers do not recognize the COMPACT attribute.
- COMPACT is a deprecated attribute.

## Associated Elements

DIR, DL, MENU, OL, UL

CONTENT="name_*value*"

The CONTENT attribute provides text or character information.

- The value of CONTENT depends on the value of the HEAD element's PROFILE attribute.
- If CONTENT is a list of keywords, each must be separated by a comma.
- *name_value* can include characters and/or special characters from the supported character set.
- For special characters, use the following syntax: &#*D*; (where *D* is a decimal character) or &#x*H*; (where *H* is a hexadecimal character).
- Special characters are case-sensitive.

## Associated Element

META

CONTROLS

The CONTROLS attribute inserts a set of controls so that you can play an embedded video clip. This is a Microsoft-defined attribute.

- Most browsers do not support Microsoft-defined attributes.

## Associated Element

IMG (Microsoft-only attribute)

---

COORDS="*coords_1, coords_2, coords_3[..., coords_n]*"

The COORDS attribute is a list containing the coordinates of a shape.

- Use commas to separate the individual coordinates.

## Associated Element

A

---

DATA="*data_url*"

The DATA attribute specifies the URL of a document that includes object data to be embedded in the current document.

- *data_url* is an absolute or relative Universal Resource Locator.

## Associated Element

OBJECT

---

DATAFLD="*ds_col_name*"

The DATAFLD attribute specifies the column name from the file that provides the data source object. This is a Microsoft-defined attribute.

- Most browsers do not support Microsoft-defined attributes.

## Associated Elements

A, APPLET, BUTTON, DIV, FRAME, IFRAME, IMG, LABEL, MAR-
QUEE, OBJECT, PARAM, SELECT, SPAN, TEXTAREA

---

DATAFORMATAS="HTML" | "TEXT"

The DATAFORMATAS attribute indicates whether the data
for this element is formatted as *plain text* (that is, unformatted
ASCII) or HTML. This is a Microsoft-defined attribute.

- Most browsers do not support Microsoft-defined attributes.

## Associated Elements

BUTTON, DIV, LABEL, MARQUEE, PARAM, SPAN

---

DATAPAGESIZE="*num_records*"

The DATAPAGESIZE attribute indicates the number of
records included in a repeated table. This is a Microsoft-defined
attribute.

- According to Microsoft documentation, DATAPAGE-
  SIZE "sets the number of records displayed in a data
  bound repeated table."
- Most browsers do not support Microsoft-defined attributes.

## Associated Element

TABLE

---

DATASRC="ds_identifier"

The DATASRC attribute specifies the identifier of the data
source object. This is a Microsoft-defined attribute.

- Most browsers do not support Microsoft-defined attributes.

## Associated Elements

A, APPLET, BUTTON, DIV, FRAME, IFRAME, IMG, LABEL, MAR-
QUEE, OBJECT, SELECT, SPAN, TABLE, TEXTAREA

---

DATETIME=" *YYYY-MM-DD* [T*hh*:*mm*:*ssTZD*] "

The DATETIME attribute names the date and time at which a change in the document was made.

- *datetime* must follow the ISO 8601 format, *YYYY-MM-DDThh:mm:ssTZD*, where:
  - *YYYY* represents the four-digit year (e.g., 1998), delimited by a dash (-).
  - *MM* represents the two-digit month, from 01 to 12, delimited by a dash (-).
  - *DD* represents the two-digit day of the month, from 01 to 31.
  - T is a delimiter indicating the start of the time section of the format.
  - *hh* represents the two-digit hour, in military time (00 to 23), delimited by a colon (:).
  - *mm* represents the two-digit minute (00 to 59), delimited by a colon (:).
  - *ss* represents the two-digit minute (00 to 59), delimited by a colon (:).
  - *TZD* is the time-zone designator: Z (the Coordinated Universal Time (UT ), +*hh*:*mm* (the number of hours and minutes ahead of UT , or -*hh*:*mm* (the number of hours and minutes behind UT .
- The default time for *datetime* is 00:00:00.

## Associated Elements

DEL, INS

**611**

DECLARE

The DECLARE attribute indicates that you are declaring, but not *instantiating* (that is, creating and object in memory and enabling it to be addressed), the object, usually for cross-reference purposes.

- Use a following OBJECT definition to actually embed the object using an address in memory.

## Associated Element

OBJECT

---

DIR="<u>LTR</u>" | "RTL"

The DIR attribute specifies the direction in which text is displayed: left-to-right or right-to-left.

- The Unicode character set provides a bidirectional algorithm for characters. Part 7, "Webliography," lists Unicode resources on the Internet.
- If a browser does not conform to the Unicode standard, you may have to specify the direction.
- The BDO element, which specifies the direction of text, overrides the DIR attribute.
- Do not use the LANG attribute to set text direction.
- To specify direction for an entire document, add the DIR attribute to the HTML element.
- The direction that you set for a block-level element remains in effect until the end of that element and any enclosed nested elements.
- A DIR attribute set for a nested block-level element overrides the previously-set value for the higher-level block-level element.
- A DIR attribute set for a nested inline element does not override the previously-set direction value.
- You can also set text direction with some Unicode characters. The best way to set direction is with the DIR attribute and/or the BDO element.

- If you use the DIR attribute more than once within a table, the order in which the attribute is processed (that is, the order of precedence), from highest to lowest, is:
  1. An attribute set on an element within a cell's contents.
  2. An attribute set on a TH or TD cell.
  3. An attribute set on a row (TR) or group of rows (TBODY, TFOOT, or THEAD).
  4. An attribute set on a column (COL) or column group (COLGROUP).
  5. An attribute set on a table.
  6. The default value of the attribute.

## Associated Elements

A, ACRONYM, ADDRESS, B, BDO, BIG, BLOCKQUOTE, BODY, BUTTON, CAPTION, CENTER, CITE, CODE, COL, COLGROUP, DD, DEL, DFN, DIR, DIV, DL, DT, EM, FIELDSET, FORM, H1, H2, H3, H4, H5, H6, HEAD, HTML, I, IMG, INPUT, INS, ISINDEX, KBD, LABEL, LEGEND, LI, LINK, MENU, META, OBJECT, OL, OPTION, P, OPTION, Q, S, SAMP, SELECT, SMALL, SPAN, STRIKE, STRONG, STYLE, SUB, SUP, TABLE, TBODY, TD, TEXTAREA, TFOOT, TH, THEAD, TITLE, TR, TT, U, UL, VAR

---

## DIRECTION="left" | "right"

The DIRECTION attribute specifies whether scrolling is from left to right or from right to left. This is a Microsoft-defined attribute.

- DIRECTION="left" scrolls the marquee text from right to left.
- DIRECTION="right" scrolls the marquee text from left to right.
- Most browsers do not support Microsoft-defined attributes.

## Associated Element

MARQUEE (Microsoft extension)

DISABLED

The DISABLED attribute prevents a user from adding input associated with the current element or from receiving the focus (the LINK element in Microsoft Internet Explorer).

- When an element is disabled, it cannot receive focus.
- When an element is disabled, it is skipped in tab order.
- When an element is disabled, its value is not submitted when its form is submitted.
- You can change the value of the DISABLED attribute by adding a script to the element.

## Associated Elements

BUTTON, INPUT, LABEL, LINK (Microsoft-only attribute), OBJECT, OPTION, SELECT, STYLE (Microsoft-only attribute), TEXTAREA

DOWNLOAD="*download_number*"

The DOWNLOAD attribute specifies the order in which the current image is downloaded. This is a Microsoft-defined attribute.

- Most browsers do not support Microsoft-defined attributes.

## Associated Element

APPLET (Microsoft-only attribute)

DYNSRC="*dynamic_url*"

The DYNSRC (Dynamic Source) attribute names the URL of a video clip or multimedia file to be inserted in an image. This is a Microsoft-defined attribute.

- Most browsers do not support Microsoft-defined attributes.

## Associated Element

IMG (Microsoft-only attribute)

---

ENCTYPE=" *Internet_Media_Type* "

The ENCTYPE attribute specifies a valid Internet Media Type (that is, MIMETYPE) for encoding user responses to be submitted to the server.

- Use the ENCTYPE attribute if METHOD="POST".
- The default MIME type is "application/x-www-form-urlencoded".
- If you are submitting one or more files to the server, use the "multipart/form-data" MIME type.
- For more information about Internet Media Types, refer to Multipurpose Internet Mail Extensions (MIME) Part One: Format of Internet Message Bodies (ftp://ds.internic.net/rfc/rfc2045.txt) and Multipurpose Internet Mail Extensions (MIME) Part Two: Media Types (ftp://ds.internic.net/rfc/rfc2046.txt).

## Associated Element

FORM

---

EVENT=" event_name "

The EVENT attribute names the event related to the current script. This is a Microsoft-defined attribute.

- Most browsers do not support Microsoft-defined attributes.

## Associated Element

SCRIPT

---

FACE=" *typeface* "

The FACE attribute specifies a typeface.

- The typeface that you specify must be installed on your computer system.

## Associated Elements

BASEFONT, FONT

---

FOR=" *id_name* "

The FOR attribute names the control with which the current label is associated.

- *control_name* must match the value of the ID attribute of the associated control.
- You can place the FOR attribute before or after the control with which it is associated.
- You can use multiple instances of FOR to create multiple labels for the current control.
- If the FOR attribute is not associated with a control, LABEL is implicitly associated with the value of the current control.

## Associated Element

LABEL

---

FOR="element_name"

The FOR attribute names the element with which the current script is associated. This is a Microsoft-defined attribute.

- Most browsers do not support Microsoft-defined attributes.

## Associated Element

SCRIPT

FRAME="_void_" | "above" | "below" | "hsides" | "vsi
des" | "lhs" | "rhs" | "box" | "border" | "insides"

The FRAME attribute specifies the table borders that are displayed onscreen or are hidden.

- The FRAME attribute refers to formats for the TABLE
  element (that is, table borders) and is not related to
  frames of the FRAME element.
- FRAME="void" hides all borders.
- FRAME="above" displays the top border only.
- FRAME="below" displays the bottom border only.
- FRAME="hsides" displays the top and bottom borders
  only.
- FRAME="vsides" displays the left and right borders
  only.
- FRAME="lhs" displays the left border only.
- FRAME="rhs" displays the right border only.
- FRAME="box" displays all borders.
- FRAME="border" displays all borders.
- If BORDER="0", FRAME equals "void" and RULES
  usually equals "none".
- If the value of BORDER is greater than 0, FRAME
  equals "border" and RULES usually equals "all".

## Associated Element

TABLE

FRAMEBORDER="no"

The FRAMEBORDER attribute turns off the border of an
embedded object. This is a Netscape-defined attribute.

- FRAMEBORDER="no" turns off the border.
- Most browsers do not support Netscape-defined attributes.

## Associated Elements

EMBED (Netscape extension)

**617**

FRAMEBORDER="1" | "0" | "yes" | "no"

The FRAMEBORDER attribute turns on or off or specifies the appearance of borders for a frame or all frames in a frameset. For framesets, this is a Netscape-and Microsoft-defined attribute.

- FRAMEBORDER="1" turns on a three-dimensional border.
- FRAMEBORDER="0" omits a border.
- FRAMEBORDER="yes" turns on a three-dimensional border. This is a Netscape value.
- FRAMEBORDER="no" turns on a plain border. This is a Netscape value.
- Most browsers do not support Netscape- and Microsoft-defined attributes.

## Associated Elements

FRAME, FRAMESET (Netscape and Microsoft), IFRAME

FRAMESPACING=" *frame_space*"

The FRAMESPACING attribute sets spacing, in pixels, between all the frames in a frameset or in a document. This is a Microsoft-defined attribute.

- Pixels is a value representing the number of pixels based on a 640x480 resolution.
- Most browsers do not support Microsoft-defined attributes.

## Associated Elements

FRAMESET, IFRAME (Microsoft-only attribute)

GUTTER=" *gutter_pix*"

The GUTTER attribute specifies the white space, in pixels, between columns. This is a Netscape-defined attribute.

- The default gutter width is 10 pixels.
- Pixels is a value representing the number of pixels based on a 640x480 resolution.
- Most browsers do not support Microsoft-defined attributes.

## Associated Element

MULTICOL (Microsoft-only attribute)

---

HALIGN="center" | "left" | "right"

The HALIGN attribute, which is a Netscape-defined attribute and not part of HTML 4.0, horizontally aligns text within the column group.

- HALIGN="center" centers text within the cells in the column group.
- HALIGN="left" aligns text with the left margin within the cells in the column group.
- HALIGN="right" aligns text with the right margin within the cells in the column group.

## Associated Element

COLGROUP

---

 **HEIGHT is a popular attribute whose values and behavior vary, depending on the element with which it is associated at a particular time. In this appendix, you'll find several versions of HEIGHT arranged alphabetically by element name.**

N O T E

---

HEIGHT="*height_pix*"

The HEIGHT attribute specifies the height, in pixels, of the window in which the applet will run or the image will be placed.

**619**

- Pixels is a value representing the number of pixels based on a 640x480 resolution.

- If you use the HEIGHT and/or WIDTH attributes, an image may be out of proportion with the dimensions of the original image.

- Using the BORDER, HEIGHT, and/or WIDTH attributes to specify the actual size of the border, image height, and image width, respectively, can increase loading speed.

- This attribute is deprecated. Use a style sheet to specify the look of a document.

## Associated Elements

APPLET, IMG

---

HEIGHT=" *height_pix* " | " *height_meas* "

The HEIGHT attribute specifies the height of the window in which the object will be placed. This is a Netscape- and Microsoft-defined attribute.

- For Netscape browsers, HEIGHT is measured in pixels, which is a value representing the number of pixels based on a 640x480 resolution.

- For Microsoft browsers, HEIGHT is measured in pixels or using the unit of measure set by the UNITS attribute.

- If you use the HEIGHT and/or WIDTH attributes, an image may be out of proportion with the dimensions of the original image.

- Using the BORDER, HEIGHT, and/or WIDTH attributes to specify the actual size of the border, image height, and image width, respectively, can increase loading speed.

- This is a Netscape- and Microsoft-defined attribute. Most browsers do not support these types of attributes.

## Associated Element

EMBED (Netscape and Microsoft extension)

HEIGHT="*height_pix*" | *height_%*

The HEIGHT attribute specifies the height, in pixels or as a percentage of the entire height of the computer screen, of an inline frame, table, or a window in which an object or marquee will be placed. For frames and marquees, this is a Microsoft-defined attribute. For tables, this is a Netscape-defined attribute.

- *height_pix* is the default frame or table height, in pixels.
- *height_&* is the frame or table width, as a percentage of the full window width.
- If you do not specify the width of a rule, frame, or table, the browser will set it.
- Pixels is a value representing the number of pixels based on a 640x480 resolution.
- Do not enclose percentage values within quotation marks.
- Most browsers do not support Netscape- or Microsoft-defined attributes.

## Associated Element

FRAME, IFRAME, MARQUEE (Microsoft extension), OBJECT, TABLE (Netscape-only attribute)

HEIGHT="*height_pix*"

The HEIGHT attribute specifies the height, in pixels, of the white-space block in the current document or of a layer window. This is a Netscape-defined attribute.

- For SPACER the HEIGHT attribute is in effect only when TYPE="BLOCK".
- Pixels is a value representing the number of pixels based on a 640x480 resolution.
- Most browsers do not support Netscape-defined attributes.

## Associated Elements

LAYER (Netscape extension), SPACER (Netscape extension)

---

HIDDEN="<u>FALSE</u>" | "TRUE"

The HIDDEN attribute indicates whether a plug-in application appears in the window. This is a Netscape-defined attribute.

- HIDDEN="FALSE" hides the plug-in.
- HIDDEN="TRUE" creates a plug-in.
- HIDDEN="TRUE" overrides the HEIGHT and WIDTH specifications.
- Most browsers do not support Netscape-defined attributes.

## Associated Element

EMBED (Netscape extension)

---

HREF="*link_url*"

The HREF attribute specifies a URL for a link.

- Within the A and AREA elements, the URL refers to an area within the current document, to another document, or to a program.
- Within the LINK element, the URL refers to another document or program.
- The URL is either absolute or relative.

## Associated Elements

A, AREA, LINK

---

HREF="*base_url*"

The HREF attribute defines an absolute URL used to complete relative URLs in the current document.

## Associated Element

BASE

---

 **HSPACE is a popular attribute whose values and behavior vary, depending on the element with which it is associated at a particular time. In this appendix, you'll find several versions of HSPACE arranged alphabetically by element name.**

NOTE

---

HSPACE="*horiz_pix*"

The HSPACE attribute is the horizontal area, in pixels, between the left margin of the page and the left margin of the applet window, image, or object.

- Pixels is a value representing the number of pixels based on a 640x480 resolution.
- This attribute is deprecated. Use a style sheet to specify the look of a document.

## Associated Elements

APPLET, IMG

---

HSPACE="*horiz_pix*"

The HSPACE attribute is the horizontal area, in pixels, between the left and right sides of the object and other text, graphics, links on the current page, or inline frame. This is a Netscape- or Microsoft-defined attribute.

- Pixels is a value representing the number of pixels based on a 640x480 resolution.
- Most browsers do not support Netscape- or Microsoft-defined attributes.

## Associated Elements

EMBED (Netscape extension), IFRAME (Netscape-only attribute)
MARQUEE (Microsoft extension)

HSPACE=" *horiz_pix"* | *horiz_%*

The HSPACE attribute is the horizontal area, in pixels or as a
percentage of the full-screen, between the left margin of the
page and the left margin of the applet window, image, or object.

- Pixels is a value representing the number of pixels
  based on a 640x480 resolution.
- Do not enclose percentage values within quotation
  marks.
- This attribute is deprecated. Use a style sheet to specify
  the look of a document.

## Associated Element

OBJECT

HSPACE=" *horiz_pix"*

The HSPACE attribute is the horizontal area, in pixels, in which
the table will fit. This is a Netscape-defined attribute.

- The browser will scale the table to fit within the specified space.
- Most browsers do not support Netscape-defined attributes.
- Pixels is a value representing the number of pixels
  based on a 640x480 resolution.

## Associated Element

TABLE

HTTP-EQUIV="*HTTP-header-field-name*"

The HTTP-EQUIV attribute binds the META information to an HTTP response header.

- HTTP-EQUIV is equivalent to the NAME attribute.
- The value of HTTP-EQUIV depends on the value of the HEAD element's PROFILE attribute.
- *HTTP=header-field-name* must begin with an uppercase or lowercase letter, followed by any combination of letters, numbers, hyphens, and periods.

## Associated Element

META

ID="*id_name*"

The ID attribute provides a unique identifier name for one element in the current document.

- Use ID to name an *anchor*, a location to which you can jump within a document.
- Use ID within a script to refer to a particular element.
- Use ID within a style sheet to style a particular element.
- Use ID to name a declaration within the OBJECT element.
- Use ID to identify a field in a database or a document into which you are copying data from a document.
- Use ID to override the CLASS attribute.
- *id_name* cannot contain special characters.

## Associated Elements

A, ACRONYM, ADDRESS, APPLET (Microsoft-only attribute), AREA (Microsoft-only attribute), B, BASE (Microsoft-only attribute), BASEFONT (Microsoft-only attribute), BIG, BLOCKQUOTE, BODY, BR, BUTTON, CAPTION, CENTER, CITE, CODE, COL, COLGROUP, DD, DEL, DFN, DIR, DIV, DL, DT, EM, EMBED (Microsoft-only attribute),

SET, FONT (Microsoft-only attribute), FORM, FRAME (Microsoft-only attribute), FRAMESET (Microsoft-only attribute), H1, H2, H3, H4, H5, H6, HEAD (Microsoft-only attribute), HR, I, IFRAME (Microsoft-only attribute), IMG, ILAYER (Netscape-only attribute), INPUT, INS, ISINDEX, KBD, LABEL, LAYER (Netscape-only attribute), LEGEND, LI, LINK, MAP, MARQUEE (Microsoft-only attribute), MENU, OBJECT, OL, OPTION, P, OPTION, Q, S, SAMP, SCRIPT (Microsoft-only attribute), SELECT, SMALL, SPAN, STRIKE, STRONG, SUB, SUP, TABLE, TBODY, TD, TEXTAREA, TFOOT, TH, THEAD, TR, TT, U, UL, VAR.

---

ISMAP

The ISMAP attribute indicates that the embedded image is a server-side image map and will use the ISMAP program to create the image map.

- If you use server-side image maps, users with text-only browsers may have unpredictable results with ISMAP.
- Microsoft supports ISMAP="*image*", where *image* represents a particular picture.

## Associated Element

IMG

---

LANG=" *lang_code*"

The LANG attribute names the language used within a particular element.

- If a browser supports a named language code, it will interpret that language using that language's character set and styles.
- *lang_code* must begin with an uppercase or lowercase letter, followed by any combination of letters, numbers, hyphens, and periods.
- RFC 1766 is the primary language code standard for HTML documents.
- ISO 639 provides two-letter primary language codes.
- ISO 3166 provides two-letter subcodes.
- The default language code is "unknown".

- If you use the LANG attribute more than once within a table, the order in which the attribute is processed (that is, the order of precedence), from highest to lowest, is:
  1. An attribute set on an element within a cell's contents.
  2. An attribute set on a TH or TD cell.
  3. An attribute set on a row (TR) or group of rows (TBODY, TFOOT, or THEAD).
  4. An attribute set on a column (COL) or column group (COLGROUP).
  5. An attribute set on a table.
  6. The default value of the attribute.

## Associated Elements

A, ACRONYM, ADDRESS, AREA (Microsoft-only attribute), B, BASE (Microsoft-only attribute), BASEFONT (Microsoft-only attribute), BDO, BIG, BLOCKQUOTE, BODY, BUTTON, CAPTION, CENTER, CITE, CODE, COL, COLGROUP, DD, DEL, DFN, DIR, DIV, DL, DT, EM, FIELD-SET, FONT (Microsoft-only attribute), FORM, FRAMESET (Microsoft-only attribute) H1, H2, H3, H4, H5, H6, HEAD, HR (Microsoft-only attribute, HTML, I, IMG, INPUT, INS, ISINDEX, KBD, LABEL, LEGEND, LI, LINK, MAP (Microsoft-only attribute), MARQUEE (Microsoft-only attribute), MENU, META, NEXTID (Microsoft-only attribute) OBJECT, OL, OPTION, P, OPTION, Q, S, SAMP, SELECT, SMALL, SPAN, STRIKE, STRONG, STYLE, SUB, SUP, TABLE, TBODY, TD, TEXTAREA, TFOOT, TH, THEAD, TR, TT, U, UL, VAR

---

LANGUAGE="*scripting_language*"

The LANGUAGE attribute declares the scripting language of the current script.

- The LANGUAGE attribute is deprecated. Use the TYPE attribute instead.

## Associated Element

SCRIPT

LANGUAGE="<u>JAVASCRIPT</u>" | "JSCRIPT" |
"VBS[CRIPT]"

The LANGUAGE attribute declares the scripting language of the current script. This is a Microsoft-defined attribute.

- LANGUAGE=JAVASCRIPT or LANGUAGE=JSCRIPT indicates that the scripting language is JavaScript.
- LANGUAGE=VBS or LANGUAGE=VBSCRIPT indicates that the scripting language is VBScript.
- Most browsers do not support Microsoft-defined attributes.

## Associated Elements

A, ADDRESS, AREA, B, BIG, BLOCKQUOTE, BODY, BR, BUTTON, CAPTION, CENTER, CITE, CODE, DD, DFN, DIR, DL, DT, EM, FIELDSET, FONT, FORM, FRAMESET, H1, H2, H3, H4, H5, H6, HR, I, IMG, INPUT, KBD, LABEL, LEGEND, LI, MARQUEE, OBJECT, OL, OPTION, P, PRE, S, SAMP, SELECT, SMALL, SPAN, STRIKE, STRONG, SUB, SUP, TABLE, TBODY, TD, TEXTAREA, TH, THEAD, TR, TT, U, UL, VAR

LEFT="*left_pos_pix*"

The LEFT attribute specifies the leftmost position, in pixels, of the left side of a layer window. This is a Netscape-defined attribute.

- The LEFT attribute specifies an absolute position.
- Pixels is a value representing the number of pixels based on a 640x480 resolution.
- Most browsers do not support Netscape-defined attributes.

## Associated Elements

ILAYER, LAYER

LEFTMARGIN=" *lmar-num* "

The LEFTMARGIN attribute specifies the left margin, in pixels, of this document. This is a Microsoft-defined attribute.

- Most browsers do not support Microsoft-defined attributes.
- LEFTMARGIN="0" moves the margin to the left edge of the page.
- The value of LEFTMARGIN overrides the default left margin.
- Pixels is a value representing the number of pixels based on a 640x480 resolution.

## Associated Element

BODY

LINK=" #*rrggbb* " | " *color* "

The LINK attribute defines the color of the text and graphics borders of links that have not been visited or that have been visited but have been made inactive again from within your browser.

- *rrggbb* is the hexadecimal code of the color; *rr* represents the red attributes, from 00 to FF; *gg* represents the green attributes, from 00 to FF; and *bb* represents the blue attributes, from 00 to FF. Table 4.1 contains selected hexadecimal color values.
- *color* represents supported color names: red, maroon, yellow, green, lime, teal, olive, aqua, blue, navy, purple, fuchsia, black, gray, silver (the default), and white.
- Colors vary according to the graphics board and associated software installed in a computer, so it's best to view all colors and see how they work together before making a final color choice. Regardless of your color choice, there is a very good chance that some browser will interpret your colors in a very strange way.

- Both Netscape and Microsoft provide additional color names. Most browsers do not support Netscape and Microsoft attributes.
- This attribute is deprecated. Use a style sheet to specify the look of a document.

## Associated Element

BODY

---

LOOP="*number_of_plays*" | "INFINITE"

The LOOP attribute indicates the number of times that an embedded audio clip will play or marquee will scroll. This is a Microsoft-defined attribute.

- LOOP="*number_of_plays*" specifies the number of times that the audio file will play.
- LOOP="-1" specifies that the audio file will play continuously until the user displays another page.
- LOOP="INFINITE" specifies that the audio file will play continuously until the user displays another page.
- Most browsers do not support Microsoft-defined attributes.

## Associated Elements

BGSOUND (Microsoft extension), MARQUEE (Microsoft extension)

---

LOOP="*number_of_plays*"

The LOOP attribute indicates the number of times that an embedded video clip will play. This is a Microsoft-defined attribute.

- LOOP="*number_of_plays*" specifies the number of times that the video file will play.
- Most browsers do not support Microsoft-defined attributes.

## Associated Element

IMG (Microsoft-only attribute)

---

LOWSRC=" *low_res_url* "

The LOWSRC attribute specifies the URL of a low-resolution graphic to be loaded in the same location as the SRC graphic. This is a Netscape- and Microsoft-defined attribute.

- LOWSRC acts as a placeholder and hint at the appearance of the final image.
- Most browsers do not support Netscape- and Microsoft-defined attributes.

## Associated Element

IMG

---

MARGINHEIGHT=" *height_pix* "

The MARGINHEIGHT attribute is the space, in pixels, between the top and bottom margins of the frame and the contents of the frame.

- MARGINHEIGHT must be greater than 1 pixel.
- Pixels is a value representing the number of pixels based on a 640x480 resolution.

## Associated Elements

FRAME, IFRAME

---

MARGINWIDTH=" *width_pix* "

The MARGINWIDTH attribute is the space, in pixels, between the left and right margins of the frame and the contents of the frame.

- MARGINWIDTH must be greater than 1 pixel.
- Pixels is a value representing the number of pixels based on a 640x480 resolution.

## Associated Elements

FRAME, IFRAME

---

MAXLENGTH=*"maximum-length"*

The MAXLENGTH attribute sets a maximum number of characters for a text box or password text box in the current form.

- If you do not use the MAXLENGTH attribute, you can enter any number of characters or spaces in a field.
- If MAXLENGTH is greater than SIZE, the browser may have to add a method for scrolling the contents of the text box.

## Associated Element

INPUT

---

MAYSCRIPT

The MAYSCRIPT attribute allows the applet to access JavaScript. This is a Netscape-defined attribute, which is getting wider acceptance for other browsers.

- If JavaScript is accessed without permission being granted, Netscape Navigator issues an exception.
- Most browsers do not support Netscape-defined attributes.

## Associated Element

APPLET (Netscape-only attribute)

---

MEDIA=["screen"][,]["print"][,]
["projection"][,]["braille"][,]
["speech"][,]["all"]

The MEDIA attribute specifies one or more types of destination for the document.

- You can specify a single medium or several.
- MEDIA="screen" sends the information to a computer screen in a continuous layout.
- MEDIA="print" sends the information to a medium that accepts page formats or to a print preview mode.
- MEDIA="projection" sends the information to a projector.
- MEDIA="braille" sends the information to a device that produces Braille output.
- MEDIA="speech" sends the information to a speech synthesizer.
- MEDIA="all" sends the information to all devices.

## Associated Elements

LINK, STYLE

---

METHOD="<u>GET</u>" | "POST"

The METHOD attribute specifies the HTTP method used to send the form to a server that contains a form handling program.

- The submitted data is comprised of pairs of names and values.
- METHOD="GET" appends the filled-in information to a newly-created submit URL named by the ACTION attribute and using an environment variable.
- METHOD="GET" is deprecated.
- METHOD="POST" specifies a form that includes information to be sent to a server.
- METHOD="POST" may update a file or send a message.
- METHOD="POST" allows you to add more information but is more difficult to use.
- Many HTML experts strongly recommend using METHOD="POST".

## Associated Element

FORM

**633**

METHODS="functions_perf"

The METHODS attribute indicates the functions to be per-formed on an object. This is a Microsoft-defined attribute.

- Use the HTTP protocol to provide advance information about anchors and links. This can result in anchor and link icons that identify the functions to be performed.
- Most browsers do not support Microsoft-defined attributes.

## Associated Element

A

MULTIPLE

The MULTIPLE attribute allows a user to select more than one item from a selection list.

- If you omit the MULTIPLE attribute, you can only choose one item from the selection list.

## Associated Element

SELECT

NOTE NAME is a popular attribute whose values and behavior vary, depending on the element with which it is associated at a par-ticular time. In this appendix, you'll find several versions of NAME arranged alphabetically by element name.

NAME="*anchor_name*"

The NAME attribute is the unique name of an anchor.

- This attribute is the same as the ID attribute.

- When you name HTML components, elements (and their attributes) can use the names for identification and communications.
- *anchor name* can include characters and/or special characters from the supported character set.
- Values of names are case-insensitive.

## Associated Element

A

---

NAME="*applet_name*"

The NAME attribute names the current applet.

- *applet_name* allows applets in the same HTML document to communicate.
- *applet_name* must begin with an uppercase or lowercase letter, followed by any combination of letters, numbers, hyphens, and periods.
- *applet_name* can include characters and/or special characters from the supported character set.
- Special characters are case-sensitive.

## Associated Element

APPLET

---

NAME="*map_name*"

The NAME attribute names the current image map or area (Netscape-only).

- *map_name* must begin with an uppercase or lowercase letter, followed by any combination of letters, numbers, hyphens, and periods.
- *map_name* can include characters and/or special characters from the supported character set.
- Special characters are case-sensitive.
- If you give an AREA a name, remember that most browsers do not support Microsoft-defined attributes.

## Associated Elements

AREA (Netscape-only attribute), MAP

---

NAME=" *button_name* "

The NAME attribute names the current button.

## Associated Element

BUTTON

---

NAME=" *object_name* "

The NAME attribute names the embedded object. This is a Netscape- and Microsoft-defined attribute.

- *object_name* allows applets, elements, and objects in the same HTML document to communicate.
- Most browsers do not support Netscape- and Microsoft-defined attributes.

## Associated Element

EMBED (Netscape and Microsoft extension)

---

NAME=" *form_name* "

The NAME attribute names the form. This is a Netscape-defined attribute.

- Most browsers do not support Netscape-defined attributes.

## Associated Element

FORM (Netscape-only attribute)

---

NAME="frame_name" ["_black" | "_par-ent" | "_self" | "_top"]

The NAME attribute names the current frame.

- If you name a frame, you can target the frame from other windows, using the TARGET attribute within the A, AREA, BASE, FORM, LINK elements.

- *frame_name* can include characters and/or special characters from the supported character set.

- For special characters, use the following syntax: &#*D*; (where *D* is a decimal character) or &#x*H*; (where *H* is a hexadecimal character).

- Special characters are case-sensitive.

- The values _blank, _parent, _self, and _top are reserved words; that is, you cannot use these values in any other way in an HTML document. These are Microsoft-only values.

- NAME="_blank" opens the named HTML document in a new, blank, unnamed window or frame. The user must manually close the window. This is a Microsoft-only value.

- NAME="_parent" opens the named HTML document in the parent (that is, one level above) of the current window or frame. If there is no parent window or frame, the document is loaded in the current frame or window. This is a Microsoft-only value.

- NAME="_self" opens the named HTML document in the current window or frame, replacing the document that is currently displayed there. This is a Microsoft-only value.

- NAME="_top" opens the named HTML document in the top, or original, window or frame at the site. If there is no top window or frame, the document is loaded in the current frame or window. This is a Microsoft-only value.

## Associated Elements

FRAME, IFRAME

---

NAME=" *image_name* "

The NAME attribute is the name of the current image. This is a Netscape-defined attribute.

- Most browsers do not support Netscape-defined attributes.

## Associated Element

IMG (Netscape-only attribute)

---

NAME=" *input_name* "

The NAME attribute names the current input control or an object that will submitted as part of a form.

- The NAME attribute is required for TEXT, BUTTON, CHECKBOX, FILE, HIDDEN, IMAGE, PASSWORD, RADIO, RESET, SUBMIT input types.
- The NAME attribute is optional for RESET and SUBMIT input types.
- Each NAME attribute in a form should be unique. Otherwise, if you use the same name for a set of checkboxes, checks are added to all when you check one.
- You can reuse the names used for controls within the current FORM start and end tags in other forms in the current document.
- For the OBJECT element, use the NAME attribute if the embedded object is submitted with a form.

## Associated Elements

INPUT, OBJECT

---

NAME="*pair_name*"

The NAME attribute names the name-value pair to be sent via a secure form. This is a Netscape-defined attribute.

- Most browsers do not support Netscape-defined attributes.

## Associated Element

KEYGEN (Netscape extension)

NAME=" *layer_name* "

The NAME attribute is the name of the current layer. This is a Netscape-defined attribute.

- The value of the NAME and ID attributes are identical. Use the ID attribute rather than the NAME attribute.
- Most browsers do not support Netscape-defined attributes.

## Associated Element

LAYER (Netscape-only attribute)

NAME=" *name_text* "

The NAME attribute is the name, description, or identification of the contents of the current document.

- The value of NAME depends on the value of the HEAD element's PROFILE attribute.
- Commonly used values for *name_text* are "author", "refresh", "keywords", "copyright", "creation_date", and "date".
- *name_text* must begin with a letter and may be followed by any number of letters, digits, hyphens, and periods.

## Associated Element

META

NAME=" *parm_name* "

The NAME attribute names a run-time parameter.

- The inserted object already is aware of the parameter.
- *parm_name* may or may not be case-sensitive, depending on the object inserted.
- *parm_name* must begin with an uppercase or lowercase letter, followed by any combination of letters, numbers, hyphens, and periods.

- *parm_name* can include characters and/or special characters from the supported character set.

## Associated Element

PARAM

---

NAME=" *element_name* "

The NAME attribute names the current drop-down list, list box, or multiline text box.

- When you click on the Submit button, the name and the value associated with the control are submitted to the form-processing program.

## Associated Elements

SELECT, TEXTAREA

---

NOHREF

The NOHREF attribute specifies that the area does not have a link associated with it.

## Associated Element

AREA

---

NORESIZE[|RESIZE]

The NORESIZE attribute freezes the current frame at its current height and width.

- RESIZE allows a user to resize the frame. This is a Microsoft-only attribute. Most browsers do not support Microsoft-defined attributes.

## Associated Element

FRAME, IFRAME (Microsoft-only attribute)

NOSHADE

The NOSHADE attribute removes the shading from the current rule.

## Associated Element

HR

NOTAB

The NOTAB attribute removes the element from the tabbing order. This is a Microsoft-defined attribute.

- Most browsers do not support Microsoft-defined attributes.

## Associated Elements

AREA (Microsoft-only attribute), INPUT (Microsoft-only attribute)

NOWRAP

The NOWRAP attribute disables word wrap within the current document division or cell. For DIV and TABLE, NOWRAP is a Microsoft-defined attribute.

- NOWRAP increases the width of a cell to hold the current contents, however long they are.
- This attribute is deprecated. Use a style sheet to specify the look of a document.
- Most browsers do not support Microsoft-defined attributes.

## Associated Elements

DIV (Microsoft-only attribute), TABLE (Microsoft-only attribute), TD, TH

OBJECT="*serial_resource*"

The OBJECT attribute names the resource containing a *serialized* (that is, serial-by-bit rather than parallel-by-bit processing) version of the current applet.

- When the applet is loaded, the start() method will be invoked, and the init() method will not be invoked.
- The serialized applet will be deserialized.
- Attributes that were valid when the applet was serialized will not be restored.
- The APPLET element is regarded as a predecessor of the OBJECT element. Use OBJECT instead of APPLET.

## Associated Element

APPLET

---

ONABORT="*oa_script_data*"

The ONABORT attribute specifies that the referred-to script runs when the user stops the current image from loading. This is a Netscape- and Microsoft-defined attribute.

- Most browsers do not support Netscape- and Microsoft-defined attributes.

## Associated Element

IMG

---

ONAFTERUPDATE="*au_script_data*"

The ONAFTERUPDATE attribute specifies that the referred-to script runs after data has been transferred from the element to the data repository. This is a Microsoft-defined attribute.

- Microsoft documentation states that "this event only fires when the object is databound and an onbeforeupdate event has fired (the element's data has changed). This event is not cancelable."

- Most browsers do not support Microsoft-defined attributes.

## Associated Elements

APPLET, BODY, BUTTON, CAPTION, DIV, IMG, INPUT, MARQUEE, OBJECT, SELECT, TABLE, TD, TEXTAREA, TR

---

ONBEFOREUPDATE=" *bu_script_data* "

The ONBEFOREUPDATE attribute specifies that the referred-to script runs before data is transferred from the element to the data repository. This is a Microsoft-defined attribute.

- Microsoft documentation states that "this event fires when an element loses focus or the page is attempting to unload when the value of the element has changed from the value that was in the element at the time it received the focus. This event is not cancelable."
- Most browsers do not support Microsoft-defined attributes.

## Associated Elements

APPLET, BODY, BUTTON, CAPTION, DIV, HR, IMG, INPUT, OBJECT, SELECT, TABLE, TD, TEXTAREA, TR

---

ONBLUR=" *bl_script_data* "

The ONBLUR attribute specifies that the referred-to script runs when the current element loses focus (that is, it is no longer the active element).

## Associated Elements

A (Microsoft-only attribute), APPLET (Microsoft-only attribute), AREA (Microsoft-only attribute), BODY (Netscape-only attribute), BUTTON, CAPTION (Microsoft-only attribute), DIV (Microsoft-only attribute), HR (Microsoft-only attribute), IMG (Microsoft-only attribute), INPUT, LABEL, LAYER (Netscape-only attribute) MAR–

QUEE (Microsoft-only attribute), OBJECT (Microsoft-only attribute), SELECT, TABLE (Microsoft-only attribute), TD (Microsoft-only attribute), TEXTAREA, TR (Microsoft-only attribute)

---

ONBOUNCE="*bn_script_data*"

The ONBOUNCE attribute specifies that the referred-to script runs when BEHAVIOR="alternate" and the marquee text reaches a side of the window in which it is scrolling. This is a Microsoft-defined attribute.

- Most browsers do not support Microsoft-defined attributes.

## Associated Element

MARQUEE

---

ONCHANGE="*ch_script_data*"

The ONCHANGE attribute specifies that the referred-to script runs when the current element loses focus after it has gained focus and has had a value change.

## Associated Elements

INPUT, SELECT, TEXTAREA

---

ONCLICK="*cl_script_data*"

The ONCLICK attribute specifies that the referred-to script runs when a user moves the mouse pointer or other pointing device over the current element and clicks the mouse button or other pointing device button.

## Associated Elements

A, ACRONYM, ADDRESS, APPLET (Microsoft-only attribute), AREA (Microsoft-only attribute), B, BIG, BLOCKQUOTE, BODY, BUTTON, CAPTION, CENTER, CITE, CODE, COL, COLGROUP, DD, DEL, DFN, DIR,

DIV, DL, DT, EM, FIELDSET, FONT (Microsoft-only attribute), FORM, H1, H2, H3, H4, H5, H6, HR, I, IMG, INPUT, INS, KBD, LABEL, LEGEND, LI, LINK, MAP (Microsoft-only attribute), MARQUEE (Microsoft-only attribute),MENU, OBJECT, OL, OPTION, P, OPTION, Q, S, SAMP, SELECT, SMALL, SPAN, STRIKE, STRONG, SUB, SUP, TABLE, TBODY, TD, TEXTAREA, TFOOT, TH, THEAD, TR, TT, U, UL, VAR

ONDBLCLICK="*dc_script_data*"

The ONDBLCLICK attribute specifies that the referred-to script runs when a user moves the mouse pointer or other pointing device over the current element and double-clicks the mouse button or pointing device button.

## Associated Elements

A, ACRONYM, ADDRESS, APPLET (Microsoft-only attribute), AREA (Microsoft-only attribute), B, BIG, BLOCKQUOTE, BODY, BUTTON, CAPTION, CENTER, CITE, CODE, COL, COLGROUP, DD, DEL, DFN, DIR, DIV, DL, DT, EM, FIELDSET, FONT (Microsoft-only attribute), FORM, H1, H2, H3, H4, H5, H6, HR, I, IMG, INPUT, INS, KBD, LABEL, LEGEND, LI, LINK, MAP (Microsoft-only attribute), MARQUEE, (Microsoft-only attraibute) MENU, OBJECT, OL, OPTION, P, OPTION, Q, S, SAMP, SELECT, SMALL, SPAN, STRIKE, STRONG, SUB, SUP, TABLE, TBODY, TD, TEXTAREA, TFOOT, TH, THEAD, TR, TT, U, UL, VAR

ONDRAGSTART="*ds_script_data*"

The ONDRAGSTART attribute specifies that the referred-to script runs when the user starts dragging a selection or element. This is a Microsoft-defined attribute.

- For the INPUT element, only the IMAGE, PASSWORD, and TEXT types support this attribute.
- Most browsers do not support Microsoft-defined attributes.

## Associated Elements

APPLET, AREA, BODY, BUTTON, CAPTION, DIV, HR, IMG, MARQUEE, OBJECT, SELECT, TABLE, TD, TEXTAREA, TR

ONERROR=" *oe_script_data* "

The ONERROR attribute specifies a script to run when the referred-to script experiences an error. This is a Netscape- and Microsoft-defined attribute.

- Most browsers do not support Netscape- and Microsoft-defined attributes.

## Associated Element

IMG

ONFINISH=" *fn_script_data* "

The ONFINISH attribute specifies that the referred-to script runs when the marquee text has stopped scrolling. This is a Microsoft-defined attribute.

- Most browsers do not support Microsoft-defined attributes.

## Associated Element

MARQUEE

ONFOCUS=" *fc_script_data* "

The ONFOCUS attribute specifies that the referred-to script runs when the current element receives focus (that is, is made active) by the mouse pointer or other pointing device.

## Associated Elements

A (Microsoft-only attribute), APPLET (Microsoft-only attribute), AREA (Microsoft-only attribute), BODY (Microsoft-only attribute), BUTTON, CAPTION (Microsoft-only attribute), HR (Microsoft-only attribute), IMG (Microsoft-only attribute), INPUT, LABEL, LAYER (Netscape-only attribute) MARQUEE (Microsoft-only attaribute) OBJECT (Microsoft-only attribute), SELECT, TABLE (Microsoft-only attribute), TD (Microsoft-only attribute), TEXTAREA, TR (Microsoft-only attribute)

## ONHELP="*hlp_script_data*"

The ONHELP attribute specifies that the referred-to script runs when a user presses the F1 or Help key over the current element. This is a Microsoft-defined attribute.

- Most browsers do not support Microsoft-defined attributes.

## Associated Elements

A, ADDRESS, APPLET, AREA, B, BIG, BLOCKQUOTE, BODY, BUTTON, CAPTION, CENTER, CITE, CODE, DD, DFN, DIR, DIV, DL, DT, EM, FIELDSET, FONT, FORM, H1, H2, H3, H4, H5, H6, HR, I, IMG, INPUT, KBD, LABEL, LEGEND, LI, MAP, MARQUEE, MENU, OBJECT, OL, P, PRE, S, SAMP, SELECT, SMALL, SPAN, STRIKE, STRONG, SUB, SUP, TABLE, TD, TBODY, TFOOT, TEXTAREA, TH, THEAD, TR, TT, U, UL, VAR

## ONKEYDOWN="*kd_script_data*"

The ONKEYDOWN attribute specifies that the referred-to script runs when a user presses and holds a key down over the current element.

## Associated Elements

A, ACRONYM, ADDRESS, APPLET (Microsoft-only attribute), AREA (Microsoft-only attribute), B, BIG, BLOCKQUOTE, BODY, BUTTON, CAPTION, CENTER, CITE, CODE, COL, COLGROUP, DD, DEL, DFN, DIR, DIV, DL, DT, EM, FIELDSET, FONT (Microsoft-only attribute), FORM, H1, H2, H3, H4, H5, H6, HR, I, IMG, INPUT, INS, KBD, LABEL, LEGEND, LI, LINK, MAP (Microsoft-only attribute), MARQUEE (Microsoft-only attribute), MENU, OBJECT, OL, OPTION, P, OPTION, Q, S, SAMP, SELECT, SMALL, SPAN, STRIKE, STRONG, SUB, SUP, TABLE, TBODY, TD, TEXTAREA, TFOOT, TH, THEAD, TR, TT, U, UL, VAR

## ONKEYPRESS="*kp_script_data*"

The ONKEYPRESS attribute specifies that the referred-to script runs when a user presses and releases a key over the current element.

### Associated Elements

A, ACRONYM, ADDRESS, APPLET (Microsoft-only attribute), AREA (Microsoft-only attribute), B, BIG, BLOCKQUOTE, BODY, BUTTON, CAPTION, CENTER, CITE, CODE, COL, COLGROUP, DD, DEL, DFN, DIR, DIV, DL, DT, EM, FIELDSET, FONT (Microsoft-only attribute), FORM, H1, H2, H3, H4, H5, H6, HR, I, IMG, INPUT, INS, KBD, LABEL, LEGEND, LI, LINK, MAP (Microsoft-only attribute), MARQUEE (Microsoft-only attribute), MENU, OBJECT, OL, OPTION, P, OPTION, Q, S, SAMP, SELECT, SMALL, SPAN, STRIKE, STRONG, SUB, SUP, TABLE, TBODY, TD, TEXTAREA, TFOOT, TH, THEAD, TR, TT, U, UL, VAR

## ONKEYUP="*ku_script_data*"

The ONKEYUP attribute specifies that the referred-to script runs when a user releases a key over the current element.

### Associated Elements

A, ACRONYM, ADDRESS, APPLET (Microsoft-only attribute), AREA (Microsoft-only attribute), B, BIG, BLOCKQUOTE, BODY, BUTTON, CAPTION, CENTER, CITE, CODE, COL, COLGROUP, DD, DEL, DFN, DIR, DIV, DL, DT, EM, FIELDSET, FORM, H1, H2, H3, H4, H5, H6, HR, I, IMG, INPUT, INS, KBD, LABEL, LEGEND, LI, LINK, MAP (Microsoft-only attribute), MARQUEE (Microsoft-only attribute), MENU, OBJECT, OL, OPTION, P, OPTION, Q, S, SAMP, SELECT, SMALL, SPAN, STRIKE, STRONG, SUB, SUP, TABLE, TBODY, TD, TEXTAREA, TFOOT, TH, THEAD, TR, TT, U, UL, VAR

## ONLOAD="*ol_script_data*"

The ONLOAD attribute specifies that the referred-to script runs after the active browser has finished loading a window, frameset, image (Netscape- or Microsoft-only attribute), applet (Microsoft-only attribute), or layer (Netscape-only attribute).

## Associated Elements

APPLET (Microsoft-only attribute), BODY, FRAMESET, IMG
(Netscape- or Microsoft-only attribute) LAYER (Netscape-only
attribute).

---

ONMOUSEDOWN=*"md_script_data"*

The ONMOUSEDOWN attribute specifies that the referred-to
script runs when a user moves the mouse pointer or other pointing device over the current element and presses and holds down
the mouse button or pointing device button.

## Associated Elements

A, ACRONYM, ADDRESS, APPLET (Microsoft-only attribute), AREA
(Microsoft-only attribute), B, BIG, BLOCKQUOTE, BODY, BUTTON,
CAPTION, CENTER, CITE, CODE, COL, COLGROUP, DD, DEL, DFN, DIR,
DIV, DL, DT, EM, FIELDSET, FONT (Microsoft-only attribute), FORM,
H1, H2, H3, H4, H5, H6, HR, I, IMG, INPUT, INS, KBD, LABEL, LEGEND,
LI, LINK, MAP (Microsoft-only attribute), MARQUEE, (Microsoft-
only attribute), MENU, OBJECT, OL, OPTION, P, OPTION, Q, S, SAMP,
SELECT, SMALL, SPAN, STRIKE, STRONG, SUB, SUP, TABLE, TBODY, TD,
TEXTAREA, TFOOT, TH, THEAD, TR, TT, U, UL, VAR

---

ONMOUSEMOVE=*"mm_script_data"*

The ONMOUSEMOVE attribute specifies that the referred-to
script runs when a user moves the mouse pointer or other pointing device over the current element.

## Associated Elements

A, ACRONYM, ADDRESS, APPLET (Microsoft-only attribute), AREA
(Microsoft-only attribute), B, BIG, BLOCKQUOTE, BODY, BUTTON,
CAPTION, CENTER, CITE, CODE, COL, COLGROUP, DD, DEL, DFN, DIR,
DIV, DL, DT, EM, FIELDSET, FONT (Microsoft-only attribute), FORM,
H1, H2, H3, H4, H5, H6, HR, I, IMG, INPUT, INS, KBD, LABEL, LEGEND,
LI, LINK, MAP (Microsoft-only attribute), MARQUEE (Microsoft-
only attribute), MENU, OBJECT, OL, OPTION, P, OPTION, Q, S, SAMP,
SELECT, SMALL, SPAN, STRIKE, STRONG, SUB, SUP, TABLE, TBODY, TD,
TEXTAREA, TFOOT, TH, THEAD, TR, TT, U, UL, VAR

**649**

ONMOUSEOUT=*"mo_script_data"*

The ONMOUSEOUT attribute specifies that the referred-to script runs when a user moves the mouse pointer or other pointing device away from the current element.

## Associated Elements

A, ACRONYM, ADDRESS, APPLET (Microsoft-only attribute), AREA (Netscape- and Microsoft-only attribute), B, BIG, BLOCKQUOTE, BODY, BUTTON, CAPTION, CENTER, CITE, CODE, COL, COLGROUP, DD, DEL, DFN, DIR, DIV, DL, DT, EM, FIELDSET, FONT (Microsoft-only attribute), FORM, H1, H2, H3, H4, H5, H6, HR, I, IMG, INPUT, INS, KBD, LABEL, LAYER (Netscape-only attribute), LEGEND, LI, LINK, MAP (Microsoft-only attribute), MARQUEE (Microsoft-only attribute), MENU, OBJECT, OL, OPTION, P, OPTION, Q, S, SAMP, SELECT, SMALL, SPAN, STRIKE, STRONG, SUB, SUP, TABLE, TBODY, TD, TEXTAREA, TFOOT, TH, THEAD, TR, TT, U, UL, VAR

ONMOUSEOVER=*"mov_script_data"*

The ONMOUSEOVER attribute specifies that the referred-to script runs the first time a user moves the mouse pointer or other pointing device over the current element.

## Associated Elements

A, ACRONYM, ADDRESS, APPLET (Microsoft-only attribute), AREA (Netscape- and Microsoft-only attribute), B, BIG, BLOCKQUOTE, BODY, BUTTON, CAPTION, CENTER, CITE, CODE, COL, COLGROUP, DD, DEL, DFN, DIR, DIV, DL, DT, EM, FIELDSET, FONT (Microsoft-only attribute), FORM, H1, H2, H3, H4, H5, H6, HR, I, IMG, INPUT, INS, KBD, LABEL, LAYER (Netscape-only attribute), LEGEND, LI, LINK, MAP (Microsoft-only attribute), MARQUEE (Microsoft-only attribute), MENU, OBJECT, OL, OPTION, P, OPTION, Q, S, SAMP, SELECT, SMALL, SPAN, STRIKE, STRONG, SUB, SUP, TABLE, TBODY, TD, TEXTAREA, TFOOT, TH, THEAD, TR, TT, U, UL, VAR

ONMOUSEUP="*mu_script_data*"

The ONMOUSEUP attribute specifies that the referred-to script runs when a user moves the mouse pointer or other pointing device over the current element and releases a pressed-down mouse button or pointing device button.

## Associated Elements

A, ACRONYM, ADDRESS, APPLET (Microsoft-only attribute), AREA (Microsoft-only attribute), B, BIG, BLOCKQUOTE, BODY, BUTTON, CAPTION, CENTER, CITE, CODE, COL, COLGROUP, DD, DEL, DFN, DIR, DIV, DL, DT, EM, FIELDSET, FONT (Microsoft-only attribute), FORM, H1, H2, H3, H4, H5, H6, HR, I, IMG, INPUT, INS, KBD, LABEL, LEGEND, LI, LINK, MAP (Microsoft-only attribute), MARQUEE (Microsoft-only attribute), MENU, OBJECT, OL, OPTION, P, OPTION, Q, S, SAMP, SELECT, SMALL, SPAN, STRIKE, STRONG, SUB, SUP, TABLE, TBODY, TD, TEXTAREA, TFOOT, TH, THEAD, TR, TT, U, UL, VAR

---

ONREADYSTATECHANGE="*rsc_script_data*"

The ONREADYSTATECHANGE attribute specifies that the referred-to script runs when an element is ready to be loaded. This is a Microsoft-defined attribute.

- According to Microsoft documentation, this attribute "fires whenever the readyState for the object has changed. When an element changes to the loaded state, this event fires immediately before the firing of the load event."
- Most browsers do not support Microsoft-defined attributes.

## Associated Elements

APPLET, FRAME, OBJECT

ONRESET="*rs_script_data*"

The ONRESET attribute specifies that the referred-to script runs when a user clicks on the Reset button to clear the current form.

## Associated Element

FORM

ONRESIZE="*rz_script_data*"

The ONRESIZE attribute specifies that the referred-to script runs when the user resizes the selected object. This is a Microsoft-defined attribute.

- Most browsers do not support Microsoft-defined attributes.

## Associated Elements

APPLET, BODY, BUTTON, CAPTION, DIV, HR, IMG, MARQUEE, OBJECT, SELECT, TABLE, TD, TEXTAREA, TR

ONROWENTER="*re_script_data*"

The ONROWENTER attribute specifies that the referred-to script runs when the current row has been modified. This is a Microsoft-defined attribute.

- Microsoft documentation states that "this event only fires when the object is databound. This event only applies to objects that identify themselves as a data provider."
- Most browsers do not support Microsoft-defined attributes.

## Associated Elements

APPLET, BODY, BUTTON, CAPTION, DIV, HR, IMG, MARQUEE, OBJECT, SELECT, TABLE, TD, TEXTAREA, TR

ONROWEXIT=*"rex_script_data"*

The ONROWEXIT attribute specifies that the referred-to script runs before the current row is modified. This is a Microsoft-defined attribute.

- Microsoft documentation states that "this event only fires when the object is databound. This event only applies to objects that identify themselves as a data provider."
- Most browsers do not support Microsoft-defined attributes.

## Associated Elements

APPLET, BODY, BUTTON, CAPTION, DIV, HR, IMG, MARQUEE OBJECT, SELECT, TABLE, TD, TEXTAREA, TR

ONSCROLL=*"sc_script_data"*

The ONSCROLL attribute specifies that the referred-to script runs when a user moves the scroll box within the scroll bar. This is a Microsoft-defined attribute.

- Microsoft documentation states that "this notification event fires for the window object and all elements that scroll. This event does not bubble and is not cancelable."
- Most browsers do not support Microsoft-defined attributes.

## Associated Elements

BODY, BUTTON, CAPTION, DIV, TABLE, TD, TEXTAREA, TH

ONSELECT=*"sl_script_data"*

The ONSELECT attribute specifies that the referred-to script runs when a user selects some text in a text box in a form.

## Associated Elements

INPUT, SELECT, TEXTAREA

---

ONSELECTSTART=" *ss_script_data* "

The ONSELECTSTART attribute specifies that the referred-to script runs when a user starts selecting an object. This is a Microsoft-defined attribute.

- Most browsers do not support Microsoft-defined attributes.

## Associated Elements

APPLET, A, ADDRESS, B, BIG, BLOCKQUOTE, BODY, BUTTON, CAPTION, CENTER, CITE, CODE, DD, DFN, DIR, DIV, DL, DT, EM, FONT, FORM, H1, H2, H3, H4, H5, H6, HR, I, IMG, INPUT, KBD, LABEL, LI, MARQUEE, MENU, OBJECT, OPTION, P, PRE, S, SAMP, SELECT, SMALL, SPAN, STRIKE, STRONG, SUB, SUP, TABLE, TBODY, TD, TEXTAREA, TH, THEAD, TR, TT, U, UL, VAR

---

ONSTART=" *st_script_data* "

The ONSTART attribute specifies that the referred-to script runs when a loop starts. According to Microsoft documentation, the ONSTART attribute "fires when a loop begins, and when a bounce cycle begins for alternate behavior." This is a Microsoft-defined attribute.

- Most browsers do not support Microsoft-defined attributes.

## Associated Elements

MARQUEE, TEXTAREA

---

ONSUBMIT=" *su_script_data* "

The ONSUBMIT attribute specifies that the referred-to script runs when a user clicks on the Submit button to submit the current form.

## Associated Element

FORM

---

ONUNLOAD="*un_script_data*"

The ONUNLOAD attribute specifies that the referred-to script runs after the active browser has removed a document from a window or frameset.

## Associated Elements

BODY, FRAMESET

---

PAGEX="*horz_pos_pix*"

The PAGEX attribute specifies the horizontal position, in pixels, of the top left corner of the layer window within the current HTML document. This is a Netscape-defined attribute.

- This attribute is valid only for Netscape Navigator 4.0 or greater.
- Most browsers do not support Netscape-defined attributes.

## Associated Element

LAYER

---

PAGEY="*vert_pos_pix*"

The PAGEY attribute specifies the vertical position, in pixels, of the top left corner of the layer window within the current HTML document. This is a Netscape-defined attribute.

- This attribute is valid only for Netscape Navigator 4.0 or greater.
- Most browsers do not support Netscape-defined attributes.

## Associated Element

LAYER

---

PALETTE=" <u>BACKGROUND</u> " | "FOREGROUND"

The PALETTE attribute specifies that the palette used by the plug-in object becomes the background or foreground palette for the current page. This is a Netscape-defined attribute.

- PALETTE="BACKGROUND" specifies that the plug-in's palette becomes the background palette.
- PALETTE="FOREGROUND" specifies that the plug-in's palette becomes the foreground palette.
- This attribute only works for Windows-based browsers.
- Most browsers do not support Netscape-defined attributes.

## Associated Element

EMBED (Netscape extension)

---

PROFILE="*prof_url_1*"[ "*prof_url_2*"
[...*"prof_url_n"*]]

The PROFILE attribute lists one or more URLs of files containing meta information, which describe the current document.

- A profile can specify document properties such as the author, copyright information, the creation or modification date, and keywords.
- Future HTML standards will support the listing of URLS pointing to one or more meta information files.
- *url* is an absolute or relative Universal Resource Locator.
- To learn more about meta information, see the META element.

## Associated Element

HEAD

---

PROMPT="*prompt-text*"

The PROMPT attribute issues a message prompting the user for a one-line response with an unlimited number of characters.

- *prompt_text* can include characters and/or special characters from the supported character set.
- For special characters, use the following syntax: &#*D*; (where *D* is a decimal character) or &#x*H*; (where *H* is a hexadecimal character).
- Special characters are case-sensitive.
- The PROMPT attribute is deprecated.

## Associated Element

ISINDEX

---

READONLY

The READONLY attribute, when specified, does not allow a user to change input for the current element.

- You can use READONLY text to display instructions for filling in a text box.
- When an element is made readonly, it can receive focus but its value cannot be changed.
- When an element is made readonly, it is included in tab order.
- When an element is made readonly, its value is submitted when its form is submitted.
- You can change the value of the READONLY attribute by adding a script to the element.

## Associated Elements

INPUT, TEXTAREA

**657**

```
REL="Contents" | "Index" | "Glossary" |
"Copyright" | "Next" | "Previous" | "Start" |
"Help" | "Bookmark" | "Stylesheet" |
"Alternate" | "Same" | "Parent" |
"link_type_1" [ "link_type_2"
[..."link_type_n"]]
```

The REL attribute specifies the link type; that is, the type of relationship of the current link forward to the anchor or to another document.

- REL="Alternate" links to another version of the current document. Examples include documents in other languages or other media.
- REL="Bookmark" links to a specific labeled section of a set of documents.
- REL="Contents" links to a table of contents for the current site or set of documents.
- REL="Copyright" links to copyright information about the current document.
- REL="Glossary" links to a glossary of terms for the set of documents at the current site.
- REL="Help" links to a document in which you can get help, obtain additional information about this site, link to related sites, and so on.
- REL="Index" links to an index for the set of documents at the current site.
- REL="Next" links to the next document (for example, the following chapter) in a related set of documents.
- REL="Previous" links to the previous document (for example, the prior chapter) in a related set of documents. This is commonly used with the REV attribute.
- REL="Start" links to the top document (for example, the introduction to several chapters) in a related set of documents.

- REL="Stylesheet" links to an external style sheet. For detailed information about style sheets, see Part 5, Cascading Style Sheets.
- Although many browsers recognize Alternate, Bookmark, Contents, Copyright, Glossary, Help, Index, Next, Previous, Start, and Stylesheet as commonly-used link types, they are not reserved words.
- REL="Same" indicates that the developer of the current document also created the linked-to document. This value is supported by Microsoft Internet Explorer only.
- REL="Parent" indicates that the current document is the parent of the linked-to document. This value is supported by Microsoft Internet Explorer only.
- The REL attribute says that the link source is in the current document.
- The link type values are case-insensitive.
- This attribute is rarely used.

## Associated Elements

A, LINK

---

```
REV="Contents" | "Index" | "Glossary" |
"Copyright" | "Next" | "Previous" | "Start" |
"Help" | "Bookmark" | "Stylesheet" | "Alternate"
| "link_type_3" [ "link_type_4"
[..."link_type_m"]]
```

The REV attribute specifies the link type; that is, the type of relationship of the anchor back to the current link or to another document.

- REV="Alternate" links to another version of the current document. Examples include documents in other languages or other media.
- REV="Bookmark" links to a specific labeled section of a set of documents.

**659**

- REV="Contents" links to a table of contents for the current site or set of documents.
- REV="Copyright" links to copyright information about the current document.
- REV="Glossary" links to a glossary of terms for the set of documents at the current site.
- REV="Help" links to a document in which you can get help, obtain additional information about this site, link to related sites, and so on.
- REV="Index" links to an index for the set of documents at the current site.
- REV="Next" links to the next document (for example, the following chapter) in a related set of documents. This is commonly used with the REL attribute.
- REV="Previous" links to the previous document (for example, the prior chapter) in a related set of documents.
- REV="Start" links to the top document (for example, the introduction to several chapters) in a related set of documents.
- REV="Stylesheet" links to an external style sheet. For detailed information about style sheets, see *Part 5, Cascading Style Sheets*.
- The REV attribute says that the link destination is in the current document.
- The link type values are case-insensitive.
- This attribute is rarely used.

## Associated Elements

A, LINK

---

RIGHTMARGIN=*"rmar-num"*

The RIGHTMARGIN attribute specifies the right margin, in pixels, of this document. This is a Microsoft-defined attribute.

- Most browsers do not support Microsoft-defined attributes.

- RIGHTMARGIN="0" moves the margin to the left edge of the page.
- The value of RIGHTMARGIN overrides the default right margin.
- Pixels is a value representing the number of pixels based on a 640x480 resolution.

## Associated Element

BODY

---

ROWS="*row_value_1*[, *row_value_2*[...,
*row_value_n*]]"

The ROWS attribute is a top-to-bottom measurement of the frameset.

- *row_value* can be an absolute number of pixels in a top-to-bottom measurement of the frameset.
- Pixels is a value representing the number of pixels based on a 640x480 resolution.
- *row_value* can be an absolute percentage of the frameset compared to the full height of the computer screen.
- *row_value* can be the relative width (*n** or *) of the frameset to other framesets.
- *n** is a multiplier of the default relative height, and * specifies a relative value of the rest of the available space in the height (for example, if the first frameset is 3* and the second frameset is *, the first frameset will be three times higher than the second).
- An * indicator implies a multiplier value of 1.
- Do not enclose * within quotation marks.
- Browsers set absolute heights first and relative heights after that.
- The default value of ROWS is the full height of the computer screen.
- Netscape browsers require that you define ROWS or COLS.

## Associated Element

FRAMESET

---

ROWS=" *number_of_rows* "

The ROWS attribute indicates the height of the text input area, by the number of rows, one per line of text.

- If a user enters more lines than can fit the text box heighth, the browser should insert a vertical scroll bar or other means of scrolling.

## Associated Element

TEXTAREA

---

ROWSPAN=" <u>1</u> " | " *num_rows* " | " 0 "

The ROWSPAN attribute specifies the number of rows down which the current cell will extend.

- The default ROWSPAN is 1; that is, one row in the span.
- If ROWSPAN=0, the span for the current row extends the remaining rows of the table.

## Associated Elements

TD, TH

---

RULES=" <u>none</u> " | " groups " | " rows " | " cols " | " all "

The RULES attribute displays rule lines between table cells.

- RULES="none" displays no rule lines.
- RULES="groups" displays rule lines between groups of cells that have been specified with the COL, COLGROUP, TBODY, TFOOT, and/or THEAD elements.
- RULES="rows" displays rule lines between all rows in the table.

- RULES="cols" displays rule lines between all columns in the table.
- RULES="all" displays rule lines between all rows and columns in the table.
- If BORDER="0", then FRAME="void" and usually RULES="none".
- If the value of BORDER is greater than 0, FRAME="border" and usually RULES="all".

## Associated Element

TABLE

---

SCHEME="*format_id*"

The SCHEME attribute identifies a particular format for the CONTENT attribute.

- Use the SCHEME attribute when the property specified in the NAME attribute supports more than one format.
- The value of SCHEME depends on the value of the HEAD element's PROFILE attribute.
- *format_id* can include characters and/or special characters from the supported character set.
- For special characters, use the following syntax: &#*D*; (where *D* is a decimal character) or &#x*H*; (where *H* is a hexadecimal character).
- Special characters are case-sensitive.

## Associated Element

META

---

SCROLL="YES" | "NO"

The SCROLL attribute turns on or off document scrollbars. This is a Microsoft-defined attribute.

- Most browsers do not support Microsoft-defined attributes.

## Associated Element

BODY

---

SCROLLAMOUNT=" *gap_pix* "

The SCROLLAMOUNT attribute specifies the gap, in pixels, from the end of the current marquee display and the beginning of the following display. This is a Microsoft-defined attribute.

- Most browsers do not support Microsoft-defined attributes.

## Associated Element

MARQUEE (Microsoft extension)

---

SCROLLDELAY=" *millisecs* "

The SCROLLDELAY attribute specifies the time delay ,in milliseconds, from the end of the current marquee display and the beginning of the following display. This is a Microsoft-defined attribute.

- Most browsers do not support Microsoft-defined attributes.

## Associated Element

MARQUEE (Microsoft extension)

---

SCROLLING=" <u>auto</u> " | "yes" | "no"

The SCROLLING attribute specifies whether the current frame contains scrollbars.

- SCROLLING="auto" allows the browser to insert or not insert scrollbars, depending on whether the contents of the frame are larger than the on-screen display.
- SCROLLING="yes" always inserts scrollbars.
- SCROLLING="no" always omits scrollbars.

## Associated Elements

FRAME, IFRAME

---

SELECTED

The SELECTED attribute highlights the current option when a pulldown menu in a form opens and is the default.

## Associated Element

OPTION

---

SHAPE="<u>RECT</u>[ANGLE]" | "CIRC[LE]"
| "POLY[GON]" | "DEFAULT"

The SHAPE attribute is the shape of an area within a link or within a client-side map.

- SHAPE="RECT" or "RECTANGLE" indicates a rectangular shape. This shape has four coordinates, in pixels and separated by commas, which point to the corners.
- SHAPE="CIRC" or "CIRCLE" indicates a circular shape. This shape has three coordinates, in pixels and separated by commas, which point to the x-axis center, the y-axis center, and the radius.
- SHAPE="POLY" or "POLYGON" indicates a polygonal shape. This shape has three or more pairs of coordinates, in pixels and separated by commas, which point to the intersection of the x-axis and y-axis and which represent the place at which one plane ends and another begins.
- If the first and last pairs of polygon coordinates do not have the same value, a utility, htimage, provides the closing coordinates.
- SHAPE="DEF" or "DEFAULT" covers the remaining area outside the other shapes.

## Associated Elements

A, AREA

SHAPES

The SHAPES attribute indicates that the current object is an image map.

- The SHAPE attribute (see the prior attribute) in the following statement will specify the shape of the object.

## Associated Element

OBJECT

---

SIZE=[+|-]1|2|3|4|5|6|7

The SIZE attribute sets relative or absolute text size.

- SIZE is required for the BASEFONT element and optional for the FONT element.
- The default absolute size is 3. Valid values range from 1 to 7.
- The + sign increases text size by one.
- The - sign decreases text size by one.

## Associated Elements

BASEFONT, FONT

SIZE is a popular attribute whose values and behavior vary, depending on the element with which it is associated at a particular time. In this appendix, you'll find several versions of SIZE arranged alphabetically by element name.

SIZE="*rule_height*"

The SIZE attribute specifies the height, in pixels, of a horizontal rule.

- The pixels measurement is based on a 640x480 graphic resolution.

## Associated Element

HR

---

SIZE="*input_control_size*"

The SIZE attribute is the maximum starting size of the current input control.

- SIZE is measured in pixels if TYPE="BUTTON", TYPE="CHECKBOX", TYPE="FILE", TYPE="HIDDEN", TYPE="IMAGE", TYPE="RADIO", TYPE="RESET", or TYPE="SUBMIT".
- SIZE is measured in the number of characters if TYPE="TEXT" or TYPE="PASSWORD".
- The SIZE attribute affects the appearance of a text box or password text box—not the number of characters and spaces that you enter. The MAXLENGTH attribute controls the number of characters and spaces that can be entered.

## Associated Element

INPUT

---

SIZE="*no_of_rows*"

The SIZE attribute specifies the maximum number of rows (that is, items) in the selection list.

## Associated Element

SELECT

---

### SIZE="*size_pix*"

The SIZE attribute specifies the horizontal or vertical white space in the current document. This is a Netscape-defined attribute.

- If TYPE="HORIZONTAL", SIZE specifies the width of the white space.
- If TYPE="VERTICAL", SIZE specifies the height of the white space.
- Pixels is a value representing the number of pixels based on a 640x480 resolution.
- If TYPE="BLOCK", the Netscape browser ignores the SIZE attribute and uses the ALIGN, HEIGHT, and WIDTH attributes instead.
- Most browsers do not support Netscape-defined attributes.

## Associated Element

SPACER (Microsoft)

---

### SPAN="1" | "*num_cols*" | "0"

The SPAN attribute specifies the default number of columns in a column group.

- This attribute is related to the SPAN element.
- The default SPAN is 1; that is, one column in the span.
- If SPAN=0, the span for the current COL element extends the remaining width of the table.
- If the current column group contains at least one COL element, a browser ignores the SPAN setting.

## Associated Elements

COL, COLGROUP

SRC is a popular attribute whose values and behavior vary, depending on the element with which it is associated at a particular time. In this appendix, you'll find several versions of SRC arranged alphabetically by element name.

---

## SRC="*object_url*"

The SRC attribute specifies an object, such as a sound or video file, embedded on the current page. This is a Netscape- and Microsoft-defined attribute.

- *object_url* is an absolute or relative Universal Resource Locator.
- Most browsers do not support Netscape- and Microsoft-defined attributes.

## Associated Element

APPLET (Microsoft-only attribute), EMBED (Microsoft and Netscape extension)

---

## SRC="*sound_url*"

The SRC attribute specifies a sound file that plays in the background. This is a Microsoft-defined attribute.

- *sound_url* is an absolute or relative Universal Resource Locator.
- Most browsers do not support Microsoft-defined attributes.

## Associated Element

BGSOUND (Microsoft extension)

SRC="*source_url*"

The SRC attribute specifies a source file displayed within the current frame, that contains the contents of a layer window (Netscape), or whose contents are displayed instead of a layer, for browsers that do not support layers (Netscape).

- *source_url* is an absolute or relative Universal Resource Locator.

## Associated Elements

FRAME, IFRAME, ILAYER (Netscape extension), LAYER (Netscape extension), NOLAYER (Netscape extension)

SRC="*image_url*"

The SRC attribute specifies an image file that is displayed on a Submit button or inserted on the current page.

- *image_url* is an absolute or relative Universal Resource Locator.
- Use supported graphic formats: GIF, JPEG, or PNG.

## Associated Element

IMG, INPUT

SRC="*ext_script_url*"

The SRC attribute specifies a URL in which an external script to be run is stored.

- *ext_script_url* is an absolute or relative Universal Resource Locator.
- An external script has priority over an embedded script.

## Associated Element

SCRIPT

STANDBY="*message_text*"

The STANDBY attribute displays a message while the object is loading onscreen.

## Associated Element

OBJECT

START="1" | "*start_num*"

The START attribute sets a starting number for the current ordered, or numbered, list.

## Associated Element

OL

STYLE="*name_1: value_1*" [; "*name_2: value_2*"] [...; "*name_n: value_n*"]

The STYLE attribute sets styles for the current element.

- Specify the style information using the default style sheet formats for the current document.
- If you want to use the same style information for several elements, consider using the STYLE element instead of the STYLE attribute, or create a separate style sheet.
- If you use the STYLE attribute more than once within a table, the order in which the attribute is processed (that is, the order of precedence), from highest to lowest, is:
    1. An attribute set on an element within a cell's contents.
    2. An attribute set on a TH or TD cell.
    3. An attribute set on a row (TR) or group of rows (TBODY, TFOOT, or THEAD).
    4. An attribute set on a column (COL) or column group (COLGROUP).
    5. An attribute set on a table.
    6. The default value of the attribute.

## Associated Elements

A, ACRONYM, ADDRESS, APPLET (Microsoft-only attribute), AREA
(Microsoft-only attribute), B, BIG, BLOCKQUOTE, BODY, BR, BUTTON,
CAPTION, CENTER, CITE, CODE, COL, COLGROUP, DD, DEL, DFN, DIR,
DIV, DL, DT, EM, EMBED (Microsoft-only attribute), FIELDSET, FONT
(Microsoft-only attribute), FORM, H1, H2, H3, H4, H5, H6, HR, I,
IFRAME (Microsoft-only attribute), IMG, INPUT, INS, ISINDEX, KBD,
LABEL, LEGEND, LI, LINK, MAP, MARQUEE (Microsoft-only attribute)
MENU, OBJECT, OL, OPTION, P, OPTION, Q, S, SAMP, SELECT, SMALL,
SPAN, STRIKE, STRONG, SUB, SUP, TABLE, TBODY, TD, TEXTAREA,
TFOOT, TH, THEAD, TR, TT, U, UL, VAR

---

TABINDEX="*position_number*"

The TABINDEX attribute defines the position of the current
element in all the elements that a user can navigate using a Tab
or Shift+Tab key.

- *position_number* is an positive or negative integer.
- You can define a tab position to a nested element.
- You can assign any number and do not have to start
  with any particular value.
- Elements with negative position numbers cannot be
  tabbed to.
- Elements that are turned off cannot be tabbed to.
- If you assign duplicate position numbers to several elements, the tab order starts with the topmost element on
  the page.
- The order of precedence from highest to lowest is as
  follows:
  1. Elements that support TABINDEX and that have
     the lowest positive position number.
  2. Elements that support TABINDEX and that have
     the highest positive position number.
  3. Elements that do not support TABINDEX and
     that do not have a position number.

## Associated Elements

A, AREA, BUTTON, INPUT, OBJECT, SELECT, TEXTAREA

TARGET="*window*" | "_blank" | "_parent" |
"_self" | "_top"

The TARGET attribute loads a linked and named document in a particular window or frame.

- TARGET="*window*" opens the named HTML document in the window or frame named "*window*".
- The name of "*window*" must start with an uppercase or lowercase letter of the alphabet.
- The values _blank, _parent, _self, and _top are reserved words; that is, you cannot use these values in any other way in an HTML document.
- TARGET="_blank" opens the named HTML document in a new, blank, unnamed window or frame. The user must manually close the window.
- TARGET="_parent" opens the named HTML document in the parent (that is, one level above) of the current window or frame. If there is no parent window or frame, the document is loaded in the current frame or window.
- TARGET="_self" opens the named HTML document in the current window or frame, replacing the document that is currently displayed there.
- TARGET="_top" opens the named HTML document in the top, or original, window or frame at the site. If there is no top window or frame, the document is loaded in the current frame or window.
- If the TARGET attribute is not specified here but is set within the BASE element, the browser uses the TARGET set in the BASE element.
- If the TARGET attribute is not set here or within the BASE element, the named document is loaded in the current window or frame.
- If the TARGET attribute includes a name that has not been given to a frame or window, the browser creates a new window or frame, gives it that name, and loads the named document into it.

- For a practical example of TARGET usage, refer to the FRAME element in Part 4, Chapter 5.

## Associated Elements

A, AREA, BASE, FORM, LINK

---

TEXT=" #*rrggbb*" | "*color*"

The TEXT attribute defines the color of all nonlink text in the current document.

- *rrggbb* is the hexadecimal code of the color; *rr* represents the red attributes, from 00 to FF; *gg* represents the green attributes, from 00 to FF; and *bb* represents the blue attributes, from 00 to FF. Table 4.1 contains selected hexadecimal color values.
- *color* represents supported color names: red, maroon, yellow, green, lime, teal, olive, aqua, blue, navy, purple, fuchsia, black, gray, silver (the default), and white.
- Colors vary according to the graphics board and associated software installed in a computer, so it's best to view all colors and see how they work together before making a final color choice. Regardless of your color choice, there is a very good chance that some browser will interpret your colors in a very strange way.
- Both Netscape and Microsoft provide additional color names. Most browsers do not support Netscape and Microsoft attributes.
- This attribute is deprecated. Use a style sheet to specify the look of a document.

## Associated Element

BODY

---

TITLE=" *title*"

The TITLE attribute, which is related to the TITLE element, provides title information about part of a document.

- Some browsers display titles as *tool tips*, which are similar to balloon help messages. Browsers that support audio may "say" the title.
- A title can include characters and/or special characters from the supported character set.
- For special characters, use the following syntax: &#*D*; (where *D* is a decimal character) or &#x*H*; (where *H* is a hexadecimal character).
- Special characters are case-sensitive.
- When title is used with the LINK element, it may name an external style sheet.

## Associated Elements

A, ACRONYM, ADDRESS, APPLET (Microsoft-only attribute), AREA (Microsoft-only attribute), B, BASE (Microsoft-only attribute), BASEFONT (Microsoft-only attribute), BIG, BLOCKQUOTE, BODY, BR, BUTTON, CAPTION, CENTER, CITE, CODE, COL, COLGROUP, DD, DEL, DFN, DIR, DIV, DL, DT, EM, EMBED (Microsoft-only attribute), FIELDSET, FONT (Microsoft-only attribute), FORM, FRAME (Microsoft-only attribute), H1, H2, H3, H4, H5, H6, HEAD (Microsoft-only attribute), HR, HTML (Microsoft-only attribute), I, IFRAME (Microsoft-only attribute), IMG, INPUT, INS, ISINDEX, KBD, LABEL, LEGEND, LI, LINK, MARQUEE (Microsoft-only attribute), MENU, OBJECT, OL, OPTION, P, OPTION, Q, S, SAMP, SCRIPT (Microsoft-only attribute), SELECT, SMALL, SPAN, STRIKE, STRONG, STYLE, SUB, SUP, TABLE, TBODY, TD, TEXTAREA, TFOOT, TH, THEAD, TR, TT, U, UL, VAR

---

TOP="*top_pos_pix*"

The Top attribute specifies the topmost position, in pixels, of the top of a layer window. This is a Netscape-defined attribute.

- The TOP attribute specifies an absolute position.
- Pixels is a value representing the number of pixels based on a 640x480 resolution.
- Most browsers do not support Netscape-defined attributes.

## Associated Elements

ILAYER, LAYER

---

TOPMARGIN=" *tmar-num* "

The TOPMARGIN attribute specifies the top margin, in pixels, of this document. This is a Microsoft-defined attribute.

- Most browsers do not support Microsoft-defined attributes.
- TOPMARGIN="0" moves the margin to the top of the page.
- The value of TOPMARGIN overrides the default top margin.
- Pixels is a value representing the number of pixels based on a 640x480 resolution.

## Associated Element

BODY

---

TRUESPEED

The TRUESPEED attribute uses the SCROLLDELAY value as the speed of the text in a scrolling marquee. This is a Microsoft-defined attribute.

- The default TRUESPEED value is 60 milliseconds.
- Most browsers do not support Microsoft-defined attributes.

## Associated Element

MARQUEE

NOTE TYPE is a popular attribute whose values and behavior vary, depending on the element with which it is associated at a particular time. In this appendix, you'll find several versions of TYPE arranged alphabetically by element name.

---

TYPE="<u>submit</u>" | "button" | "reset"

The TYPE attribute indicates the type of button:

- TYPE="submit" submits a form.
- TYPE="button" is a button that runs a script.
- TYPE="reset" clears a form.
- A button with TYPE="submit" is a close relative of the INPUT TYPE="submit".
- A button with TYPE="reset" is a close relative of the INPUT TYPE="reset".

## Associated Element

BUTTON

---

TYPE="*Internet_Media_Type*"

The TYPE attribute specifies a valid Internet Media Type (that is, MIMETYPE) of the object, parameter, or scripting language.

- For the EMBED element, the TYPE attribute is Netscape-defined. Most browsers do not support Netscape-defined attributes.
- For the OBJECT element, the TYPE attribute works with the data named by the DATA attribute.
- If you do not use the TYPE attribute in the OBJECT element, a browser will try to determine the data type.
- For the PARAM element, this attribute, which is valid only if VALUETYPE="REF", specifies the content type of the run-time values stored at the named URL.
- For the SCRIPT element, this attribute specifies the scripting language, which must be a valid Internet Media Type.

- For more information about Internet Media Types, refer to Multipurpose Internet Mail Extensions (MIME) Part One: Format of Internet Message Bodies (ftp://ds.internic.net/rfc/rfc2045.txt) and Multipurpose Internet Mail Extensions (MIME) Part Two: Media Types (ftp://ds.internic.net/rfc/rfc2046.txt).

## Associated Element

EMBED (Netscape extension), OBJECT, PARAM, SCRIPT

---

TYPE="<u>text</u>" | "button" | "checkbox" | "file" | "hidden" | "image" | "password" | "radio" | "reset" | "submit" | "textarea"

The TYPE attribute specifies the type of input control:

- TYPE="text" creates a text box one line high.
- TYPE="button" creates a button associated with a script.
- TYPE="checkbox" creates a set of two or more check boxes. When a check box is checked, its value is submitted when the Submit button is clicked on. When two or more check boxes have the same name and are checked, all their values are submitted when the Submit button is clicked on.
- TYPE="file" is an attached file. When you attach more than one file to a particular control, the files should be placed in a MIME multipart document (that is, ENC-TYPE="multipart/form-data"), as defined in RFC 2045.
- TYPE="hidden" creates a hidden field. When you submit a form, the values of hidden fields are submitted to the form-processing program. You can use a hidden field to hold HTTP information.
- TYPE="image" creates a graphic image.
- TYPE="password" creates a text box one line high and containing a password, which is represented by asterisks or spaces when the user types it.

- TYPE="radio" creates a set of two or more radio buttons. When a radio button is filled, its value is submitted when the Submit button is clicked on. When two or more radio buttons have the same name, the value of the filled radio button is submitted when the Submit button is clicked on.
- TYPE="reset" creates a "flat" command button that when clicked on returns to the starting values set by the VALUE attributes. Fields with no starting values are cleared.
- TYPE="submit" creates a "flat" command button that when clicked on submits data from the form. If a form contains more than one Submit button, only the value of the clicked-on button is submitted when it is clicked on.
- TYPE="submit" is a close relative of a button with TYPE="submit".
- TYPE="reset" is a close relative of a button with TYPE="reset".
- TYPE="textarea" creates a multi-line text box. This is a Microsoft-defined attribute. Most browsers do not support Microsoft-defined attributes.
- For more information about Internet Media Types, refer to Multipurpose Internet Mail Extensions (MIME) Part One: Format of Internet Message Bodies (ftp://ds.internic.net/rfc/rfc2045.txt) and Multipurpose Internet Mail Extensions (MIME) Part Two: Media Types (ftp://ds.internic.net/rfc/rfc2046.txt).

## Associated Element

INPUT

```
TYPE="disc"|"square"|"circle"|"1"|"a"|
"A"|"i"|"I"
```

The TYPE attribute sets a number or a bullet format preceding a list item.

- TYPE="disc" uses filled bullets (l).
- TYPE="square" uses filled square bullets (n).
- TYPE="circle" uses unfilled circles (°).
- TYPE="1" uses Arabic numerals(for example, 1, 2, 3, and so on).
- TYPE="a" uses lowercase letters (for example, a, b, c, and so on).
- TYPE="A" uses uppercase letters (for example, A, B, C, and so on).
- TYPE="i" uses small Roman numerals (for example, i, ii, iii, iv, and so on).
- TYPE="I" uses large Roman numerals (for example, I, II, III, IV, and so on).
- A browser may or may not display bullets or numbers exactly as shown above.
- Nested lists may use different bullets or numbers.

## Associated Element

LI

---

## TYPE="*content_type*"

The TYPE attribute specifies a type name of the link, for information within the current document.

## Associated Element

LINK

---

## TYPE="1" | "a" | "A" | "i" | "I"

The TYPE attribute sets a number format for an ordered, or numbered, list:

- TYPE="1" uses Arabic numerals(for example, 1, 2, 3, and so on).
- TYPE="a" uses lowercase letters (for example, a, b, c, and so on).
- TYPE="A" uses uppercase letters (for example, A, B, C, and so on).

- TYPE="I" uses small Roman numerals (for example, i, ii, iii, iv, and so on).
- TYPE="I" uses large Roman numerals (for example, I, II, III, IV, and so on).
- A browser may display numbers differently.
- Nested lists may use different numbers.

## Associated Element

OL

---

TYPE="horizontal" | "vertical" | "block"

The TYPE attribute specifies the type of white-space area in the current document. This is a Netscape-defined attribute.

- TYPE="horizontal" indicates that a wide white-space (specified by the SIZE attribute) will be added at the location of the SPACER extension.
- TYPE="vertical" indicates that a high white-space (specified by the SIZE attribute) will be added at the location of the SPACER extension.
- TYPE="block" indicates that a white-space rectangle will be added at the location of the SPACER extension. Use the ALIGN, HEIGHT, and WIDTH attributes to specify the alignment and dimensions of the white-space block.
- Most browsers do not support Netscape-defined attributes.

## Associated Element

SPACER (Netscape extension)

---

TYPE="*style_sheet_language*"

The TYPE attribute specifies a language (that is, the Internet Media Type) for the style sheet.

## Associated Element

STYLE

**681**

TYPE="<u>disc</u>" | "square" | "circle"

The TYPE attribute sets a bullet in an unordered, or bulleted, list.

- TYPE="disc" uses filled bullets (l).
- TYPE="square" uses filled square bullets (n).
- TYPE="circle" uses unfilled circles (°).
- A browser may or may not display the bullets exactly as shown above.
- Nested lists may use different bullet symbols.

## Associated Element

UL

UNITS="<u>PIXELS</u>" | "EN"

The UNITS attribute specifies the unit of measure for the HEIGHT and WIDTH attributes. This is a Microsoft-defined attribute.

- UNITS="PIXELS" specifies that pixels are the unit of measure.
- UNITS="EN" specifies that the unit of measure is half the current point size of text.
- Pixels is a value representing the number of pixels based on a 640x480 resolution.
- Most browsers do not support Microsoft-defined attributes.

## Associated Element

EMBED (Microsoft extension)

URL="*this_url*"

The URL attribute names the URL of the current HTML document. This is a Microsoft-defined attribute.

- Most browsers do not support Microsoft-defined attributes.

## Associated Element

META

URN="*urn*"

The URN attribute names a uniform resource name (URN) for the target document specified with the TARGET attribute. This is a Microsoft-defined attribute.

- Most browsers do not support Microsoft-defined attributes.

## Associated Element

A

USEMAP="*map_url*"

The USEMAP attribute specifies a client-side image map that is displayed in a document or form.

- *map_url* is an absolute or relative Universal Resource Locator.
- *map_url* either includes an object directly in a document or links to another document or program.
- USEMAP may be supported in the future for the INPUT element.

## Associated Elements

IMG, OBJECT

VALIGN="<u>middle</u>" | "top" | "bottom" | "baseline"

The VALIGN attribute vertically aligns the contents of table cells or, as a Microsoft-defined attribute, a caption or legend.

- VALIGN="middle" centers data between the top and bottom edges of the current cell. As a Microsoft-defined attribute, VALIGN="middle" aligns a table.

- VALIGN="top" aligns data with the top edge of the current cell. As a Microsoft-defined attribute, VALIGN="top" aligns a caption or legend with the top of a table, a set of fields, or a table.

- VALIGN="bottom" aligns data with the bottom edge of the current cell. As a Microsoft-defined attribute, VALIGN="bottom" aligns a caption or legend with the bottom of a table, a set of fields, or a table.

- VALIGN="baseline" aligns one line of text in the current row on an invisible baseline.

- The baseline value does not affect subsequent lines of text.

- If you use the VALIGN attribute more than once within a table, the order in which the attribute is processed (that is, the order of precedence), from highest to lowest, is:

  1. An attribute set on an element within a cell's contents.
  2. An attribute set on a TH or TD cell.
  3. An attribute set on a row (TR) or group of rows (TBODY, TFOOT, or THEAD).
  4. An attribute set on a column (COL) or column group (COLGROUP).
  5. An attribute set on a table.
  6. The default value of the attribute.

## Associated Elements

CAPTION (Microsoft-only attribute), COL, COLGROUP, LEGEND (Microsoft-only attribute), TABLE (Microsoft-only attribute), TBODY, TD, TFOOT, TH, THEAD, TR

VALUE is a popular attribute whose values and behavior vary, depending on the element with which it is associated at a particular time. In this appendix, you'll find several versions of VALUE arranged alphabetically by element name.

VALUE="*button_value*"

The VALUE attribute sets the initial value for a button.

## Associated Element

BUTTON

VALUE="*initial_value*"

The VALUE attribute sets the initial value for a form control.

- VALUE is required if TYPE="RADIO" or TYPE="CHECKBOX".
- When you click on a Reset button, a control returns to the starting values specified by the VALUE attribute. If you do not specify VALUE, the control is cleared.
- A form button value becomes the button's name.

## Associated Element

INPUT

VALUE="*cur_num*"

The VALUE attribute sets the current number for a list item.

- *cur_num* can include characters and/or special characters from the supported character set.
- For special characters, use the following syntax: &#D; (where D is a decimal character) or &#xH; (where H is a hexadecimal character).
- Special characters are case-sensitive.

## Associated Element

LI

---

VALUE="*submitted_value*"

The VALUE attribute sets the submitted value for an option.

- If you do not specify VALUE, the default value is the content of the OPTION element.

## Associated Element

OPTION

---

VALUE="*parm_value*"

The VALUE attribute provides a value for the parameter defined by the NAME attribute.

- The object determines the validity of the value. HTML cannot evaluate value's validity.

## Associated Element

PARAM

---

VALUETYPE="<u>DATA</u>" | "REF" | "OBJECT"

The VALUETYPE attribute specifies the type of the VALUE attribute: string or URL.

- VALUETYPE="DATA" is a string. The value is passed to the object after special characters are *resolved* (that is, converted).
- VALUETYPE="REF" is the URL of the file in which the run-time values is stored. The URL is passed to the object without any resolution. If VALUETYPE="REF, you should also use the TYPE attribute.
- VALUETYPE="OBJECT" is a URL for an OBJECT declaration in the current document. The OBJECT declaration must include an ID attribute that defines the declaration.

## Associated Element

PARAM

---

VERSION=" *dtd_url* "

The VERSION attribute specifies the URL for the Document Type Definition (DTD) of the HTML standard for the elements and attributes of the current document (for example, "http://www.w3.org/TR/WD-html40-970708/HTML4.dtd").

## Associated Element

HTML

---

VISIBILITY=" INHERIT " | "SHOW" | "HIDE"

The VISIBILITY attribute specifies whether a layer is visible. This is a Netscape-defined attribute.

- VISIBILITY="INHERIT" shows the layer if its parent is visible or hides the layer if its parent is hidden.
- If the current layer does not have a parent, it is visible.
- VISIBILITY="SHOW" displays the layer.
- Visible layers on top of visible layers can hide all or part of the contents of the underneath layers.
- VISIBILITY="HIDE" hides the layer.
- A hidden layer is still within the pages in the current document.
- Most browsers do not support Netscape-defined attributes.

## Associated Elements

ILAYER, LAYER

---

VLINK=" # *rrggbb* " | " *color* "

The VLINK attribute defines the color of the text and graphics borders of links that have been visited.

- *rrggbb* is the hexadecimal code of the color; *rr* represents the red attributes, from 00 to FF; *gg* represents the green attributes, from 00 to FF; and *bb* represents the blue attributes, from 00 to FF. Table 4.1 contains selected hexadecimal color values.
- *color* represents supported color names: red, maroon, yellow, green, lime, teal, olive, aqua, blue, navy, purple, fuchsia, black, gray, silver (the default), and white.
- Colors vary according to the graphics board and associated software installed in a computer, so it's best to view all colors and see how they work together before making a final color choice. Regardless of your color choice, there is a very good chance that some browser will interpret your colors in a very strange way.
- Both Netscape and Microsoft provide additional color names. Most browsers do not support Netscape and Microsoft attributes.
- This attribute is deprecated. Use a style sheet to specify the look of a document.

## Associated Element

BODY

---

VOLUME=" *vol_num* "

The VOLUME attribute specifies how loud or soft the background sound file will play. This is a Microsoft-defined attribute.

- Valid values for this attribute are -10,000 to 0.
- VOLUME="0" is the loudest volume.
- Most browsers do not support Microsoft-defined attributes.

## Associated Element

BGSOUND

**N O T E** VSPACE is a popular attribute whose values and behavior vary, depending on the element with which it is associated at a particular time. In this appendix, you'll find several versions of VSPACE arranged alphabetically by element name.

VSPACE="*vert_pix*"

The VSPACE attribute is the vertical area, in pixels, between the top margin of the page and the top margin of the applet window, image, or object.

- Pixels is a value representing the number of pixels based on a 640x480 resolution.
- This attribute is deprecated. Use a style sheet to specify the look of a document.

## Associated Elements

APPLET, IMG

VSPACE="*vert_pix*"

The VSPACE attribute is the vertical area, in pixels, of the top and bottom of the object and other text, graphics, and links on the current page. This is a Netscape- and Microsoft-defined attribute.

- Pixels is a value representing the number of pixels based on a 640x480 resolution.
- Most browsers do not support Netscape-defined attributes.

## Associated Elements

EMBED (Netscape extension), MARQUEE (Microsoft extension)

---

VSPACE="vert_pix"|vert_%

The VSPACE attribute is the vertical area, in pixels or as a percentage of the full-screen, between the top margin of the page and the top margin of the applet window, image, or object.

- Pixels is a value representing the number of pixels based on a 640x480 resolution.
- Do not enclose percentage values within quotation marks.
- This attribute is deprecated. Use a style sheet to specify the look of a document.

## Associated Element

OBJECT

---

VSPACE="*vert_pix*"

The VSPACE attribute is the vertical area, in pixels, in which the table will fit. This is a Netscape-defined attribute.

- The browser will scale the table to fit within the specified space.
- Most browsers do not support Netscape-defined attributes.
- Pixels is a value representing the number of pixels based on a 640x480 resolution.

## Associated Element

TABLE

---

**WIDTH is a popular attribute whose values and behavior vary, depending on the element with which it is associated at a particular time. In this appendix, you'll find several versions of WIDTH arranged alphabetically by element name.**

WIDTH="*width_pix*"

The WIDTH attribute specifies the width, in pixels, of the window in which the applet will run or the image will be placed.

- Pixels is a value representing the number of pixels based on a 640x480 resolution.
- If you use the HEIGHT and/or WIDTH attributes, an image may be out of proportion with the dimensions of the original image.
- Using the BORDER, HEIGHT, and/or WIDTH attributes to specify the actual size of the border, image height, and image width, respectively, can increase loading speed.
- This attribute is deprecated. Use a style sheet to specify the look of a document.

## Associated Elements

APPLET, IMG

WIDTH="*width_pix*"|*width_%*|*0\**|*n\**

The WIDTH attribute indicates the absolute width of the column, in pixels, or as a percentage of the full-screen width, or the relative width of the column to other columns in the current table or column group.

- *width_pix* is the default absolute column width, in pixels.
- Pixels is a value representing the number of pixels based on a 640x480 resolution.
- *width_&* is the absolute column width, as a percentage of the full window width.
- 0* automatically sets each column to its minimum relative width; that is, wide enough to fit the widest contents.
- *n\** is a multiplier of the default relative width, and * specifies a relative value of the rest of the available space in the table (for example, if the first column is 3*

and the second column is *, the first column will be three times wider than the second).

- An * indicator implies a multiplier value of 1.
- Do not enclose * or percentage values within quotation marks.
- Browsers set absolute widths first and relative widths after that.
- The WIDTH for a particular COL-described column overrides the WIDTH settings for the COLGROUP in which the column is embedded.

## Associated Element

COLGROUP

---

WIDTH="*width_pix*" | "*width_meas*"

The WIDTH attribute specifies the width of the window in which the object will be placed. This is a Netscape- and Microsoft-defined attribute.

- For Netscape browsers, WIDTH is measured in pixels, which is a value representing the number of pixels based on a 640x480 resolution.
- For Microsoft browsers, WIDTH is measured in pixels or using the unit of measure set by the UNITS attribute.
- If you use the HEIGHT and/or WIDTH attributes, an image may be out of proportion with the dimensions of the original image.
- Using the BORDER, HEIGHT, and/or WIDTH attributes to specify the actual size of the border, image height, and image width, respectively, can increase loading speed.
- This is a Netscape- and Microsoft-defined attribute. Most browsers do not support these types of attributes.

## Associated Element

EMBED (Netscape and Microsoft extension)

WIDTH=*"width_pix"*|*width_%*

The WIDTH attribute specifies the width, in pixels or as a percentage of the entire width of the computer screen, of a horizontal rule, inline frame, table, or window in which an object or marquee will be placed. For marquees and frames, this is a Microsoft-defined attribute.

- *width_pix* is the default rule, frame, or table width, in pixels.
- *width_&* is the rule, frame, or table width, as a percentage of the full window width.
- If you do not specify the width of a rule, frame, or table, the browser will set it.
- Do not enclose percentage values within quotation marks.
- Pixels is a value representing the number of pixels based on a 640x480 resolution.
- Most browsers do not support Microsoft-defined attributes.

## Associated Elements

FRAME, HR, IFRAME, MARQUEE (Microsoft extension), OBJECT, TABLE

WIDTH=*"width_pix"*

The WIDTH attribute specifies the width, in pixels, of the white-space block in the current document. This is a Netscape-defined attribute.

- The WIDTH attribute is in effect only when TYPE= "BLOCK".
- Pixels is a value representing the number of pixels based on a 640x480 resolution.
- Most browsers do not support Netscape-defined attributes.

## Associated Element

LAYER (Netscape extension), SPACER (Netscape extension)

---

WIDTH="*width_pix*"

The WIDTH attribute specifies the width of all columns, in pixels, in a MULTICOL area of a document. This is a Netscape-defined attribute.

- If you do not specify WIDTH, the browser subtracts the gutter width (the GUTTER attribute) from the window width and divides by the number of columns (the COLS attribute).
- Pixels is a value representing the number of pixels based on a 640x480 resolution.
- Most browsers do not support Netscape-defined attributes.

## Associated Element

MULTICOL (Netscape extension)

---

WIDTH="*text_block_width*"

The WIDTH attribute sets a maximum line width.

- *text_block_width* is an integer representing the width, in characters, of the formatted text block.
- To meet the width specification, a browser may increase or decrease the font size or adjust the left and/or right indention.
- For the OPTION element, *width* is an integer representing the width, in characters, of the formatted text block. The browser may change the font size or adjust the indention.
- Not all browsers support the use of WIDTH.

## Associated Element

OPTION, PRE

**694**

WIDTH="*width_pix*"

The WIDTH attribute specifies the width of a table cell, in pixels. This is a Microsoft-defined attribute.

- If you do not specify the WIDTH of a table, the browser will set it.
- Pixels is a value representing the number of pixels based on a 640x480 resolution.
- Most browsers do not support Microsoft-defined attributes.

## Associated Elements

TD (Microsoft-only attribute), TH (Microsoft-only attribute)

WRAP="OFF" | "HARD" | "SOFT" | "PHYSICAL" | "VIRTUAL"

The WRAP attribute indicates whether the text wraps when it reaches the right margin of the text box. This is a Netscape- and Microsoft-defined attribute.

- WRAP="OFF" turns off word wrap. Explicit line breaks break text. This is a Netscape- and Microsoft-defined attribute.
- WRAP="HARD" wraps words, and line breaks are included in the data sent when the form is submitted. This is a Netscape-defined attribute.
- WRAP="SOFT" wraps words, and line breaks are not included in the data sent when the form is submitted. This is a Netscape-defined attribute.
- WRAP="PHYSICAL" wraps words. This is a Microsoft-defined attribute.
- WRAP="VIRTUAL" wraps words and submits the text as it was typed. This is a Microsoft-defined attribute.
- Most browsers do not support Netscape-and Microsoft-defined attributes.

## Associated Element

TEXTAREA (Netscape-only attribute)

---

Z-INDEX="*order_num*"

The Z-INDEX attribute specifies the numerical order of the current layer. This is a Microsoft-defined attribute.

- This attribute must be a positive integer.
- The topmost layer must have a higher number than any other layer.
- The bottom layer must have a lower number than any other layer.
- Nested layers are above their parents in the stack of layers.
- Most browsers do not support Microsoft-defined attributes.

## Associated Elements

ILAYER, LAYER

# APPENDIX C

# HTML Editors and Utilities

The Internet contains a wealth of resources, including downloadable freeware, shareware, and trial versions of HTML editors and utilities as well as fact sheets about the programs:

- **Commercial programs**: Typically, you cannot try commercial programs before buying, although sometimes a software publisher provides a trial or demonstration version.
- **Trial versions**: Many commercial software publishers provide these incomplete or limited programs, also known as *demonstration programs* (demos), so that you can try before buying. A trial version may be an older version of the program, may expire on a particular date, or may not include all the features of the commercial software.
- **Shareware programs**: These programs usually contain every feature and function; you are expected to buy a license after you try the program for a set number of days. In return, the author may send you program disks, manuals, and notices of problems or new releases.
- **Freeware programs**: As you might imagine, these programs are available at no cost. Freeware programs can be just as good as shareware or commercial programs.

This appendix provides information about HTML editors and utilities with which you can create and enhance Web pages. In the first section is a list of many HTML editors for several platforms. On the concluding pages are lists of HTML utilities of all types.

# HTML Editors

This section lists HTML editors.

### 1-4-All HTML Editor

(http://www.mmsoftware.com/14All/) is a Windows 95/NT HTML editor.

### Aardvark Pro

(http://www.tmgnet.com/aardvark/) is an HTML editor for Windows 95/NT/3.x.

### Adobe PageMill

(http://www.adobe.com/prodindex/pagemill/main.html) is an HTML editor for Windows 95/NT and Macintosh. For more information about PageMill, see *Part 1*.

### ANT_HTML

(http://telacommunications.com/ant/) is a document conversion tool for Windows and the Macintosh. Both shareware and trial versions are available.

### AOLPress

(http://www.aolpress.com/press/index.html) is an HTML editor for both Windows 95/NT/3.x and Macintosh computers.

### ASHE (A Simple HTML Editor)

(ftp://ftp.cs.rpi.edu/pub/puninj/ASHE/README.html) is a freeware program with which you can edit HTML documents on UNIX computers.

### Aspire-x

(http://www.aspire-x.com/) is a text-based HTML editor for Windows 95/NT/3.x computers. This is a shareware program.

### AsWedit

(ftp://sunsite.doc.ic.ac.uk/packages/www/asWedit/) is a UNIX-based program that edits HTML for X Window and Motif systems.

### ATRAX the Web Publisher

(http://www.winwareinc.com/atrax.html) is a shareware HTML editor for Windows 95/NT.

### BBEdit

(http://www.barebones.com/bbedit.html), an HTML editor for the Macintosh, is a commercial program with a trial version.

### City University HTML Editor

(http://web.cs.city.ac.uk/homes/njw/htmltext/htmltext.html) is a X windows and UNIX HTML editor. This is a freeware program.

### Claris Home Page

(http://www.claris.com/products/claris/clarispage/clarispage.html ) is a commercial HTML editor for Windows 95/NT and Macintosh computers. A trial version is available.

### CMed

(http://www.users.highway1.com.au/~cmathes/) is a Windows 95/NT HTML editor.

### CoffeeCup HTML Editor++

(http://www.coffeecup.com/editor/) is a Windows 95/NT HTML editor.

### DiDaPro

(http://www.faico.net/dida/) is a small HTML editor for Windows 95/NT/3.x.

### Einstein HTML

(http://www.algonet.se/~perji/index.htm) is a shareware HTML editor for Windows.

### E-Publish

(http://www.stattech.com.au/) is a set of Internet authoring tools for Windows 95/NT/3.x. These programs require 8 megabytes of RAM.

### FlexED

(http://www.infoflex.com.au/flexed.htm) is a shareware HTML editor for Windows 95/NT/3.x.

### Hippie 97

(http://pages.prodigy.com/Hippie/) is a Windows 95/NT HTML editor that supports Prodigy pages. You must also have a recent version of Microsoft Internet Explorer.

### HomeSite

(http://www.allaire.com/) is an HTML editor for Windows 95/NT. Shareware and freeware versions are available.

### HotDog

(http://www.sausage.com/hotdog32.htm) is a popular HTML editor for Windows 95/NT for computers running at least 16 megabytes of RAM. Several versions are available.

### HoTMetaL PRO

(http://www.softquad.com/products/hotmetal/) is a commercial HTML editor for Windows, Macintosh, and UNIX. For more information about HoTMetaL PRO, see *Part 1*.

### HTML Assistant Pro

(http://www.brooknorth.com/) is a Windows-based HTML editor.

### HTML Author

(http://www.salford.ac.uk/iti/gsc/htmlauth/summary.html) is a Word for Windows template that you can use to create and edit HTML documents. This is a shareware program.

### HTMLed

(http://www.ist.ca/htmled/) is a Windows 95/NT/3.x HTML editor. This is a shareware program.

### HTML-Ed

(http://www.wilmington.net/bmtmicro/catalog/html-ed.html) is a small shareware HTML editor for OS/2.

### html-helper-mode

(http://www.santafe.edu/~nelson/tools/) is a UNIX HTML editor. This is a freeware program.

### HTML-HyperEditor

(http://www.lu.se/info/Editor/HTML-HyperEditor.html) is a freeware HTML editor for the Macintosh. English and Swedish language versions are available.

### HTML Notepad

(http://www.cranial.com/software/htmlnote/) is a small Windows 95/3.x HTML editor. This is a shareware program.

### HTMLpad

(http://intermania.com/htmlpad/index.html) is a Windows 95/NT shareware HTML editor.

### HTML Pro

(http://www.ts.umu.se/~r2d2/files/HTML_Pro_info.html), a shareware HTML editor for the Macintosh, provides two views of the current page: the source code and the page as it will look when browsed.

### HTML Studio

(http://www.program.com/panacea/) is a 32-bit shareware HTML editor that runs under OS/2 Warp.

### The HTML Wizard

(http://www.gnv.com/HTMLWizard/) is a 32-bit HTML editor for OS/2.

### HTML Writer

(http://www.public.asu.edu/~bottger/) is a Windows-based HTML editor also known as HTML Edit. This is an inexpensive shareware program.

### HypeType Edit

(http://users.aol.com/nutfact/hypeedit.htm) is a Windows-based HTML editor. This is a freeware program.

### LiquidFX

(http://www.psylon.com/) is an HTML editor for Windows 95/NT. It requires 8 megabytes of RAM.

### Luckman's WebEdit Pro

(http://www.luckman.com/webeditpro/) is a Windows 95/NT HTML editor.

### Microsoft FrontPage

(http://www.microsoft.com/products/prodref/62_ov.htm) is a commercial program for Windows and Macintosh computers. For more information about FrontPage, see *Part 1*.

### Microsoft Internet Assistant

(http://www.microsoft.com/word/internet/ia/) is an add-in to Word for Windows 95 and Windows 95/NT.

### Mocha Shop

(http://www.fred.net/drescher/dl.html) is a freeware HTML editor for Windows 3.x.

### MyInternetBusinessPage

(http://www.mybusinesspage.com/) is a shareware HTML editor for Windows 95/3.x.

### Myrmidon

(http://206.86.175.148/index.shtml) is a Macintosh program that converts documents to Web pages. Freeware and commercial versions are available.

### NetObjects Fusion

(http://www.netobjects.com/) is a Windows 95/NT HTML editor.

### PageSpinner

(http://www.algonet.se/~optima/pagespinner.html) is a Macintosh HTML editor. This is a shareware program.

## Phoenix

(http://www.bsd.uchicago.edu/ftp/pub/phoenix/README) is a freeware HTML editor for UNIX. This is an alpha (prerelease) program.

## Quicksite

(http://www.deltapoint.com/) is a Windows 95 HTML editor that requires 16 megabytes of RAM.

## Simple HTML Editor (S H E)

(http://www.lib.ncsu.edu/staff/morgan/simple.html) is a HyperCard stack with which you can create HTML documents on a Macintosh.

## SpHyDir

(http://pclt.cis.yale.edu/pclt/sphydir/SPHYDIR.HTM) is a Structured Professional Hypertext Directory Manager for OS/2 Warp. This shareware program is designed to manage large documents or libraries.

## SpiderPad

(http://www.sixlegs.com/spidrpad.htm) is a Windows 95/NT HTML editor.

## Symposia Pro

(http://www.grif.fr/prod/sympro.html) is a Windows and UNIX commercial program that combines a Web browser and an HTML editor. Symposia Pro also supports the XML standard.

## TC-Director

(http://www.tashcom.com/) is a shareware HTML editor for Windows 95/3.x.

## tkHTML

(http://www.cobaltgroup.com/~roland/tkHTML/tkHTML.html) is a UNIX-based HTML editor. This is a shareware program.

## Web Elite

(http://www.safety.net/webelite/) is an HTML editor for Windows 95/NT. This is a shareware program.

## WebExpress

(http://www.mvd.com/webx.htm) is a Windows 95/NT/3.x HTML editor.

## WebMagic

(http://www.sgi.com/Products/WebFORCE/WebMagic/index.ht ml) is a commercial HTML editor for Silicon Graphics workstations.

## Web Media Publisher

(http://www.wbmedia.com/publisher/) is a 32-bit Windows-based HTML editor. This is a shareware program.

## Web Publisher

(http://www.skisoft.com/) converts word-processing documents to HTML files.

## Web Weaver

(http://www.mcwebsoftware.com/) is a Windows 95/NT HTML editor.

## WebWorks Publisher

(http://www.quadralay.com/Company/products.html) converts FrameMaker documents to HTML. Windows, Macintosh, and UNIX commercial and trial versions are available.

## WebWriter

(http://www.geocities.com/CapitolHill/2519/WEBWRITE.HTM ) is Windows 3.x HTML editor. This is a freeware program.

## World Wide Web Weaver

(http://www.miracleinc.com/) is a Macintosh-based HTML editor. This is a shareware program.

# HTML Utilities

This section provides links to utilities that can help you enhance your Web pages.

### ACDSee

(http://www.acdsystems.com/) is an image viewer, editor, and organizer running under Windows 95/NT/3.x.

### Applet Widget Kit

(http://www.siliconjoy.com/index.html) is a Windows 95/NT utility allows nonprogrammers to create Java-based animations.

### Banner*Show

(http://www.webgenie.com/Software/Banner/) creates Java or JavaScript rotating banners. This is a Windows 95/NT utility.

### BK HTML Body Builder

(http://bk.base.org/body/) is a Windows 95/NT utility that helps you choose attributes and values for the BODY element. This is freeware.

### Bookworm

(http://www.sausage.com/bookworm.htm) is a Windows 95/NT utility with multilink jump boxes. This program requires 8 megabytes of RAM.

### Broadway

(http://www.sausage.com/broadway.htm) is a Windows 95/NT Java marquee utility. This program requires 8 megabytes of RAM.

### Cart32 Shopping Cart System

(http://www.ozarksonline.com/cart32/) is a CGI program that enables you to build an online retail system. This Windows 95/NT utility requires 16 megabytes of RAM.

### Clikette

(http://www.sausage.com/clikette.htm) creates Java-based three-dimensional buttons on which you can click to go to multiple links. This Windows 95/NT program requires 8 megabytes of RAM.

### ColorMaker

(http://www.danere.com/ColorMaker/) is a Windows 95/NT utility that enables you to choose colors for an HTML document. You must have VB40032.DLL to run this program.

### Color Manipulation Device

(http://www.meat.com/software/cmd/) is an easy-to-use Windows 95/NT/3.x program that you can run to select colors for the page background, text, and links.

### Crosseye

(http://www.sausage.com/crosseye.htm) is a Windows-based image map editor. This is a shareware program.

### Egor

(http://www.sausage.com/egor.htm) is a Windows-based Java animator. Both shareware and demo programs are available.

### Flash

(http://www.sausage.com/flash.htm) scrolls Java-based text on the status bar. This is a Windows 95/NT utility.

### FrameGang

(http://www.sausage.com/framgang.htm) is a Windows 95/NT/3.x utility that helps build pages with frames. This utility requires 8 megabytes of RAM.

### GIF Builder

(http://iawww.epfl.ch/Staff/Yves.Piguet/clip2gif-home/GifBuilder.html) creates animated GIF files and converts graphic files. This program is Macintosh freeware.

### GIF Construction Set

(http://www.mindworkshop.com/alchemy/gifcon.html) is a GIF image editing and animation program. This is a Windows shareware program.

### Graphics Workshop

(http://www.mindworkshop.com/alchemy/gww.html) converts images from one file type to another. Also included are editing features. This is a Windows shareware program.

### GuestBook

(http://www.webgenie.com/Software/Guestar/) is a Windows 95/NT utility that creates a guest book.

### Hot Chilli

(http://www.ozramp.net.au/~maxzmije/) is a Windows 95/NT utility that creates Java-based special effects. This utility requires 16 megabytes of RAM.

### HTML Grinder

(http://www.matterform.com/grinder/index.html) contains 20 HTML tools for the Macintosh.

### Joe Boxer's Bigger, Dumber Utility Library

(http://www.joeboxer.com/utilities.html) provides Windows and Macintosh freeware and shareware programs for enhancing Web pages and to take advantage of all the multimedia files when browsing.

### List2HTM

(http://home.earthlink.net/~naturalsoft/list2htm.htm) converts lists and directories into HTML code.

### LiveImage

(http://www.mediatec.com/) edits image maps. This is a Windows 95/NT program.

### Lview Pro 16

(http://www.cycor.ca/Manual/lview.htm) is a graphic file viewer running under Windows. This is a shareware program.

### Net-It Now

(http://www.net-it.com/) is a Windows 95/NT utility that converts documents into Java-enhanced Web pages. This requires 8 megabytes of RAM.

### Paint Shop Pro

(http://www.jasc.com/) creates and edits graphic images. This is a Windows shareware program.

### SiteFX

(http://www.sausage.com/sitefx.htm) is a set of Java applications for Windows 95/NT. This utility requires 8 megabytes of RAM.

### Swami

(http://www.sausage.com/swami.htm) is a Java-based text animation shareware utility for Windows 95/NT. This utility requires 8 megabytes of RAM.

### Thumbsplus

(http://www.cerious.com/) organizes image, metafile, font, and multimedia files. This is a Windows shareware program. The developers are working on a Macintosh version.

### VuePrint

(http://www.hamrick.com/) is a program with which you can view and print images. Both 32- and 16-bit Windows versions are available.

### WebEd Image Mapper

(http://www.ozemail.com.au/~kread/mapper.html) is a map file editor for Windows. The Pro version allows import and export. Commercial and shareware versions are available.

### WebImage

(http://www.group42.com/) creates animated GIFs, edits image maps, and creates and edits other images. This is a Windows shareware program.

### Weenies

(http://www.sausage.com/weenies.htm) are GIF images that can be animated.

# INDEX

# Index

DECLARE attribute, 391, 392, 612
declaring, an object, 391, 392
  the document type, 53–54
decreasing, space between bullet and list item, 160, 212
  space between number and list item, 166
defining, area of image map, 373–76
  base font size, 72
  definition list, 117–119
  definition term, 120–22
  floating frames, 358–60
  frame, 342–54
  glossary, 117–119
  HTML document, 141–42
  pane within desktop, 342–54
  set of frames, 355–57
  table, 247–56
  table body, 257–60
  table cell data, 261–70
  table footer, 271–74
  table header, 281–83
  table heading, 275–80
  table row, 284–88
definition, pairing term and, 117–119, 120–22
definition description, 99–101, 117–119, 120–22
definition list, defining, 117–119
definition term, defining, 120–22
  identifying, 105–107
  pairing with definition, 117–119, 120–22
definitions on same line
  inserting terms and, 117–119, 120–22
DEL element, 102–104
  attributes, 102–104
  notes, 103–104
  purpose, 102
  syntax, 102
demonstration versions, 699
demos, 699
deprecated elements, 566
deprecated, defined, 518
describing, HTML document, 163–65
  term, 99
description, definition, 117–119, 120–22
  providing document, 163–65
  stating a definition, 99–101
DFN element, 105–7
  attributes, 105–6
  example, 107
  notes, 107
  purpose, 105
  syntax, 105
dialup, defined, 518
DIR attribute, 55, 56, 62, 64, 67, 74, 75, 78, 81, 82, 90,
  93, 96, 99, 102, 105, 108, 112, 113, 117, 120, 123, 130,
  134, 141, 143, 146, 149, 152, 156, 160, 166, 171, 175,
  178, 181, 184, 187, 190, 194, 197, 198, 201, 204, 206,
  209, 212, 217, 234, 239, 243, 244, 247, 249, 257, 258,
  261, 262, 271, 272, 275, 276, 281, 282, 284, 285, 290,
  291, 294, 297, 301, 302, 303, 304, 305, 306, 307, 308,
  317, 319, 320, 322, 325, 328, 329, 334, 335, 377, 378,
  391, 393, 612–13
DIR element, 108–11
  attributes, 108–10
  example, 110
  notes, 110
  purpose, 108
  syntax, 108
DIRECTION attribute, 414, 415, 613
direction, specifying text, 55, 56, 62, 64, 67, 74, 75, 78,
  81, 82, 90, 93, 96, 99, 102, 105, 108, 112, 113, 117,
  120, 123, 130, 134, 141, 143, 146, 149, 152, 156, 160,
  166, 171, 175, 178, 181, 184, 187, 190, 194, 197, 198,
  201, 204, 206, 209, 212, 217, 234, 239, 243, 244, 247,
  249, 257, 258, 261, 262, 271, 272, 275, 276, 281, 282,
  284, 285, 290, 291, 294, 297, 301, 302, 303, 304, 305,
  306, 307, 308, 317, 319, 320, 322, 325, 328, 329, 334,
  335, 377, 378, 391, 393, 612–13
directories, HTML (Webliography), 550–52
DISABLED attribute, 156, 197, 290, 291, 301, 302, 303,
304, 305, 306, 307, 308, 319, 320, 325, 334, 335, 614
DISPLAY property, 463
displaying, all table borders, 247, 248
  borders between rows and columns, 247, 248
  horizontal borders between table groups, 247, 248
  inside table borders, 247, 248
  large font text, 75–77
  left and right table borders, 247, 248
  menu list, 160–62
  outside table borders, 247, 248
  text in a smaller font, 187–89
  top and bottom table borders, 247, 248
  word list, 105–7
DIV element, 112–16
  attributes, 112–15
  example, 115
  notes, 115
  purpose, 112
  syntax, 112
division or section, marking new, 112–16
division, aligning, 112
DL element, 117–19
  attributes, 117–19
  example, 119
  notes, 119
  purpose, 117
  syntax, 117
document, creating an HTML, 13–27
  defining an HTML, 141–42
  embedding an object in, 405–7
  including a script in, 399–400
  inserting hidden comments in a, 52
  introducing an HTML, 134–35
  naming the location of a, 55–61
  sample HTML, 26
  showing a link to another, 156–58
  specifying margins of, 81, 82
  specifying the title for HTML, 204–5
  type, declaring, 53–54
Document Type Definition. *See also* DTD.
document type definition, defined, 11. *See* DTD.
domain name registration (Webliography), 548–49
Domain Name System, defined, 519
domain name, defined, 519
domain name, registering, 30–31, 548–49
domain, defined, 518–19
download, defined 519
drop-down list box, naming, 325, 326
drop-down list or list box, inserting option in, 325–27
drop-down lists, inserting in form, 325–27
DT element, 120–22
  attributes, 120–22
  notes, 122
  purpose, 120
  syntax, 120
DTD, defined, 11, 519
dynamic HTML, defined, 519
DYNSRC attribute, 377, 378, 614–15

## E

editors, HTML, 700–6
  HTML (Webliography), 540
electronic mail. *See* e-mail.
element, defined, 519–20
elements
  !, 52
  !DOCTYPE, 53–54
  A, 27, 55–61
  ACRONYM, 62–63
  ADDRESS, 64–66
  APPLET, 366–72
  AREA, 373–76
  attributes, 23
  B, 24, 67–69
  BASE, 25, 70–71
  BASEFONT, 72–73
  BGSOUND, 402–3
  BIG, 12, 75–77

**716**

# Index

# Index

# Index

# Index

# Index

**728**